A GUIDE TO CRITERION-REFERENCED TEST CONSTRUCTION

Other books edited by Ronald A. Berk

Criterion-Referenced Measurement: The State of the Art
Educational Evaluation Methodology: The State of the Art
Handbook of Methods for Detecting Test Bias

A GUIDE TO CRITERION-REFERENCED TEST CONSTRUCTION

EDITED BY RONALD A. BERK

The Johns Hopkins University Press • Baltimore and London

The Johns Hopkins University Press, Baltimore, Maryland 21218
The Johns Hopkins Press Ltd., London

Library of Congress Cataloging in Publication Data
Main entry under title:

A Guide to criterion-referenced test construction.

Rev. and enl. ed. of: Criterion-referenced measurement. c1980.
Bibliography
Includes index.
1. Criterion-referenced tests—Congresses. I. Berk, Ronald A. II. Johns Hopkins University National Symposium on Educational Research (1st: 1978: Washington, D.C.). Criterion-referenced measurement.
LB3060.32.C74G85 1984 371.2'6 84-47955
ISBN 0-8018-2417-6

To Marissa

CONTENTS

PREFACE

THIS BOOK IS a major revision and extension of an earlier work, *Criterion-Referenced Measurement: The State of the Art* (Johns Hopkins University Press, 1980). It did not seem appropriate to label the book as a second edition because six new chapters have been added, three of the previous chapters have undergone considerable revision, and two others have been updated. The new title, *A Guide to Criterion-Referenced Test Construction*, reflects this volume's stronger orientation toward practitioners, especially classroom teachers, district and state level test makers, and test publishers.

Decisions regarding the contents of this volume have been guided by the limitations acknowledged in *Criterion-Referenced Measurement* and by the response to that book by students, researchers, and practitioners. Also, since the earlier book was a product of the 1978 Johns Hopkins University National Symposium on Educational Research, its structure and contents were limited by the scope of the symposium. The most important omissions identified over the past five years have been addressed in the current book.

The state-of-the-art concept advanced at the symposium and in the subsequent book has been de-emphasized here. Although the review section in each chapter can be regarded as a state-of-the-art assessment of a particular step in the test construction process, the total work does not provide a comprehensive assessment of the state of the art of criterion-referenced measurement and evaluation. Topics outside of the domain of test construction, such as score use and interpretation, would require attention in order to justify state-of-the-art coverage of the field.

The challenge of improving upon an existing work cannot be met without the cooperation and assistance of professionals who are committed to the project. Foremost among these professionals are the eight authors who graciously added new material, eliminated obsolete or redundant material, revised and reorganized existing material, and completed editorial corrections. The quality of the contributions reflects their very positive attitude almost as much as their expertise. Inasmuch as this book represents my fourth volume with the Johns Hopkins University Press, it is also appropriate to acknowledge and to thank the outstanding editors with whom I have worked and from whom I have learned so much: Wendy Harris, Mary Lou Kenney, Barbara Lamb, Anders Richter, Miriam Tillman, Henry Tom, and Jackie Wehmueller. My association with this staff has proven to be extremely rewarding, and my writing and editing have been influenced greatly by their advice, criticism, and, above all, standards for book publishing. Finally, I express my sincere appreciation to Karen A. Simmons for typing several sections of the book and for her assistance in preparing the final version of the manuscript.

A GUIDE TO CRITERION-REFERENCED TEST CONSTRUCTION

INTRODUCTION

RONALD A. BERK

BACKGROUND

AMONG THE MANY developments in educational measurement over the past 50 years, the emergence of criterion-referenced testing has been one of the most dramatic. An emphasis on mastery-proficiency-competency has permeated all levels of education, occupational licensure and certification (particularly in medicine and the allied health fields), and business and industry. Commercial test publishers have committed substantial resources to the production of criterion-referenced testing systems and diagnostic-prescriptive instructional packages for decision making at the classroom level. The back-to-basics trend and the state mandates for minimum competency testing in education have provided additional impetus to the movement since 1970. With 39 states requiring competency test performance for high school graduation certification and/or grade level promotion and the report by the National Commission on Excellence in Education (1983) calling for "Five New Basics," the role of criterion-referenced measurement is expected to become increasingly prominent.

A Brief History

The current momentum for generating tests that are designed expressly for interpreting an individual's performance in terms of what he or she can and cannot do irrespective of the performance of other students has a rather uneven history. The concept of an absolute versus relative standard of measurement can be traced to the work of Thorndike (1913), Flanagan (1951), Nedelsky (1954), and Ebel (1962). The research into and application of this concept, however, did not begin formally until the 1960s.

1960s. The term *criterion-referenced* was first coined in 1962 by Glaser and Klaus (1962). The distinction between a *criterion-referenced* and a *norm-referenced* test was defined in Robert Glaser's (1963) seminal essay (see Nitko, chapter 1).* For the remainder of the 1960s there was a sparsity of

*Citations to the present volume are indicated by the word *chapter*. Citations to chapters in other volumes are indicated by the abbreviation *chap*.

major research activity on the topic until publication of the article by Popham and Husek in 1969, which seemed to provide the stimulation needed to arouse the measurement community. Their article amplified Glaser's distinction between criterion-referenced and norm-referenced measurement, and also enumerated the advantages and disadvantages of the two approaches in instructional decision making. An explosion of interest in and research on the topic occurred in the following decade.

1970s. Just prior to 1978, Hambleton, Swaminathan, Algina, and Coulson (1978) estimated that more than 600 papers had been written on criterion-referenced testing. Many of these papers appeared in a variety of journals, monographs, and books, but a proportionately greater number were unpublished in the form of conference presentations and reports by school districts, state departments of education, and research and development laboratories. Apparently much of the research proceeded independently, with little regard for potentially comparable work. This observation can be illustrated by the confusion over terminology in the titles and contents of the papers. Although some researchers consistently used the label "criterion-referenced test," it was not uncommon to find the terms *domain-referenced test*, *objectives-referenced test*, *competency-based test*, *proficiency test*, and *mastery test* used interchangeably in the literature. When this confusion is coupled with the diverse forms in which the research existed, the body of research could be characterized as published, unpublished, redundant, and fragmented.

This state of the research literature in the 1970s indicated a need for synthesis and direction. The first response to this need was the chapter on criterion-referenced measurement authored by Jason Millman (1974). He furnished an organization and a description of the technical issues that did not appear to have existed previously. During 1974 a monograph was also published on the technical problems in criterion-referenced measurement which was edited by Chester W. Harris, Marvin C. Alkin, and W. James Popham (1974). In 1977 Victor R. Martuza produced the first measurement textbook that integrated norm-referenced and criterion-referenced test construction procedures. There were also five publications or events in 1978 that addressed the problem: (1) Hambleton et al.'s (1978) trenchant review article on the major technical topics, such as standard setting, validity, and reliability, (2) the special issue of the *Journal of Educational Measurement* devoted to standard setting which was edited by Lorrie A. Shepard, (3) W. James Popham's (1978) book, *Criterion-Referenced Measurement*, which was the first single-author volume on the topic, (4) the American Educational Research Association Topical Conference on "Minimum Competency Achievement Testing," and (5) the Johns Hopkins University National Symposium on Educational Research, which tackled "Criterion-Referenced Measurement: The State of the Art." Subsequently, there was an edited monograph on competency-based measurement by Bunda and Sanders (1979), a monograph on criterion-referenced testing by Brown (1980), edited volumes by Jaeger and Tittle (1980) and Berk (1980) based on the aforementioned conferences, and a special 1980 issue of *Applied Psychological Measurement* examining the criterion-referenced testing technology which was guest edited by Ronald K. Hambleton.

1980s. All of these contributions helped advance research and practice at a highly technical level. The published and unpublished papers since 1980 have followed a similar course, perhaps due, in part, to the popularity of latent trait approaches to test development and their application to criterion-referenced measurement.

TECHNICAL STANDARDS FOR TEST CONSTRUCTION

The *Standards for Educational and Psychological Tests* (APA/AERA/NCME Joint Committee, 1974) has served as the guide to and, in essence, the "bible" of acceptable measurement practices for the construction and use of norm-referenced tests. Unfortunately, no set of standards has been established by a joint committee of national experts for criterion-referenced tests. While it is possible to search through the *Standards* and extract some standards relevant to criterion-referenced tests, the product of this effort will be far from adequate. A recent draft of the next edition of the *Standards*, titled *Joint Technical Standards for Educational and Psychological Testing* (AERA/APA/NCME Joint Committee, in preparation), suggests that much more attention will be devoted to standards for criterion-referenced tests. In fact, it is expected that this edition will contain separate sections dealing exclusively with standards for certification testing in elementary and secondary education and for professional and occupational licensure and certification.

In addition to the *Standards*, test makers can turn to the list of questions compiled by Hambleton (1982), which is the extension of an earlier work by Hambleton and Eignor (1978). These questions are the most up-to-date and comprehensive collection of guidelines for building and evaluating criterion-referenced tests. Thirty-eight questions written for test makers and test users relate to seven key technical areas: (1) the objectives, (2) the items, (3) test administration, (4) the mastery standard, (5) validity, (6) reliability, and (7) scoring and score interpretation.

The statistical procedures, guidelines, and recommendations given in this volume are consistent with Hambleton's (1982) questions and with those standards germane to criterion-referenced tests in both the 1974 edition and the new edition of the *Standards*. Indeed, the chapter coverage of each topic goes far beyond any single set of technical standards. Moreover, the concluding "Guidelines for Practitioners" sections in the chapters can serve collectively as the most explicit set of standards for constructing criterion-referenced tests currently available.

PURPOSES OF THE BOOK

This book has three major purposes: (1) to evaluate what has been done, (2) to suggest what still needs to be done, and (3) to recommend what should be done in criterion-referenced test construction. It attempts to examine systematically the most pressing practical problems and thorny technical issues that test makers confront.

The first purpose requires a synthesis of the research that has accumulated over the past 20 years. This synthesis consists of a critical review of alternative methods, strategies, and statistics in order to bring into sharp focus the important issues that have been resolved and those that need resolution.

The second purpose concentrates on the conclusions from the research review in order to pinpoint gaps in the research that need to be filled. Certainly sifting through the published and unpublished works on the topic can help identify avenues for further study. However, the difficulties experienced in applying test construction methods can also indicate directions for investigation.

The third purpose also builds on the findings of the review. The research results are translated into forms that are meaningful and useful to practitioners. Alternative approaches are proffered, where possible, so that a test maker is not restricted to a single strategy for attacking a technical problem encountered in the test construction process. The approaches are directed at the most recent applications of the testing technology, which include mastery testing for instructional decisions at the classroom level, minimum competency testing for promotion and graduation decisions at the school district and state levels, competency testing for occupational licensure and certification by boards and agencies, and employment testing for performance appraisal in business and industry. The recommendations reflect the technical standards for acceptable criterion-referenced measurement practices.

ORGANIZATION OF THE BOOK

The book is divided into 11 chapters. The topics covered are arranged sequentially and correspond to the major steps in developing a criterion-referenced test, from defining the type of test through the analysis of its technical characteristics. The length of each chapter and the number of chapters addressing a given topic typically are a function of the scope and complexity of the material. For example, there are three chapters dealing with reliability; chapter 9 provides a framework for selecting an appropriate index and chapters 10 and 11 describe the computation and interpretation of the various indices.

The chapters suggest answers to 14 fundamental questions:

1. How can "criterion-referenced test" be defined?
2. What are the most effective strategies for defining a content domain?
3. What methods can be used to generate the items?
4. How can the test be constructed by computer?
5. How can the test be administered by computer?
6. What are the procedures for conducting an item analysis?

7. How can sex, racial, and ethnic bias in the items be detected?
8. How can test length be determined?
9. What are the best methods for setting a performance standard?
10. What types of validity evidence should be obtained?
11. How can the validity of the scores be measured?
12. What is the most appropriate reliability index?
13. How can the reliability of mastery-nonmastery classifications be estimated?
14. How can the dependability of the scores be estimated?

The answers are differentiated for different test makers, especially classroom teachers, district and state level test specialists, and test publishers.

For ease of use by researchers and practitioners, each chapter is organized into five main sections: (1) "Introduction," which defines the topic and explains its contribution to the test development process; (2) "Review," which presents a critical survey of all major strategies, methods, conceptualizations, and statistics related directly to the topic; (3) "Suggestions for Future Research," which lists the specific types and areas of research that still need attention; (4) "Guidelines for Practitioners," which furnishes recommendations on the best strategy/method/statistic for tests constructed by classroom teachers, district and state level specialists, test publishers, and other test makers; and (5) "References," which supplies a comprehensive bibliography of the most important journal articles, book chapters, books, monographs, and unpublished documents on the topic.

INTENDED USES OF THE BOOK

Consistent with its structure, contents, and orientation, this book is intended for use as a textbook in a graduate level course on criterion-referenced measurement or in a measurement seminar. It should serve as a supplementary volume in an introductory measurement course for upper level undergraduate and graduate students in education and psychology where a balanced presentation of norm-referenced and criterion-referenced measurement is desired (i.e., most measurement tests concentrate almost exclusively on norm-referenced measurement and classical test theory). For this use, the technical material in chapters 6, 10 and 11, which presumes the reader has had intermediate to advanced statistics courses, should be de-emphasized. Only the concepts discussed in these chapters should be presented.

The book can also serve as a handbook and resource for the following audiences: (1) classroom teachers who construct their own mastery tests and/or need to be able to evaluate the quality of commercially produced tests; (2) district and state level test makers who are involved in minimum competency testing; (3) specialists in licensing and certification agencies who develop competency tests and set passing scores; (4) industrial psychologists who construct tests for the performance assessment of employees; and (5) researchers who are interested in investigating the technical issues in criterion-referenced measurement.

REFERENCES

AERA/APA/NCME Joint Committee. *Joint technical standards for educational and psychological testing*. Washington, DC: American Psychological Association, in preparation.

APA/AERA/NCME Joint Committee. *Standards for educational and psychological tests* (rev. ed.). Washington, DC: American Psychological Association, 1974.

Berk, R. A. (Ed.). *Criterion-referenced measurement: The state of the art.* Baltimore, MD: Johns Hopkins University Press, 1980.

Brown, S. *What do they know? A review of criterion-referenced assessment*. Edinburgh, Scotland: Scottish Education Department, 1980.

Bunda, M. A., & Sanders, J. R. (Eds.). *Practices and problems in competency-based measurement*. Washington, DC: National Council on Measurement in Education, 1979.

Ebel, R. L. Content standard test scores. *Educational and Psychological Measurement*, 1962, *22*, 15–25.

Flanagan, J. C. Units, scores, and norms. In E. F. Lindquist (Ed.), *Educational measurement*. Washington, DC: American Council on Education, 1951. Pp. 659–763.

Glaser, R. Instructional technology and the measurement of learning outcomes: Some questions. *American Psychologist*, 1963, *18*, 519-521.

Glaser, R., & Klaus, D. J. Proficiency measurement: Assessing human performance. In R. M. Gagné (Ed.), *Psychological principles in systems development*. New York: Holt, Rinehart and Winston, 1962. Pp. 419–474.

Hambleton, R. K. Advances in criterion-referenced testing technology. In C. R. Reynolds & T. B. Gutkin (Eds.), *The handbook of school psychology*. New York: Wiley, 1982. Pp. 351–379.

Hambleton, R. K., & Eignor, D. R. Guidelines for evaluating criterion-referenced tests and test manuals. *Journal of Educational Measurement*, 1978, *15*, 321–327.

Hambleton, R. K., Swaminathan, H., Algina, J., & Coulson, D. B. Criterion-referenced testing and measurement: A review of technical issues and developments. *Review of Educational Research*, 1978, *48*, 1–47.

Harris, C. W., Alkin, M. C., & Popham, W. J. (Eds.). *Problems in criterion-referenced measurement* (CSE Monograph Series in Evaluation, No. 3). Los Angeles: Center for the Study of Evaluation, University of California, 1974.

Jaeger, R. M., & Tittle, C. K. (Eds.). *Minimum competency testing: Motives, models, measures, and consequences*. Berkeley, CA: McCutchan, 1980.

Martuza, V. R. *Applying norm-referenced and criterion-referenced measurement in education*. Boston: Allyn and Bacon, 1977.

Millman, J. Criterion-referenced measurement. In W. J. Popham (Ed.), *Evaluation in education: Current applications*. Berkeley, CA: McCutchan, 1974. Pp. 311–397.

National Commission on Excellence in Education. *A nation at risk: The imperative for educational reform*. Washington, DC: U.S. Government Printing Office, April 1983. (Stock No. 065-000-00177-2).

Nedelsky, L. Absolute grading standards for objectives tests. *Educational and Psychological Measurement*, 1954, *14*, 3–19.
Popham, W. J. *Criterion-referenced measurement*. Englewood Cliffs, NJ: Prentice-Hall, 1978.
Popham, W. J., & Husek, T. R. Implications of criterion-referenced measurement. *Journal of Educational Measurement*, 1969, *6*, 1–9.
Thorndike, E. L. *Educational psychology* (Vol. 1). New York: Teachers College, Columbia University, 1913.

1 DEFINING "CRITERION-REFERENCED TEST"

ANTHONY J. NITKO

INTRODUCTION

EXAMINEES' SCORES on virtually all educational and psychological tests need to be *referenced* before meaningful interpretations can be made. Referencing a score means comparing it to something external to the test in order to enhance the interpretation given an examinees' test performance.

Norm-referencing

Very early in the history of educational and psychological measurement test users recognized that raw scores were difficult to interpret. The social and scientific context of the late nineteenth and early twentieth centuries led educators and psychologists to endorse a viewpoint that made *relative* ability important to measure. Various types of derived scores were proposed and tried over the years, and today most published tests rather routinely report a more or less standard set of derived scores which communicate examinees' relative ability and enhance the interpretation of raw scores: percentile ranks, linear standard scores, normalized standard scores, and grade-equivalent scores.

Derived scores such as these are constructed in a way that conveys to the knowledgeable test interpreter information about an examinee's standing relative to others in a defined group. A "defined group of other examinees" is called a *norm group*, and since derived scores reference a raw score to the norm group, they are called *norm-referencing scores*. Tests especially built to maximize the usefulness of norm-referencing are called *norm-referenced tests*.

Although the four types of norm-referencing scores mentioned earlier are widely used, there are many other types of norm-referencing scores. A more complete description of them can be found in any standard testing and measurement textbook or in a readable book specializing in norm-referencing by Howard B. Lyman (1978).

This chapter has been adapted from Nitko (1980, pp. 461–485), published by the American Educational Research Association, Washington, DC.

Norm-referencing is useful when the information needed about an examinee is related to the examinee's relative ability or relative attainment. The potential interpretive value of norm-referencing depends on the relevance of the norm group to the decision being made and on the clarity with which the composition of the norm group is specified. Suppose your percentile rank on a mathematics test is 98, for example. In order to understand your relative mathematics ability it is important to know whether the norm group is comprised of a representative sample of the nation's fifth graders or a representative sample of the nation's adults. For some decisions a more specific norm group, such as "college applicants majoring in engineering," is more relevant to understanding an examinee's relative ability than is a nonspecific norm group such as "adults in general."

Norm-referencing Is Insufficient

For a great many educational and psychological uses of tests, you need to know more about the examinee than norm-referenced information. You may have scored higher than 98% of the individuals who have taken a mathematics test—whoever they may be—but what kinds of mathematics concepts do you know or what mathematics problems can you solve? How do you go about solving such problems? Is your mathematics skill limited to elementary arithmetic computations? Were the mathematics problems on the test selected because they are typical, practical problems, or are they abstract, theoretical problems? Do the problems require routine, easily memorized procedures for solution, or do they require creative, novel thinking for solution?

Questions such as these become important when the intended use of a test extends beyond identifying the relative ability of examinees. Identifying the relative ability of pupils may be important in forming "high," "middle," and "low" groups for mathematics instruction, for example, but before effective instruction can be carried out, you need to know the kinds of mathematics concepts each pupil understands and the kinds of difficulties each pupil experiences when solving mathematics problems.

Criterion-referencing

For some tests, referencing schemes other than norm-referencing is possible. When a derived score or other referencing procedure enhances raw score interpretation by communicating an examinee's behavior repertoire, rather than an examinee's ability relative to other examinees in the norm group, it is said to be *criterion-referenced*. Tests built especially to enhance the usefulness of criterion-referencing are called *criterion-referenced tests*. A test can provide both norm-referencing and criterion-referencing information.

Because the theories of mental abilities prevailing during the early part of this century were concerned primarily with identifying relative differences among individuals, measurement specialists focused their attention on developing and using norm-referencing schemes. However, by 1962 Robert Glaser and David Klaus saw the need for criterion-referenced measurement in connection with military and industrial training. Glaser began a program of research and development based on the application of psychological principles to school learning environments, and in that context he expanded the original idea a year later (Glaser, 1963):

> Underlying the concept of achievement measurement is the notion of a continuum of knowledge acquisition ranging from no proficiency at all to perfect performance. An individual's achievement level falls at some point on the continuum as indicated by the behaviors he displays during testing. The degree to which his achievement resembles desired performance at any specified level is assessed by criterion-referenced measures of achievement or proficiency. The standard against which a student's performance is compared when measured in this manner is the behavior which defines each point along the achievement continuum. The term "criterion," when used in this way, does not necessarily refer to final end-of-course behavior. Criterion levels can be established at any point in instruction as to the adequacy of an individual's performance. In other words, the specific behaviors implied at each level of proficiency can be identified and used to describe the specific tasks a student must be capable of performing before he achieves one of these knowledge levels. It is this sense that measures of proficiency can be criterion-referenced.
>
> Along such a continuum of attainment, a student's score on a criterion-referenced measure provides explicit information as to what the individual can or cannot do. Criterion-referenced measures indicate the content of the behavioral repertory, and the correspondence between what an individual does and the underlying continuum of achievement. Measures which assess student achievement in terms of a criterion standard thus provide information as to the degree of competence attained by a particular student which is independent of reference to the performance of others. (p. 519)

Criterion-referencing can be used together with norm-referencing to come to a more complete understanding of an individual. Many published criterion-referenced tests provide both kinds of referencing. Figure 1.1 illustrates how this dual referencing might be done with a hypothetical elementary school arithmetic test. The figure shows that raw scores on the test can be referenced both to location in a group (e.g., percentile ranks) and to a criterion-referencing scale of arithmetic complexity. While it is possible to use both referencing schemes for some tests, it is unlikely that the same test can provide optimal information for both norm-referencing and criterion-referencing (Hambleton & Novick, 1973; Nitko, 1970).

REVIEW OF THE MANY DEFINITIONS OF CRITERION-REFERENCING

Glaser's proposal to articulate the raw scores on a test to a scale or continuum of competence seems straightforward, but the literature on criterion-referencing employs so many different variations of criterion-referencing that defining it can become confusing. Not only do different writers use the term differently, but some writers may use the term differently within the same article (Gray, 1978). It is helpful in understanding the nature of criterion-referencing to adopt a broad definition to distinguish criterion-referencing

Figure 1.1. Hypothetical example of two ways to reference test scores: criterion-referencing and norm-referencing

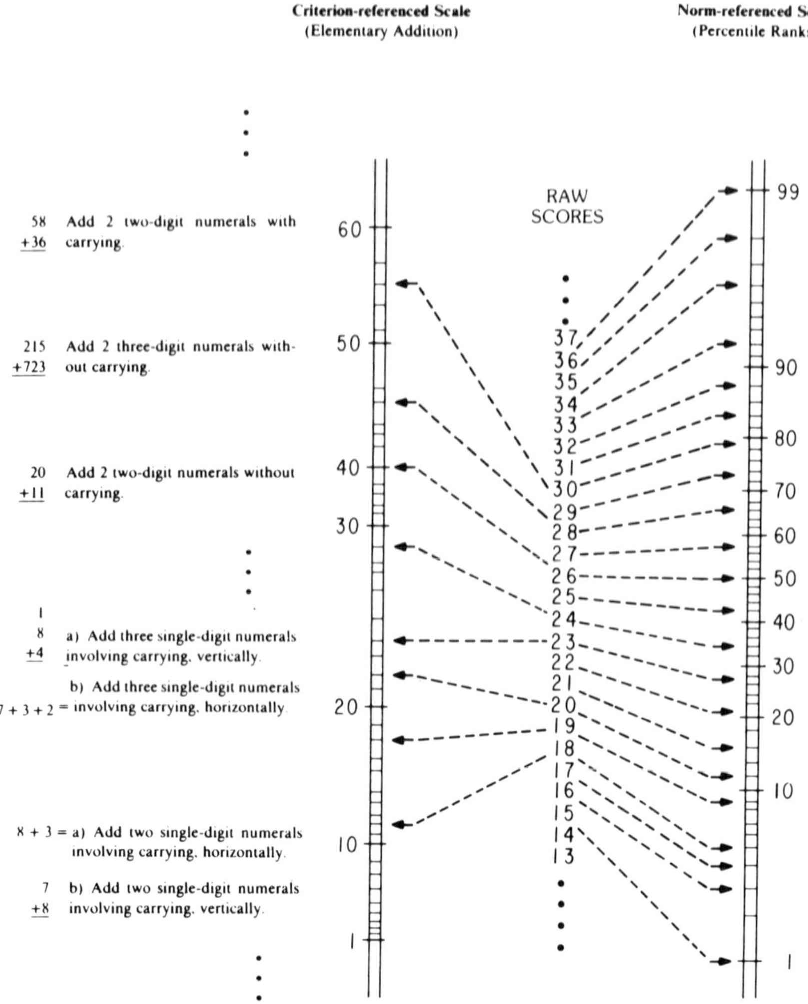

Source: Reprinted with permission from Nitko, Anthony J. "Distinguishing the Many Varieties of Criterion-referenced Tests." *Review of Educational Research*, 1980, *50*, 461–485, Figure 1 (p. 464). Copyright 1980, American Educational Research Association, Washington, DC. Specific addition examples taken from Cox and Graham (1966, p. 148).

from other similar-sounding schemes, and then to classify the various kinds of criterion-referencing schemes which fit this broad definition. In this way you come to understand to what kinds of tests the various suggestions made for test development, for reliability and validity determination, and for test usage can be applied.

Broad Definition of Criterion-referencing

Each kind of criterion-referenced test is designed to reference an examinee's score to a different behavior domain, and different tests may accomplish this referencing in different ways. There is neither an agreed-upon definition of criterion-referencing nor a preferred criterion-referencing scheme, since the most useful scheme will depend on the nature and purpose of the test. A broad definition, however, can be used as a basis for delimiting the nature of the concept:

> *A criterion-referenced test is one that is deliberately constructed to yield measurements that are directly interpretable in terms of specified performance standards.* Performance standards are generally specified by defining a class or domain of tasks that should be performed by the individual. Measurements are taken on representative samples of tasks drawn from this domain, and such measures are referenced directly to this domain for each individual measured. [Criterion-referenced tests] . . . are specifically constructed to support generalizations about an individual's performance relative to a specified domain of tasks. . . . (In the instructional context, such a domain of tasks may be termed a *domain of instructionally relevant tasks*. The insertion of the qualifiers "instructionally relevant" serves to delimit the domain to those tasks, the learning of which is the goal of instruction. The term tasks includes both content and process). (Glaser & Nitko, 1971, p. 653)

As can be inferred from this definition, criterion-referenced test scores must be referenced to a well-defined domain of tasks or behaviors. A domain is *well defined* if it is clear which categories of performance or which kinds of tasks are and are not potential test items. A basic use of criterion-referencing is to generalize an examinee's status from the relatively few items which happen to be on a test to the larger performance domain from which the items were sampled, and to do so in a way that permits a test user to make a statement about the examinee's behavior repertoire. Thus, a well-defined domain is a necessary condition for criterion-referencing. Since building a test requires much more than simply defining a domain, a well-defined domain, while a necessary condition for any criterion-referenced test, is not a sufficient condition.

Two General Categories of Criterion-referenced Tests

Table 1.1 shows one way of classifying various criterion-referenced tests. The column headings show that domains can be well-defined, ill-defined, or undefined. Ill-defined and undefined domains cannot form the basis for building a criterion-referenced test, and so tests developed from these two

Table 1.1. A Scheme for Classifying and Distinguishing Criterion-referenced Tests

	Well-defined and Ordered Domains	Well-defined But Unordered Domains	Ill-defined Domains	Undefined Domains
Basis for Test Development	Ordering based on judgments of the social or aesthetic quality of an examinee's product or performance	Specifying the stimulus properties of the items to be included in the domain	Poorly articulated behavioral objectives	No attempt to define a domain to which test performance is referenced
	Ordering based on which level of difficulty or complexity a topic or subject is learned	Specifying the stimuli and the responses in the domain	Defining the domain only in terms of the particular items on the test	Using a cut-off score, but not defining a performance domain
	Ordering based on degree of proficiency with which a complex skill is performed	Specifying the "diagnostic" categories of the domain		
	Ordering based on prerequisite sequences for acquiring an intellectual or psychomotor skill	Specifying the abstractions, traits, or constructs that define the domain		
	Basis for Test Development			
	Ordering based on an empirically defined latent test	Other ways of specifying the domain are possible		
	Ordering on other bases is possible			

Source: Reprinted with permission from Nitko, Anthony J. "Distinguishing the Many Varieties of Criterion-referenced Tests." *Review of Educational Research*, 1980, *50*, 461–485, Table 1 (p. 466). Copyright 1980, American Educational Research Association, Washington, DC.

categories cannot be called criterion-referenced under the broad definition adopted here, even though some test developers may claim otherwise.

Only the first two categories of Table 1.1 provide a basis for classifying criterion-referenced tests. Within the group of tests referenced to well-defined domains, we can distinguish between domains that are *ordered* and domains that are *unordered*. In some cases, the behaviors comprising a domain can be ordered along a continuum of achievement. One kind of achievement continuum, for example, consists of ordering behaviors in a sequence of learning prerequisites; a test may be built which references a learner's performance to this sequence. The table shows five subcategories of ordered domains, but it may be possible to identify other bases for ordering domains.

Not all domains can be ordered along a continuum of achievement, even though it is possible to define a domain quite well. It is usually not possible to order in a scale, for example, items within a very specific, narrow domain such as that implied by a single behavioral objective.

Distinguishing between ordered and unordered domains is not meant to imply that one is preferred to the other. Furthermore, it should be noted that in differing applications, the same domain could be considered both ordered and unordered. For example, a narrow behavioral objective such as "adding three single-digit numerals involving carrying" implies a domain of items that is essentially unorderable. In some applications, however, this narrow domain could be considered as a small portion of a broad domain of elementary arithmetic performance. Within this broad domain, these narrow portions may be orderable along a scale even though items within each narrow portion may not. This is essentially what had been done by Cox and Graham (1966) to order the arithmetic domain illustrated in Figure 1.1. It is possible, too, that a domain considered unorderable may one day become orderable if someone discovers the means for so doing.

Tests Referenced to Well-defined and Ordered Domains

Table 1.2 provides examples of tests for various categories of well-defined and ordered domains. The tests named in the table were included to illustrate the various categories and should not be considered as representative or exhaustive of the field. Further, many of these tests are no longer used, often because they were crude, were unreliable, or contain outdated content. You can find illustrations of the older tests cited in this table (and in Table 1.3) in Starch (1916) and Chapman and Rush (1917). Note that older tests were not called criterion-referenced since the term was not invented until 1962.

Social or esthetic quality. An examinee's test performance can be judged according to its social merit or aesthetic quality and compared to a domain of performances for interpretation. In this case, a domain is considered to be all the various nuances of quality with which a certain category of tasks can be performed. These nuances of performance are then ordered along a continuum of aesthetic quality or social merit as established by one or more judges. This is what Rev. George Fisher, the headmaster of an English school, did in

Table 1.2. Categories of Criterion-referenced Tests Based on Well-defined and Ordered Domains

Basis for Scaling or Ordering the Defined Domain of Behavior[a]	Examples[b]
Judged social or esthetic quality of the performance	Rev. George Fisher's Scale Books (Chadwick, 1864) E. L. Thorndike's Handwriting (1910) and Drawing (1913) Scales
Complexity or difficulty level of the subject matter	Ayres's Spelling Scale (1915) Glaser's Criterion-referenced Measures I (1962, 1963) Cox and Graham's Arithmetic Scale (1966)
Degree of proficiency with which complex skills are performed	Harvard-Newton English Composition Scales (Ballou, 1914) Glaser's Criterion-referenced Measures II (1962, 1963) Perhaps certain sports events or physical fitness tests
Prerequisite sequence for acquiring intellectual and psychomotor skills	Gagné's Learning Hierarchies (1962) Piagetian Development Scales (Gray, 1978) Infant Development Scales (Uzgiris & Hunt, 1966)
Location on an empirically defined latent trait	Connolly, Nachtman, and Pritchett's arithmetic tests (1971) Other tests built with latent trait models (e.g., Rasch, 1960, or Birnbaum, 1968), provided they are referenced to well-defined and ordered domains of behavior.

Source: Adapted from Nitko (1980, p. 468) with permission of the American Educational Research Association, Washington, DC.

[a]Other bases for scaling are possible.

[b]Examples are meant to be illustrative rather than representative or exhaustive.

1864 (Chadwick, 1864). Fisher developed "scale books" containing specimens of pupils' school work, which he ordered according to his personal judgment of merit or quality. Each degree of handwriting quality, for example, was assigned a numerical merit rating. A pupil's handwriting was compared to specimens in the scale book until a close match to one of the specimens was found. The numerical value of that scale-book specimen become the pupil's handwriting score.

Edward L. Thorndike and his students developed a number of achievement quality scales during the early part of this century, including handwriting (1910) and drawing (1913). Rather than relying on his personal judgment to order handwriting and drawing specimens, Thorndike used psychophysical scaling techniques which required several judges to order the same specimens. The data from these judges were used to establish a quality scale with numerical values, each value associated with one or more actual handwriting specimens. Specimens forming this scale ranged from barely legible to copybook perfect. During the days when quality handwriting was an important school outcome, thousands of these handwriting specimen scales were used by pupils and teachers throughout the nation (Thorndike, 1918).

Subject matter difficulty or complexity. A test developer might be able to order the tasks in the domain according to their difficulty or complexity for a population of persons. A test is then developed which references an examinee's score to this domain to reveal to which level of difficulty or complexity a topic or subject has been learned. Glaser (1963) and his co-workers (Glaser & Cox, 1968; Glaser & Klaus, 1962) wrote about this type of criterion-referencing, so in Table 1.2 I have referred to this as "Glaser's Criterion-referenced Measures I." Cox and Graham (1966) used a Guttman (1950) scaling technique to order arithmetic problems in a scale that could be used to identify the most complex problem a pupil could perform correctly (see Figure 1.1).

These scales do not order behavior according to social merit or aesthetic quality, as do the scales in the first category, nor do the behaviors in this scale of complexity represent verified learning sequences or prerequisites, as do the scales described in what follows. Rather, they stand as psychometric scales, ordering tasks on the basis of difficulty.

Degree of proficiency. A test developer may consider the domain to be a complex intellectual or psychomotor skill and order the various degrees of proficiency with which this skill can be performed. Tests referenced to this domain might, for example, distinguish the performance level of a master machinist from apprentice or journeyman levels (Glaser & Klaus, 1962). In Table 1.2, I have called this category "Glaser's Criterion-referenced Measures II."

These scales are ordered on the basis of the quality of performance, of course, but here quality is defined as proficiency rather than as aesthetics or complexity. To develop such scales may require an analysis of the difference between an "expert's" behavior and a "novice's" behavior (cf. Chi & Glaser, 1980; Hively, 1970; Simon & Simon, 1978). The performance of experts is likely to be both quantitatively and qualitatively different from that of novices. An expert's performance of a complex task, for example, may require fewer and more efficiently performed subbehaviors than the performance of a novice on the same task.

Prerequisite learning or developmental sequences. The behaviors in a domain may be orderable on the basis of a hierarchy of learning or developmental prerequisites. A hierarchical ordering of learning prerequisites is based on the "psychological structure of the subject-matter . . . an ordering of behaviors in a sequence of prerequisite skills so that competence in an early task in the sequence facilitates learning of later tasks in the sequence" (Glaser & Nitko, 1971, p. 636). The most familiar learning hierarchies are those of

Gagné (1962, 1968; Gagné, Major, Garstens, & Paradise, 1962; Gagné & Paradise, 1961).

A domain of behaviors may be orderable in terms of a developmental sequence. Gray (1978), Uzgiris and Hunt (1966, 1968), and Hunt (1975) used ordinal scales of development in this way.

Latent trait location. Sometimes the domain of behavior represents a single dimension or factor, called a *latent trait*, which is hypothesized to underlie the performance of specific behaviors. If so, it might be possible to scale the tasks in the domain along this dimension using one of the various latent trait models. (See the *Journal of Educational Measurement*, 1977, *14*(2), for an introduction to this topic.) Connolly, Nachtman, and Pritchett (1971) have developed such a test in which items within each of 14 topics in arithmetic are scaled according to their location in each topical area.

Note that it is not latent trait analysis in general that is criterion-referenced. Rather, latent trait analysis might be used to help order the tasks comprising a domain so that an examinee's test score may be referenced to the domain in a way that reveals the specific behaviors of which the examinee is capable. This does not flow automatically from an application of latent trait measurement theory, but requires that the domain of tasks be unidimensional and that the items (tasks) be orderable on a number line representing this dimension. The resultant test scores must be capable of being interpreted in terms of the specific behaviors in the domain an examinee is likely to be able to perform.

Tests Referenced to Well-defined and Unordered Domains

Not all well-defined domains of tasks can be ordered. In fact, it is probable that a great many of the domains that educators define as important representations of school learning outcomes cannot be ordered. However, you can develop criterion-referenced tests for many of these unorderable domains, provided you can define them well.

Table 1.3 provides examples of tests for several categories of such domains. Because space is limited for this chapter, all of these examples cannot be described in detail, so it will be necessary for you to check the reference cited. It should be noted that most of the literature on criterion-referencing deals with tests based on unordered domains, usually without acknowledging that criterion-referencing applies to ordered domains as well. This is important to keep in mind when reading the literature because many of the suggestions for developing and using tests based on unordered domains do not apply to tests referenced to ordered domains.

Focusing on stimulus properties. One way to define a domain precisely is to describe in great detail the stimulus properties of the items within it. In this context, "stimulus properties" means the surface features of items that the test developer believes will affect performance: for example, the syntax fea-

Table 1.3. Categories of Criterion-referenced Tests Based on Well-defined but Unordered Domains

Basis for Delineating the Behavior Domain[a]	During Test Development Emphasis is Placed on:	Examples[b]
Stimulus Properties of the Domain and the Sampling Plan of the Test	Defining content and content strata	Starch's English Vocabulary Test (1916) Ebel's Content-standard English Vocabulary Test (1962)
	Specifying stimulus properties of item domains	Hively's Item Forms (1966; Hively, Patterson & Page, 1966; Hively, 1968) Osburn's Item Forms (1968)
Verbal Statements of Stimuli and Responses in Domain	Behavioral objectives with or without the cut-off score ("criterion") specified	Tests based on Mager's Type of Objectives (1962) Curriculum Embedded Tests of IPI Mathematics (Cox & Boston, 1967) Popham and Husek's Criterion-referenced Testing (1969) Harris and Stewart's Criterion-referenced Testing (1971)
	Elaborated descriptions of behaviors and stimuli	Popham's Criterion-referenced Tests (1975, 1978) IOX Objectives-based Tests: Amplified Objectives (Popham, 1972, 1974) IOX Test Specifications (Popham, 1978, 1980, 1981)

"Diagnostic" Categories of Performance	Identifying entry-level behaviors	Hunt and Kirk's Tests of School Readiness (1974)
	Identifying behavior components missing from a complex performance	Tests built on Resnick's Components Analysis (Resnick, Wang, & Kaplan, 1973)
		Gagné's Two-Stage Testing (1970)
	Identifying and categorizing erroneous responses	Glaser, Damrin, and Gardner's "Tab-Item" Technique (1954)
		Nesbit's CHILD Program (1966)
		Hsu's Computer-Assisted Diagnostic Tests (Hsu & Carlson, 1972)
	Identifying erroneous processes	Beck's Blending Algorithm (Beck & Mitroff, 1972)
		Interviews to determine what processes were used in responding to test tasks
Abstractions, Traits, or Constructs	Specifying specific behaviors or categories of behaviors that delimit the abstraction, trait, or construct	Tests based on the *Taxonomy of Educational Objectives* (Bloom, 1956)
		Certain basic skills survey tests, e.g., ITBS, MAT

Source: Adapted from Nitko (1980, p. 472–473) with permission of the American Educational Research Association, Washington, DC.
[a]Other bases for delineating exist.
[b]Examples are meant to be illustrative rather than representative or exhaustive.

tures of a sentence, the type of word in a vocabulary item, or the magnitude of the numbers in each position of an arithmetic problem.

Identifying stimulus properties of items that potentially affect performance is important when you are developing a test because a particular form of a test will be but a small sample of items from the domain. If this sample is not representative of the important stimulus features of the tasks in the domain, the test will likely provide less accurate information about the behaviors an examinee is able to perform. Identifying the stimulus features during the development of a test allows you to construct a sampling plan and to draw a representative sample of items from the domain—a sample that contains items having all the important stimulus features implied by the domain. This ideal is not always attained, however, because what is known about how the stimulus properties of items relate to examinee performance is limited.

Focusing on both stimuli and responses. The most common way to define a domain has been for the test developer to state both the stimuli and the responses that comprise a domain. This statement may take the form of a behavioral objective. Many people believe that behavioral objectives are necessary for criterion-referencing, but this is not entirely correct (Nitko, 1980).

Popham (1980) has argued that behavioral objectives as usually written are not sufficient to define a domain unambiguously because they are too variable in their form, content, and level of difficulty. He suggests that an "IOX Test Specification" be written in which the form, stimulus features, and response features of items in the domain be described along with precise instructions on how the items are developed from the stimulus materials. This elaborated statement of stimuli and responses may require several hundred words rather than the 10 or 20 typically comprising a behavioral objective. See Popham (1978, 1981, chapter 2) for further details.

Focusing on diagnostic categories. There may be some overlap between tests in this category and tests in the preceding categories. A behavior domain may be defined in terms of (a) entry-level behavior needed for an upcoming instructional sequence, (b) behavior components that are part of a complex performance, (c) erroneous behavior(s) made in response to subject matter learning, or (d) erroneous processes used to solve problems. Usually it is necessary to use special techniques to construct items capable of detecting erroneous or incomplete responses. For example, it may be necessary to limit the stimulus materials presented to the examinee to those that are known to have a high probability of eliciting an erroneous response from the examinee who is disposed toward making a particular kind of error. Or, it may be necessary to use a two-stage testing procedure in which the second stage is used to pinpoint the specific nature of an erroneous response.

Focusing on behaviors that delimit an abstraction, trait, or construct. Another way to define a domain is to describe the particular behaviors that comprise the test developer's definition of a particular trait or construct, such as spelling ability, map reading, or reading comprehension. Although simply stating the construct name is not sufficient for defining the domain well, some test developers go beyond this by delineating the specific behaviors that comprise the construct. If, by so doing, it is clear to test users which items are and are not included in the domain, then such tests would be appropriately included under the criterion-referenced test label.

What Criterion-referencing Is Not

Criterion-level confusion. One confusion about criterion-referencing is the misconception that the term means using a *cut-off score* or a *passing score*. Criterion-referencing does not require cut-off or passing scores, although certain practical applications of criterion-referenced tests may require the use of cut-off scores.

You may establish a cut-off score on any test—criterion-referenced or not. If you simply set 80% as "passing" for a test, for example, this certainly does not mean that you can reference the score to a well-defined domain and describe an examinee's performance with respect to the behaviors in that domain. It is the ability of the test to give information about the examinee's status with respect to the behaviors in the domain that makes a test criterion-referenced, not the fact that the test is used with a cut-off score.

Criterion-measure confusion. Sometimes tests are built to predict an examinee's status on another test or another measure. For example, a scholastic aptitude test is built in order to help predict a college applicant's college grades. The variable to be predicted is termed the *criterion* variable. Thus, college grade average is the criterion measure for a scholastic aptitude test. The research that is conducted to establish that a test is useful in predicting an examinee's status on a criterion variable is called *criterion-oriented* or *criterion-related* validity research.

These uses of the term "criterion" are different from its use in connection with criterion-referencing.

Closely Related Concepts

Domain-referencing. Domain-referencing is quite similar to criterion-referencing, referring to the ability of a test to be used to describe an examinee's status on a well-defined domain of behaviors. In fact, it might be desirable to use "domain-referencing" instead of "criterion-referencing." However, for a variety of reasons, testing specialists have come to the conclusion that "criterion-referencing" should remain the preferred term (Hambleton, Swaminathan, Algina, & Coulson, 1978; Popham, 1978).

A special use of domain-referencing has been proposed by Wells Hively (1966, 1970; Hively, Patterson, & Page, 1968) in the context of instructional design and evaluation. For Hively and his associates, behavioral objectives proved too vague for the kind of instructional research and development in which they were engaged. The solution was to define operationally a domain in terms of *item forms* (see, for example, Hively et al., 1968; Popham, chapter

2). This led to the following description of domain-referencing (cited in Hively, Maxwell, Rabehl, Sension, & Lundin, 1973):

The basic notion underlying domain-referenced achievement testing is that certain important classes of behavior in the repertoires of experts (or amateurs) can be exhaustively defined in terms of structured sets or *domains* of test items. Testing systems may be *referenced* to these domains in the sense that a testing system consists of rules for sampling items from a domain and administering them to an individual (or sample of individuals from a specified population) in order to obtain estimates of the probability that the individual (or group of individuals) could answer any given item from the domain at a specified moment in time. Domains of test items are structured and built up through the specification of stimulus and response properties which are thought to be important in shaping the behavior of individuals who are in the process of learning to be experts. These properties may be thought of as stratifying large domains into smaller domains or subsets. Precise definition of a domain and its subsets makes statistical estimation possible. This provides the foundation for precise diagnosis of the performance of individuals over the domain and its subsets. In addition, clear specification of the properties used to structure the domain makes possible inductive generalization beyond the domain to situations which share those properties. That is, once we have diagnosed a student with respect to a defined domain we may be able to predict his behavior (in a non-statistical, inductive fashion) in natural situations which have some properties in common with the test items within the domain (Hively, 1970). (p. 15)

Objectives-referenced testing. This term refers to the situation in which a test has behavioral objectives corresponding to each item. Objectives-referenced tests can be criterion-referenced tests if (a) objectives are written to define a domain and (b) items are representative samples of behavior from this domain. Objectives-referenced tests are not criterion-referenced if behavioral objectives are written after the items are written. One can take any test and make up verbal statements of behavior to describe each item. However, such a collection of items, not representing a well-defined behavior domain, is likely to be a poor basis for generalizing an examinee's test performance. These after-the-fact procedures are classified as ill-defined domains in Table 1.1.

Single-objective testing. A single behavioral objective can be used to define a domain of tasks. If a test is designed to infer an examinee's status on this domain of tasks, then it is likely to be a criterion-referenced test of the type identified as the second category in Table 1.3.

Mastery testing. A *mastery test* is any test used to provide information relevant to the decision about whether a pupil has "mastered" a given instructional goal. Mastery may mean different things in different instructional contexts. For example, Chi and Glaser (1980) summarized cognitive psychology views that imply that "experts" or "masters" exhibit different behaviors and may employ different internal cognitive processes than do "nonmasters" or "novices" when attempting to answer the same test items. Mastery tests measuring these different kinds of behaviors and processes could be quite different in content from the mastery tests currently being used. Currently, "mastery" is conceived as "knowing more of" a domain. For example, a "master" is often considered to be a pupil who can answer correctly 85% of the items, while a "nonmaster" can only answer correctly fewer than 85% of the items. These two concepts of mastery are in sharp contrast to each other. The former emphasizes qualitative differences between masters and nonmasters, while the latter emphasizes quantitative differences.

Although a mastery decision *need not* be based on a criterion-referenced test, it would be difficult to imagine that a mastery decision *should not* be based on a criterion-referenced test. A mastery decision begs the question, "Mastery of what?" The answer to such a question would need to be linked to a well-defined domain of performance. Given the current state of the art, it seems reasonable to assert that the "mastery of what" question would be best answered by delineating clearly the domain of relevant behaviors of which the learner has command.

SUGGESTIONS FOR FUTURE RESEARCH

Research and development of criterion-referencing procedures are needed on both the ordered and the unordered sides of the domain ledger. Of the several categories of criterion-referencing described previously, I suggest two areas in which future research is sorely needed because of the current and likely future demands of educational and societal needs:

1. *Glaser criterion-referenced measurement II*. You will recall that this category of referencing calls for articulating test scores to a domain that can be ordered as levels of proficiency, a qualitative scaling of behaviors along a novice-expert continuum. Research related to such test development will need to focus initially on describing the nature of competence in a specific kind of performance or knowledge area and the relation of competent performance to cognitive process. Such research will undoubtedly reveal that there is not an underlying unidimensional continuum, and thus existing mathematical models will be difficult, if not impossible, to apply to this psychometric problem. Defining and measuring competence seems to be an important societal concern, however, even though a scientific understanding of the psychological processes differentiating levels of competence is still largely lacking. It is to be expected, therefore, that there will be a lag between experimental research and practical test development. Once an operational version of a test has been developed it will be possible to explore the potential uses of competence measurements in classroom practice, thereby moving cognitive-psychology process research out of the laboratory and into the school.
2. *Diagnostic categories of performance*. The development of practical tools for identifying the nature of pupil errors is a second area of research and

development that seems to have important payoffs for school learning. As Glaser (1981) pointed out:

> An important skill of teaching is the ability to synthesize from a student's performance an accurate picture of a student's misconceptions that lead to error. This task goes deeper than identifying incorrect errors and pointing these out to the student: It should identify the nature of the concept or rule that the student is employing that governs his [or her] performance in some specific way (in most cases, the student's behavior is not random or careless, but is driven by some underlying misconceptions or by incomplete knowledge). (p. 10)

Glaser's paper summarizes some of the research that has been done to identify types of pupil errors and offers ideas about the directions in which future research should proceed. It would seem that efficient and formal procedures (tests) would be of great benefit to teachers, especially those lacking the skill or time to apply informal procedures. Furthermore, once patterns of erroneous behavior are properly identified, it should be possible to redirect pedagogical methods to avoid the initial erroneous learning on the part of the pupil.

It seems important to both instructional theory and practice that research and development be undertaken in the preceding two areas. More than likely, these two areas are complementary: Learning about the nature of incompetence ("diagnosis") helps define the nature of competence. The researcher working in these areas is likely to need to use skills and knowledge in several areas, including cognitive psychology, psychometrics, and instructional practice (pedagogy).

GUIDELINES FOR PRACTITIONERS

This chapter described the rather abstract concept of criterion-referencing, a concept that is still in the process of being formulated by workers in the field. Nevertheless, the practitioner can apply this abstract information about the nature of criterion-referencing in the following ways:

1. Carefully read articles, chapters, and books about criterion-referencing to discern the type of criterion-referencing being discussed. Writers will often not explicate the variety to which their suggestions apply, so it will be up to you to determine it.
2. Recognize that most statements about criterion-referencing—be they positive or negative—apply primarily to one or two types and not to the entire field. Reviewing the varieties described in Tables 1.1, 1.2, and 1.3 should make this clear.
3. Recognize that different decisions will imply the use of different kinds of information and perhaps different kinds of tests. Criterion-referencing may be important to some decisions, but different decisions may require different kinds of criterion-referencing. It is an oversimplication to state that "a criterion-referenced test is needed." Rather, it is essential for you

to be specific about the nature of the information you need and about the kind of criterion-referencing that might provide this information.

4. Recognize that norm-referenced data are needed to interpret fully an examinee's criterion-referenced test performance. Look for the important norm-referenced information in the materials that accompany the criterion-referenced test(s) you are planning to purchase. Criterion-referencing and norm-referencing provide complementary information.
5. Criterion-referenced tests are often recommended when decisions of mastery and/or minimum competency are being made. Recognize that there are several conceptions of mastery and competence. Be sure that the criterion-referenced test you adopt is built on a theoretical framework consistent with your conception of mastery and/or competence. (You should be able to articulate your conception of mastery in rather precise terms.)
6. Recognize that most practical work in criterion-referencing, including technical suggestions for ascertaining reliability and validity, has been related to unordered behavior domains, especially the first two categories of Table 1.3. Not all authors explain this. As a result, many of the suggestions (in this book and elsewhere) for improving the quality of criterion-referenced testing do not apply to all categories of criterion-referenced tests.

REFERENCES

Ayres, L. P. *A measuring scale for ability in spelling*. New York: Russell Sage Foundation, 1915.

Ballou, F. W. Scales for the measurement of English composition. *Harvard-Newton Bulletins* (No. 2). Cambridge: Harvard University, 1914.

Beck, I. B., & Mitroff, D. D. *Comprehension during the acquisition of decoding skills*. Pittsburgh: Learning Research and Development Center, University of Pittsburgh, 1972.

Birnbaum, A. Chapters 17–20. In F. M. Lord & M. R. Novick, *Statistical theories of mental test scores*. Reading, MA: Addison-Wesley, 1968.

Bloom, B. S. (Ed.). *Taxonomy of educational objectives. Handbook I: Cognitive domain*. New York: McKay, 1956.

Chadwick, E. Statistics of educational results. *The Museum, A Quarterly Magazine of Education, Literature, and Science*, 1864, *3*, 479–484.

Chapman, J. C., & Rush, G. P. *The scientific measurement of classroom products*. Boston: Silver, Burdette, 1917.

Chi, M. T. H., & Glaser, R. The measurement of expertise: Analysis of the development of knowledge and skill as a basis for assessing achievement. In E. L. Baker & E. S. Quellmalz (Eds.), *Educational testing and evaluation: Design, analysis, and policy*. Beverly Hills, CA: Sage, 1980. Pp. 37–47.

Connolly, A. J., Nachtman, W., & Pritchett, E. M. *KeyMath Diagnostic Arithmetic Test*. Circle Pines, MN: American Guidance Service, 1971.

Cox, R. C., & Boston, M. E. *Diagnosis of pupil achievement in the Individually Prescribed Instruction Project* (Working Paper No. 15). Pittsburgh: Learning Research and Development Center, University of Pittsburgh, 1967.

Cox, R. C., & Graham, G. T. The development of a sequentially scaled achievement test. *Journal of Educational Measurement*, 1966, *3*, 147-150.

Ebel, R. L. Content standard test scores. *Educational and Psychological Measurement*, 1962, *22*, 15-25.

Gagné, R. M. The acquisition of knowledge. *Psychological Review*, 1962, *69*, 355-365.

Gagné, R. M. Learning hierarchies. *Educational Psychologist*, 1968, *6*, 1-9.

Gagné, R. M. *The conditions of learning* (2nd ed.). New York: Holt, Rinehart and Winston, 1970.

Gagné, R. M., Major, J. R., Garstens, H. L., & Paradise, N. E. Factors in acquiring knowledge of a mathematical task. *Psychological Monographs*, 1962, *76* (7, Whole No. 526).

Gagné, R. M., & Paradise, N. E. Abilties and learning sets in knowledge acquisition. *Psychological Monographs*, 1961, *75* (14, Whole No. 518).

Glaser, R. Instructional technology and the measurement of learning outcomes. Some questions. *American Psychologist*, 1963, *18*, 519-521.

Glaser, R. *The future of testing: A research agenda for cognitive psychology and psychometrics* (Technical Report No. 3). Pittsburgh: Learning Research and Development Center, University of Pittsburgh, 1981.

Glaser, R., & Cox, R. C. Criterion-referenced testing for the measurement of educational outcomes. In R. Weisgerber (Ed.), *Instructional processes and media innovation.* Chicago: Rand McNally, 1968.

Glaser, R., Damrin, D. E., & Gardner, F. M. The tab item: A technique for the measurement of proficiency in diagnostic problem-solving tasks. *Educational and Psychological Measurement*, 1954, *14*, 283-293.

Glaser, R., & Klaus, D. J. Proficiency measurement: Assessing human performance. In R. M. Gagné (Ed.), *Psychological principles in systems development.* New York: Holt, Rinehart and Winston, 1962. Pp. 419-474.

Glaser, R., & Nitko, A. J. Measurement in learning and instruction. In R. L. Thorndike (Ed.), *Educational Measurement* (2nd ed.). Washington, DC: American Council on Education, 1971. Pp. 625-670.

Gray, W. M. A comparison of Piagetian theory and criterion-referenced measurement. *Review of Educational Research*, 1978, *48*, 223-249.

Guttman, L. The basis for scalogram analysis. In S. A. Stouffer, L. Guttman, E. A. Suchman, P. F. Lazarsfeld, S. A. Star, & J. A. Clausen (Eds.), *Studies in social psychology in World War II* (Vol. 4): *Measurement and prediction.* Princeton, NJ: Princeton University Press, 1950.

Hambleton, R. K., & Novick, M. R. Toward an integration of theory and method for criterion-referenced tests. *Journal of Educational Measurement*, 1973, *10*, 159-170.

Hambleton, R. K., Swaminathan, H., Algina, J., & Coulson, D. B. Criterion-referenced testing and measurement: A review of technical issues and developments. *Review of Educational Research*, 1978, *48*, 1-47.

Harris, M. L., & Stewart, D. M. *Application of classical strategies to criterion-referenced test construction: An example.* Symposium paper presented at the annual meeting of the American Educational Research Association, New York, February 1971.

Hively, W. *Preparation of a programmed course in algebra for secondary school teachers: A report to the National Science Foundation.* Minneapolis: Minnesota National Laboratory, Minnesota State Department of Education, 1966.

Hively, W. *Domain-referenced achievement testing.* Symposium paper presented at the annual meeting of the American Educational Research Association, Minneapolis, March 1970.

Hively, W., Maxwell, G., Rabehl, G., Sension, D., & Lundin, S. *Domain-referenced curriculum evaluation: A technical handbook and a case study from the MINNEMAST project* (CSE Monograph Series in Evaluation, No. 1). Los Angeles: Center for the Study of Evaluation, University of California, 1973.

Hively, W., Patterson, H. L., & Page, S. A. A "universe-defined" system of arithmetic achievement tests. *Journal of Educational Measurement*, 1968, *5*, 275–290.

Hsu, T. C., & Carlson, M. *Computer-assisted testing.* Pittsburgh: Learning Research and Development Center, University of Pittsburgh, 1972.

Hunt, J. M. Implications of sequential order and hierarchy in early psychological development. In B. X. Friedlander, G. M. Sterritt, & G. E. Kirk (Eds.), *Exceptional infant* (Vol. 3). New York: Brunner/Mazel, 1975.

Hunt, J. M., & Kirk, G. E. Criterion-referenced tests of school readiness: A paradigm with illustrations. *Genetic Psychology Monographs*, 1974, *90*, 143–182.

Lyman, H. B. *Test scores and what they mean* (3rd ed.). Englewood Cliffs, NJ: Prentice-Hall, 1978.

Mager, R. F. *Preparing instructional objectives.* Palo Alto, CA: Fearon, 1962.

Nesbit, M. Y. *The CHILD Program: Computer help in learning diagnosis of arithmetic scores* (Curriculum Bulletin 7–E–B). Miami, FL: Dade County Board of Public Instruction, 1966.

Nitko, A. J. Criterion-referenced testing in the context of instruction. In *Testing in turmoil: A conference on problems and issues in educational measurement.* Greenwich, CT: Educational Records Bureau, 1970.

Nitko, A. J. Distinguishing the many varieties of criterion-referenced tests. *Review of Educational Research*, 1980, *50*, 461–485.

Osburn, H. G. Item sampling for achievement testing. *Educational and Psychological Measurement*, 1968, *28*, 95–104.

Popham, W. J. *Developing IOX objectives-based tests: Procedural guidelines* (Technical Paper No. 8). Los Angeles: Instructional Objectives Exchange, August 1972.

Popham, W. J. Selecting objectives and generating test items for objectives-based tests. In C. W. Harris, M. C. Alkin, & W. J. Popham (Eds.), *Problems in criterion-referenced measurement* (CSE Monograph Series in Evaluation, No. 3). Los Angeles: Center for the Study of Evaluation, University of California, 1974. Pp. 13–25.

Popham, W. J. *Educational evaluation.* Englewood Cliffs, NJ: Prentice-Hall, 1975.

Popham, W. J. *Criterion-referenced measurement.* Englewood Cliffs, NJ: Prentice-Hall, 1978.

Popham, W. J. Content domain specifications. In R. A. Berk (Ed.), *Criterion-referenced measurement: The state of the art.* Baltimore, MD: Johns Hopkins University Press, 1980. Pp. 15–31.

Popham, W. J. *Modern educational measurement.* Englewood Cliffs, NJ: Prentice-Hall, 1981.

Popham, W. J., & Husek, T. R. Implications of criterion-referenced measurement. *Journal of Educational Measurement*, 1969, *6*, 1–9.

Rasch, G. *Probabilistic models for some intelligence and attainment tests.* Copenhagen: Danish Institute for Educational Research, 1960.

Resnick, L. B., Wang, M. C., & Kaplan, J. Task analysis in curriculum design: A hierarchically sequenced introductory mathematics curriculum. *Journal of Applied Behavior Analysis*, 1973, *6*, 679–710.

Simon, D. P., & Simon, H. A. Individual differences in solving physics problems. In R. S. Siegler (Ed.), *Children's thinking: What develops?* Hillsdale, NJ: Erlbaum, 1978.

Starch, D. *Educational measurements.* New York: Macmillan, 1916.

Thorndike, E. L. Handwriting. *Teacher's College Record*, 1910, *11*, 1-93.

Thorndike, E. L. A scale for measuring achievement in drawing. *Teacher's College Record*, 1913, *14*, 345-382.

Thorndike, E. L. The nature, purposes, and general methods of measurement of educational products. In G. M. Whipple (Ed.), *The seventeenth yearbook of the National Society for the Study of Evaluation* (Part II): *The Measurement of educational products.* Bloomington, IL: Public School Publishing Co., 1918.

Uzgiris, I. C., & Hunt, J. M. *An instrument for assessing infant psychological development.* Urbana: Psychological Development Laboratory, University of Illinois, 1966.

Uzgiris, I. C., & Hunt, J. M. *Ordinal scales of infant psychological development: Information concerning six demonstration films.* Urbana: Psychological Development Laboratory, University of Illinois, 1968.

2 SPECIFYING THE DOMAIN OF CONTENT OR BEHAVIORS

W. JAMES POPHAM

INTRODUCTION

CREATIVITY IS a uniformly cherished commodity. Hence, what self-respecting test development agency would not want its item-writing staff to be simply brimming with Faulkner-like folks or Hemingway clones? After all, almost all test items hinge on the way writers use words, and creatively woven words make for better reading than stodgy ones.

But, contrary to the common adoration of creativity in any form, there is a phase in the development of criterion-referenced tests when freewheeling creativity is to be shunned, and that is when item writers are actually nutsing and boltsing out a pile of test items. The remainder of this analysis will constitute an effort to demonstrate why we should wish to put a clamp on such creativity and how we might go about effectively stifling the fervor of the inventive item writer.

To realize why anyone would have the effrontery to rail against creativity, it is requisite to look hard at criterion-referenced tests and decide why they were spawned in the first place. Unlike their norm-referenced predecessors, which rely chiefly on the relative status of an examinee's performance in relationship to the performances of those in a normative group, criterion-referenced tests are supposed to tell us what it is that examinees can or can't do. The phrase "What examinees can or can't do," is deceptively simple, since it fails to communicate all that vividly just how much difficulty is actually embedded in the task of spelling out even a run-of-the-mill "can or can't do," much less a complicated one.

If a criterion-referenced test doesn't unambiguously describe just what it's measuring, it offers no advantage over norm-referenced measures. And therein comes the crunch, since to describe the set of behaviors ostensibly being measured by a criterion-referenced test we are almost totally dependent on verbal symbols—on words.

Although it's true that in certain fields, such as the hard sciences, for example, people can describe phenomena by employing sophisticated measuring instruments and tons of numbers, we do not have that luxury when describing an examinee's performance on an educational test. Think about the process of educational measurement for a moment and you'll see why we must depend totally upon verbal precision if we ever hope to describe satisfactorily what it is that an examinee's performance really means.

In the typical case, a student attempts to answer a flock of test items; some he answers correctly and some he doesn't. A raw score of, say, 45 correct out of 60 items is obtained. What does that score mean? In what conceivable way does it signify what the examinee "can or can't do"? Well, in a norm-referenced world, of course, we'd quickly consult our norm table and discover that a raw score of 45 is equivalent to the 86th percentile; hence, all would be well. All would be well, that is, if we only wanted to know how a person scoring 45 on the test stacked up against other people. But if we want to know what the 45 scorer "can or can't do," norm tables don't offer much solace.

To get a fix on what our student's score really means, of course, we could say that raw score of 45 represented a 75% mastery of the 60 possible items. And that kind of an assertion would make good sense *if* (*a*) 60 items represented a relatively homogeneous collection of instances for the student to exhibit a *single* skill, and (*b*) the nature of those 60 items has been described well enough for us to know precisely what they're trying to measure. Those are truly substantial *ifs*.

Let's start off with condition (*b*), a reversal of the traditional alphabetic sequence. Note that one condition requisite for rendering an accurate interpretation of what an examinee's test performance signifies is a lucid description of the nature of the items on the test. It is because we know how an examinee responds to particular stimuli that we can infer something about what those responses signify. The more clearly we understand what the stimuli are to which the examinee responds, the more accurate our inferences are apt to be. Thus, an indispensable element necessary to render accurate interpretations of examinees' test performances is a carefully crafted description of the type of test item being employed to measure a particular skill, attitude, etc. (The bulk of this analysis will be devoted to a scheme for providing such descriptions.)

Now let's return to condition (*a*), since it is here where unbridled creativity will get us in a peak of trouble. Assume that we have carved out a decent description of what a test's items are supposed to be like, that is, we've in essence set forth the rules that govern the creation of the test items. In other words, we have explicated a set of *test specifications*. Now, if those specifications are going to convey with veracity what's being measured, then it is necessary for the test items to be totally congruent with the limits that constitute those specifications. If all of the items on the test are, in fact, congruent with the test's specifications, then those items will be sufficiently homogeneous to allow us to make sense of an assertion that "Johnny has mastered 75% of the items measuring this competency."

We can represent such a blissful situation pictorially, as seen in Figure 2.1, where a tight descriptive scheme (test specifications) plus congruent test items yields an unerring interpretation of what an examinee's test performance means, and permits us to characterize that test performance according to the proportion of items that the examinee can answer correctly. Since the items on the test constitute a sample of the possible items that could be generated to assess the behavior in question, we can place considerable confidence in the legitimacy of our interpretation.

On the other hand, if either or both of these elements are missing, as seen in Figure 2.2, then the interpretations we make of an examinee's test performance are likely to be meaningless. A fuzzy set of test specifications makes all sensible test interpretations impossible. Incongruent items further muddy the interpretive waters. Put them both together, as in Figure 2.2, and you will surely have nonsensical interpretations.

Where we do need creativity is in the development of highly communicative descriptive schemes that lay out the rules for item writers. These descriptive schemes, deftly fashioned, will simultaneously (1) constrain item writers so

Figure 2.1. Requisite elements for an accurate interpretation of examinee performance on a criterion-referenced test

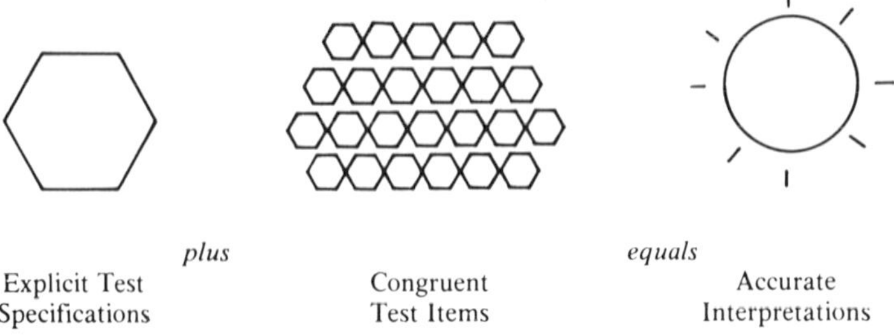

Figure 2.2. Elements accounting for an inaccurate interpretation of examinee performance on a criterion-referenced test

that they can produce congruent items and (2) communicate to those who must interpret examinees' test performances.

Where we do *not* need creativity is in the writing of items that match those descriptive constraints. Item writers need to be bright. This is not a setting where dullards will shine. But they need to employ their brightness in dutifully cleaving to the admonitions set forth in the test's specifications. Creative departures from the rules in the specifications will create items that, albeit innovative, fail to mesh with those specifications and thus contribute to interpretive confusion. It is to forestall the generation of incongruent, or runaway, test items that so much attention must be given to the generation of test specifications.

Once truly constraining test specifications have been devised, then a necessary but not sufficient condition for accurate test interpretation is present. An additional necessary condition is that the item writers follow those specifications to the letter. Following-to-the-letter writing of items is inconsistent with creative writing of items.

If you cannot quell an item writer's zest for invention, send that individual scurrying to more congenial pursuits, such as sculpture, gymnastics, or erotic dance.

REVIEW OF SPECIFICATION STRATEGIES

How, then, can we head off the incongruent test item? Assuming that we have rounded up a staff of bright but compliant item writers, how do we deter them from generating aberrant items?

Let's turn to a consideration of how we can best prepare item-writing rules, that is, test specifications, that truly aid item writers in the construction of congruent items. To deal with this problem it would be delightful if we could consult the research literature and draw upon the pioneering efforts of empirically oriented investigators who have engaged in hand-to-hand, but experimental, combat with test specifications—and won.

But, sadly, research dealing with the particulars of test specifications is almost totally nonexistent. To illustrate, in their recent comprehensive review of research dealing with criterion-referenced measurement, Hambleton, Swaminathan, Algina, and Coulson (1978) cited only the work of Ebel (1962) and Hively, Patterson, and Page (1968) when the topic of test specifications was discussed. Neither the Ebel nor the Hively analysis is actually an empirical investigation of, for example, the efficacy of varying forms of test specification. They are, instead, conceptual observations regarding how one might design constraints so that more readily interpretable test performance is possible. Even so, however, since Hively and his colleagues actually applied measurement insights in the creation of many test instruments, his observations (1968, 1973) have been particularly useful to a number of individuals working with criterion-referenced test construction.

Lacking solid research bases for our work with criterion-referenced test specifications, it seems necessary to rely on our best experience-based hunches about what sorts of test specification will prove serviceable. The reader will, it is hoped, be lenient since from this point forward I must draw heavily on my personal experiences in attempting to stumble on a salubrious test specification strategy. These experiences extend over a 10-year period and are chiefly drawn from projects carried out by the Instructional Objectives Exchange (IOX), a Los Angeles agency specializing in the development of criterion-referenced tests.

Behavioral Objectives

When IOX was born in 1968, it was intended that it serve as a clearinghouse for behavioral objectives so that busy educators who needed such objectives would not have to engage in wheel reinvention. Contained in the booklets of behavioral objectives that IOX tossed forth upon an eager flock of educators were scores of behaviorally stated objectives and sample test items to illustrate how each objective might be measured. Sometimes we included a half dozen sample items per objective, sometimes fewer.

Although I was spending a major chunk of my professional time attempting to drum up educator acceptance of behavioral objectives, particularly as a vehicle for curriculum and instructional planning, it did not take the IOX staff long to realize that as delimiting devices for item writers, behavioral objectives were inadequate. Given their typically terse form, behavioral objectives left far too many decisions to the item writer.

Different IOX staff members who were attempting to come up with sample items for the same objective would usually whip up items that bore scant resemblance to one another. It was clear—behavioral objectives, whatever their virtues for curriculum and instruction, were too abbreviated to constrain item writers.

Item Forms

When IOX decided to expand its development work to include criterion-referenced tests, we sought out the advice of the best persons we could find to tell us how to build the specifications to govern our test development efforts. Those individuals, in our view, were Wells Hively, then of the University of Minnesota, and Jason Millman, then and forever of Cornell University. During the summer of 1971, Wells and Jay offered our staff wise counsel on how to whomp up winning criterion-referenced testing devices.

At first we tried to employ the *item form* scheme that Hively et al. (1968) had used in their Minnesota efforts. The item form was a highly detailed set of rules for creating test items of what was hoped to be a homogeneous nature. Although Wells had used item forms almost exclusively in connection with the assessment of mathematics and science skills, he was convinced that his approach could not be employed in the measurement of more elusive quarries. An example of Hively's item forms is found in appendix A.

We gave item forms a solid try. They were detailed and, when well formulated, quite constraining. But with the kinds of examinee behavior that we were attempting to measure, we ended up with too many item forms and, even worse, two few item writers who were willing to pay attention to them.

In retrospect, it is now quite obvious that we were working with classes of behavior that were too minuscule. Although the size of our behavior domains approximated those used by Wells and his cohorts in Minnesota, the "chunks" of examinee behavior that we were attempting to measure were just too small. We were overwhelming ourselves with hyperspecificity.

Amplified Objectives

The experience with Wells and Jay had proved illuminating in a number of ways, one of which was that we needed far more delimiting detail than we were able to squeeze out of the objectives in our behavioral objectives collections. The guidance of Millman and Hively also led us to move toward fewer, larger scope objectives. As a consequence, we tried developing criterion-referenced tests for, say, Reading Comprehension 4–6,and measured the key skills in that grade range with, for example, only 30 to 40 separate criterion-referenced tests. In our previous collections of behavioral objectives we might have had as many as 100 or 200 objectives to cover that same grade range.

Because we wanted to maintain some continuity with our major efforts prior to that time, namely, serving as a brokerage for behavioral objectives, and yet recognizing that we needed more detailed constraints for our criterion-referenced item writers, we adopted the descriptive phrase *amplified objectives*.

An amplified objective was, as its title suggests, a more elaborate version of a behavioral objective. Our amplified objectives hovered in specificity somewhere between (*a*) our previous telegraphic behavioral objectives and (*b*) Hively's item forms. An example of an IOX amplified objective is included in appendix B. Amplified objectives represented an IOX attempt at compromise. We wanted to add more specificity, but not too much. We were shooting for just the right balance between clarity and conciseness. We missed.

As it turned out, although the IOX amplified objectives did tie down item writers considerably, there was far too much slack still remaining. The amplified objectives, with the possible exception of those in mathematics, allowed item writers—and test interpreters—too much latitude. Although as an effort in test specification the IOX amplified objectives represented a valiant attempt, they fell short on the delimitation scale.

A Limited Focus Strategy

Given our less than lustrous success in subduing the problem of appropriate specificity level, the IOX staff spent at least a year or so in wound licking and allied endeavors. The more we pondered the dilemma, the bigger the dilemma seemed to be. The crux of the problem was that as we ladled in additional spoonfuls of specificity, we were simultaneously reducing the likelihood that our item writers, and, by the same token, classroom teachers, would ever pay attention to the resulting superspecific descriptions.

We had tried the terseness of behavioral objectives; they were not sufficiently constraining. We had tried item forms; they were too detailed. We had attempted to take the middle ground with amplified objectives; they had proved to be insufficiently precise. We were troubled.

But after rumination, not to mention desperation, we bumbled our way toward what currently seems to be a viable hope of hopping our dilemma's horns. We concluded that if we could only retain the descriptive rigor of item forms, yet figure out a way to get item writers and teachers to heed that heightened specificity, we would have a winner. Our discussions led us in the direction of limiting our measurement focus to a smaller number of assessed behaviors, but conceptualizing these behaviors so that they were larger scale, important behaviors that subsumed lesser, en route behaviors.

By using a *limited focus* measurement strategy (Popham, 1978), we were able to create a small enough number of test descriptors so that item writers and teachers would attend to them. We could employ a level of descriptive detail requisite to foster precise communication with item writers as well as those who must make sense out of an examinee's test performance.

Although we are not measuring all of the good things that should be measured in the world, and make no pretense at doing so, we are at least confident that we're doing a good job of measuring what we say we're measuring. Limited focus is the key element in the current efforts of IOX to develop criterion-referenced tests that are both (1) sufficiently specific to communicate properly to test users and (2) sufficiently targeted to be of utility to busy classroom teachers.

IOX Test Specifications

The current effort of IOX to delimit the class of behaviors being assessed by a criterion-referenced test we refer to as *test specifications*. We have adopted the more general descriptive phrase, test specifications, to permit us over time to sharpen our approach to circumscribing a set of measured behaviors.

Our current versions of test specifications have greatly benefited from Hively's item form strategies, only applying that approach to more substantial lumps of examinee behavior. Examples of current IOX test specifications in the cognitive, affective, and psychomotor domains are provided in appendix C. There are four (and sometimes five) components of a set of IOX test specifications.

General description. The initial component of a set of IOX criterion-referenced test specifications is a one- or two-sentence general description of what it is that the test measures. The purpose of the general description is to provide a succinct overview of the set of behaviors to be described more fully later in the specifications.

In some criterion-referenced test specifications this component is referred to as an "objective." Yet, because many criterion-referenced tests will be used as preinstruction status determiners, not necessarily as measures of whether instructional intentions have been achieved, the phrase "general description" appears to be more defensible.

It should be apparent that a test specifier would have to possess the gift of prophecy in order to anticipate with certainty what a complete set of test specifications, particularly the subsequent stimulus-attributes and response-attributes sections, will look like. Accordingly, the general description statement is often phrased tentatively when one commences a set of test specifications. Indeed, it usually ends up looking quite different as a consequence of the more detailed analysis that occurs as the remaining components of the test specification are explicated.

Sample item. The next component in a set of IOX test specifications is a sample item, complete with directions to the student, that might be used in the test itself. Such illustrative items are usually easy to supply, since the test frequently consists of a number of relatively short items. Therefore, it is a simple matter to select one of these items for illustrative purposes. Sometimes, when the test is more complicated and the items more lengthy, it becomes difficult to supply a sample item. Nonetheless, an illustrative item is always provided as the second component of each set of test specifications.

There are two reasons for providing a sample item. First, some people using the specifications, particularly busy individuals, may find their need for test description satisfied with the general description statement and the illustrative item alone. Such people, if forced to read the entire set of specifications, might avoid it completely. But they can be abetted by the communication, albeit incomplete, provided by the specification's general description plus sample item.

The second purpose of the sample item is to provide format cues for those who must generate the items that will constitute the test. Of course, it often makes little difference what the format of a given type of test is. For instance, is it really important whether a true/false item presents the examinee with T/F or F/T options? Undoubtedly not. Yet, there are instances when format variations do seem to be important. In such cases an illustrative item can go a long way toward setting forth the preferred form in which items are to be constructed.

Stimulus attributes. In a test an examinee is presented with some sorts of stimuli that, in general, are designed to yield a response. In the third component of IOX criterion-referenced test specifications, the attributes of this stimulus material are set forth.

In the stimulus-attributes section of the test specifications we must set down all the influential factors that constrain the composition of a set of test items. This means that we must first think through exactly what those factors are and how they can be most accurately and succinctly described. We have to decide how to cope with content considerations. Just how should a range of eligible content be most effectively circumscribed? Anything less than the most rigorous standards of intellectual scrutiny will result in specifications that are imprecise or, worse, misleading.

Response attributes. The final component of a set of IOX test specifications focuses on the examinee's response to the elements generated according to the stimulus-attributes section. Only two types of response on the part of the examinee exist. The examinee can either *select* from response options presented in the test—for example, as in true/false or multiple-choice questions—or the examinee can *construct* a response—for example, as in essay, short-answer, or oral presentations. Thus, only *selected responses* or *constructed responses* will be encountered, and in the response-attributes section of the specifications the rules regarding these two response possibilities will be treated.

If the test involves a selected response, then rules must be provided for determining not only the nature of the correct response, but also the nature of the wrong-answer options. For instance, in a multiple-choice test it would be imperative to state first the guidelines for creating the correct answer. Next, the test specifier must spell out the various classes of wrong-answer option that might constitute any item's distractors. It is not appropriate merely to indicate that such distractors will be "incorrect." Instead, the precise nature of these wrong answers must be carefully explicated.

But although the difficulties of delineating the response-possibilities section for selected response sorts of test are considerable, they become almost trivial when a test specifier attempts to spell out the response-attributes section of specifications for tests involving constructed responses. Here the task is to explain the criteria that permit reliable judgment of the adequacy of examinees' constructed responses. Ideally, these criteria would be so well formulated that determining the acceptability of any constructed response would be simple. Realistically, however, criteria possessing such precision can rarely be created. The test specifier will have to think as lucidly as possible about such criteria, and even then there may be more slack in this section of the specifications than we would like.

Specification supplement. There are instances in which our IOX test specifications deal with sets of content—for example, a series of rules or a list of important historical figures. If we included this content information in either the stimulus-attributes or the response-attributes section, we would have created a set of specifications too voluminous for the typical reader. Beyond that, by being obliged to wade through such lengthy content citations, a reader of the specifications might actually be distracted from some of the important noncontent-specification statements. In such cases it is often convenient to include a supplement at the close of the specifications that sets forth such information. Such a supplement is obviously optional.

SUGGESTIONS FOR FUTURE RESEARCH

Given the essentially anecdotal nature of the foregoing remarks, it is more than apparent that we need research, and lots of it, dealing with the procedures for spelling out test specifications and subsequently generating test items that mesh with those specifications.

Chiefly, we need to assess the efficacy of varied procedures for constraining criterion-referenced item writers. The approach to test specifications used at IOX constitutes only one way to play that game. There may be other, markedly better, specification strategies that should be tried out, then empirically honed. Berk (1980) has described six strategies for specifying content domains and items with criterion-referenced tests. The adequacy of these and other such strategies must be investigated without delay (see also Roid, chapter 3).

We need to abandon the intuitively derived, experience-based schemes for generating criterion-referenced tests. We must move toward an experimentally tested technology of criterion-referenced test construction.

GUIDELINES FOR PRACTITIONERS

This analysis will be terminated by a series of observations, some even related to one another, regarding the rigors of rapping out test specifications for criterion-referenced tests. As will soon be apparent to the reader, these musings will be a far piece from anything even mildly definitive.

Realistic Expectations

When we use a phrase like *test specifications*, some folks naively assume that we're really tying down all the loose ends in a domain of examinee behaviors. It isn't so.

It would be glorious if we could so precisely circumscribe a domain of important examinee behaviors that we would know with complete and all-consuming clarity just what it is that the examinee "can or can't do." But to create a set of specifications that captured that much detail would surely force us to create a major opus of several hundred pages in length. Remember, we're talking about an *important*, hence undoubtedly complex, examinee behavior. As it is, many IOX test specifications run five or more single-spaced pages in length. And specifications of that length begin to tax severely the item writer's, and certainly the classroom teacher's, patience.

With respect to the degree of constraint that any test specification of reasonable length can exert, it probably makes sense to think of a continuum something like that seen in Figure 2.3, where we have a range of specificity

Figure 2.3. A range of specificity for the descriptive schemes employed with criterion-referenced tests

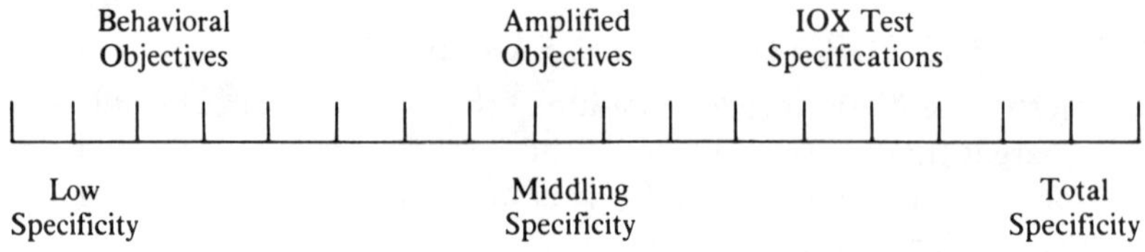

that at the left is little more detailed than a behavioral objective and, accordingly, permits multiple interpretations. At the right we have a voluminous (almost inconceivably detailed) set of test specifications. The rigor of interpretability increases, of course, as one moves from left to right. Even with the descriptive detail currently contained in the IOX test specifications, there is still a certain degree of imprecision associated with the interpretation of test performance. Until humans start functioning like computers, there probably always will be.

But even though the efforts of criterion-referenced testing specialists, for the foreseeable future, will fall short of total delimitation, there are clearly substantial clarity dividends over the less descriptive schemes represented at the left of the specificity continuum.

Homogeneity

Once upon a time, when I was younger and foolisher, I thought we could create test specifications so constraining that the test items produced as a consequence of their use would be *functionally homogeneous*, that is, essentially interchangeable. But if we use the difficulty of an item as at least one index of the item's nature, then it becomes quite obvious that even in such teensy behavior domains as measuring the student's ability to multiply pairs of double-digit numbers, the task of $11 \times 11 = ?$ is lots easier than $99 \times 99 = ?$

About the only way we can ever attain functional homogeneity is to keep pruning the nature of the measured behavior so that we're assessing ever more trifling sorts of behavior. That would be inane. We can, however, if we do a smashing job in creating test specifications, achieve sets of items that are *derivatively homogeneous*, that is, that can be judged as having been derived from the same set of specifications (Popham, 1980). We can apply something akin to a test specification paternity test in order to show that the behavioral domain delimited by the test specifications, a domain that includes items of differing difficulty levels, is the legitimate home of all the items on the test.

Art with a Capital A

At no point in the test development process for criterion-referenced measures is it more apparent that we are employing art, rather than science, than when the general nature of the behavioral domain to be tested is initially conceptualized.

Particularly in view of our current predilection toward larger behavioral domains that (1) effectively coalesce smaller, en route behaviors yet (2) maintain sufficient descriptive rigor to communicate effectively, these conceptualizations become artistic endeavors of no small shakes. I am constantly distressed that so few of our staff members seem to possess the ability to corral apparently diverse, yet related, sets of subskills, then blend them into a new, subsuming skill that serves as the focus for the measurement.

I am even more distressed that I am unable to teach people how to go about this conceptualization process. I can explain how I personally do it, and I can get a few other staff members to engage in similar introspection, but I have been completely unable to reduce the process to a form that is directly teachable—complete with practice exercises, etc.—to others.

With respect to the conceptualizing of such behavioral domains, as well as a galaxy of other phases of criterion-referenced test development, it is so apparent that we're still nibbling on a cake whose frosting may be technology but whose many layers are art, art, and more art.

APPENDIX A: AN ILLUSTRATIVE ITEM FORM

ITEM FORM 3.15[a]

Comparing numerosity of sets by one-to-one correspondence.

GENERAL DESCRIPTION

The child is given either two or three sets of "counters," each having approximately 20 members (or less). The sets may have the same number of members or they may differ by one member. The child is asked to show whether or not the sets have the same number of members, without counting.

STIMULUS AND RESPONSE CHARACTERISTICS

Constant for all Cells

Only standard "counters" (small colored disks) are used. Each set of counters is a different color (red, green or yellow).

Distinguishing between cells

Number of sets compared (two or three). Whether or not the sets have the same number of objects. Approximate number of objects in each set (about 5, about 13, or about 21).

Varying with Cells

No variation.

CELL MATRIX

Approximate Number of Objects in Sets	Number of Sets Compared: 2 — Equality Relations: $N_a = N_b$	$N_a \neq N_b$	3 — Equality Relation: $N_a = N_b = N_c$	$N_a = N_b \neq N_c$	$N_a \neq N_b \neq N_c$
5	(1)	(4)	(7)	(10)	(13)
13	(2)	(5)	(8)	(11)	(14)
21	(3)	(6)	(9)	(12)	(15)

[a]Originally developed by Bruce Mussell.

ITEM FORM SHELL

MATERIALS 1. Set of counters (a) 2. Set of counters (b) 3. Set of counters (c)	
DIRECTIONS TO E	SCRIPT
Place the above sets near either edge (and the middle) of the test board as shown above. Then say:	Show me if these (**d**) sets (point) have the same number of members.
If S begins to count or says "I don't know how," say:	In class you paired objects to tell if two sets had the same number of members. Please show me if these (**d**) sets have the same number of members.
When S has finished, say:	Do they have the same number of members?
Keep a running record of what S does and says.	

REPLACEMENT SCHEME

Sets of Counters (a) = red, (b) = green, (c) = yellow Number of objects in each set:

Cell 1: (a) 5; (b) 5
Cell 2: (a) 13; (b) 13
Cell 3: (a) 21; (b) 21
Cell 4: (a) 5; (b) 6
Cell 5: (a) 13; (b) 14
Cell 6: (a) 21; (b) 22
Cell 7: (a) 5; (b) 5; (c) 5
Cell 8: (a) 13; (b) 13; (c) 13
Cell 9: (a) 21; (b) 21; (c) 21
Cell 10: (a) 5; (b) 5; (c) 6
Cell 11: (a) 13; (b) 13; (c) 14
Cell 12: (a) 21; (b) 21; (c) 22
Cell 13: (a) 5; (b) 6; (c) 7
Cell 14: (a) 13; (b) 14; (c) 15
Cell 15: (a) 21; (b) 22; (c) 23

Script (d):

Cells 1 through 6: "two"
Cells 7 through 15: "three"

SCORING SPECIFICATIONS

Child should state correctly (yes or no) whether or not the sets have the same number of members. He should also carry out a detectable one-to-one pairing operation.

Source: Reprinted with permission from Hively, Wells; Maxwell, Graham; Rabehl, George; Sension, Donald; and Lundin, Stephen. *Domain-Referenced Curriculum Evaluation: A Technical Handbook and a Case Study from the MINNEMAST Project, 1973*, Appendix 3, Item form 3.15. (p.69). Copyright 1973, Center for the Study of Evaluation, University of California, Los Angeles.

APPENDIX B: AN ILLUSTRATIVE IOX AMPLIFIED OBJECTIVE FOR A THIRD-GRADE LEVEL READING COMPREHENSION SKILL

DETERMINING SEQUENCE FROM TENSE AND WORDS THAT SIGNAL ORDER

Objective
The student will correctly identify the sequence of three sentences by determining order from tense and words that signify order.

Sample Item
Directions. Read the three sentences. Then mark an "X" next to the answer that arranges the sentences in the proper order.

Example
A. Once there were only candles for lighting the home.
B. Later there were dim electric lights.
C. Tesla thought of a way to make the electric lights brighter.
___a) A,C,B ___b) A,B,C ___c) C,A,B

Amplified Objectives

Testing Situation
1. The student will be given three sentences and will identify their proper sequence on the basis of verb tenses and signal words.
2. Three sentences containing signal words and/or changes in verb tense will be provided.
3. Vocabulary will be familiar to the third grader.

Response Alternatives
1. Three possible orderings of the sentence will be given.
2. At least one distractor should *not* consist of a random ordering. It should maintain the first event as first, varying only the second and third events.
3. The other distractor may be any other incorrect ordering of the events.

Criterion of Correctness
The correct answer will be the order that can be determined on the basis of one of the following:

1. Words that signify sequence, e.g., afterwards, finally, then, before, during, now, next, lastly, later, earlier, meanwhile, long ago, once;
2. Verb tense (future, past, present).

APPENDIX C: ILLUSTRATIVE SETS OF IOX CRITERION-REFERENCED TEST SPECIFICATIONS

COGNITIVE DOMAIN

DETERMINING MAIN IDEAS

General Description
The student will be presented with a factual selection such as a newspaper or magazine article or a passage from a consumer guide or general-interest book. After read-

ing that selection, the student will determine which one of four choices contains the best statement of the main idea of the selection. This statement will be entirely accurate as well as the most comprehensive of the choices given.

Sample Item

Directions. Read the selections in the boxes below. Answer the questions about their main ideas.

THE COLD FACTS

Had you lived in ancient Rome you might have relieved the symptoms of a common cold by sipping a broth made from soaking an onion in warm water. In Colonial America you might have relied on an herbal concoction made from sage, buckthorn, goldenseal, or bloodroot plants. In Grandma's time, lemon and honey was a favorite cold remedy, or in extreme cases, a hot toddy laced with rum. Today, if you don't have an old reliable remedy to fall back on, you might take one of thousands of drug preparations available without prescription. Some contain ingredients much like the folk medicines of the past; others are made with complex chemical creations. Old or new, simple or complex, many of these products will relieve some cold symptoms, such as a stopped-up nose or a hacking cough. But not a single one of them will prevent, cure, or even shorten the course of the common cold. *Source*: Reprinted with permission from *Test specifications, IOX Basic Skill Tests: Secondary level Reading*. Los Angeles: The Instructional Objectives Exchange, 1978, pp. 21–24.

1. Which one of the following is the best statement of the main idea of the article you just read?
   a. Old-fashioned herbal remedies are more effective than modern medicines.
   b. There are many kinds of relief, but no real cures, for the common cold.
   c. Some of today's cold preparations contain ingredients much like those found in folk remedies of the past.
   d. Americans spend millions of dollars a year on cold remedies.

Stimulus Attributes

1. Each item will consist of a reading selection followed by the question "Which one of the following is the best statement of the main idea of the (article selection) you just read?" Eligible reading selections include adaptations of passages from factual texts such as general-interest books and consumer guides and pamphlets. Care should be taken to pick selections of particular interest to young adults and to avoid selections which may in the near future appear dated. Each reading selection will be titled, will be at least one paragraph long, and will contain between 125 and 250 words. Not more than 1,000 words of reading material can be tested in any set of five items. At least two of the five items in any set of five items must contain reading selections that are more than one paragraph long.
2. If necessary, the following modifications may be made to a selection used for testing:
   a. A title may be added if the selection does not have one, or if the selection represents a section of a longer piece whose title would not be applicable to the excerpt. If a title is added, it should be composed of a brief, interest-getting and/or summarizing group of words.
   b. A selection may be shortened, but only if the segment which is to be used for testing makes sense and stands as a complete unit of thought without the parts which have been omitted. If necessary, minor editing can be done to a reading selection which represents a shortening of a longer piece, but

this editing should be for the purposes of clarity and continuity only, and not for the purposes of increasing or decreasing the difficulty level, or changing the content, of the text.

3. Reading selections used for testing should not exceed a ninth-grade reading level, as judged by the Fry readability formula.

Response Attributes

1. A set of four single-sentence response alternatives will follow each reading selection and its accompanying question. All of these statements must plausibly relate to the content of the reading selection, either by reiterating or paraphrasing portions of that selection or by building upon a word or idea contained in the selection.
2. The three incorrect response alternatives will each be based upon a lack of one of the two characteristics needed by a correct main idea statement: *accuracy* and *appropriate scope*. A correct main idea statement must be accurate in that everything it states can be verified in the text it describes. It must have appropriate scope in that it encompasses all of the most important points discussed in the text that it describes.
3. A distractor exemplifies a *lack of accuracy* when it does any one or more of three things:
   a. Makes a statement contradicted by information in the text.
   b. Makes a statement unsupported by information in the text. (Such a statement would be capable of verification or contradiction if the appropriate information were available.)
   c. Makes a statement incapable of verification or contradiction; that is, a statement of opinion. (Such statements include value judgments on the importance or worth of anything mentioned in the text.)
4. A distractor exemplifies a *lack of appropriate scope* when it does one of two things:
   a. Makes a statement that is too narrow in its scope. That is, the statement does not account for all of the important details contained in the text.
   b. Makes a statement that is too broad in its scope. That is, the statement is more general than it needs to be in order to account for all of the important details contained in the text.
5. The important points which must be included in a main idea statement are those details which are emphasized in the text by structural, semantical, and rhetorical means such as placement in a position of emphasis, repetition, synonymous rephrasing, and elaboration. Whether any given main idea statement contains all of the important points that it should is always debatable rather than indisputable. The nature of the question asked on this test, i.e., select the *best* main idea statement from among those given, attempts to account for this quality of relative rather than absolute correctness.
6. The distractors for any one item must include at least one statement that lacks accuracy and one statement that lacks appropriate scope. On a given test, between 10 and 20 percent of the distractors should be sentences taken directly from the text.
7. The correct answer for an item will be that statement which is both entirely accurate and of the most appropriate scope in relation to the other statements given. If a sentence in the text itself qualifies as the best main idea statement which can be

formulated about the selection, that sentence may be reiterated as a response option. No more than 20 percent of the items on a given test may have as their correct answer a main idea statement which is a direct restatement of a sentence in the text.

AFFECTIVE DOMAIN

TEST SPECIFICATIONS: COULD YOU DECREASE STRESS?

General Description

This measure is designed to assess children's perceived self-efficacy in being able to manage stress. Children are presented with a series of situations which might serve as barriers to managing stress and are asked to indicate if they could decrease their stress, given each situation.

Sample Item

Directions. Read each question. Then put a check (√) under the answer that best tells if you could decrease your stress. Stress is what you feel when you are nervous about something.

Could you decrease your stress if . . .	Certainly Yes	Probably Yes	Maybe	Probably Not	Certainly Not
1. . . . you had to help at home rather than play with your friends?	______	______	______	______	______

Stimulus Attributes

1. An item will specify a situation which might serve as a barrier to managing stress and will require individuals to indicate if they could decrease stress in the described situation. The item will be written in the second person and will refer to someone's participation or feelings, for example, "You felt that something bad was going to happen."
2. The situations presented in the test items will involve, directly or indirectly, physical stress, symbolic stress, overload, frustration, or deprivation.
3. Situations will be selected to be applicable to most individuals. For example, a situation describing an individual's being busy because of taking care of a sibling will not be used because potential respondents might not have siblings. Situations in which individuals are generally busy, however, would be appropriate.
4. Each item will be 18 words or fewer in length. The words used will not exceed the fourth-grade level of the *IOX Basic Skills Word List*, except for the following words: *decrease*, *stress*.

Response Attributes

1. The following five response options will be available for each item: CERTAINLY YES, PROBABLY YES, MAYBE, PROBABLY NOT, and CERTAINLY NOT.
2. Children are to use the response options to indicate their ability to decrease stress in the specified situation. Respondents place a check in the appropriate space to the right of each item.

Scoring and Interpretation

1. The rationale underlying this measure is that the more often children indicate that they can with certainty decrease stress, the stronger the perceived efficacy of those children in being able to manage stress.
2. Point values are assigned to items according to the certainty of the respondents in being able to decrease stress as follows: CERTAINLY YES = 5, PROBABLY YES = 4, MAYBE = 3, PROBABLY NOT = 2, CERTAINLY NOT = 1.
3. A total score can be computed by adding the point value of every response. An average score can be computed by dividing the total score by the number of responses. High total or average scores reflect a strong perceived ability to decrease stress.

Measure Format

1. The following plan indicates the key characteristics of the "Could You Decrease Stress?" inventory developed from these test specifications.

Item	*Cause of Stress*
1	Frustration
2	Physical stress
3	Overload
4	Symbolic stress
5	Deprivation
6	Overload
7	Symbolic stress
8	Deprivation
9	Frustration
10	Physical stress
11	Symbolic stress
12	Deprivation
13	Overload
14	Deprivation
15	Physical stress
16	Symbolic stress
17	Frustration
18	Physical stress
19	Frustration
20	Overload

PSYCHOMOTOR DOMAIN

PHYSICAL FITNESS

General Description

Students will show an improvement in physical fitness (stronger respiratory muscles, improved strength and pumping efficiency of the heart, increased amount of blood circulation and improved muscle tone) by attaining a rating of at least "Good" on a 12-minute fitness test.

Sample Item

Directions. (To be read by the teacher.) Today I am going to check your overall physical fitness. Choose a partner. You are going to take turns acting as a lap counter and running the fitness course. The person taking the fitness test will have 12 minutes to walk and run as far as possible while the lap counter marks in a notebook the number of laps made around the track. When I call, "Stop," the lap counter will observe where you are on the track and mark in the notebook the final distance. Each pole on the track is 110 yards apart and once around the track is 440 yards. The total distance is computed by multiplying the number of laps around the track by 440 yards, adding the number of yards completed on the last lap, then dividing this total by 1,760 to obtain the distance in miles. Remember, you are to do this test at a comfortable pace. If you experience nausea, dizziness, shortness of breath, fatigue or lightheadedness, you are to stop. Ready........Begin!

Stimulus Attributes

1. Testing will take place on a track or field on which a quarter-mile oval or circular course is set and distances are marked each 110 yards with a flag, pole, or chalk.
2. All students participating in the fitness test must have been checked by the school physician and certified as eligible for regular physical education classes.
3. Participants will be verbally advised of the following before testing begins:
    a. Students will team up with another student who will act as a lap counter and calculate distances at completion of the 12-minute period.
    b. Students will walk or run around the fitness course as many times as possible within the time period.
    c. At the end of 12 minutes, runners and lap counters will exchange roles and the test will be run again until all students in the class have participated.
    d. Students experiencing fatigue, shortness of breath, lightheadedness, or nausea will stop immediately.

Response Attributes

1. Students will walk or run around a quarter-mile course as many times as possible within a 12-minute period.
2. Distance completed by each student will be recorded by a peer. At the end of the 12-minute period, the total number of miles run be each student will be obtained by dividing the number of yards completed by 1,760 yards. Distance of less than a lap (440 yards) will be rounded off to the nearest quarter lap attained (110 yards).
3. The fitness rating may be obtained for the mileage of each student by consulting a chart prepared by K. Cooper in *The New Aerobics* (New York: Bantam, 1972. P. 30). For example, if a male student runs 1.65 miles, his fitness rating would be "good;" for a female who runs that distance, the rating would be "excellent."

REFERENCES

Berk, R. A. A comparison of six content domain specification strategies for criterion-referenced tests. *Educational Technology*, 1980, *20*, 49–52.

Ebel, R. L. Content standard test scores. *Educational and Psychological Measurement*, 1962, *22*, 15–25.

Hambleton, R. K., Swaminathan, H., Algina, J., & Coulson, D. B. Criterion-referenced testing and measurement: A review of technical issues and developments. *Review of Educational Research*, 1978, *48*, 1–47.

Hively, W., Maxwell, G., Rabehl, G., Sension, D., & Lundin, S. *Domain-referenced curriculum evaluation: A technical handbook and a case study from the MINNE-MAST Project* (CSE Monograph Series in Evaluation, No. 1). Los Angeles: Center for the Study of Evaluation, University of California, 1973.

Hively, W., Patterson, H. L., & Page, S. A. A "universe-defined" system of arithmetic achievement tests. *Journal of Educational Measurement*, 1968, *5*, 275–290.

Popham, W. J. *Criterion-referenced measurement*. Englewood Cliffs, NJ: Prentice-Hall, 1978.

Popham, W. J. *Modern educational measurement*. Englewood Cliffs, NJ: Prentice-Hall, 1981.

3 GENERATING THE TEST ITEMS

GALE H. ROID

INTRODUCTION

FOLLOWING THE SPECIFICATION of the purpose and design of a criterion-referenced test, the challenging step of writing the actual test items arrives. With the press of deadlines and hectic schedules, it is very tempting to find a convenient list of objectives or some reference materials and start writing draft items. For some subject matter areas and for some classroom tests that may be used only once, an informal or objectives-based method of item writing may be the only reasonable and efficient choice. However, when one wishes to design criterion-referenced instruments for sophisticated interpretive or diagnostic purposes, extra time spent on the rules for generating items may pay rich dividends.

In contrast to informal approaches, the focus of this chapter will be on methods of item writing that have been variously described as domain-referenced (Hively, 1974), operationally defined (Bormuth, 1970; Osburn, 1968), algorithmic (Durnin & Scandura, 1973), and forming a technology of item writing (Roid & Haladyna, 1980, 1982). These are typically contrasted with objectives-based approaches (see Popham, chapter 2) and are described in typologies of achievement tests as having well-defined domains (Nitko, 1980, chapter 1; Wardrop et al., 1982).

Several scientific and practical advantages accompany the use of item-writing technologies: (1) the explicit description of item-writing methods so that researchers can replicate the types of test instruments used in published studies, (2) the public disclosure of item-writing methods, for use in large-scale evaluation studies with political or social impact, (3) increased efficiency in producing multiple test forms for use in mastery-testing (and -retesting)

Appreciation is expressed to Western Psychological Services for support and resources during the preparation of this chapter. Some of the background work for this chapter was previously supported by research contract MDA 903-77-C-0189 from the Advanced Research Projects Agency of the Department of Defense and a grant from the National Institute of Education while I was at the Teaching Research Division, Oregon State System of Higher Education.

systems, and (4) greater potential for linking tests to instructional methods and materials (Anderson, 1972; Berk, 1980; Bormuth, 1970; Millman, 1974; Shoemaker, 1975).

Further motivation for exploring item-writing methods comes from the exciting developments in diagnostic achievement testing, with its link to contemporary cognitive psychology (Glaser, 1981; Haertel & Calfee, 1983; Nitko, 1980), and increasing interest in the component processes of student test item performance (e.g., Carroll & Maxwell, 1979; Brown & Burton, 1978). This work is bringing into question the assumption that achievement and aptitude tests are or must be unidimensional, and forcing more attention to the different rules or cognitive strategies that different students use to solve achievement test items of the problem-solving type. Birenbaum and Tatsuoka (1983) have shown, for example, that the "factorial structure of the [achievement test] data is highly affected by the existence of different algorithms underlying the student response patterns"(p. 23). Specific attention to the construction of test items would allow these latent cognitive processes of students to be uncovered and new subtest scores based on these processes to be derived so that psychometric qualities of the test could be improved compared to conventional total scores (Birenbaum & Tatsuoka, 1983). In this way, diagnostic information about the erroneous rules used by students (problem-solving "bugs") could be uncovered and provided to teachers as feedback. Presumably, this will only be possible if achievement test items have been specifically written to provide such diagnostic information; hence the interest in algorithmic item-writing methods.

This chapter will briefly describe three major types of item-writing technologies: (1) procedural methods such as item forms and linguistic transformations, (2) theory-based methods such as the mapping sentence method and some of the newer cognitive-component methods, and (3) diagnostic methods such as Scandura's (1977) algorithmic approach and several methods derived from experimental cognitive psychology. An overview and listing of methods is provided in Table 3.1. Examples and references for each will be given, including a review of the strengths and weaknesses of the various approaches. The chapter concludes with suggestions for future research and guidelines for practitioners.

REVIEW OF ITEM-WRITING METHODS

Earlier reviews of the emerging technology of item writing (Berk, 1980; Engel & Martuza, 1976; Roid & Haladyna, 1980) typically emphasized a continuum of methods from the informal to the objectives-based to the algorithmic. Now, with further development and perspective on the field of item writing, it is possible to differentiate further the "algorithmic" end of the continuum into the three major types of methods that will be the topics of discussion in this chapter. However, before proceeding, it should be acknowledged that the categories chosen are somewhat arbitrary. For example, some

Table 3.1. Categories of Item-writing Methods and the Basic References to Their Development

Category/Method	Developers
I. Procedural	
A. Item Forms	Hively, Patterson, and Page (1968), Osburn (1968)
B. Linguistic Transformations	Bormuth (1970), Finn (1975), Conoley and O'Neil (1979), Roid and Haladyna (1982)
II. Theory-based	
A. Mapping Sentences	Guttman (1959, 1970), Guttman and Schlesinger (1967), Castro and Jordan (1977), Berk (1978)
B. Testing Concepts, Rules, and Principles	Markle and Tiemann (1970), Tiemann, Kroeker, and Markle (1977), Tiemann and Markle (1983)
C. Factor-based Item Construction	Guilford (1967), Meeker and Meeker (1975)
III. Diagnostic	
A. Algorithmic	Scandura (1970, 1977), Durnin and Scandura (1973)
B. Cognitive Strategy	Brown and Burton (1978), Glaser (1981), Birenbaum and Tatsuoka (1982, 1983)

diagnostic methods are also clearly theory based. Also, the number of different, well-described methods is small, and they remain difficult to categorize exactly because of their evolving, developmental characteristics.

In addition, it should be noted at the start that the use of any method of item writing should be accompanied by the time-honored collection of "conventional wisdom" represented in the lists of good item-writing principles. Practical guidelines for writing quality test items have been compiled by Coffman (1971), Conoley and O'Neil (1979), Ebel (1979), Gronlund (1982), Roid and Haladyna (1982), and others. These guidelines frequently give examples of multiple-choice, true-false, matching, and constructed-response items written well or poorly to point out the common flaws in test item construction. These lists of common flaws are invaluable in screening proposed item generation algorithms, especially if the intention is to generate large numbers of items automatically.

The lists of flaws can be grouped under two major principles of good item writing: (1) the reduction of guessing factors or clues susceptible to test-wiseness, and (2) the elimination of extraneous ability factors such as speed of reading or attention-to-detail capacity. For example, in multiple-choice items, writers are instructed to make the distractors grammatically parallel and of similar length to avoid cuing the correct answer. Or, lengthy item distractors that require the reading of redundant material are seen as injecting too much unnecessary reading into the item. Basically, the task of item writing is to create measures of the true achievement dimensions desired, not of extraneous abilities such as test-wiseness or related skills such as logical thinking, reading ability, or speed of information processing.

Procedural Item-writing Methods

Item forms. The method of item forms was developed by Hively (1974) and his colleagues (Hively, Patterson, & Page, 1968). Item forms employ a fixed syntactical structure having one or more variable element, each of which has a defined replacement set (Osburn, 1968). For example, a question on a measurement-statistics exam might ask for the proper choice of a correlational index, given two variables, each of which may be dichotomous or continuous. This question could be analyzed as an item form because it defines a class of related questions depending on the type of variables specified: "Given an (A) variable that measures (X), and a (B) variable that measures (Y), use the data in Table (C) to compute an appropriate correlational index." Table (C) could even be generated by computer, using randomly selected numbers designed to match the requirements of the problem. Presumably, such an item form could result in nearly an infinite number of unique items, if one counts the number of possible combinations of data.

For further information about the use of item forms, and the related method of amplified objectives, see chapter 2 by Popham. For references to the computerization of item forms, see chapter 4 by Millman, who discusses the development of a computer language specifically designed for the programming of item forms. Item forms are briefly described here because they are an example of a procedural method not requiring a theoretical or research basis for the design or selection of items.

Linguistic transformations. Bormuth (1970) and subsequent work by Finn (1975) formed the basis of a class of methods that attempt to transform prose or instructional discourse into test questions. The methods were developed from research on reading comprehension, and evolved from early work on cloze test procedures (Bormuth, 1967; Taylor, 1953, 1957). The goal of Bormuth's work was to produce a truly operationally defined method of developing questions directly linked to reading materials or instructional discourse. In addition to methods of transforming sentences from instructional prose, Bormuth advocated the development of methods based on intersentence syntax. Conoley and O'Neil (1979) extended the methods further, to items at the level of application or principle learning. Due to the brevity of the present review, focus will be on an example of sentence transformation. The reader is encouraged to explore the original references to cloze procedures and the Bormuth methodology, perhaps beginning with an overview such as chapter 6 in Roid and Haladyna (1982). Also, Berk (1979) provides a valuable comparison of cloze and linguistic transformation procedures that will be helpful in applying these methods.

Instructors have for years relied on their scanning of written instructional materials to suggest the important ideas, concepts, and principles embedded in the content of their classes. The Bormuth methods simply take this process a step further and attempt to objectify the way in which prose material is transformed into test questions. Also, linguistic transformations make one very aware of the enormous number of test items that could be created from any prose segment, such as the chapter from a book. If items are written informally, by constructing the first items that come to mind, systematic coverage of the material is not assured, nor is there any documentation of the criteria used to select an item. The precise relationship between the test items and the instructional materials must be known, especially in the realm of program evaluation, where an achievement test may be designed to measure the degree of knowledge and skill retained by the student who has been exposed to a set of instructional materials or methods, or the evaluation cannot be described as rigorous in its sampling of the material taught. Therefore, although the transformation of prose material into questions has the inherent flaw of being easily degenerated into a testing of trivial item content, the method remains conceptually attractive for rigorous assessment projects where important content is sampled.

Therefore, the first task in using sentence transformation methods is to find a way to identify the important sentences in prose material. Finn (1978) recommended an objective method of searching for key words in text based on research on the *standard frequency index* of words in American textbooks (Carroll, Davies, & Richman, 1971). If a word is relatively rare in textbooks, and yet appears in the prose material being examined, that word is probably a "high information" word—one that labels an important concept or idea—for the student who reads the material. This fact can be used in an informal way rather easily by anyone who scans a written document, searching for the unique words that are not often seen in other documents but that are highlighted or defined in the text. If one liberalizes this further to include unique phrases, a very powerful technique for identifying important content in prose becomes available. For example, in the present chapter, if one were to scan from the beginning to the present sentence, certain unique phrases such as "algorithmic method," "linguistic transformation" and "standard frequency index" would emerge as phrases that are not often discussed in education or psychology texts, or in texts on measurement, for that matter. These key phrases would probably be the topics of test questions based on this chapter.

Roid and Haladyna (1982, chap. 6) present other possible methods of identifying the important sentences in prose material in preparation for sentence transformations. These include the scanning of statements of objectives or instructional goals, outlines and topic sentences, and having teachers or content experts select the important sentences in a passage. Another approach suggested by Anderson's (1972) work on the importance of paraphrase in the accurate assessment of reading comprehension is the writing of summary or "mediating" sentences that would be similar to item forms. The teacher or content experts would write these sentences as a way of summarizing the important themes in the written material. Variable elements in the sentences could be sampled to create many parallel test items. For example, from a chapter in a measurement course on item writing, a summarizing sentence could be constructed such as: "Given an item in (A) subject matter, with an item flaw (B), written in the (C) item format, would you categorize the flaw as related to (1) test-wiseness, (2) guessing, or (3) the measurement of an extraneous skill?"

Detailed steps for implementing sentence transformation methods are given elsewhere (Roid & Haladyna, 1982, chap. 6). However, to illustrate the essential features of the method, an example is presented in Table 3.2. First the well-written text on oceans (see Table 3.2) was examined, and a chapter on plankton was chosen as an example. An informal method of item transformation was then completed in order to show how feasible the method would be for those not equipped with an analysis of word frequencies, etc. The concept developed by Finn (1978) and Roid and Finn (1978) was used to identify a key word noun that would tap an important idea in the content of the chapter. A study of key word nouns in the chapter revealed such words as *krill*, *euphausiidae*, and, of course, *plankton*. Finding the key sentences in the passage was somewhat complicated by the fact that the author used a great deal of anaphora, referring back to previous words and phrases, and a flowery, interesting style. One of the major facts was isolated in one paragraph, listed as "Original Text" in Table 3.2. The first task was to identify the basic structure or key elements of the idea underlying the sentences, and then to replace the anaphoric phrases with the actual nouns (e.g., "these creatures" is linked back to "animals"). Extra clauses that add additional or separate detail to the basic idea of the sentences are dropped (e.g., "forms a vast layer of living soup"). The basic sentence is transformed into a Wh- form by placing the word "What" at the beginning of the item stem. Distractors that contrast

Table 3.2. Example of Sentence Transformation Method

Original Text:	"These little plants are eaten by animals scarcely larger than themselves, and the whole plant-animal mixture forms a vast layer of living soup in the upper levels of the ocean. . . . The name, plankton, has been given to these creatures."
Source:	Clarke (1960)
Key Elements:	". . . plants are eaten by animals. . . . The name, plankton. . . ."
Verbatim Test Item:	What animals eat the little plants in the sea's upper layers? a. krill b. euphausiidae c. plankton d. herring
Paraphrased Test Item:	What feeds regularly on the tiny, floating plant-life near the ocean's surface? ______

with the key word "plankton" were chosen from the nearby text, to complete the verbatim, multiple-choice form of the item. For the more difficult task of measuring comprehension, with constructed response, a fill-in item using paraphrasing was then written to parallel the verbatim item.

It should be noted that the example given in Table 3.2 cannot be completely defined in operational terms, as originally intended by Bormuth (1970). However, I believe the more flexible use of the technique, with the item writer's choice entering to a great extent, to be more practical and of more immediate and widespread use. The rigorous and rather automated methods of transforming randomly selected sentences tend occasionally to result in items that are odd, too easy, or otherwise trivial (e.g., the clerical method of distractor development in Roid, Haladyna, Shaughnessy, & Finn, 1979; or in Roid & Wendler, 1983). The technology of intelligently transforming complex textual material just has not advanced to the degree that a fully operational method will result consistently in quality test items. The psychometric properties of the partially objective, writer's choice method, such as shown in Table 3.2, have been demonstrated by Roid and Wendler (1983). They found that a sentence transformation method with writer's choice of distractors resulted in less sex bias and greater internal consistency than did an objectives-based method.

Theory-based Methods

Another category of item-writing methods includes those based on a theory or research foundation that dictates the steps used to construct a set of items. In nearly every case, these methods are an outgrowth of research in areas outside of achievement testing, such as the study of attitudes, conceptual learning, or the nature of intelligence. Table 3.1 lists the methods in this category, which will be discussed in turn.

Mapping sentences. Similar to the way in which item forms are created, mapping sentences are written with variable elements (called *facets*) that define variations in wording that could be used to create a large number of parallel sentences. However, the major difference in the two approaches is that mapping sentence methods were intended to be verified by empirical research (typically using some form of cluster analysis or smallest-space analysis) that documents the relationship between the theoretical structure of the items and actual data. In practice, the mapping sentence method has been applied informally without the verification step. Both the formal and the informal application of the method will be discussed.

Structural facet theory (Guttman, 1959; Foa, 1968) and its subsequent application to scale development and item writing (Guttman & Schlesinger, 1967; Guttman, 1970; Runkel & McGrath, 1972) forms the basis of a method that has become identified with one of its major features— the mapping sentence. An actual example of the application of facet theory to attitude-scale development by one of Guttman's colleagues will provide a good introduction to the logic and processes involved in rigorous use of the technique.

Dancer (1983) studied a group of 6 items that measured the frequency of feelings of hostility. Using Guttman's (1968) smallest-space analysis (Lingoes, 1977), she had identified the 6 items as forming a region in geometric space defined by data from 1,158 subjects who responded to a 36-item questionnaire including the hostility items. Using a mapping sentence presented in Levy and Guttman (1981) defining the universe of items that describe one's well-being and adjustment, Dancer was able to classify each of the items on the 36-item scale. The next step was to explore the match between the mapping sentence and real data. This was done using a partial-order scalogram analysis (Dancer, 1983) calculated on a random sample of 90 subjects, using the 6 hostility items. The analysis is a nonmetric, special case of multidimensional scalogram analysis (Lingoes, 1977) that examines the response patterns of each subject on the 6 items. Each individual is then represented in a multidimensional, geometric space (in this case using two dimensions). Also, the analysis includes an output diagram showing patterns of item responses such as is illustrated in Figure 3.1. A fictitious ordering of patterns for 3 items is shown in Figure 3.1 to provide a simplified example of the method used by Dancer (1983). The researcher's task is to examine the subject diagrams (applying knowledge about subgroups of subjects) and item diagrams such as Figure 3.1 to identify conceptually meaningful regions that define the underlying dimensions of the data. Results showed clearly that two dimensions described the items: intensity of hostility and the object to which hostility was directed. Items included references to "breaking things when mad" (hostility toward objects), hostility toward others, and a self-directed anger. These results suggest that a mapping sentence, with the two facets of intensity and direction, would well represent (or generate) the items. And, more importantly, to measure more thoroughly the underlying dimensions of "hostility," a much larger number of items could be written than the original 6.

Now, one must make the intuitive leap from the attitude or personality realm into the achievement domain, in order to see how the mapping sentence method, and facet theory, can be applied to criterion-referenced tests. First of all, as was mentioned earlier, the method has a practical application immediately if one focuses only on the mapping sentence itself, without doing the computerized data analyses. Table 3.3, for example, shows a possible mapping sentence for a topic in American literature, the "greatness of Mark Twain's *Huckleberry Finn*." Although this example has not been verified empirically on data from literary critics, it is clear that breaking the topic into a general sentence with several facets is very helpful in a practical understanding of what could be tested. If one wishes to have an empirically validated set of questions, a study would need to be conducted of representative questions generated on the topic of *Huckleberry Finn* that were completed by different groups such as (1) expert critics in American literature, (2) graduate students in literature, (3) other students and novices, to suggest but a few. Such a study might reveal that certain dimensions underlying the items define the acknowledged criteria by which experts judge the novel, and that additional

Figure 3.1. Patterns of responses to three hostility items depicted in two-dimensional space

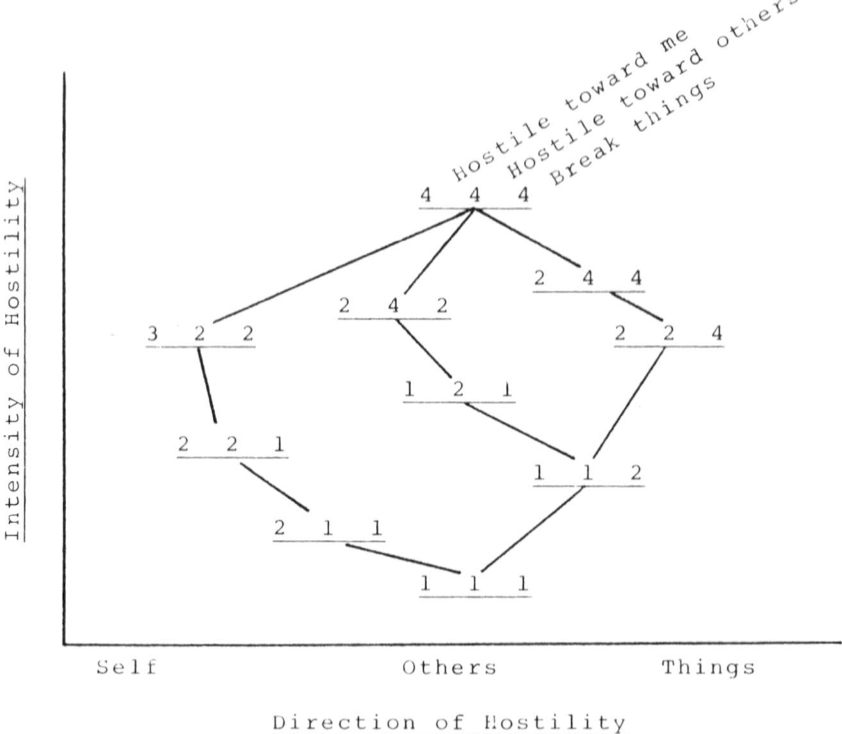

Note: Item responses were 1 = "none or little of the time," 2 = "some of the time," 3 = "a good part of the time," 4 = "most or all of the time."

Source: This figure was adapted from Dancer (1983) with permission of the author, but has been abbreviated and changed from a data-referenced display to a purely illustrative figure.

items can be written to tap these dimensions more thoroughly. To date, it is not clear that anyone has attempted such an empirical extension of facet theory into the realm of achievement testing, but the potential of such a technique is intriguing.

For further examples and guidelines for developing mapping sentences for criterion-referenced tests, the reader is referred to the articles by Berk (1978) and Guttman and Schlesinger (1967), chapter 8 in Roid and Haladyna (1982), and the general reference work of Runkel and McGrath (1972).

Testing concepts, rules, and principles. One of the best examples of systematic item writing based on theories of learning and teaching is the work of Tiemann and Markle (1983). By integrating the considerable research on

Table 3.3. Example of a Mapping Sentence in American Literature

Mapping Sentence:	"The greatness of *Huckleberry Finn*'s (A) is in Mark Twain's (B) the (C)."
Facet Elements:	(A)
	topic or theme
	character development
	form
	style
	social commentary
	(B)
	attention to
	choice of
	departure from
	(C)
	relationship of Huck and Jim.
	moral struggle of Huck.
	Divinity of the River.
	use of realistic American dialects.
	picaresque novel form.
	past grandiose "literary" style.
Possible Short-Answer Essay Question Form:	
	"Briefly describe three episodes from the novel *Huckleberry Finn* that are examples of its greatness of (A) in Mark Twain's (B) the (C)."

Source: Derived from a reading of Trilling (1948).

concept and rule learning, Tiemann and Markle developed a training package (Markle & Tiemann, 1970) that demonstrated how to analyze concepts in a variety of subject matter areas from art to zoology. The basic theory of concept learning implemented by the technique included three ideas: (1) that students must learn to discriminate between examples and nonexamples of a concept, (2) that students must generalize from teaching examples to a broader set of examples, and (3) that testing the understanding of concepts must include both examples and nonexamples *different* from those used in teaching the concepts.

In the Tiemann and Markle system, concepts are defined as classes of entities, the members of which share some properties in common. Some concepts and their subject matter areas are soliloquy (literature), synonym (grammar), mercantilism (history), element (chemistry), and reliability estimate (measurement). For each concept, the critical and variable attributes of examples and nonexamples can be specified. For instance, in the concept "insect," one of the critical attributes is that it must be an invertebrate with six jointed legs, but the size of the legs or the presence of wings are attributes that can vary across both examples and nonexamples.

Tiemann, Kroeker, and Markle (1977) showed that a set of related concepts can be coordinated so that examples used to teach one concept may be used as nonexamples for another concept. They examined the related concepts of positive and negative reinforcement, punishment and extinction, and they were able to devise a criterion-referenced system of questions. The domain for the items was specified by the critical and variable attributes of the examples and nonexamples used in teaching and testing. Again, examples used in teaching were excluded from the tests so that true comprehension could be assessed (Anderson, 1972).

Recently Tiemann and Markle (1983) have extended the method to include the analysis of rules and principles, which can be viewed as statements of the relationship among concepts. It is often easier to identify rules or principles in instructional materials or teaching exercises than it is to begin by finding the more elemental concepts. For example, in the realm of writing and copyediting, a general rule for using compound words is: "When a temporary compound is used as an adjective before a noun, it is often hyphenated to avoid misleading the reader." Examples of compound words from this chapter would include "item-writing (method)" and "attitude-scale (development)." A thorough study of the rule reveals that a number of fundamental concepts in language arts and grammar are embedded in it: "temporary compound," "adjective," and "noun." By providing a comprehensive list of examples and nonexamples of each concept, it is possible to construct a huge domain of teaching and testing items for assessing understanding of the rule.

Learning to use the Tiemann and Markle approach takes study time and some feedback from colleagues or subject matter experts. An excellent place to begin is the training workbook (Tiemann & Markle, 1983), which includes many practical exercises.

Factor-based item construction. An interesting area of item development that has indirect implications for criterion-referenced testing is the assessment of cognitive abilities from the perspective of factor analysis. Decades of work have been invested by Guilford (1956, 1967, 1981) and others (e.g., Guilford, Hoepfner, & Petersen, 1965; Meeker, 1969; Meeker & Meeker, 1975) in the development of objective tests for the assessment of the many dimensions hypothesized by Guilford's (1967) Structure-of-Intellect (SOI) model. In the process of developing a number of ingenious types of items, research on the SOI model has been guided by empirical data and a factor-based theory in the purposeful design of test items.

Although no direct parallel in achievement testing comes to mind, as one studies the SOI tests in detail it becomes clear that the method has a definite application in the area of achievement testing. Only recently has there been a more widespread recognition of the possible role of factor analysis (and other multidimensional techniques) in the study of criterion-referenced tests. Hambleton (1980, chapter 8) mentions Guttman scalogram analysis and factor analysis as possible methods of exploring the construct validity of criterion-referenced tests. The recent work of Reckase (1979) and Birenbaum and Tatsuoka (1982, 1983) suggests that the multidimensional nature of achievement tests will become a topic of increased attention, and perhaps factor analysis will be one of many analytical methods used to explore the dimensionality of criterion-referenced tests. Kingsbury and Weiss (1979), for example, used factor analysis to demonstrate that achievement test data collected before instruction showed a different factor structure than data collected after instruction.

An example of items used in the *SOI Learning Abilities Tests* (Meeker & Meeker, 1975) is shown in Figure 3.2. These items are sample items that are part of the test directions for 3 of the 26 subtests in the battery. They are described by a trigram of three letters that refer to the three dimensions in Guilford's model: (1) operations: cognition, memory, evaluation, convergent

Figure 3.2. Items from the SOI Learning Abilities Tests

1. **C**ognition of **F**igural **S**ystems (CFS)

2. **C**ognition of **S**ymbolic **S**ystems (CSS)

1, 3, 5, ___	6 ☐	7 ☐	10 ☐	9 ☐

3. **C**ognition of se**M**antic **S**ystems (CMS)

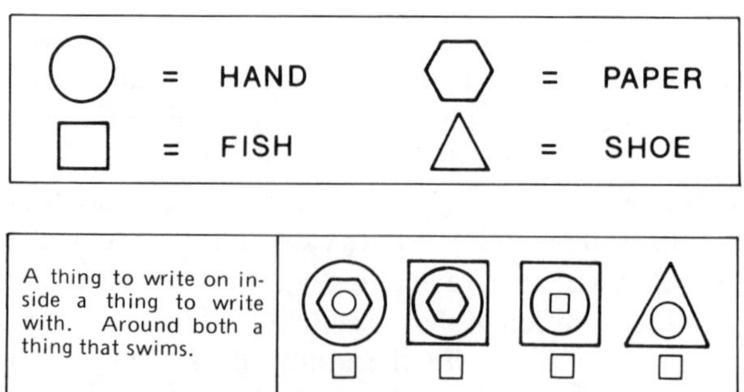

Source: From the *SOI Learning Abilities Test*, Form A, by Mary Meeker and Robert Meeker, Copyright 1975 by Mary Meeker. Reproduced by permission of the publisher, Western Psychological Services, 12031 Wilshire Blvd., Los Angeles, CA 90025.

production, and divergent production; (2) contents: figural, symbolic, semantic, and behavioral; and (3) products: units, classes, relations, systems, transformations, and implications. The three items in Figure 3.2 vary only on the content dimension that represents figures, numbers, and words.

The value of this factor-based approach to item writing may be the rigor with which theory and empirical research can be used to sample comprehensively a full range of possible tasks and content areas with items specifically designed to measure hypothesized dimensions of those areas. Certainly, many investigators have criticized the actual dimensions and even the underlying SOI model (Horn, 1979; Sternberg, 1979), but most have recognized the ingenious nature of the test development effort (Cronbach, 1970, p. 339). What remains to be seen is whether applications in achievement testing, stimulated by the search for examples that will match the new multidimensional latent trait models (e.g., Reckase, 1979), will be forthcoming.

Diagnostic Methods

Algorithmic methods. One of the most widely referenced methods of item writing was proposed by Scandura (1970, 1977). Durnin and Scandura (1973) described the method as an algorithmic approach with more potential for diagnosing the problem-solving errors of students than the method of item forms. The choice of the term "algorithm" comes from the fact that problem-solving behavior, particularly in mathematics and quantitative areas of natural and social sciences, can be described by a flow chart that is similar to a computer algorithm. If the algorithm is an accurate representation of the procedures that students use in solving problems, then the algorithm can be used to simulate the "paths" students can take through the various steps in problem solution. Also, the steps in the algorithm, once listed and described, can be used to develop a universe of possible problems, and to track student errors and incorrect choices.

Table 3.4 presents a sample problem in arithmetic, analyzed from an algorithmic viewpoint. Two algorithms are listed. The first was adapted from Durnin and Scandura (1973) and is a systematic method of summing the first two addends and then adding each successive number. The second, informally created for this table, is a contrasting algorithm that sums pairs of addends, and includes an attempt to increase the speed of problem solution through the pairing of those numbers that sum to 10. The two contrasting algorithms are presented to emphasize that even for a simple problem, there are multiple strategies or rules that students can use to solve a problem. By anticipating and specifying the steps in such rules before a test is developed, one can design rather sophisticated diagnostic information into the items. Diagnostic information may be derived from problems that exaggerate certain errors that students are known to make. One of many possible examples might be to overload a problem such as presented in Table 3.4 with pairs of numbers that have sums greater than 10 to test the accuracy of the student's "carrying" into the tens position. Another example would be to include a set

Table 3.4. Analysis of Algorithms for an Addition Problem

Problem:	Addition of multiple, single-digit addends (Four or more addends)
Example:	$3 + 7 + 4 + 9 + 5 = \underline{(?)}$
Algorithm 1:	1. Sum the first two addends. 2. If the sum equals 10 or more, go to Step 4, otherwise go to Step 3. 3. Add the units digit of the sum to the next addend and go back to Step 2. 4. Add 1 to whatever is in the tens place and go back to Step 3 if there is another addend, otherwise to Step 5. 5. Write down the sum and stop.
Algorithm 2:	1. Add successive pairs of two addends and write out these temporary sums to the side, including any remaining single addend. If any pairs add to ten, even if nonadjacent, add them together first. 2. Add the "ones digits" of the temporary sums, incrementing the tens place by 1 as many times as required. 3. If the number of temporary sums is large (e.g., greater than 5), repeat Step 1 for these sums. 4. Write down the final sum.

of items that have many pairs of addends that sum to exactly 10 to test for the presence of the efficiency strategy mentioned in algorithm 2 in Table 3.4 through the recording of response time. (For further information about the method the reader is referred to Durnin and Scandura, 1973; Scandura, 1970, 1977; and Scandura and Durnin, 1978.)

Other diagnostic methods. An increasing number of studies are appearing in the measurement literature concerning the design of achievement tests that are measuring separate components or steps in the performance of students on test items of the problem-solving type. By providing separate subtests or scores for each component or step, tests of problem solving can become more diagnostic of student errors. Because no formal names for such methods have been coined, and few detailed examples of sample items have been provided in the literature, they will be described in rather general terms.

Brown and Burton (1978) used information-processing models of student performance on addition and subtraction problems as a method of simulating the problem-solving operations commonly used by elementary students. The study used a concept from computer programming to describe errors embedded in student problem-solving strategies. These errors are called "bugs," and any programmer is familiar with the process of "debugging" a computer program. By documenting the common bugs that students acquire, anticipated wrong answers to questions can be recorded and used to identify the presence of particular errors. Remedial instruction in mathematics or statistics can be seen as a process of "debugging" the incorrect algorithms used by students in solving calculation problems. Also, the work of Brown and Burton, Scandura, and others highlights the importance of knowing the algorithms initially taught to a student, so that diagnostic tests can be linked to the actual algorithms used in learning.

Birenbaum and Tatsuoka (1983) have devised methods for scoring arithmetic tests based on the underlying algorithms used by students to solve each item. They were successful in eliminating the variability in test scores due to "the fact that students can sometimes get right answers by following the wrong rule." Patterns of student responses to signed-number problems, for example, were intensely analyzed, and students were interviewed to find the incorrect algorithms being used to solve these problems. For instance, some students converted subtraction problems into addition problems, ignoring the signs of each number. New scoring methods gave a score of "1" only when a correct answer was achieved by using an error-free algorithm. In other words, students were not given credit for a "correct" answer obtained by an erroneous strategy. Results showed that the internal consistency was greater (.93 versus .84) for the new scoring methods, and the factor structure of the rescored items was greatly simplified.

In order for the Birenbaum and Tatsuoka (1983) scoring method to be used, presumably a sufficient number of items needs to be written to uncover the majority of common algorithms used by students in solving a set of problems. Therefore, their work has direct implications for the technology of item writing. Also, the approach is a further example of a "bootstrapping" method of item writing that could be very valuable. After an initial field testing of a group of items, the dimensionality underlying the test items is examined using cluster analysis, multidimensional scaling, or factor analysis, or through attempts to fit multicomponent latent trait models (e.g., Reckase, 1979; Stegelmann, 1983; Whitely, 1981). Then, the adequacy of the items for measuring the latent cognitive components of student test performance is assessed. If too few items are present to assess one or more of the underlying cognitive strategies or components, the test can be expanded accordingly. A similar bootstrapping procedure was recommended in the discussion of mapping sentences presented earlier.

In the design of achievement tests for reading, the work of Curtis and Glaser (1983), Drum, Calfee, and Cook (1980), and Hoepfner (1978), among many others, points in the direction of increasing attention to the writing of items that measure important cognitive components in the reading process. Curtis and Glaser (1983) described four areas of cognitive functioning in reading—word decoding, semantic access, sentence processing, and discourse analysis—that have implications for the design of achievement test items. In-depth testing of speed and accuracy of word recognition, and more precise determination of the student's knowledge of word meanings, are possible through branching technology and the timing of responses, particularly if microcomputers can be used. Curtis and Glaser (1983) and Hoepfner (1978) have provided a number of examples of items from published achievement tests that do measure depth of knowledge of word meanings. However, the problem is that item selection procedures are typically based on psychometric characteristics of items, rather than on the cognitive-component functions they embody. Drum et al. (1980) discuss another level of concern—that surface features of reading test items, such as sentence length, syntactic complexity, and plausibility of distractors, are expected to influence the complexity of the cognitive processes students use to answer each question. At the same time, if these important features of items are not systematically varied, the overall test score becomes a mixture of item scores having an unspecified complexity. In Birenbaum and Tatsuoka's (1982) terminology, the resulting tests are multidimensional, but they are not amenable to diagnostic subtest scoring because systematic subgroupings of items may not have been included.

SUGGESTIONS FOR FUTURE RESEARCH

Computer Applications

The growing use of computers in all phases of testing and test development will surely influence the directions of future research on item writing for criterion-referenced tests. The implementation of item forms on microcomputers will make possible increasing research on their application to practical learning tasks. Progress in the field of linguistic transformations may require computerization in order to make the methods more immediately useful to busy educators. For example, similar to the microcomputer software that computes readability indices and corrects spelling errors as part of word processing, a software package could identify key words in a passage and print them for the textbook writer or reading test developer. The Carroll et al. (1971) word-frequency index, which could be made accessible by such a processor, could be used to find those nouns that have a standard frequency index of 60 or less (as recommended by Roid & Finn, 1978). The sentences in which the identified words occur could then be available for printing, and, perhaps, could be partially processed for possible use as test questions. Research teams may be composed of linguistics, cognitive psychologists, and educators if the technology of sentence transformation or other, more complex, linguistic transformations is to progress further. The integration of Bormuth's (1970) work with the contemporary work on cognitive components of reading (e.g., Curtis & Glaser, 1983) is a major challenge.

Another interesting application of microcomputers is in the development of programs that combine instruction and sophisticated diagnostic testing. Scandura (1981) has developed a system called RULE-TUTOR that implements a diagnostic, branching procedure for assessing a student's mastery of algorithms for solving problems such as those in basic mathematics. With as few as three items, one can diagnose the student's mastery of the rules of problem solving, assuming that one has a hierarchically structured content area and an algorithmic analysis of the problems, such as was done by Durnin and Scandura (1973) and Scandura (1982). The development of computer-based diagnostic testing is certainly an area where sophisticated item-writing technologies will be needed.

Linking Teaching and Testing

Additional research is needed to guide practitioners in matching the appropriate item-writing methods to particular instructional tasks. Perhaps the concept of task structures (Baker & Herman, 1983) will help in this regard, but the practical guidelines such as those currently used by the U.S. Navy (Ellis & Wulfeck, 1983) also need extension into the broader areas of school learning. Although the Navy method begins with performance objectives, rather than domain specifications, it is extremely comprehensive in including most of the item-writing methods discussed in this chapter, and it provides a means of matching task and content characteristics to test item formats in the realm of skills training. It uses the Instructional Quality Inventory system (Montague, Ellis, & Wulfeck, 1983; Roid & Haladyna, 1982, chap. 11), which categorizes all objectives and test items into a grid composed of tasks (Remember, Use-Unaided, Use-Aided) by contents (Facts, Concepts, Procedures, Rules, Principles). Other typologies (e.g., Miller, Williams & Haladyna, 1978), methods of analysis (e.g., Merrill, Reigeluth, & Faust, 1979), and systems (e.g., the PLANA system of Schott, Neeb, & Wieberg, in press) may be useful schemas for matching item types with instructional requirements.

Components of Achievement Performance

As Guttman (1970) insightfully observed, there have been many theories of test scores, but few theories of content structure and specification. It is ironic, therefore, that the growing recognition of the usefulness of item response theories such as the Rasch model (Rasch, 1980) and the three-parameter model (Lord, 1980) has also highlighted the unidimensionality assumption of achievement tests. With increased attention to item response theory has come rather immediate concern for multicomponent and multidimensional models (Reckase, 1979; Whitely, 1981). One hopes that the excitement over the statistical aspects of multidimensional test analysis will not distract researchers from the conceptual and research tasks ahead in specifying the components of achievement performance. The methods proposed by Scandura (1982) for analyzing content areas, especially basic mathematics, are an excellent example of new analytical methods that attempt to uncover prototypic strategies or rules used to solve problems such as those found on many achievement tests.

The complex challenge ahead will be to extend further the important work begun on decomposing test item performance into its cognitive or information-processing components. Stimulated by work on intelligence (Sternberg, 1977, 1979, 1981) and aptitude testing (e.g., Whitely, 1977, 1981), researchers can begin to search for the component processes underlying achievement test performance, with the recognition that new test-scoring and statistical models (e.g., Birenbaum & Tatsuoka, 1983; Stegelmann, 1983) will be awaiting the computer entry of real data.

A prototypical study by cognitive psychologists that could serve as a model for empirical research on the components of test item performance is the study of the block-design test by Schorr, Bower, and Kiernan (1982). This study actually consisted of four experiments in which the task of assembling a set of blocks to match a design was progressively studied by examining two sets of variables: (1) the stimulus characteristics and task complexity of each item, and (2) the problem-solving strategies used by students. Of course, the interaction between item attributes and strategies was also examined. The results showed that the number of interior edges (those edges of the blocks not occurring on the periphery of the design) and the number of solid-colored blocks in the design were important determiners of item difficulty; symmetry and type of overall pattern were also influential factors. The study provides a rigorously empirical basis on which block-design items can be graded in difficulty and systematically varied to sample a full range of complex problem-solving behavior. In addition, it was found that there were predominantly two strategies employed by subjects: "analytical," in which subjects proceeded nearly one block at a time, and "synthetic," in which subjects used a gestalt impression of the entire design.

The Schorr et al. (1982) study suggests some interesting possibilities for research on underachievement and learning disabilities where both task characteristics and learner characteristics are examined in the intensive study of types of achievement test items. For example, in reading comprehension research, the cognitive components suggested by the test item features described by Drum et al. (1980) could be examined in interaction with learner characteristics such as broad versus narrow scanning (Santostefano, 1978). One hopes that through such experiments we can learn which features of test item design are crucial for the thorough sampling of the cognitive skills and strategies used by students in achievement test items of the problem-solving type.

Multidimensional Analysis of Criterion-referenced Tests

A final area of new research will undoubtedly be the study of the multidimensional nature of achievement test data. Just as factor analysis has often motivated psychologists to add or subtract certain items from personality and ability tests because of a desire to measure factors, perhaps educational test developers will begin to create test items to measure the underlying dimensions of new multidimensional, multicomponent achievement tests. The upsurge in interest in item response theories has brought an increased interest in the determination of test dimensionality (Green, Lissitz, & Mulaik, 1977; McDonald, 1981; Smith, 1980). New methods of factor analysis that recognize the problem of factoring dichotomous items may also stir interest in this much-neglected area.

Gorsuch and Yagel (1982) recommended two types of analysis: item parcel procedures and hierarchical factor analysis. Cattell (1956, 1974) has used a technique called item parceling for decades, but its usage has somehow escaped the attention of educational test developers. Three types of item parceling have been used: informal, radial, and suppressor parceling. Each will be briefly described here. Informal item parcels are miniscales composed of three to seven items judged to be similar in content which are then scored, and the parcel scores are subjected to a factor analysis. Radial parcels are defined by an initial factor analysis that extracts a large number of factors. Then, an examination of the pattern of factor loadings is used to form parcels of similar items. In suppressor parceling, each grouping of items is composed of three or more items that differ systematically along some "nuisance" dimension that needs to be suppressed in order to study the "true" factor structure. For example, items that are high, medium, or low on guessing or testwiseness influence (as determined by some empirical index of these influences) would be placed in each parcel. The resulting factor analysis of the parcel scores would have neutralized the influence of the nuisance variable(s).

Gorsuch and Dreger (1979) described a computer program for doing hierarchical factor analysis that has been recommended for use with dichotomous items by Gorsuch and Yagel (1982). As Gorsuch (1983, chap. 11) explained in more detail, higher-order factors are extracted from the correlations among lower-order factors. If nuisance factors are present among the lower-order factors (e.g., factors due solely to item difficulty) they will be preempted by higher-order factors, which may provide more meaningful definition of the underlying dimensions of the test items. The Gorsuch and Dreger (1979) analysis method allows correlated factors to be extracted. Wherry and Wherry (1969) developed another hierarchical program, based on the work of Wherry (1959), which extracts uncorrelated factors. Examples of the application of hierarchical analysis are provided in Gorsuch (1983, chap. 11) and in studies such as Wallbrown, Blaha, and Wherry (1973). My current research is suggesting that hierarchical factor analysis may empirically verify that achievement test items can be grouped into sets defined by instructional objectives used to write the items.

In a series of important studies, Muthén (1978, 1981) and Muthén and Christofferson (1981) have developed a factor-analytic model specifically for dichotomous items. A generalized computer program, which performs other functions of structural equation modeling, is also under development and is efficient in analyzing 20 to 25 variables at a time (Muthén, 1982). Research on the dimensionality of groups of achievement test items would certainly be an important application of these new methods.

As mentioned earlier in this chapter, there are two purposes for exploring the dimensionality of criterion-referenced achievement tests. First, the empirical determination of the dimensions underlying test item response data may suggest ways to write additional items having identified dimensional qualities. Second, the construct validity of the resulting criterion-referenced test is at stake (see Hambleton, chapter 8), and the ultimate purpose of writing each item on the test should be to contribute to the validity of the measure.

GUIDELINES FOR PRACTITIONERS

First some general recommendations will be discussed, and then specific guidelines for teachers/instructors, large-scale survey testing, certification testing, and program evaluation will be proposed. Clearly, a general statement can be made that objectives-based item-writing methods continue to be more widely applied than the kind of operationally defined, criterion-referenced methods that were the major focus of this chapter. An encouraging trend, however, is that operationally defined methods have been recommended for certain types of objectives (e.g., concept-based methods for concept and rule learning, in Ellis and Wulfeck, 1982), and for certain types of subject matter (e.g., the algorithmic method of Scandura for mathematics, in Berk, 1980). The objectives- and domain-based approaches were seen as incompatible in the past, but in practical applications, both approaches can coexist. In fact, there is further evidence that item response theory has important functions in criterion-referenced testing (Haladyna & Roid, 1981, 1983), and that a rigorous, statistical theory of test scores and criterion-referenced item development can be used together to increase the measurement precision of testing procedures. This chapter has emphasized the further importance of the new multidimensional, multicomponent item response models, which similarly should be seen as compatible with criterion-referenced item writing.

An unfortunate past trend has been to expect that if items have been constructed by operationally defined rules or other criterion-referenced methods, they will automatically have certain desirable psychometric properties. Also, there may have been a generalized fear that we should not tamper with such items even if they have flaws for fear of disturbing domain score inferences. However, a strong recommendation of this chapter is to use field testing and experimental applications of draft criterion-referenced item collections in order to study the dimensionality and underlying student cognitive strategies that can be uncovered only from empirical analysis of data and close work with students. In addition to validity evidence, studies of dimensionality may greatly stimulate the comprehensive design of truly diagnostic criterion-referenced tests by suggesting new item types that can be developed.

Teachers, Instructors, and Trainers

As Shepard (chapter 7) points out, the limited time available to practicing teachers, trainers, and instructors for the development of tests cannot be stretched to include the complex analyses and field testing that would accompany the development of the theory-based or diagnostic methods described in this chapter. By being aware of the need for such methods, however, the teacher can be sensitive to the search for instructional materials and tests that are diagnostic of the cognitive components used by students to solve mathematics problems, for example, in the classroom.

At an informal level, there is no reason why certain principles of item writing cannot be applied without the definitive application of all the steps required by one of the operational methods. Several examples come to mind. First, item forms continue to be a useful tool for suggesting possible test questions, even if they are not precisely specified or used to create full universes of items. Taking statements of objectives or goal statements and turning them into item forms is often possible by just using informal judgment. Also, the related method of mapping sentences, excluding the empirical verification of each facet, is equally useful in adapting statements of objectives, or themes found in textbooks. For instance, a geography book may describe each of five regions of the United States, with details given on four types of cities: (1) manufacturing centers, (2) trading centers, (3) transportation hubs, and (4) farming-support cities. This should rather immediately suggest two facets with five and four elements, respectively, and 20 possible resulting questions.

In terms of linguistic methods, the sentence transformation method has actually been used for centuries in an informal way, and there is no reason to stop now, with the refinement that important sentences are selected and paraphrasing is used to test comprehension. The concept of key word nouns is a powerful one that is extremely helpful, in a very practical way, for identifying the important content that has been presented to students in reading assignments.

Finally, the informal application of diagnostic methods of item writing would surely pay rich dividends in teaching, especially in areas of remedial instruction. Without having to construct a full algorithm with all its flow chart steps, the teacher can note the common kinds of strategies a student uses to solve a mathematics or science problem, and then ensure that a few items are included that would show the typical errors created by students who use an incorrect method to solve the problem. Surely, teachers have been doing this for years, but it has never been formally labeled as an algorithmic method of test construction. Perhaps a deeper appreciation that students do in fact have unique cognitive strategies developed in their own ways to solve problems will do much to stimulate attention to diagnostic testing.

Large-scale Survey Testing

In the case of school district, state, or national assessments, and published achievement batteries, the importance and scale of the projects often allow for much more elaborate test item development than is feasible for teachers. In this arena, the new extension of Tiemann and Markle's (1983) concept-based approach to rule and principle learning would be highly recommended. It seems that there is hardly a subject matter area that is not filled with principles and rules, the bases of which are important concepts that have not yet been systematically analyzed.

As the methodology of diagnostic methods develops further, it will be exciting to see large-scale survey tests emerge that measure the cognitive components embedded in student performance in reading or mathematics. Furthermore, the application of new scoring procedures, such as those advocated by Birenbaum and Tatsuoka (1983), would allow the documentation of the frequency (e.g., in a district or state) of common erroneous strategies for solving arithmetic problems. At the same time, the possibility of such new scores should encourage the development of arithmetic subtests sensitive to the common errors made by students.

With the proliferation of microcomputers in schools, colleges, and other institutions, it is recommended that survey-testing projects explore the feasibility of using microcomputer-administered, branching-type diagnostic tests, using the kinds of diagnostic item-writing methods mentioned by Curtis and Glaser (1983) for reading. Certainly, if tests and data collection were done on floppy discs, with only small, representative samples of students employed, such survey testing could be found to be cost effective. The goal of such efforts would be to assess speed of response and other factors that cannot be adequately measured by paper-and-pencil methods.

For test publishers, a very obvious kind of recommendation would be to have all test item writers read similar reference works on item-writing methods, so that, at a minimum, they can be equipped with "the modern tools of the trade" even if an operationally defined method is not used for an entire test or subtest. Then, using some of the contemporary methods for studying the underlying dimensions or latent cognitive processes that may be embedded in the test item performance of students, items can be evaluated in ways that go beyond conventional item analysis.

Certification Testing

The importance of the decisions derived from certification and licensure testing programs is so great that they clearly deserve the extra time and resources required to implement the more rigorous item-writing methods. Of course, a note of practicality must be inserted here due to the fact that often such tests rely on the help of content experts who may draft the actual items, rather than on item writers who are trained in the operationally defined methods described in this chapter.

Again, one of the promising new developments recommended is the extension of concept-based testing to rules and principles (Tiemann & Markle, 1983). Certainly, knowledge of principles is a key element of most professions, and experience shows that content experts can recognize rather quickly that certain key principles will need to be tested. What will continue to be difficult, however, is to complete the kind of concept analysis necessary to create truly criterion-referenced collections of examples and nonexamples of key concepts. Perhaps realistically the goal should be to experiment with some concept analysis without expecting that an entire test or test section could be based on such analyses.

Another promising avenue of test item development in the area of diagnostic methods would be stimulated by the exemplary work of Sternberg and Wagner (1983) in the specification of the adaptive intelligence of people such as psychologists and attorneys in their everyday work. By uncovering the cognitive skills, strategies, and components that characterize the highly functioning professional in an area of certification, test items tapping those dimensions could be designed. Some of these skills may be very "product" or "performance" oriented, implying an expensive kind of nonwritten testing, but some components are bound to be amenable to ingenious types of paper-and-pencil testing.

Program Evaluation

Evaluation projects for local programs or locally produced materials will probably follow the guidelines described for teachers, as described previously. However, for widely distributed or published programs and materials, the value of a well-documented assessment of learning effects may be great enough to warrant rather elaborate application of some of the item-writing techniques described in this chapter. Because the methods of item forms, linguistic transformations, concept-based analyses, and algorithmic approaches were specifically developed to link instructional materials with tests, they should have an important role in such applications.

Perhaps a major developer of instructional materials or textbooks would find it economically feasible to implement the kind of computerized key word search described in the section on future research. As long as tests created from sentence transformations are clearly labeled as verbatim recall of key words, they would seem to have at least a partial role in the evaluation of textual material. Verbatim recall can be used as a baseline to compare other effects, such as comprehension or the learning of important themes covered in a text.

Of particular interest to instructional materials developers are the diagnostic methods, such as Scandura's, which assess the problem-solving strategies used by students, particularly in basic arithmetic areas. If students are asked to solve arithmetic problems using particular rules or steps, then test items could be designed to discover whether or not students actually used the rules or steps recommended. For example, if students are taught a method of estimating the result in long division before completing the problem, test items that measure accuracy of estimation could be included. If one discovered that students were unable to estimate accurately, one would question whether or not the instructional program had adequately covered this skill. Perhaps, one would find that students have reverted to their own strategies or rules for solving long division, and that these are quite different from those taught in the instructional program. Even if this were done for only a few problem-solving procedures within a set of materials, the transfer of a given skill could be systematically sampled. Otherwise, the problem-solving errors of some students may be inextricably buried within a multidimensional total score, as shown by Birenbaum and Tatsuoka (1983).

Conclusion

The technology of item writing is developing in some intriguing new ways, especially in the direction of supporting the search for the latent cognitive components or cognitive strategies that underlie student performance on criterion-referenced test items. The question of the dimensionality of achievement tests is surfacing as a major new concern, and can only be stimulating to the field of item writing, which has suffered somewhat from the philosophy that a unidimensional set of items can be written by an individual equipped with a pencil and paper and familiarity with the subject matter. The precision of educational measurements will continue to progress as it is increasingly recognized that the writing of items should be a data-based process. Major steps in this process are (1) review of existing research on the cognitive components in an achievement domain prior to item writing, (2) drafting items, (3) field testing to identify item flaws *and* to assess the dimensions (or lack thereof) underlying item performance, and (4) revision and extension of items to meet the needs suggested by research and data analysis. Because this process is time consuming and expensive, it is often avoided. However, if item writing is to progress beyond an informal art, the attitudes and procedures of the research investigator need to be injected into the item development process. Also, future criterion-referenced test development projects that include teams composed of content experts, linguists, cognitive psychologists, statistical and measurement consultants, and teachers will undoubtedly provide some interesting new examples of creative item writing.

REFERENCES

Anderson, R. C. How to construct achievement tests to assess comprehension. *Review of Educational Research*, 1972, *42*, 145-170.

Baker, E. L., & Herman, J. L. Task structure design: Beyond linkage. *Journal of Educational Measurement*, 1983, *20*, 149-164.

Berk, R. A. The application of structural facet theory to achievement test construction. *Educational Research Quarterly*, 1978, *3*, 62-72.

Berk, R. A. The relative merits of item transformations and the cloze procedure for the measurement of reading comprehension. *Journal of Reading Behavior*, 1979, *11*, 129-138.

Berk, R. A. A comparison of six content domain specification strategies for criterion-referenced tests. *Educational Technology*, 1980, *20*, 49-52.

Birenbaum, M., & Tatsuoka, K. On the dimensionality of achievement test data. *Journal of Educational Measurement*, 1982, *19*, 259-266.

Birenbaum, M., & Tatsuoka, K. The effect of a scoring system based on the algorithm underlying the students' response patterns on the dimensionality of achievement test data of the problem solving type. *Journal of Educational Measurement*, 1983, *20*, 17-26.

Bormuth, J. R. Comparable cloze and multiple-choice comprehension test scores. *Journal of Reading Behavior*, 1967, *10*, 291-299.

Bormuth, J. R. *On the theory of achievement test items*. Chicago: University of Chicago Press, 1970.

Brown, J. S., & Burton, R. R. Diagnostic models for procedural bugs in basic mathematics skills. *Cognitive Science*, 1978, *2*, 155-192.

Carroll, J. B., Davies, P., & Richman, B. *Word frequency book*. Boston: Houghton-Mifflin, 1971.

Carroll, J. B., & Maxwell, S. Individual differences in ability. *Annual Review of Psychology*, 1979, 603-640.

Castro, J. G., & Jordan, J. E. Facet theory attitude research. *Educational Researcher*, 1977, *11*, 7-11.

Cattell, R. B. Validation and intensification of the Sixteen Personality Factor Questionnaire. *Journal of Clinical Psychology*, 1956, *12*, 205-214.

Cattell, R. B. Radial parcel factoring versus item factoring in defining personality structure in questionnaires: Theory and experimental checks. *Australian Journal of Psychology*, 1974, *26*, 103-119.

Clarke, A. C. *The challenge of the sea*. New York: Holt, Rinehart and Winston, 1960.

Coffman, W. E. Essay examinations. In R. L. Thorndike (Ed.), *Educational measurement* (2nd ed.). Washington, DC: American Council on Education, 1971. Pp. 271-302.

Conoley, J. C., & O'Neil, H. F., Jr. A primer for developing test items. In H. F. O'Neil, Jr. (Ed.), *Procedures for instructional systems development*. New York: Academic Press, 1979. Pp. 95-127.

Cronbach, L. J. *Essentials of psychological testing* (3rd ed.). New York: Harper and Row, 1970.

Curtis, M. E., & Glaser, R. Reading theory and the assessment of reading achievement. *Journal of Educational Measurements*, 1983, *20*, 133-148.

Dancer, L. S. *On the multidimensional structure of suicidal behavior: Analysis of data from the Suicide Probability Scale*. Unpublished paper, University of Texas, Austin, 1983.

Drum, P. A., Calfee, R. C., & Cook, L. K. The effects of surface structure variables on performance in reading comprehension tests. *Reading Research Quarterly*, 1980, *16*, 486-513.

Durnin, J., & Scandura, J. M. An algorithm approach to assessing behavior potential: Comparison with item forms and hierarchical technologies. *Journal of Educational Psychology*, 1973, *65*, 262-272.

Ebel, R. L. *Essentials of educational measurement* (3rd ed.). Englewood Cliffs, NJ: Prentice-Hall, 1979.

Ellis, J. A., & Wulfeck, W. H. *Handbook for testing in Navy schools*. San Diego, CA: Navy Personnel Research and Development Center, 1982.

Engel, J. D., & Martuza, V. R. *A systematic approach to the construction of domain-referenced multiple-choice test items*. Paper presented at the annual meeting of the American Psychological Association, Washington, DC, September 1976.

Finn, P. J. A question writing algorithm. *Journal of Reading Behavior*, 1975, *7*, 341-367.

Finn, P. J. Word frequency, information theory, and cloze performance: A lexical marker-transfer feature theory of processing in reading. *Reading Research Quarterly*, 1978, *13*, 508-537.

Foa, U. G. Three kinds of behavioral changes. *Psychological Bulletin*, 1968, *70*, 460-473.

Glaser, R. A research agenda for cognitive psychology and psychometrics. *American Psychologist*, 1981, *36*, 923-936.

Gorsuch, R. L. *Factor analysis* (2nd ed.). Hillsdale, NJ: Erlbaum, 1983.

Gorsuch, R. L., & Dreger, R. M. "Big jiffy": A more sophisticated factor analysis and rotation program. *Educational and Psychological Measurement*, 1979, *39*, 209-214.

Gorsuch, R. L., & Yagel, J. C. *Exploratory item factor analysis*. Unpublished paper, Fuller Graduate School of Psychology, Pasadena, California, 1982.

Green, S. B., Lissitz, R. W., & Mulaik, S. A. Limitations of coefficient alpha as an index of test unidimensionality. *Educational and Psychological Measurement*, 1977, *37*, 827-838.

Gronlund, N. E. *Constructing achievement tests* (3rd ed.). Englewood Cliffs, NJ: Prentice-Hall, 1982.

Guilford, J. P. The structure of intellect. *Psychological Bulletin*, 1956, *53*, 267-293.

Guilford, J. P. *The nature of human intelligence*. New York: McGraw-Hill, 1967.

Guilford, J. P. Higher-order structure-of-intellect abilities. *Multivariate Behavioral Research*, 1981, *16*, 411-435.

Guilford, J. P., Hoepfner, R., & Peterson, H. Predicting achievement in ninth-grade mathematics from measures of intellectual-aptitude factors. *Educational and Psychological Measurement*, 1965, *25*, 659-682.

Guttman, L. A structural theory for intergroup beliefs and actions. *American Sociological Review*, 1959, *24*, 318-328.

Guttman, L. A general nonmetric technique for finding the smallest coordinate space for a configuration of points. *Psychometrika*, 1968, *33*, 469-506.

Guttman, L. Integration of test design and analysis. In *Proceedings of the 1969 Invitational Conference on Testing Problems*. Princeton, NJ: Educational Testing Service, 1970.

Guttman, L., & Schlesinger, I. M. Systematic construction of distractors for ability and achievement testing. *Educational and Psychological Measurement*, 1967, *27*, 569-580.

Haertel, E., & Calfee, R. School achievement: Thinking about what to test. *Journal of Educational Measurement*, 1983, *20*, 119-132.

Haladyna, T. M., & Roid, G. H. The role of instructional sensitivity in the empirical review of criterion-referenced test items. *Journal of Educational Measurement*, 1981, *18*, 39-53.

Haladyna, T. M., & Roid, G. H. A comparison of two approaches to criterion-referenced test construction. *Journal of Educational Measurement*, 1983, *20*, 271-282.

Hambleton, R. K. Test score validity and standard-setting methods. In R. A. Berk (Ed.), *Criterion-referenced measurement: The state of the art*. Baltimore, MD: Johns Hopkins University Press, 1980. Pp. 80-123.

Hively, W. Introduction to domain-referenced testing. *Educational Technology*, 1974, *14*(6), 5-10.

Hively, W., Patterson, H. L., & Page, S. A. A "universe-defined" system of arithmetic achievement tests. *Journal of Educational Measurement*, 1968, *5*, 275-290.

Hoepfner, R. Achievement test selection for program evaluation. In M. J. Wargo & D. R. Green (Eds.), *Achievement testing of disadvantaged and minority students for educational program evaluation*. Monterey, CA: CTB/McGraw-Hill, 1978.

Horn, J. The rise and fall of human abilities. *Journal of Research and Development in Education*, 1979, *12*, 59-78.

Kingsbury, G. G., & Weiss, D. J. *Relationships among achievement level estimates from three characteristic curve scoring methods* (Research Report 79-3). Minneapolis: Department of Psychology, University of Minnesota, April 1979.

Levy, S., & Guttman, L. On the multivariate structure of well-being. In I. Borg (Ed.), *Multidimensional data representations: When and why*. Ann Arbor, MI: Mathesis Press, 1981.

Lingoes, J. C. (Ed.). *Geometric representations of relational data*. Ann Arbor, MI: Mathesis Press, 1977.

Lord, F. M. *Applications of item response theory to practical testing problems*. Hillsdale, NJ: Erlbaum, 1980.

Markle, S. M., & Tiemann, P. W. *Really understanding concepts*. Champaign, IL: Stipes, 1970.

McDonald, R. P. The dimensionality of tests and items. *British Journal of Mathematical and Statistical Psychology*, 1981, *34*, 100-117.

Meeker, M. *The structure of intellect: Its interpretation and uses*. Columbus, OH: Merrill, 1969.

Meeker, M., & Meeker, R. *Structure of Intellect (SOI) Learning Abilities Tests*. El Segundo, CA: SOI Institute, 1975. (Also available from Western Psychological Services, Los Angeles, CA.)

Merrill, M. D., Reigeluth, C. M., & Faust, G. W. The instructional quality profile: A curriculum evaluation and design tool. In H. F. O'Neil, Jr. (Ed.), *Procedures for instructional systems development*. New York: Academic Press, 1979. Pp. 165-204.

Miller, H. G., Williams, R. G., & Haladyna, T. M. *Beyond facts: Objective ways to measure thinking*. Englewood Cliffs, NJ: Educational Technology Publications, 1978.

Millman, J. Criterion-referenced measurement. In W. J. Popham (Ed.), *Evaluation in education: Current applications*. Berkeley, CA: McCutchan, 1974. Pp. 311-397.

Montague, W. E., Ellis, J. A., & Wulfeck, W. H. Instructional quality inventory: A formative evaluation tool for instructional development. *Performance and Instruction*, 1983, *22*(5), 11-14.

Muthén, B. Contributions to factor analysis of dichotomous variables. *Psychometrika*, 1978, *43*, 551-560.

Muthén, B. Factor analysis of dichotomous variables: American attitudes toward abortion. In E. Borgatta & D. J. Jackson (Eds.), *Factor analysis and measurement in sociological research: A multidimensional perspective*. San Francisco: Sage, 1981.

Muthén, B. LACCI: *Latent variable analysis with dichotomous, ordered categorical, and continuous indicators*. Los Angeles: Graduate School of Education, University of California, 1982.

Muthén, B., & Christofferson, A. Simultaneous factor analysis of dichotomous variables in several groups. *Psychometrika*, 1981, *46*, 407-419.

Nitko, A. J. Distinguishing the many varieties of criterion-referenced tests. *Review of Educational Research*, 1980, *50*, 461-485.

Osburn, H. G. Item sampling for achievement testing. *Educational and Psychological Measurement*, 1968, *28*, 95-104.

Rasch, G. *Probabilistic models for some intelligence and attainment tests*. Chicago: University of Chicago Press, 1980.

Reckase, M. D. Unifactor latent trait models applied to multifactor tests: Results and implications. *Journal of Educational Statistics*, 1979, *4*, 207-230.

Roid, G. H., & Finn, P. J. *Algorithms for developing tests questions from sentences in instructional materials* (NPRDC Technical Report No. 78-23). San Diego, CA: Navy Personnel Research and Development Center, 1978.

Roid, G. H., & Haladyna, T. M. The emergence of an item-writing technology. *Review of Educational Research*, 1980, *50*, 293-314.

Roid, G. H., & Haladyna, T. M. *A technology for test-item writing*. New York: Academic Press, 1982.

Roid, G. H., Haladyna, T. M., Shaughnessy, J., & Finn, P. J. *Item writing for domain-based tests of prose learning*. Paper presented at the annual meeting of the American Educational Research Association, San Francisco, April 1979.

Roid, G. H., & Wendler, C. L. W. *Item bias detection and item-writing technology*. Paper presented at the annual meeting of the American Educational Research Association, Montreal, April 1983.

Runkel, P. J., & McGrath, J. E. *Research on human behavior: A systematic guide to method*. New York: Holt, Rinehart and Winston, 1972.

Santostefano, S. *A bio-developmental approach to clinical child psychology: Cognitive controls and cognitive-control therapy*. New York: Wiley, 1978.

Scandura, J. M. Role of rules in behavior: Toward an operational definition of what (rule) is learned. *Psychological Review*, 1970, *77*, 516-533.

Scandura, J. M. *Problem solving: A structural/process approach with instructional implications*. New York: Academic Press, 1977.

Scandura, J. M. Microcomputer systems for authoring, diagnosis, and instruction in rule-based content. *Educational Technology*, 1981, *21*, 13-19.

Scandura, J. M. Structural analysis (cognitive tasks): A method for analyzing content. Part I: Background and experimental findings. *Journal of Structural Learning*, 1982, *7*, 101-114.

Scandura, J. M., & Durnin, J. Assessing behavior potential: Adequacy of basic theoretical assumptions. *Journal of Structural Learning*, 1978, *6*, 3-47.

Schorr, D., Bower, G. H., & Kiernan, R. Stimulus variables in the block design task. *Journal of Consulting and Clinical Psychology*, 1982, *50*, 479-487.

Schott, F., Neeb, K. E., & Wieberg, H. J. W. A general procedure for the construction of content-valid items for goal-oriented teaching and testing. *Studies in Educational Evaluation*, in press.

Shoemaker, D. M. Toward a framework for achievement testing. *Review of Educational Research*, 1975, *45*, 127-148.

Smith, J. K. On the examination of test unidimensionality. *Educational and Psychological Measurement*, 1980, *40*, 885-889.

Stegelmann, W. Expanding the Rasch model to a general model having more than one dimension. *Psychometrika*, 1983, *48*, 259-267.

Sternberg, R. J. *Intelligence, information processing, and analogical reasoning: The componential analysis of human abilities*. Hillsdale, NJ: Erlbaum, 1977.

Sternberg, R. J. The nature of mental abilities. *American Psychologist*, 1979, *34*, 214-230.

Sternberg, R. J. Testing and cognitive psychology. *American Psychologist*, 1981, *36*, 1181-1189.

Sternberg, R. J., & Wagner, R. K. *Measuring "intelligence in the real world."* Paper presented at the annual meeting of the American Educational Research Association, Montreal, April 1983.

Taylor, W. L. Cloze procedure: A new tool for measuring readability. *Journalism Quarterly*, 1953, *30*, 414-438.

Taylor, W. L. "Cloze" readability scores as indices of individual differences in comprehension and aptitude. *Journal of Applied Psychology*, 1957, *41*, 12-26.

Tiemann, P. W., Kroeker, L. P., & Markle, S. M. *Teaching verbally-mediated coordinate concepts in an on-going college course*. Paper presented at the annual meeting of the American Educational Research Association, New York, April 1977.

Tiemann, P. W., & Markle, S. M. *Analyzing instructional content: A guide to instruction and evaluation* (2nd ed.). Champaign, IL: Stipes, 1983.

Trilling, L. Introduction. In M. Twain, *The adventures of Huckleberry Finn*. New York: Holt, Rinehart and Winston, 1948.

Wallbrown, F., Blaha, J., & Wherry, R. J. The hierarchical factor structure of the Wechsler Preschool and Primary Scale of Intelligence. *Journal of Consulting and Clinical Psychology*, 1973, *41*, 356-362.

Wardrop, J. L., Anderson, T. H., Hively, W., Hastings, C. N., Anderson, R. I., & Muller, K. E. A framework for analyzing the inference structure of educational achievement tests. *Journal of Educational Measurement*, 1982, *19*, 1-18.

Wherry, R. J. Hierarchical factor solutions without rotation. *Psychometrika*, 1959, *24*, 45-51.

Wherry, R. J., & Wherry, R. J., Jr. WHEWH program. In R. J. Wherry (Ed.), *Psychology department computer programs*. Columbus, OH: Department of Psychology, Ohio State University, 1969.

Whitely, S. E. Some information-processing components of intelligence test items. *Applied Psychological Measurement*, 1977, *1*, 465-476.

Whitely, S. E. Measuring aptitude processes with multicomponent latent trait models. *Journal of Educational Measurement*, 1981, *18*, 67-83.

4 INDIVIDUALIZING TEST CONSTRUCTION AND ADMINISTRATION BY COMPUTER

JASON MILLMAN

INTRODUCTION

COMPUTER-ASSISTED TESTING (CAT) is jogging in many directions. Its pace has quickened somewhat in recent years, and its efforts are being more widely disseminated than before, although adoptions are still several laps behind. But of particular interest to me is the variety of forms that CAT is taking.

Regardless of the approach followed, CAT almost invariably results in an individualization of testing. Individualization occurs when examinees are tested one at a time as they sit in front of a computer screen. Individualization also occurs when examinees are presented with items that are, in some sense, uniquely their own.

Tests that have been produced or administered by computers to date have for the most part been used to make criterion-referenced inferences. It does not have to be that way, of course. But, as will be pointed out, many of the CAT schemes require careful attention to the content of the items, and such scrutiny is consonant with criterion-referenced inferences.

Several topics related to computers and testing will not be addressed. Methods of item writing, including how to specify domains, will not be discussed unless those methods are a necessary part of the CAT approach. Excellent reviews of item-writing techniques for criterion-referenced tests are available elsewhere (see, for example, Berk, 1980; Hambleton & Eignor, 1979; Martuza, 1979; Popham, 1978, chapter 2; Roid, chapter 3; Roid & Haladyna, 1982). Testing within a computer-managed instructional system is not covered either, except as one or more of the general approaches identified in this chapter are incorporated in the system. Also omitted is a discussion of computerized classroom monitoring techniques that *simultaneously* record and summarize from a group of examinees the answers to test items or self-reports of the examinee's understanding, level of interest, or attention (see Rogers, 1982). Computer-assisted item selection, test analysis, scoring, record keeping, and interpretation will not be treated, nor will computer hardware and personnel requirements and costs. These topics and other concerns related to the installation and operation of CAT systems have been discussed by Hsu and Nitko (1983) and by Lippey (1974).

REVIEW OF INDIVIDUALIZED TESTING

Traditional Attempts to Individualize Testing

The earliest examples of mental tests were individually administered tests. The Binet tests, which date back to the beginning of this century, are administered to one examinee at a time. Such tests permit flexibility in administration, since the examinee's performance dicates the questions that are administered. Testing proceeds from middle-difficulty items to either increasingly less difficult on more difficult items for the examinee. Testing terminates when several easy questions in a row are answered correctly and several difficult questions in a row are missed. The assumption is made that, if administered, even easier items would be answered correctly or even more difficult items would be missed, so further testing is unnecessary.

Individual administration of tests has several advantages. First, up to a point, items whose difficulty levels match the examinee's level of functioning can be chosen. Second, in addition to test tasks, which are written on paper, individual administration can facilitate the use of a variety of other tasks. Third, rapport with the examinee can be easily established, which can increase the examinee's motivation to do well. Fourth, the examiner can secure additional assessment information through the observation of nontest behaviors.

Individual administration of tests using a live examiner also has several disadvantages. First, nontest information observed may not be reliable and valid. Second, examiners differ in their ability to motivate examinees, which can differentially affect test performance. Third, one-on-one test administrations are costly, time consuming, and require a trained examiner.

Publishers of major standardized group-administered achievement tests have attempted to provide some individualization in their test offerings. Most of the companies have two or more forms of their tests that are parallel in content and in statistical properties. Thus, repeated testing of the same individual need not be conducted using the same form. However, the number of alternate forms is usually limited, each form is expensive to make, and individualization is only partially achieved, in that any given form of the test is shared by a large number of examinees.

In addition to providing multiple forms of equivalent difficulty and content, test publishers often provide several forms having different levels of difficulty. Here, some degree of individualization can come about by the choice of level. A problem arises, however, when a form designed primarily for students at one grade level is administered to students at a different grade level. The content of the test items differs among the forms at the several levels of the test, and thus in attempting to match the difficulty level of a form to a student's actual level of functioning, a mismatch in test content can occur.

Issues related to out-of-level testing have received a considerable amount of attention by testing specialists (Arter, 1982; Gabriel, Arter, & Demaline, 1980).

The availability of equivalent forms of tests and of forms that span several levels of ability represents only a crude attempt at individualizing testing. Computerized testing makes it possible to have a greater number of test "forms" so that individuals can be administered tests that are more uniquely their own.

Sequential Analysis Testing

For years, quality control experts have used sequential analysis procedures (Wald, 1947) for testing batches of manufactured products. The procedure consists of sampling components from each batch to see if the batch meets a prespecified quality standard. Sampling continues until the inspector is confident that the batch is above the standard and can be accepted or is confident the batch is below the standard and should be rejected. More samples of components will be needed from batches of borderline quality than from batches that are clearly above or below the standard. This is necessary in order to have sufficient evidence to determine whether the borderline batches should be accepted or rejected.

The same approach can be applied to criterion-referenced testing. It is hypothesized that each examinee has a true level of functioning, which is the *unknown* proportion of all the possible items in a large collection of items that the examinee can answer correctly. Examinees are administered items until the evidence is clear cut that the examinee's true level of functioning is above or below the passing standard. Computer administration facilitates this process, since an examinee's answer must be corrected before it is known whether additional test items need be given.

Sequential testing usually involves the use of items that are similar in content and difficulty level, but the procedure could be used with any group of pass/fail items that are considered to be a random sample from a larger collection of items. The procedure could also be used in conjunction with other test administration methods to develop a rule for when to stop testing.

Note that the individualization in sequential testing is manifested in the number of items administered. All examinees can start out receiving the same items; it is the number of items needed to make a pass/fail decision that is individualized. That number can vary markedly from one individual to another, but those individuals near the passing standard receive the largest number of test items.

Ideally, examinees should pass the test if their true levels of functioning exceed or equal the passing score and should fail the test otherwise. However, since complete testing is impractical, some mistakes must be tolerated. The test user specifies this tolerance for error, from which it is possible to calculate standards for when to stop testing. These termination standards indicate whether the evidence is sufficient, given the degree of error one is willing to tolerate, to make a pass or fail decision for the examinee, or whether it is necessary to continue testing.

Table 4.1 contains a procedure for calculating the termination standards. For the example shown in Table 4.1, if 20 items are administered, the examinee needs to answer 18 or more correctly to pass or 10 or fewer to fail. An examinee who scores between 11 and 17, inclusive, is administered a 21st item, and the examinee's new score is compared to the termination standards for a 21-item test. Testing continues until the examinee's score falls outside the termination standards corresponding to the number of items administered, or until some predetermined maximum test length is reached.

Table 4.1. Procedures for Determining Termination Standards in Sequential Analysis Testing

Definitions:

c	The criterion or passing score
p_0	A value less than c such that mistakenly passing an examinee whose true level of functioning is p_0 or greater is considered of no practical consequence
p_1	A value more than c such that mistakenly failing an examinee whose true level of functioning is p_1 or less is considered of no practical consequence
α	The probability one is willing to tolerate of incorrectly passing an examinee whose true level of functioning is actually less than p_0
β	The probability one is willing to tolerate of incorrectly failing an examinee whose true level of functioning is actually more than p_1
r_n	The number of items, out of n items administered, that must be answered right (r) before the examinee is passed
w_n	The number of items, out of n items administered, that must be answered wrong (w) before the examinee is failed

Formulas:

$$k = 1\Big/\left(\log\frac{p_1}{p_0} - \log\frac{1-p_1}{1-p_0}\right) \qquad a = (k)\log\frac{1-p_0}{1-p_1}$$

$$b_1 = (k)\log\frac{1-\beta}{\alpha} \qquad b_0 = (k)\log\frac{\beta}{1-\alpha}$$

$$r_n = b_1 + a(n) \qquad w_n = b_0 + a(n)$$

Example:

$$c = .75; \quad p_0 = .65; \quad p_1 = .80; \quad \alpha = .10; \quad \beta = .05$$

$$k = 1\Big/\left(\log\frac{.80}{.65} - \log\frac{.20}{.35}\right) = 3.00 \qquad a = (3.00)\log\frac{.35}{.20} = .73$$

$$b_1 = (3.00)\log\frac{.95}{.10} = 2.93 \qquad b_0 = (3.00)\log\frac{.05}{.90} = -3.77$$

$r_{20} = 2.93 + .73(20) = 17.53$ or, rounding *up* to the next larger integer, 18

$w_{20} = -3.77 + .73(20) = 10.83$ or, rounding *down* to the next smaller integer, 10

Source: Adapted from Wald (1947).

Using the example in Table 4.1, the relation between test length and termination standards, expressed in percent scores, is shown graphically in Figure 4.1. As additional items are administered, an examinee's true level of functioning can be estimated more precisely. Consequently, as illustrated in Figure 4.1, the termination standards approach the passing score as test length increases. And as test length increases, only the relatively few examinees whose test performances remain near the passing score will continue to be tested.

Traditional Item Banking

The most frequent way computers are used to generate tests requires the items to be stored or "banked" in the computer exactly as they might appear in a test. Typically the text for hundreds or thousands of test items, together with cataloging information, such as the topic or instructional objective referenced by the item, is entered onto a computer disk. The collection of items is called the *item bank* or item pool. A test is constructed by assembling a sample of questions from the item bank.

Because many more items are in the bank than will be used on any single test, it is possible to produce multiple test forms having different items arranged in different orders. Traditional item banking fosters individualization

Figure 4.1. Termination standards as a function of n in sequential analysis testing

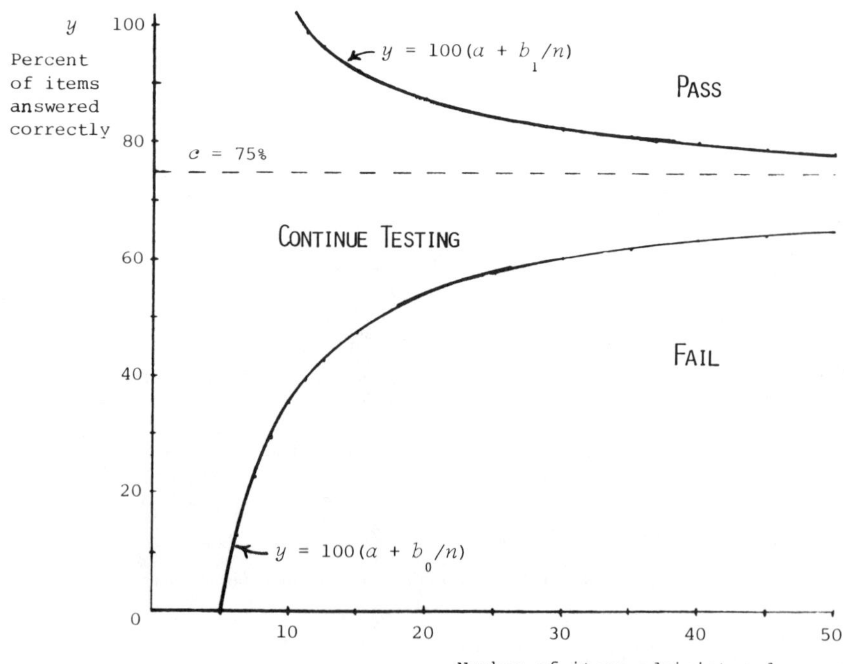

of testing not only because different tests can be produced, but, more importantly, because different users can obtain tests that reference different sections of the item bank. For example, if a user wishes to develop a test on objectives 1, 37 and 86, such a test can be constructed for those objectives. It is this customized test construction feature that makes item banks so popular.

Although a population of items exists in traditional item banking, it would be stretching the concept of criterion-referencing or domain-referencing to call tests generated from such a population criterion-referenced tests. That is because the population of items cannot be clearly described without telling about each of the items. When a student obtains a score of 80%, for example, it is not very descriptive to say that the student knows 80% of the items stored in the computer, or even to say that the student knows 80% of the test items about unit 37 that are stored in the computer. Knowing that a student answered correctly two questions out of three on objective 86.4 does not convey much information about the student's competence with respect to that objective, because the objective alone is not an adequate description of the three items. Without knowing more about those particular items, for example, whether they were difficult or easy, their content, and how the questions were asked, we are hard pressed to evaluate the student's competence.

Although the items in the bank are traditionally categorized by curriculum unit or instructional objective, that categorization is not necessary. Rubincam and Olivier (1978) and Hiscox and Brzezinski (1980) favor plans in which each item is classified by several descriptors that identify several subject matter and other features of the item. For example, a multiple-choice item about the vitamin content of orange juice might have associated with it the following descriptors: nutrition, orange juice, vitamins, vitamin C, multiple choice, etc. An advantage of this way of referencing items is that it frees the system from adherence to a single curriculum or a single way of organizing the subject matter. The item pool thereby could be easily transferred to users who structure the subject matter in different ways, provided an agreed-upon vocabulary is used. Possible disadvantages include the extra effort in categorizing items and the greater difficulty in being able to characterize what is in the bank.

Test users wishing to implement the traditional item-banking approach need first to decide whether they will construct their own collection of items or use those that appear in one of over one hundred available collections. Depending, in part, on that decision, it may be necessary to classify the items by objective or otherwise code them so that they can be retrieved during the test construction phase. Furthermore, unless one uses the services of a publisher like Prentice-Hall, which supplies customized tests that are already printed, the user will need hardware and software computer support.

Fortunately, many modest test construction programs are available for microcomputers (for a listing, see Hsu & Nitko, 1983). The Northwest Regional Educational Laboratory is preparing a list of computerized test construction software programs that are transportable to local schools and colleges. Banks of items are also becoming available on disks for immediate use on the Apple or similar microcomputers (e.g., PRISM, marketed by The Psychological Corporation, and Academic Hallmarks, distributed through P.O. Box 998, Durango, CO 81301). For an extensive listing of names and addresses of item bank users and a description of their banks, see Hiscox and Brzezinski (1980). Millman and Arter (in press) have raised many questions that potential users of item banks should consider.

Item Program Banking

One variation of traditional item banking is storing computer programs instead of finished items. A program, when selected and executed, produces an item. A different test item can be produced each time the item-generating program is executed by having random functions within the program. For example, the modified BASIC program:

```
X = RND (1,500)

Y$ = " is a prime number. True or False?"

PRINT X; Y$
```

would, on successive executions, yield such items as:

437 is a prime number. True or False?

315 is a prime number. True or False?

63 is a prime number. True or False?

When a collection of item programs is stored in the computer, the potential is present for creating large numbers of items. Every test composed of items generated from the item programs will be unique because it is unlikely that specific test questions will be repeated.

Fremer and Anastasio (1969) were among the first to use the computer to generate tests using item program banking. Other researchers using similar schemes include Vickers (1973), Olympia (1975), and Wasik (1979). Coursewriter, TUTOR, and similar languages used to write computer-assisted instructional programs frequently have functions that help in writing test item programs. The most elaborate high-level language devised specifically for writing test items has been provided by Millman and Outlaw (1978). This language is illustrated next.

One way to proceed in constructing item programs is to list a prototype item that references an instructional objective. Assume the item is:

Half of the individuals in a class will score above the median score for the class.

A. True

B. False

Answer: A. True

The instructor can then consider ways of changing the item, ways that may or may not affect which option is correct. For example, instead of "half," "fifty percent" may be used. Instead of scores of individuals in a class, data values in a frequency distribution could be the example. Furthermore, the question could ask about being below instead of above the median, or ask about the mean instead of the median. These options can be displayed in the form shown in Table 4.2, which resembles both an item form and a mapping sentence. (For a further discussion of items forms and mapping sentences, see Berk, 1978, Millman, 1974, Popham, chapter 2, Roid, chapter 3, and Roid and Haladyna, 1982.)

From the form in Table 4.2, an item program can easily be written. Such a program, which uses the Millman and Outlaw language, appears in Table 4.3. Repeated executions of the program in Table 4.3 produce 16 variations, since one of two choices at point A in the form (Table 4.2) can be combined with one or two choices at point B, which in turn can be combined with two choices each at points C and D. Note that the choice at point B′ will agree with the choice at point B, so that the examples ("individuals . . . class"; "values . . . distribution") do not get mixed when a single version of the item is printed. Line 230 in Table 4.3 ensures this.

The user might then think of additional ways to test the same principle. For example, the form in Table 4.4 can lead to a second item program, and the test generation computer routine could be set up so that only one of the two item programs on this principle would be executed for any given test.

It has been my experience that the activity of writing the mapping sentences—attempting to expand the content, considering what are and are not reasonable examples, etc.—became reflected in my instruction, for example, as I was forced to clarify my course content objectives. The activity also provided me with a richer and more varied conception of what I was trying to teach (Millman, 1982).

Table 4.2. An Example of a Mapping Sentence

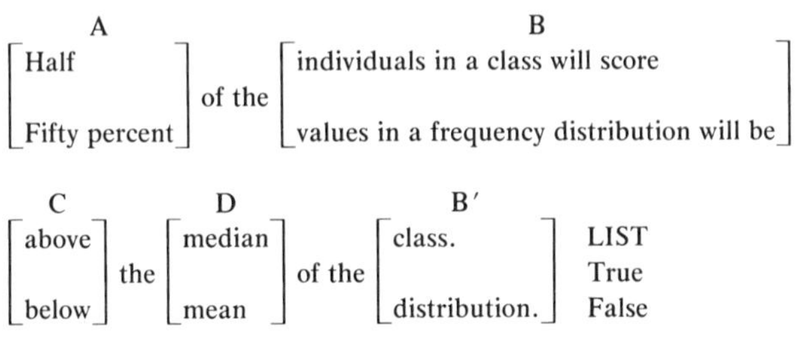

Answer: If Choice D = 1 (median), then True; else False.

Table 4.3. An Example of an Item-generating Program

```
 10 FROM
 20 "Half "
 30 "Fifty percent "
 40 CHOOSE AT RANDOM
 50 "of the "
 60 FROM
 70 "individuals in a class will score "
 80 "values in a frequency distribution will be "
 90 CHOOSE AT RANDOM
100 FROM
110 "above "
120 "below "
130 CHOOSE AT RANDOM
140 "the "
150 FROM
160 "median "
170 "mean "
180 CHOOSE AT RANDOM
190 "of the "
200 FROM
210 "class."
220 "distribution."
230 CHOOSE CHOICE (90)
240 LIST2
250 "True"
260 "False"
270 IF CHOICE (180) = 1 THEN ANSWER "A. True"
280 ELSE ANSWER "B. False"
```

Table 4.4. An Alternative Mapping Sentence to Table 4.2

<table>
<tr><td></td><td>A</td><td></td></tr>
<tr><td>The chances are</td><td>[even
50-50
equally likely]</td><td>that any observation in a set of data</td></tr>
</table>

<table>
<tr><td></td><td>B</td><td></td><td>C</td><td></td><td>B′</td><td></td><td></td></tr>
<tr><td>will be</td><td>[above
below]</td><td>the</td><td>[median
mean]</td><td>as will be</td><td>[below
above]</td><td>it.</td><td>LIST
True
False</td></tr>
</table>

Answer: If Choice C = 1 (median), then True; else False.

Adaptive Testing

Measurement on a scale. Measurement of an individual is most precise when the highest discriminating items are used, and these items tend to be the ones that are neither too difficult nor too easy for that individual. As long as individuals vary on the attribute being measured, however, some items on a given test will be difficult for some examinees and easy for others; consequently, the precision of measurement will suffer.

Several procedures for dealing with this less-than-optimum precision are available. Most commonly, the test constructor uses items that range over moderate levels of difficulty, thus attempting to have a high level of precision of measurement for most examinees at the sacrifice of precise measurement of examinees at the extreme levels of ability. Minimum competency examinations, however, will be composed of items that are bunched at the easy end of the difficulty continuum, thus preventing precise discriminations among the most able. The reverse is true for scholarship examinations, where a preponderance of hard items works against the precise measurement of the less able.

Adaptive testing, often called response contingent or tailored testing, or, less frequently, programmed or branched testing, has, as one of its goals, the increased precision of measurement for all examinees. Adaptive testing can tailor the items that are administered to the examinee's ability as estimated from the examinee's performance on previously administered items. In adaptive testing, the items that are given to the examinee are contingent upon the examinee's previous responses. By selecting discriminating items that are matched to the individual's ability, more precise measurement can take place, or alternatively, fewer items are needed to reach the same level of precision that is possible when a single set of test items is administered to all the examinees.

An example of adaptive testing, at a somewhat crude level, is the "routing" or "locator" test that is used to decide which one of several main tests that differ in difficulty level should be administered. If the examinee scores well on the routing test, a difficult second test is given; if the individual scores poorly on the routing test, an easy test is given next. Weiss and Betz (1973) described several variations of this two-stage testing procedure.

A computer is not needed to administer a two-stage testing design as described. The examinee merely waits until the routing test is scored before beginning the main test. Even if continuous branching procedures are used, in which the choice of each item to be administered is contingent on the response to the previous item, special test-printing formats can still circumvent the need for computer administration (see Lord, 1971).

If computers are used in test administration, however, it is possible to invoke powerful mathematical models to estimate, after each item response, an examinee's ability on the underlying achievement or aptitude continuum being measured. The next item chosen for administration from an item bank is then that one which, when answered, will be especially informative about the examinee's ability. The process normally results in more difficult items being administered after correct answers and easier items being administered after incorrect answers. Testing usually continues until an examinee's ability can be estimated by the mathematical model to a desired degree of accuracy.

Item response theory, sometimes called latent trait theory, almost always provides the mathematical basis for item selection and ability estimation. (However, see Cliff, 1975; Cudeck, Cliff, and Kehoe, 1977; and McCormick and Cliff, 1977, for an alternative basis and accompanying computer programs.) Questions remain in the minds of many experts about which specific item response models work best. Many technical problems and the stringent requirements in order for the item response models to be valid have led some observers to argue for caution in their use (McLean & Ragsdale, 1983; Traub & Wolfe, 1981). Nevertheless, the use of computerized adaptive testing within an item response theory framework is likely to increase as some major testing programs have adopted or are seriously considering adopting such testing (Green, Bock, Humphreys, Linn, & Reckase, 1982; Urry, 1977). Procedures for conducting computerized adaptive testing based on item response theory may be obtained from Lord (1980) and Wright and Stone (1979).

Diagnosis. The capability of the computer to select the items presented to the examinees contingent on their responses to previous items makes possible a diagnostic evaluation of the examinee's ability (Choppin & McArthur, in press; Scandura 1981a, 1981b). Representative problems are constructed and the steps, rules, operations, or decisions required to solve each problem are identified. By presenting the examinee with several tasks, some of which require certain steps and some of which do not, it is possible to discern which specific parts of the rule-governed operations the examinee knows. Such diagnostic information is extremely useful for prescribing appropriate instruction in which the unlearned portions of the rule are presented.

Simulation. The response-contingent capability of computers can permit the presentation of problems realistically, in that the examinees can be given feedback about the consequences of their actions, much as in real life. For example, patient management problems (McGuire, Solomon, & Forman, 1976) are well suited for computer presentation. In such problems, a medical case is presented, and the "doctor" (the examinee) indicates what actions should be taken. These actions might include examining some aspect of the patient's physical condition, ordering laboratory tests, or prescribing medication or other treatments. Results of each of these actions are made known to the doctor, who then proceeds with further treatment. The sequence of actions taken can then be assessed against standards of approved practice provided by experts. Since every examinee may proceed along a different path toward solving the problem, the scoring of the examinees' response patterns is not straightforward.

Automated Question Generating

In all of the examples of CAT discussed thus far, the user constructs the questions to appear on the tests. Even in the case of item program banking, the test constructor must identify all of the content that could appear in an item.

A few attempts have been made to have the computer generate the actual wording of the test items. In one approach developed by Braby, Parrish, Guitard, and Aagard (1978), an item-writing program is constructed that is appropriate for several different tasks that have a common form. For example, the authors constructed a program to produce items to test whether examinees can recognize symbols. The symbols could be Morse code, chemical compounds, or weather map abbreviations. The test constructor merely enters into the computer the codes, their meaning, and some other basic information; the writing of the questions and the testing of the examinees are then taken over by the computer.

Another approach to automated item writing is to have the computer generate questions from passages of text that have been previously entered into the computer. Noncomputer-based schemes for identifying ways of unambiguously transforming sentences of text into questions were devised by Bormuth (1970) and Anderson (1972). Their efforts were then expanded by Finn (1975) and by Stevens and O'Neill (1974). To date, perhaps the most ambitious effort to computerize the item-writing process has been described by Wolfe (1975). The approach is syntactic rather than semantic, because only the form of the sentence, and not its meaning, is considered. As Wolfe stated:

> A pure syntactic approach has many limitations, of course. First, the student is required to give verbatim parts of the original text in his [or her] answers. Second, it is well known that many English sentences are syntactically ambiguous and can only be parsed correctly when their meaning is taken into account. (p. 104)

Nevertheless, Wolfe reports encouraging results in having the computer identify sentence patterns and, in accordance with procedures built into the computer routines, in writing appropriate questions and answer criteria for the identified pattern.

The foregoing automated question-generating approaches have been developed for use within a computer-assisted instruction context. The approaches include procedures for automated scoring of examinee responses and the feedback of results.

Comparison of Procedures

A comparison of the approaches to individualized testing appears in Table 4.5. The first three procedures do not use computers and thus have no items stored in the computer. Automated question-generating approaches, the last procedure shown in the table, also do not have items in the computer but, instead, have rules for operating on the subject matter content (e.g., symbols and their meaning, text passages) to produce test items.

Evaluation of CAT

The variety of features in and purposes of CAT approaches preclude a simple evaluation that applies to all variations. However, the following general comments, grouped by evaluation criteria, seem appropriate.

Table 4.5. Comparison of the Procedures to Individualize Testing

Procedure Name	Primary Purpose	Description of the Items in the Computer	Administered by Computer?	What Is Administered?
Individually administered tests	To provide an accurate estimate of the examinee's ability to perform a variety of tasks	None	No	Performance tasks graded by difficulty
Multi-form tests	To allow the examinee multiple chances to pass the test; to show change	None	No	Statistically parallel tests
Multi-level standardized tests	To match the difficulty level of the test to the examinee's ability; to show long-term change	None	No	One of several possible levels of the test
Sequential analysis testing	To determine an examinee's status relative to a standard	Items homogeneous in content and difficulty	Yes	A random sample of items from the item pool
Traditional item banking	To produce a test that has curricular validity	Items categorized by instructional objectives or topics	Usually not, but could be	Tests custom-made to match local curricula
Item program banking	To allow the examinee many opportunities to pass the test; to show change	"Items" are computer programs that generate items when executed	Usually not, but could be	Content parallel tests different for each examinee
Adaptive testing				
Measurement on a scale	To maximize the precision of the estimate of each examinee's ability by using a minimum number of test items	Single factor items; heterogeneous in difficulty; high in discrimination; low in susceptibility to guessing	Usually	Items selected on the basis of the examinee's performance on the previous items
Diagnosis	To diagnose student learning deficiencies	Items classified by the elemental skills or knowledges tested	Usually	
Simulation	To present problem-solving tasks realistically	Information and a series of options for each step in a problem-solving task	Usually not, but could be	
Automated question generation	To automate the writing of test items	None	Yes	Computer-written test items

Cost. Many ingredients contribute to the cost of a CAT system: computer equipment, maintenance, and supplies; computer program purchase or development; acquisition or development and installation of item banks; time of examinees (discussed shortly); and so forth. Rapid changes in computer products and the accompanying prices make precise cost estimates impossible and true cost values unstable. It is worth noting, however, that although one-time, fixed costs are significant, when computer support is already available, the *incremental* fixed costs to make a CAT system operational may be small. Furthermore, cost efficiency becomes more evident when a system is in place for some time. Computers are very effective at repetitive tasks, such as generating multiple tests from a single item pool, and their value becomes more apparent as the cumulative use of the system increases. Also, CAT systems generally have the flexibility to make changes easily in the item pool that may be necessary due to a shift in curricular emphasis, to newly acquired empirical evidence of item quality, or to other factors.

Capability to measure what is desired. Questions that can be asked by paper-and-pencil tests can be asked by computer. One possible qualification is the type of item that contains graphical or pictorial material. Such items are not easily produced on computer screens. Although the technology exists (e.g., the METAFORM System from Intran Corporation), it is not widely and inexpensively available. On the other hand, some features of the computer enhance testing capability over that provided by paper-and-pencil instruments. The real time clock feature of computers makes measuring response latency particularly easy, and the response contingent (adaptive testing) capability of computers assists in the measurement of complex problem-solving skills.

Feasibility. Two aspects of the feasibility of CAT have already been mentioned, namely, cost and the capability to measure what is desired. If the notion of feasibility is limited to getting a system up and running, then CAT is very feasible. Hundreds of operating systems and the increasingly available computer software for microcomputers are a testimonial to the claim that CAT systems are feasible. One exception is automated question-generating systems that use text as the content source. Such systems, commendable as they may be, are still primitive at this time.

Contribution to instruction. The capability of some CAT systems to diagnose learning problems represents an obvious link to instruction. The necessity to consider the curriculum in item-banking and item-program-banking CAT schemes is another link. When item pools are large, or item program banking is used, then having practice examinations, make-up examinations, and repeated testing all become feasible. These different types of testing support learning in individually paced or group mastery-learning contexts (Millman, 1982). CAT can be combined with computer-managed instructional systems to support the latter. A recent example of how extensive this interaction can be for microcomputers is the MIMS Systems by CTB/McGraw-Hill. When examinees are given control over the presentation of test-like exercises, as is possible in some computer-managed instructional contexts, it is possible that at least conscientious and reflective learners will benefit. One would hope that the capability of some CAT systems to provide immediate feedback on whether or not an examinee's answer is correct would result in greater learning. Empirical research is not clear on this point, however (Bender, 1975; Gialluca & Weiss, 1980).

Precision of measurement; testing time. Precision and time are two sides of the same coin. Item response theory-based systems of adaptive testing can substantially reduce average testing time without loss in precision, or can substantially increase precision for a fixed testing time. Other CAT systems do not have this advantage. However, when the goal of the testing program is to estimate the average ability of a group, systems like item program banking surpass the precision of measurement of conventional testing (Lord, 1977). This superiority of item program banking is due to the characteristic that each examinee receives different items, and the domain of test content is thereby sampled more extensively than in conventional testing, where a single sample of items is administered to all examinees.

Security. Cheating on tests is a recognized and undesired problem that jeopardizes the validity of test score interpretations and the fairness of the test process. CAT can essentially eliminate cheating when each examinee receives a unique test. Whether examinees are tested together in a group or at different times, test security is not a problem as long as examinees are presented with different items.

Concern for the individual. One can argue that CAT is a mechanical process devoid of caring; but so are cars, food processors, and dental drills. Perhaps what is at issue is not that a machine produces the test, but the legitimate fear that the best interests of the examinee will not be served if the testing system is too rigid and insensitive.

Testing by computer, however, can celebrate rather than retard flexibility and opportunity, and therefore can exhibit a concern for the individual. One dimension of *flexibility* is test administration. Since CAT systems can assure test security, test administrations can occur at the convenience of the examinee rather than on a set day. A second dimension of flexibility is test difficulty. The response contingent, adaptive character of some CAT systems makes it possible to assure a comfortable fit between the difficulty of the test items and the examinee's ability. *Opportunity* can be increased because CAT systems facilitate the production of many different test versions and thus encourage users to allow examinees to have practice and repeated-testing opportunities. One theme of this chapter has been that CAT and the individualization of testing are interrelated.

Ease of scoring. For each examinee, individual items must be scored, and the performance on each of the items usually needs to be aggregated to provide a total score for the entire test. When a pool of items exists, the correct answers to objective items can be entered into the computer together with the text of the items, and scoring can be performed easily and automatically by the computer. A CAT system like item program banking requires that an item-scoring procedure be included in the item program. Satisfactory computer scoring is less easy to obtain for open-response test items, but several efforts to have computer scoring of answers in the form of text exist (e.g., Lawlor, 1982; Wolfe, 1975).

Obtaining a single score for the entire test can be troublesome when each examinee takes a different test. The need to use a method that can estimate fairly the total test scores is particularly acute in adaptive testing, when examinees are purposely given tests that differ in difficulty. The mathematical models that support such testing systems provide formulations for estimating an appropriate score for each individual that take into account the difficulty of the test.

Fairness. The issue of fairness, just mentioned, arises in CAT because usually all examinees do not take the same test. Some examinees may be given more difficult tests than other examinees. CAT advocates, such as Green et al. (1982), respond to such a concern as follows:

> The questions differ, but the area of skill or knowledge assessed is the same on all test forms, and every candidate has the same opportunity. . . . It should be noted that the concept of fairness involves equal opportunity, not equal treatment. In a track-and-field meet, each competitor must have the same chance at the high jump, but fairness does not require that a person who can't clear a six-foot high jump nevertheless be given a chance at seven feet. . . . In the same way, a CAT provides every candidate the same initial opportunity. (p. 13)

Another aspect of fairness is freedom from bias. In CAT, examiner bias is controlled because the computer is not influenced by the race, the sex, or the other characteristics of the examiner. The bias of the item writer is also reduced in some CAT systems that replace idiosyncratically produced items, which rely on the intuitive skills and standards of the item writer, with a replicable, scientific procedure that can be made public (Roid & Haladyna, 1982).

SUGGESTIONS FOR FUTURE RESEARCH

The proliferation of CAT schemes is unaccompanied by careful evaluations. The value of the alleged benefits of CAT listed previously needs to be assessed. For example, a cost analysis of CAT systems should consider the hidden costs of time as well as the touted savings in time. The comparative validity of standard item formats and measures based on simulations or other nontraditional approaches should be studied.

In addition to evaluations of the effectiveness and cost of current CAT schemes, technical research on how to operate CAT better is needed. Research topics might include how best to incorporate graphical or other external materials in the test items, how to construct tests that fit the mathematical models being used (or vice versa), and how to make the entire system easier to use by classroom teachers and by other practitioners.

GUIDELINES FOR PRACTITIONERS

Unless more than modest resources are available, practitioners should not attempt to develop and implement a CAT system of their own design. A list of questions that developers of item banks should consider has been provided by Millman and Arter (in press). Other concerns have been expressed by Lippey (1974). If practitioners wish to adopt a CAT system that is operating elsewhere, special care should be taken to assure that (a) any items that are an integral part of the system meet the adopters' standards of curricular relevance and quality, (b) the system will perform the tasks desired, (c) the system will operate on the adopters' computer equipment, and (d) the adopters have the resources to implement and maintain the system.

Practitioners who seek customized tests produced by commercial publishers should be concerned primarily with the first two of these requirements. Teachers having access to microcomputers may wish to select test-writing computer programs written specifically for and known to be compatible with their equipment (Hsu & Nitko, 1983). Although such systems may be very modest in their capability, more sophisticated systems for microcomputers are anticipated.

In summary, CAT systems differ widely in their purpose, design, and development. This diversity plus the rapid changes in computer technology and supporting software preclude a simple evaluation of CAT. Its promise appears to be great, and watching it progress in the years ahead should be exciting.

REFERENCES

Anderson, R. C. How to construct achievement tests to assess comprehension. *Review of Educational Research*, 1972, *42*, 145–170.

Arter, J. A. *Out-of-level versus in-level testing: When should we recommend each?* Paper presented at the annual meeting of the American Educational Research Association, New York, March 1982.

Bender, B. *The effects of an answer-until-correct procedure with response contingent feedback on learning to solve problems in statistics*. Unpublished master's thesis, Cornell University, 1975.

Berk, R. A. The application of structural facet theory to achievement test construction. *Educational Research Quarterly*, 1978, *3*, 62–72.

Berk, R. A. A comparison of six content domain specification strategies for criterion-referenced tests. *Educational Technology*, 1980, *20*, 49–52.

Bormuth, J. R. *On the theory of achievement test items*. Chicago: University of Chicago Press, 1970.

Braby, R., Parrish, W. F., Guitard, C. R., & Aagard, J. A. *Computer-aided authoring of programmed instruction for teaching symbol recognition* (Report No. 58). Orlando, FL: Training Analysis and Evaluation Group, Department of the Navy, June 1978.

Choppin, B., & McArthur, D. L. Computerized diagnostic testing. *Journal of Educational Measurement*, in press.

Cliff, N. Complete orders from incomplete data: Interactive ordering and tailored testing. *Psychological Bulletin*, 1975, *82*, 289–302.

Cudeck, R. A., Cliff, N., & Kehoe, J. F. TAILOR: A fortran procedure for interactive tailored testing. *Educational and Psychological Measurement*, 1977, *37*, 767–769.

Finn, P. J. A question writing algorithm. *Journal of Reading Behavior*, 1975, *7*, 341–367.

Fremer, J., & Anastasio, E. J. Computer-assisted item writing: I, Spelling items. *Journal of Educational Measurement*, 1969, *6*, 69–74.

Gabriel, R. M., Arter, J. A., & Demaline, R. E. *Functional level testing: Selecting the right test level* (Workshop Package, Title I Technical Assistance Centers). Portland, OR: Northwest Regional Educational Laboratory, 1980.

Gialluca, K. A., & Weiss, D. J. *Effects of immediate knowledge of results on achievement test performance and test dimensionality* (Report 80-1). Minneapolis: Psychometric Methods Program, Department of Psychology, University of Minnesota, January 1980.

Green, B. F., Bock, R. D., Humphreys, L. G., Linn, R. L., & Reckase, M. D. *Evaluation plan for the Computerized Adaptive Vocational Aptitude Battery* (Report 82-1). Baltimore, MD: Department of Psychology, The Johns Hopkins University, May 1982.

Hambleton, R. K., & Eignor, D. R. *A practitioner's guide to criterion-referenced test development, validation, and test score usage* (Report No. 70). Amherst: Laboratory of Psychometric and Evaluative Research, School of Education, University of Massachusetts, 1979.

Hiscox, M. D., & Brzezinski, E. J. *A guide to item banking in education*. Portland, OR: Northwest Regional Educational Laboratory, June 1980.

Hsu, T. C., & Nitko, A. J. *Microcomputer testing software teachers can use*. Paper presented at the ECS Large-scale Assessment Conference, Boulder, CO, June 1983.

Lawlor, J. Evaluating textual responses. In J. Lawlor (Ed.), *Computers in composition instruction*. Los Alamitos, CA: Southwest Regional Laboratory for Educational Research and Development, 1982. Pp. 75–81.

Lippey, G. (Ed.). *Computer-assisted test construction*. Englewood Cliffs, NJ: Educational Technology Publications, 1974.

Lord, F. M. The self-scoring flexilevel test. *Journal of Educational Measurement*, 1971, *8*, 147–151.

Lord, F. M. Some item analysis and test theory for a system of computer-assisted test construction for individualized instruction. *Applied Psychological Measurement*, 1977, *1*, 447–455.

Lord, F. M. *Applications of item response theory to practical testing problems*. Hillsdale, NJ: Erlbaum, 1980.

Martuza, V. R. *Domain definition/item generation for criterion-referenced tests: A review and directions for future research*. Paper presented at the annual meeting of the Eastern Educational Research Association, Kiawah Island, SC, February 1979.

McCormick, D. J., & Cliff, N. TAILOR-APL: An interactive computer program for individual tailored testing. *Educational and Psychological Measurement*, 1977, *37*, 771–774.

McGuire, C. H., Solomon, L., & Forman, P. *Clinical simulations: Selected problems in patient management* (2nd ed.) New York: Appleton-Century-Crofts, 1976.

McLean, L. D., & Ragsdale, R. G. The Rasch model for achievement tests: Inappropriate in the past, inappropriate today, inappropriate tomorrow. *Canadian Journal of Education*, 1983, *8*, 71–76.

Millman, J. Criterion-referenced measurement. In W. J. Popham (Ed.), *Evaluation in education: Current applications*. Berkeley, CA: McCutchan, 1974. Pp. 311-397.

Millman, J. A system for generating unique tests by computer and its use in a mastery learning setting. In P. R. Baumann (Ed.), *Computer based instruction*. Albany: Faculty Grants for the Improvement of Undergraduate Instruction, State University of New York, 1982. Pp. 99–106.

Millman, J., & Arter, J. A. Issues in item banking. *Journal of Educational Measurement*, in press.

Millman, J., & Outlaw, W. S. Testing by computer. *AEDS Journal*, 1978, *11*, 57–72.

Olympia, P. L. Computer generation of truly repeatable examinations. *Educational Technology*, 1975, *15*, 53-55.

Popham, W. J. *Criterion-referenced measurement*. Englewood Cliffs, NJ: Prentice-Hall, 1978.

Rogers, D. H. *A new instrument for classroom data collection: The in-class student self-report instrument*. Paper presented at the joint meeting of the Evaluation Network and the Evaluation Research Society, Baltimore, October 1982.

Roid, G. H., & Haladyna, T. M. *A technology for test-item writing*. New York: Academic Press, 1982.

Rubincam, I., & Olivier, W. P. *A non-hierarchical computerized test item data base*. Paper presented at the annual meeting of the Association of Educational Data Systems, Atlanta, May 1978.

Scandura, J. M. Microcomputer systems for authoring, diagnosis, and instruction in rule-based content. *Educational Technology*, 1981, *21*, 13–19. (a)

Scandura, J. M. Problem-solving in schools and beyond: Transitions from the naive to the neophyte to the master. *Educational Psychologist*, 1981, *16*, 139–150. (b)

Stevens, J. D., & O'Neill, Jr., H. F. *Suggestions for development of test items*. Austin Computer-Assisted Instruction Laboratory, University of Texas, 1974.

Traub, R. E., & Wolfe, R. G. Latent trait theories and the assessment of educational achievement. *Review of Research in Education*, 1981, *9*, 377–435.

Urry, V. W. Tailored testing: A successful application of latent trait theory. *Journal of Educational Measurement*, 1977, *14*, 181–196.

Vickers, F. D. Creative test generators. *Educational Technology*, 1973, *13*, 43–44.

Wald, A. *Sequential analysis*. New York: Wiley, 1947.

Wasik, J. L. GENTEST: A computer program to generate individualized objective test forms. *Educational and Psychological Measurement*, 1979, *39*, 653–656.

Weiss, D. J., & Betz, N. E. *Ability measurement: Conventional or adaptive*? (Research Report 73–1). Minneapolis: Psychometric Methods Program, Department of Psychology, University of Minnesota, 1973.

Wolfe, J. H. Automatic question generation from text: An aid to independent study. In R. Colman & P. Lorton (Eds.), *Proceedings of the ACM SIGCSE-SIGCUE technical symposium: Computer science and education*. New York: Association for Computing Machinery, 1975. Pp. 104–112.

Wright, B. D., & Stone, M. H. *Best test design: Rasch measurement*. Chicago: MESA Press, 1979.

5 CONDUCTING THE ITEM ANALYSIS

RONALD A. BERK

INTRODUCTION

ONCE THE TEST ITEMS have been generated, they need to undergo a review process to identify structural flaws and to determine whether they function or "behave" consistently with the purposes for which they were constructed. Several researchers have critically examined and studied this process, primarily from a technical perspective in terms of instructional sensitivity statistics (Berk, 1978, 1980; Brown, 1980, chap. 4; Haladyna & Roid, 1981; Harris & Pearlman, 1977; Roid & Haladyna, 1982, chap. 13; van der Linden, 1981), item equivalence (Wilcox, 1977a), item stability (Wilcox, 1977b), and item response theory (van der Linden, 1981). Less attention has been given to the judgmental procedures or logical analysis of the items (Berk, 1980; Hambleton, 1980b; Roid & Haladyna, 1982, chap. 12).

The use of both judgmental and statistical methods is essential in order to evaluate item validity. The choice of methods is contingent on the type of criterion-referenced test and the procedures employed to write the items. If the test is built from objectives-based specifications using traditional item construction rules and a performance standard is to be set to make mastery decisions, then analyses must be performed to appraise whether the items (1) measure their respective instructional and behavioral objectives and (2) differentiate between masters and nonmasters of those objectives. In addition, the items must be free of structural flaws that could cue or confuse the student. The extent to which the items are *valid* for these purposes depends on the outcomes of two analyses. The first is concerned with the establishment of item-objective congruence or the degree of relationship between each item and the objective it is intended to measure. The second involves statistical procedures designed to express the degree of relationship between the intent of each item and the responses of students to each item.

Similar methods should also be considered for minimum competency tests, which are usually developed from academic and life skills with objective item formats. The test scores are used for pass-fail decisions of grade-to-grade promotion and/or graduation certification (for details, see Berk, in press). Like the items on teacher-made mastery tests, minimum competency test items need to be scrutinized with a judgmental review and statistical analyses. The difference is that the procedures are executed by committees and professional test makers of the state level instead of by individual teachers.

These various item analysis methods that are required for mastery and minimum competency tests are unnecessary and, in fact, undesirable for "domain-referenced" tests, where the items are actually drawn randomly from a domain or pool of items (Haladyna & Roid, 1983). It has been argued that in domain-referencing (see Nitko, chapter 1) the use of item statistics for refining and selecting the items would theoretically destroy the defining character of the test, thereby weakening the interpretability of the domain score. Furthermore, given the precision of the strategies that are frequently employed to generate the item domain (see Roid, chapter 3), the need to assess congruence between the items and the domain specifications or to search for flaws in the items seems questionable.

The single category of analysis essential for all criterion-referenced tests pertains to detecting sex, racial, or ethnic bias in the items. Bias can be a source of invalidity just as the mismatch between an item and an objective can be. Judgmental reviews and statistical studies are needed to pinpoint the source of possible bias and decide the appropriate course of action to eliminate it.

The purpose of this chapter is to survey the major judgmental and statistical item analysis techniques that teachers and district and state level test makers can use to assess the effectiveness of criterion-referenced test items. The advantages and disadvantages of the techniques are noted and the most promising approaches are identified. Finally, specific recommendations are provided to guide future research and current practices.

REVIEW OF ITEM ANALYSIS PROCEDURES

Several item analysis procedures have been devised expressly for criterion-referenced tests. The procedures involve four different phases of analysis: (1) a judgmental review to assess item-objective congruence and content bias, (2) statistical analyses to evaluate the effectiveness of the items, (3) a judgmental review of the statistical results to determine whether the items should be selected, revised, or discarded, and (4) choice response analyses to identify what part(s) of an item requires revision or replacement. In this section of the chapter, various procedures are critically examined according to these four phases by which a teacher or district or state level test maker would conduct an item analysis.

Judgmental Review

Item-objective congruence. The most important item characteristic is item-objective congruence. It is concerned with the extent to which an item measures the objective it is intended to measure. Congruence is determined by a judgmental process. The items are reviewed in relation to the list of instructional and behavioral objectives and the table of domain specifications. At least three criteria are employed to determine the congruence or match between the items and the objectives: (1) behavior, (2) content, and (3) hierarchical classification.

Since the items are generated from the statements of objectives, the behavioral (verb) and content components of the objectives should be reflected in the format and content of the items. Agreement in terms of the first two criteria is typically built in during the item construction phase. These aspects of congruence, however, still merit attention before administering the test. Occasionally, verbs in the behavioral objectives suggesting essay questions (e.g., explain) are mismatched with complex multiple-choice items. Either the objectives should be corrected or the items should be rewritten.

The time devoted to establishing congruence should be concentrated on the third criterion. More disagreements seem to occur regarding item and objective classifications in the cognitive, affective, and psychomotor taxonomies than with the preceding criteria. When the items are examined according to those hierarchical schemes, it is not uncommon to find discrepancies, particularly at the middle and upper levels of the cognitive domain. The discrepancies can be identified by using the test draft as an item checklist against which the classification categories can be compared. An item-by-item analysis can be conducted to ascertain whether the initial intent of each objective is, in fact, realized in each item. Some test makers tend to construct items at lower levels of cognition than the specifications originally indicated. For an objective classified at the application level, for example, it is not surprising to find that the corresponding item has been written at the knowledge level. This incongruence may be due to confusion over what constitutes measures at the different levels of the hierarchy or to the process by which the objectives are developed.

If the item is the predominant consideration when the objective is being written, the type of behavioral outcome is often restricted by the test maker's knowledge of test items. To the extent that the domain specifications are defined in the context of some preconceived notion of what the items should look like, the resulting objectives and their classifications are developed to fit the items rather than the reverse. This method creates problems in assuring the link with the content domain. The assessment of congruence will usually reveal inconsistencies between the item and the specifications. Under those conditions the test maker has two choices: either modify the objectives and their classifications to correspond with the items or rewrite the items to correspond with the existing classifications.

The foregoing procedures can be extended to items developed at the district and state levels. The difference lies in the number of persons judging the characteristic. Instead of individual teacher judgment at the classroom level, the collective judgment of a panel of content specialists is required (Dahl,

1971). Three approaches to assessing congruence using content specialists have been described by Rovinelli and Hambleton (1977): (1) an index derived from Hemphill and Westie's (1950) index of homogeneity of placement, (2) a rating scale in the format of a semantic differential, and (3) a matching task that is analyzed using the chi-square test of independence. The empirical comparison among the methods revealed that the index that quantifies the degree of agreement among the individual judgments provides the most meaningful measure of congruence. For specific guidelines on this procedure and several others, the reader is referred to Hambleton's discussion of item validity (chapter 8).

Regardless of the method employed to determine item-objective congruence, it is crucial that when discrepancies occur, the appropriate corrections be made. A judgment of congruence is a *necessary but not sufficient condition for test score validity*. If it cannot be stated unequivocally that the items measure the objectives, then any other characteristic becomes meaningless. The interpretability of the test scores in terms of objectives hinges on the congruence between the items and the objectives.

Content bias. Once it has been established that the items do appear to measure their respective objectives, each item should be examined for content bias. Any language in an item that is stereotypic of a particular sex or of a racial or ethnic subpopulation should be removed. Also, words and phrases that are culture specific or offensive to a given group should be eliminated. Tittle (1982) has presented numerous review forms that have been employed by test publishers for this purpose. However, one convenient form prepared by Hambleton (1980a), shown in Table 5.1, can be used by test makers at any level. In addition to the questions in this form, attention should be given to the characteristics of the persons and the situations described in the items to assure fair representation in the work roles and life styles of sex, racial, and ethnic groups, especially females and minorities.

These reviews should be conducted by classroom teachers for the tests they develop and by specially formed panels for competency tests constructed at the school (grade or department), district, and state levels. The panels should be composed of professional educators and lay persons representative of the appropriate subpopulations (e.g., males, females, blacks, whites, Hispanics). The individual teacher and the panel should carefully review the test items using a structured checklist or other set of guidelines (see Table 5.1) and make specific recommendations on the revision or elimination of those items judged questionable.

Although test publishers commit a substantial amount of time and resources for the content bias review of norm-referenced tests (Green et al., 1982), test makers at the local level have not been very sensitive to the issues of content bias in criterion-referenced and minimum competency tests. Only recently have they addressed the topic of item bias (e.g., Christie & Casey, 1983). There are legal, ethical, and technical reasons why such sensitivity is essential. The consequences of not considering bias as a source of invalidity in

Table 5.1. Item Review Form to Detect Bias

Reviewer: ______________ Date: ______________ Objective: ______________

This review form has been designed to assist in the identification of test items which may reflect sex, cultural, racial, regional and/or ethic content bias and stereotyping. Place your name, the date, and the objective number at the top of the review form.

In the spaces at the right under the heading "Test Item Number" provide the numbers of the test items you will review. When the number of test items for review exceeds ten, use a second review form.

Next, read each test item and answer the six questions below. Use "✓" for YES, "X" for NO, "?" for UNSURE, and "NA" for NOT APPLICABLE. When your rating is negative ("X" or "?"), indicate what you think is the problem in the test item and suggest a revision on your copy of the test item.

When you have completed your review task, staple the test items to your review form(s) and return.

	Test Item Number									
1. Is the item free of *offensive* sex, cultural, racial, regional and/or ethnic content?										
2. Is the item free of sex, cultural, racial, and/or ethnic stereotyping?										
3. Is the item free of language which could be offensive to a segment of the examinee population?										
4. Is the item free from descriptions which could be offensive to a segment of the examinee population?										
5. Will the activities described in the item be equally familiar (or equally unfamiliar) to all examinees?										
6. Will the words in the item have a common meaning for all examinees?										

Source: Revised version of Hambleton (1980a) review form by Ronald K. Hambleton, May 1981. Reprinted with permission of the author.

the test scores may eventually be felt in the courtroom (e.g., *Larry P. et al.* v. *Wilson Riles et al.*, 1979, 1984).

Statistical Analyses

After the various item reviews have been completed and a draft version of the test is ready for administration, the test maker should plan a field test with one or more samples of students. The response data obtained from the students can be used to evaluate the effectiveness of the items in terms of whether they function in the manner in which they were intended. The steps in the process include the selection of criterion groups, gathering informal student feedback, computing difficulty, discrimination, and homogeneity statistics, and conducting an item bias study. The following presentation is an extension of Berk's (1978) "consumers' guide" survey of item statistics.

Selection of criterion groups. The first consideration in the use of item statistics is the selection of the students to whom the items should be administered. The majority of the statistics are based on pretest-posttest repeated measurements from one group or two independent measurements from two different groups. Only four statistics are computed from one set of data gathered from one group (Brennan, 1972; Epstein, 1977; Engel & LaDuca, 1977; Pettie & Oosterhof, 1976).

The choice of which groups to use depends upon their availability and the purpose of the test. Since a criterion-referenced test is employed in most instances to identify masters and nonmasters of a set of objectives, sample selection translates into the following question: *Who should be able to master the objectives and who should not?* Two categories of student are of interest—those who would be *successful* (masters) and those who would be *unsuccessful* (nonmasters) on the objectives. In essence, these groups are samples of *actual* masters and nonmasters. For the majority of instructional programs for which tests are developed, the groups will consist of students who have and students who have not been exposed to the instruction, respectively. It is likely that most if not all students will perform poorly on the test prior to instruction. If this level of performance is not obtained, either the items are failing to function as expected or the objectives have been taught previously. When the latter appears to be the explanation, the justification for the instruction needs to be examined. In the case of the successful group, which is tested after the instruction has been completed, performance should be quite high. That is, most if not all of these students should master the objectives.

These two groups of students chosen for the item analysis are often referred to as *criterion groups*. Their selection is based on some criterion of current or future performance. This may be success in the instructional program in which the test will be used or success in a subsequent program, i.e., unit, course, grade level. The former often suggests summative decision making at one point in time, whereas the latter denotes placement decision making within a predictive context. Placement in a program that contains sequentially arranged units each represented by an instructional objective presumes that a student's success in any single unit is prerequisite for success in the following unit (see Glaser & Nitko, 1971). Therefore, a group of students that has successfully completed the entire program can serve as one of the criterion groups for validating the placement test items. The same group may also be employed in the validation of items used for summative decisions about individual mastery at the conclusion of the program.

A clear definition of the criterion is essential. Three approaches for identifying criterion groups are described in this section: (1) preinstruction-postinstruction measurements, (2) uninstructed-instructed groups, and (3) contrasting groups. The first two approaches entail the selection of intact samples judged to contain both masters and nonmasters (Berk, 1976, 1978,

1980). The last-named approach requires that the samples be composed by individually picking each master and nonmaster (Livingston & Zieky, 1982). All of the approaches are applicable to criterion-referenced tests used for diagnostic (or placement) decisions as well as summative decisions. Variations of the uninstructed-instructed and contrasting groups approaches can be employed with minimum competency tests used for grade promotion and graduation decisions. The advantages and disadvantages of each approach are noted.

The *preinstruction-postinstruction measurements method* has been an integral part of mastery learning and diagnostic-prescriptive teaching for several years (Block, 1971; Block & Burns, 1976; Carroll, 1963, 1970). It involves *testing one group of students twice*, before instruction (preinstruction) and after instruction (postinstruction). Students are commonly tested with the same set of items on the two occasions. Alternatively, a parallel or equivalent set of items can be used on the second administration.

The advantage of measuring students before and after instruction is that it permits the teacher to examine individual as well as group gains. These data can be particularly useful in assessing progress from one unit to the next. Information on gains cannot be obtained from any other type of design.

One major disadvantage of the approach, however, pertains to the impracticality of administering the posttest. The analysis cannot be conducted until the instruction has been completed. Hence, any instructional application of the measure would likely be deferred until the following year. A second disadvantage concerns the amount of time allowed between the pretest and posttest. When the administrations are in close succession, it is possible for the students' performance on the pretest to influence their performance on the posttest. One way to obviate this problem of testing effect would be to develop an equivalent set of items. If this is unfeasible due to practical constraints or the extreme specificity of the objectives (i.e., no other items could be developed), it is recommended that the intervening period between the administrations be extended a reasonable length of time so that the carry-over effect of memory from the initial testing can be minimized. This extension should not be as long as four months or longer, to avoid incurring the effect of maturation, inasmuch as simply growing older could improve a student's achievement performance. This growth would confound the measurement of gain to which the teacher wishes to attribute the effect of instruction. Improvement as a result of instruction and maturation become inextricably mixed when several months pass before the posttest is administered. The item analysis is designed to focus only on the change in item responses due to instruction.

In order to expedite computation of the item statistics, the results of the two measurements should be displayed in the form of a student × item matrix. This format is shown in Table 5.2. The table consists of the item scores (0, 1) of 10 students who were administered five items both before and after instruction. The students were assigned a score of 1 for a correct response and 0 for an incorrect response or no response (omit). The rationale for scoring an omit

Table 5.2. Student × Item Matrix for Preinstruction-Postinstruction Measurements

	Preinstruction Item					Postinstruction Item				
Student	1	2	3	4	5	1	2	3	4	5
1	0	0	1	1	1	1	0	1	1	1
2	0	1	1	1	0	1	1	1	1	1
3	0	1	0	1	1	1	1	1	1	1
4	0	0	0	1	1	1	1	0	1	1
5	0	0	1	1	0	1	0	0	1	1
6	0	0	0	1	0	1	1	0	1	0
7	0	1	1	1	1	1	0	0	1	1
8	0	0	1	1	0	1	0	1	1	0
9	0	0	0	1	0	1	1	0	1	1
10	0	0	1	1	0	1	1	1	1	1

as 0 relates to the purpose of the test. Since a criterion-referenced test assesses how much a student knows unaffected by speed of response, no time limit is imposed. Therefore, when students are given ample time to complete the test, it can be assumed that if a student did not respond to an item, it was because he or she did not know the correct answer.

The *uninstructed-instructed groups approach* is a form of the "known-groups" technique employed for many years in the validation of personality tests (Cronbach & Meehl, 1955; Edwards, 1970, chap. 4; Wiggins, 1973, chap. 6). Only during the past decade has this technique been applied to criterion-referenced measurement (Henrysson & Wedman, 1974; Jackson, 1970; Klein & Kosecoff, 1976; Millman, 1974; Zieky, 1973). It involves *testing two separate groups of students at the same point in time*, one group that has not received instruction (uninstructed group) and a second group that has received instruction (instructed group).

The known-groups technique compares one group of persons known by independent means to possess more of the specified trait/attribute with a second group known to possess much less. In the validation of a criterion-referenced test, the trait of interest is *knowledge*. The acquisition of knowledge in most content domains is a continuous process. Learning to read, write, and solve mathematical problems occurs gradually throughout a person's formal schooling. Improvement in these areas is frequently accompanied by improvement in the other subject areas. Since students learn at different rates, at any given time the students within a single classroom will vary in the amount of knowledge they possess. Therefore, in general, it can be expected that students in an instructed group will possess *more knowledge* related to a set of instructional objectives and an uninstructed group will possess much less. There are only two special cases where a group might know all or nothing. Those cases will be discussed shortly.

The uninstructed-instructed groups approach requires that the two groups be identified on the basis of *independent, informed teacher judgment*. Students in one or more classrooms who have not received instruction or who are known to be deficient on the objectives to be assessed may serve as the uninstructed group. Conversely, students in other classrooms who have received "effective" instruction on the objectives may comprise the instructed group. This group, in the judgment of the teacher, should have demonstrated *success* in the instructional unit. Whether this success pertains to a current or subsequent unit depends on the orientation of the test. Student performance on written assignments, quizzes, and other classroom tasks is often the available information a teacher must rely upon for guidance in making the judgment.

The students chosen for the instructed group should be as similar as possible to those in the uninstructed group in ability level and all other relevant characteristics. Although the groups will often be unequal in size, the proportional distributions of the characteristics should be equivalent. For example, if one group has 60% boys and 40% girls, this balance should be maintained in the second group. The only real difference that should exist between the uninstructed and instructed groups is in exposure to the instructional treatment.

While the approach is applicable to most testing situations, there are two instances where possessing or not possessing the knowledge necessary to master objectives will be characterized as *all* or *nothing*: (1) where basic skills or minimum competencies are being measured and (2) where no prior knowledge on objectives can be expected due to the nature of the content domain. The former is concerned with the "all"; the latter emphasizes the "nothing."

When basic skills or *minimum competencies* are to be assessed, complete mastery by the instructed group is desirable. If a test is designed to identify children who cannot succeed or function at a minimum level, the criterion *successful* group that is chosen must by definition unequivocally perform at least at that level and most likely could perform at a higher level. This means the group should be able to demonstrate total mastery, or 100% performance, on the set of minimum skills. If this does not occur, it is possible that the skills may not be "minimum." The criterion *unsuccessful* group should perform at less than total mastery. The actual performance could be expected to range from 0 to less than 100%. This group should consist of the type of children to be identified by the test.

The item validation of a placement test to determine reading readiness, for example, would require the selection of children who clearly can and cannot read. In other areas, such as learning disabilities and English as a second language, the criterion groups would consist of children who possess and do not possess specific disabilities and those who are native English speakers and speakers of English as a second language (e.g., Hispanic Americans), respectively. Evidence of these different characteristics can often be found in school records. Again, teacher judgment plays a significant role in locating the children.

The procedure has implications for other competency-based decisions in course placement, grade level placement, high school graduation certification, and functional literacy. For example, to validate the items on a minimum competency test used to determine which students should receive a high school diploma (or certificate of attendence), competence must be defined operationally in terms of the actual test performance of individuals who have been judged by their teachers, immediate supervisors, or similar persons as competent on an appropriate collection of skills (e.g., Christie & Casey, 1983). Teacher nominations of masters and nonmasters of academic skill objectives in reading, mathematics, and writing can be used effectively. For survival-level skills, occupational groups of unskilled and service workers could be compared with unemployed adults or junior high school students. The competency groups are frequently accessible through the coordinators of work-study programs in local districts.

Dissimilar to the above, where 100% mastery is desirable for the instructed or minimally competent group, is the case where *no prior knowledge* can be expected for the uninstructed group. This occurs in courses that introduce the student to completely unfamiliar content, e.g., a foreign language. A test administered prior to the instruction would yield results that unequivocally demonstrate nonmastery or 0 performance. For the purposes of validation, there is no need to administer the test to uninstructed students who are expected to know nothing about the content. Item and test performance can be assumed to equal 0. The test must be administered, however, to an instructed group.

The advantage of the uninstructed-instructed group approach is one of practicality. The item analysis can be conducted at one point in time, prior to instruction, if an instructed group of students is concurrently available. This can facilitate the immediate use of the test for mastery-nonmastery decisions during the program being taught.

One disadvantage is the difficulty of defining suitable criteria for identifying the groups. All variations of the criterion-groups model have this difficulty. The test maker must confront the crucial issue of how to *define operationally the criterion of success* in terms of the designated target groups. The process of defining "master," "competent," "minimally competent," or "successful" represents the Achilles heel of the approach. The more objectivity that can be incorporated into the process, the better. Informed judgment as described previously is one step in that direction. However, regardless of the rigor imposed on the specification of selection criteria and the systematic and standardized procedures used with each teacher (or supervisor), there is no known strategy for objectifying the judgments. One must accept this scientific imprecision in the context of the state of the art and proceed to the next steps, or reject the approach. If the judgmental process is not credible or intuitively convincing, the statistical methods that follow from that premise will be meaningless.

Another disadvantage that is inherent in the approach is the problem of assuring group equivalence. Since randomly assigning students to instructed (competent) and uninstructed (incompetent) groups is generally unfeasible and inappropriate, the test maker may need to explain differences in group performance that may not be attributable to the instruction, e.g., age, sex, ability level, socioeconomic background. Perhaps the best strategy to prevent this charge from arising would be to control deliberately for possible extraneous factors in the initial selection of the groups and exhibit caution in interpreting the item analysis results.

The scoring and presentation of the item data for the uninstructed and instructed groups is identical to the preinstruction-postinstruction approach. Table 5.3 displays a student × item matrix with item scores on five items administered to one group of 10 uninstructed students and a second group of 10 instructed students.

The most common criticism of the preceding two intact-group approaches is that only rarely would the assumption of "instructed student equals true master" be satisfied completely (Hambleton, Swaminathan, Algina, & Coulson, 1978; Shepard, 1980). Usually there will be a few instructed students who are clearly nonmasters and a few uninstructed students who may be masters of the objective. In addition, the base rate in both approaches is assumed to be 50%, which may not be an accurate representation of mastery in the population.

These assumptions are troublesome because they can markedly affect the item statistics. In particular, the estimates of item discrimination may be deflated to the extent that the equivalence of instructed students and masters and of uninstructed students and nonmasters is not real. Furthermore, the data can be misleading and incorrect if the sample sizes do not reflect the incidence of mastery in the classroom or grade level.

The *contrasting-groups approach* can be viewed as a refinement of the intact-group approaches inasmuch as it specifically addresses the aforementioned criticisms. Again based on teacher judgment, this strategy requires a

Table 5.3. Student × Item Matrix for Uninstructed and Instructed Groups

	Uninstructed Group Item						Instructed Group Item				
Student	1	2	3	4	5	Student	1	2	3	4	5
1	0	0	1	1	1	1	1	1	1	1	1
2	0	1	1	1	0	2	1	1	0	1	1
3	0	1	0	1	1	3	1	1	1	1	1
4	0	0	0	1	1	4	0	0	1	1	1
5	0	0	1	1	0	5	1	0	1	1	0
6	0	0	0	1	0	6	1	1	1	1	1
7	0	1	1	1	1	7	1	0	0	1	1
8	0	0	1	1	0	8	0	1	0	1	0
9	0	0	0	1	0	9	1	0	1	1	0
10	0	0	1	1	0	10	1	1	1	1	1

teacher to choose only those students he or she is certain are either definite masters or nonmasters of the objectives measured by the test. By hand picking each student to compose the mastery and nonmastery samples, the borderline student who is too close to call a master or nonmaster is excluded. The composition of "definites" will tend to maximize item discrimination.

This process of criterion-group selection avoids the assumption of equating instruction with mastery. Therefore, it has the key advantage of including only those students judged to be definite masters and nonmasters in the respective groups. Another advantage is that the sample of masters reflects the base rate in the population. For example, if a classroom of, say, 20 students, constitutes the entire population, then the identification of 12 masters and 6 nonmasters provides proportional representation for that population, where the base rate is 60%.

Despite these important advantages of the contrasting-groups approach, there are several disadvantages that tend to diminish their impact. First, it is not clear at what point in the instruction a teacher should or could identify a definite group of masters and nonmasters. The number in each group will be quite disproportionate either prior to or after instruction, and the incidence rate may be very low during instruction. This identification problem must be resolved before one can recommend a point in time when the test should be administered to the two groups. Second, individually composing each group is logistically more difficult and time consuming than using intact groups, especially when populations other than a single classroom are considered. Third, the sample sizes drawn from one or two classes may be too small to yield reliable item statistics. If either sample contains fewer than 20 students, the data can be very misleading. Finally, the difficulties of defining suitable criteria for identifying the students and of assuring group equivalence, which were mentioned already in the context of the uninstructed-instructed groups approach, also apply to contrasting groups.

Informal student feedback. Immediately following the administration of the items to the criterion groups, informal student feedback on the items can be obtained. Frequently, only the masters are involved in the procedures because the nonmasters typically convey frustration instead of information. The procedure entails conducting a classroom discussion or individual interviews to elicit student reactions to the items and test structure. Much can be learned about test quality from a student critique that otherwise would not be disclosed from a quantitative analysis. The feedback can provide valuable insights and directions for improving the test. Specific test weaknesses such as item ambiguity and cuing, miskeyed answers, inappropriate vocabulary, and unclear item and test directions can be revealed by asking leading questions pertinent to the item content and structure, test directions, and test format. Such questions may include the following:

1. Did any of the items seem confusing?
2. Did you find any item with no correct answer?

3. Did you find any item with more than one correct answer?
4. Were there any words in the items that you did not know?
5. Did you have any difficulty understanding what to do as you worked through the test?

Since students commonly are not requested to participate or assist in the test improvement process, the novelty of the experience may produce a flood of responses. In many cases, the first question yields more information than may be anticipated. As students become attuned to the procedure, however, the quantity of feedback will diminish and the quality of the feedback can be expected to improve. The 5 to 10 minutes often needed to conduct this analysis coupled with the valuable knowledge the analysis provides the test maker should demonstrate its utility and worth as an attractive adjunct to the statistical measures.

Item difficulty. The difficulty of an item is the percentage of persons who answer the item correctly (percent pass). It is computed using the formula:

$$DIFF = \frac{C}{N} \times 100,$$

where:

C = number of students who answer the item correctly and
N = total number of students in the group.

The index is equivalent to the mean of the item (the proportion of students who got the item right) multiplied by 100.

Difficulty index values can range from 0 to 100. The higher the index, the easier the item. When all students answer the item correctly, the index equals 100; when all students respond incorrectly, the index is 0.

It is important that estimates of difficulty be obtained for both criterion groups. If difficulty levels are determined only for those students who have received the instruction, there is no way of knowing whether the students would have performed similarly without the instruction; for example, an easy item after instruction may have also been easy prior to instruction.

Item discrimination. The index of item discrimination measures the performance changes (pretest-posttest) or differences (uninstructed-instructed; incompetent-competent) between the criterion groups. This is consistent with the notion that a criterion-referenced test should maximize discrimination between groups and minimize discriminations among individuals within any one group (Glaser, 1963). Differences that occur between the groups are presumed to be attributable to the effect of instruction (Wedman, 1973, 1974a). The interpretation of the index in terms of the instructional program has prompted some proponents of the technique to refer to item discrimination as a measure of *instructional sensitivity*.

The vast array of indices found in the literature suggests that there is no single best method for estimating discrimination. Invoking the "law of parsi-

Table 5.4. Evaluation of Item Discrimination Indices
(*All were judged manually calculable and easily interpretable*)

Index	Statistic	Definition	Source	Comments
DIS_{PPD} (pretest-posttest difference)	Proportion	Proportion of students who answered item correctly on posttest minus proportion who answered it correctly on pretest	Cox and Vargas (1966); Tucker and Vargas (1974); Vargas (1969)	Range of values is -1.00 to $+1.00$. *Advantages:* Easy to compute and to interpret. *Disadvantage:* Index is not sensitive to individual performance changes, only to total group gain or loss.
DIS_{UIGD} (uninstructed-instructed group difference)	Proportion	Proportion of students in the instructed group who answered item correctly minus proportion in uninstructed group who answered it correctly	Klein and Kosecoff (1976); Levin and Marton (1971); Marton (1973)	Range of values is -1.00 to $+1.00$. Correlates .70 and .12 with DIS_{PPD} (Crehan, 1974; Wedman, 1974b). Relationship with DIS_{PPD} is contingent upon how closely instructed group resembles postinstruction group. *Advantages:* Same as DIS_{PPD}, plus index can be computed at the beginning of instruction. *Disadvantage:* Same as DIS_{PPD}, but index is a function of the data base rather than of the statistic.
DIS_{IG} (individual gain)	Proportion	Proportion of students who answered item incorrectly on pretest and correctly on posttest	Roudabush (1973)	A correction for guessing using the Marks and Noll (1967) procedure is optional. Range of values is -1.00 to $+1.00$ with correction and 0 to $+1.00$ without correction.

				Advantage: Measures directly the proportion of students who actually gained from the instruction. *Disadvantage:* Assumptions underlying the correction for guessing are questionable.
DIS_{NG} (net gain) or *ESI* (external sensitivity index)	Proportion	DIS_{IG} minus proportion of students who answered item incorrectly on both pretest and posttest	Kosecoff and Klein (1974)	Extends DIS_{IG} by considering the performance of all students who answered the item incorrectly on the pretest (i.e., only those students who could have gained from instruction). Correction for guessing is optional. Range of values is -1.00 to $+1.00$ with or without correction. *Advantages:* Represents net individual gains and losses as a result of the instruction. Yields more conservative values than preceding indices. *Disadvantage:* Same as DIS_{IG}.

mony" in this context, it is possible to extract four approaches that are conceptually and computationally simple yet statistically sound. These manually calculable indices are evaluated in Table 5.4 according to two criteria: (1) *practicability* in terms of the ease which the statistic could be computed and interpreted and (2) *meaningfulness* in the context of the test development process. The first two indices are based on the item difficulties expressed as proportions; the last two are based on the item response outcomes of the preinstruction-postinstruction measurements, i.e., incorrect-correct ($0 \rightarrow 1$) and incorrect-incorrect ($0 \rightarrow 0$). The former are the simplest in that they are computed directly from the difficulty levels (p values or item means) for the criterion groups; the latter are the most sensitive to pretest-posttest item score gains.

The choice of which of the four indices to use may be determined initially by the criterion groups available for the analysis. There is only one index for the case of uninstructed-instructed groups or incompetent-competent groups. Since discrimination is defined as the difference between two proportions or item means, the index can be applied to a variety of item formats. It can be used with multipoint items (0, 1, 2, . . .) as well as dichotomous items (0, 1). In fact, a test of the statistical significance of the index such as the t-test between independent samples drawn from independent populations and an estimate of effect size to evaluate the practical significance of the index are appropriate and can be quite informative (see, for example, Berk & DeGangi, 1983, chap. 4).

Among the three indices intended for preinstruction-postinstruction measurements, DIS_{PPD} appears to be the simplest, but it is insensitive to individual gains. That is, when a positive or negative value is obtained, the index does not indicate which students or how many students actually improved in performance; for example, some students may gain from the instruction even though the overall group performance may yield a negative index.

To overcome the limitations of the DIS_{PPD} index the specific individual performance changes from pretest to posttest need to be considered. There are four possible item response outcomes: (1) correct→correct ($1 \rightarrow 1$); (2) correct→incorrect ($1 \rightarrow 0$); (3) incorrect→correct ($0 \rightarrow 1$); (4) incorrect→incorrect ($0 \rightarrow 0$). A slight reorganization of the preinstruction-postinstruction scores on the five items from Table 5.2 can be used to demonstrate these four response trends. These trends are shown in Table 5.5.

The scores on item 5, for example, reveal that students 1, 3, 4, and 7 answered the item correctly on both occasions, students 2, 5, 9, and 10 improved their performance, and students 6 and 8 did not improve. Therefore, it is possible to determine the number of students who changed or did not change their status on the two measurements. The four outcomes can be summarized in a 2×2 contingency table, as presented in Table 5.6.

The DIS_{IG} and DIS_{NG} indices are derived from these outcomes. The former is based on the n_3 frequency or n_3/N; the latter employs both n_3 and n_4 or $(n_3 - n_4)/N$. Without incorporating the correction for guessing, DIS_{NG}

Table 5.5. Item Scores for Preinstruction-Postinstruction Measurements

	Item									
	1		2		3		4		5	
Student	Pre	Post	Pre	Post	Pre	Post	Pre	Post	Pre	Post
1	0	1	0	0	1	1	1	1	1	1
2	0	1	1	1	1	1	1	1	0	1
3	0	1	1	1	0	1	1	1	1	1
4	0	1	0	1	0	0	1	1	1	1
5	0	1	0	0	1	0	1	1	0	1
6	0	1	0	1	0	0	1	1	0	0
7	0	1	1	0	1	0	1	1	1	1
8	0	1	0	0	1	1	1	1	0	0
9	0	1	0	1	0	0	1	1	0	1
10	0	1	0	1	1	1	1	1	0	1

Table 5.6. Four Outcomes of Preinstruction-Postinstruction Measurements

		Posttest	
		Correct	Incorrect
Pretest	Correct	n_1	n_2
	Incorrect	n_3	n_4

Note: n_1 = Number of students who answered the item correctly on both pretest and posttest;
n_2 = Number of students who answered the item correctly on the pretest and incorrectly on the posttest;
n_3 = Number of students who answered the item incorrectly on the pretest and correctly on the posttest;
n_4 = Number of students who answered the item incorrectly on both pretest and posttest;
$N = n_1 + n_2 + n_3 + n_4$.

uses more information and possesses a greater range of possible values than DIS_{IG}. It is also statistically more sensitive than DIS_{PPD} since it takes into account the individual gains and losses resulting from the instruction rather than just the total group gain or loss. Overall, the DIS_{NG} index yields a more conservative estimate of item discrimination than either DIS_{PPD} or DIS_{IG}.

The foregoing measures of item discrimination provide evidence of item validity. In general, the intent of the test items to discriminate between students who have and students who have not been exposed to instruction on a set of objectives is concurrently validated with group performance on the items. The external criterion was informed teacher judgment about the students' success/failure in a well-defined segment of instruction. It served as the basis for selecting the criterion groups. Given the persistent validation problem of obtaining a satisfactory criterion of success, teacher judgment should prove adequate for estimating validity at the classroom level. Certainly a more reliable, comprehensive alternative would be desirable. At present, however, such an alternative does not seem to be available.

Since the empirical item validation process is inherent in the test item analysis, its interpretation is subject to the conditions under which the item analysis is performed. The fact that each analysis is uniquely related to the set of objectives, students' abilities and attributes, and instructional procedures characteristic of each classroom implies that *test items that are valid for one class may not be valid for other classes*. Test makers should not attempt to generalize the results beyond the context for which the items were originally designed.

In addition to the four discrimination indices just reviewed, 13 other indices were also identified in the literature. They are evaluated in Table 5.7 using the aforementioned criteria. These indices were judged less practical than the previous indices since they could not be computed efficiently without a computer program and, in some cases, very specialized programs. Hence, they may be of limited value and utility for teacher-made tests and for competency tests in many school districts. Most of the indices do not simply measure the extent to which an item differentiates between criterion groups. Additional factors are considered (e.g., interitem correlations) that tend to complicate the computation and interpretation of item discrimination. For this reason the indices are listed in order of increasing overall complexity. The major disadvantages or deficiencies of the indices are listed.

The last two indices described in the table deserve special attention. Both are derived from either the one-parameter (Rasch) or three-parameter logistic model. If a minimum competency test or other type of mastery test is developed at the district or state level using latent trait analysis, then one of these indices may be appropriate. The special requirements for computing the *z*-difference or item information function, such as sample size, model assumption, and computer program, suggest that this item analysis procedure should not be conducted in isolation. For example, test items that are calibrated on a Rasch scale should be evaluated statistically for characteristics other than dis-

Table 5.7. Evaluation of Item Discrimination Indices
(In order of increasing overall complexity)

Index	Statistic	Definition	Source	Comments
Maximum possible gain	Proportion	Proportion of maximum possible difference accounted for by obtained difference (DIS_{PPD}); extension of DIS_{PPD} index	Brennan (1974); Brennan and Stolurow (1971)	Correlates from .71 to .92 with DIS_{PPD} (Haladyna & Roid, 1981; Wedman, 1974b). *Advantage:* Takes into account potential for an item to demonstrate change from pretest to posttest. *Disadvantages:* Very susceptible to overemphasizing small gains. With high $DIFF_{Pre}$, a small gain in $DIFF_{Post}$ results in a large index; with low $DIFF_{Pre}$, the same gain results in a low index. Range of values and interpretation are different from most other indices.
B index	Proportion	Same as DIS_{UIGD}, but criterion groups are determined by mastery standard applied to one instructed group	Brennan (1972); Hsu (1971)	Equal to the sample value of Peirce's θ when item response is taken as the predictor and the upper-lower groups define the criterion (Harris & Wilcox, 1980). *Advantage:* Index requires only one test administration. *Disadvantages:* Decision validity of the mastery standard becomes a necessary condition for the validity of *B*. *B* cannot be computed when all or none of the students meet the standard. Interpretation of index values is rather unorthodox, i.e., ideal index is 0.

Table 5.7. *(continued)*

Index	Statistic	Definition	Source	Comments
ISI (internal sensitivity index)	Proportion	Proportion of students answering item correctly who were nonmasters on pretest and masters on posttest minus proportion answering item correctly who were nonmasters on both testings	Kosecoff and Klein (1974)	Intended to measure whether an item discriminates between students (correctly answering item) who were nonmasters before instruction and masters after instruction. Range of values is −1.00 to +1.00. *Disadvantages:* Decision validity of the mastery standard becomes a necessary condition for the validity of *ISI*. Index values are dependent on the number of students who answered the item correctly on the posttest; that is, an *ISI* of +1.00 can result when only one student who was a nonmaster on the pretest and master on the posttest answers the item correctly. Interpretation of such values can be confusing.
Combined groups item-total *r*	Correlation	Application of traditional item-total *r* to sample consisting of both criterion groups	Haladyna (1974); Helmstadter (1972)	Correlates from .64 to .86 with DIS_{PPD} (Bernknopf & Bashaw, 1976; Haladyna & Roid, 1981). *Advantage:* Index can be computed with most norm-referenced test item analysis programs, such as ITEMAN (Berk & Griesemer, 1976). *Disadvantage:* Index is not sensitive to which students are scoring high or low (masters or nonmasters), and therefore may not measure discrimination between designated criterion groups.

Item-criterion partial r	Correlation	Correlation of item scores with criterion group classification (0, 1), holding total score constant	Darlington and Bishop (1966); Millman (1974, pp. 369–370)	Several items per iteration method that takes into account interitem correlations is recommended item selection procedure; method is designed to maximize test validity. *Disadvantages:* Computation and item selection process are more complicated than that of preceding indices. Content and importance of objective being assessed are not considered. Index requires a specialized item analysis program or partial correlation program.
Change-item r	Correlation	Correlation of item change scores (-1, 0, $+1$) with total change scores from pretest to posttest	Saupe (1966)	Designed originally to maximize reliability of change scores (Stanley, 1967; Webster, 1957) or validity with a criterion variable (Webster, 1956). *Disadvantages:* Most complex correlational approach requiring computation of six different covariances. Variance restriction on pretest or posttest scores will limit index values. Content and importance of objective being assessed are not considered in the item selection process. Index requires a specialized item analysis program, such as CHANGE-SCORE (Berk & Griesemer, 1977).
r^2	Analysis of variance (or phi coefficient)	Proportion of total item variance explained by preinstruction-postinstruction measurements	Herbig (1975, 1976)	Based on analysis of variance with repeated measures from pretest-posttest item administrations. For a 2×2 table, r^2 equals ϕ^2 (Harris & Pearlman, 1977). *Disadvantage:* Inappropriate statistic for measuring instructional sensitivity. Indicates stability of item response rather than change in response from pretest to posttest (see Wilcox, 1977b).

Table 5.7. *(continued)*

Index	Statistic	Definition	Source	Comments
	Multiple regression	Stepwise regression analysis with items entered as predictor variables and criterion group classification serving as the criterion variable; analysis incorporates interitem correlations	Millman (1974, pp. 367–368)	*Disadvantages:* Analysis requires a relatively large sample size. There is no item discrimination index; selection is based on inclusion in prediction equation. Item regression coefficients are used to weight item scores with no consideration given to the objective the items measure.
3 Bayesian indices	Bayes' theorem	$B1$: Probability that a student has knowledge, given that the student gets the item right $B2$: Probability that the student does not have knowledge, given that the student gets the item wrong $B3$: Probability of making a right decision due to either mastery or nonmastery	Helmstadter (1974)	Probabilities for all three indices are estimated from pretest, posttest, and combined pretest-posttest item difficulties. Correlate moderately high with DIS_{PPD} and combined-groups item-total r (Haladyna & Roid, 1981). *Disadvantages:* Indices are highly influenced by difficulty and are unstable across samples (Haladyna & Roid, 1981). $B1$ tends to increase as $DIFF_{Pre}$ and $DIFF_{Post}$ approach 0; $B3$ is largest when the two *DIFF*s are very high or very low (ceiling and floor effects). They are statistically and computationally complex.
z-difference	One-parameter (Rasch) logistic model	Normalized difference between item difficulty estimates from criterion groups (instructed and uninstructed)	Haladyna and Roid (1981)	Derived from latent trait analyses of the test for two samples. Correlates .87 with DIS_{PPD} (Haladyna & Roid, 1981). *Advantages:* Conceptually analogous to DIS_{PPD}. Only one item parameter, difficulty, is estimated.

				Disadvantages: Index requires two test administrations. It is statistically and computationally complex, requiring the computer program BICAL (Wright & Mead, 1978). Assumptions of no guessing and equal discrimination are not practical. Relatively large sample sizes of 200 or more are needed. Interpretation of index values is complicated.
Item information function	One- or three-parameter logistic model	Discriminating power of an item around the latent mastery score, where the item must show a high probability of a successful response for latent continuum values to the right of the mastery score	Hambleton and de Gruijter (1983); van der Linden (1981); (see also Birnbaum, 1968; Lord, 1980, sects. 5.4 and 11.11; van Naerssen, 1977)	Derived from a latent trait analysis of the test. *Advantages:* Index requires only one test administration and uses only the population-invariant item characteristic curve. *Disadvantages:* Most conceptually, statistically, and computationally complex index. Analysis requires relatively large sample sizes of 500 or more (three-parameter) and a special computer program, such as BICAL (Wright & Mead, 1978) or LOGIST (Wood, Wingersky, & Lord, 1976). Index is dependent on the mastery standard. Interpretation of index values is complicated.

crimination power, especially sex and racial bias (see Ironson, 1982). A series of analyses of item difficulty, discrimination, and bias based on the same logistic model can serve to justify those requirements and the expenses involved as well as provide useful data to evaluate item validity.

Item homogeneity. Four statistics that relate to item-objective congruence are evaluated in Table 5.8. These homogeneity measures are intended to verify statistically that items congruent with an instructional objective behave similarly on a single testing or on repeated testings (pretest-posttest). The assumption that the items should yield identical difficulty indices or change scores is questionable. Such "homogeneity" may be unrealistic and, in fact, undesirable in cases where a variety of skills may define the content of an instructional objective that encompasses several weeks of instruction or longer. The generality-specificity of the objective will probably determine the meaningfulness of the homogeneity statistics.

Item bias. Beyond the judgmental review of item content described previously, there are statistical procedures test makers should consider to investigate item bias. These procedures are appropriate for minimum competency tests and other criterion-referenced tests constructed according to the mastery or domain-referenced model. Since extensive critiques of item bias statistics have been presented by Angoff (1982) and Ironson (1982), only a brief discussion of these statistics is given in this section. Interested readers should consult these references for details on the execution of the statistical analyses.

An item is biased if individuals with the same ability have an unequal probability of answering the item correctly as a function of their group membership (cf. Pine, 1977; Scheuneman, 1979). Operationally, bias is inferred from differences in performance between groups. The focus of an item bias study is to detect discrepancies in item performance between specific groups (e.g., males and females, blacks and whites, Hispanics and whites), while controlling for ability differences. There are three major alternative strategies a test maker can use to search for bias: (1) plan a study using a true experimental design with a statistic such as analysis of variance or analysis of covariance (see Schmeiser, 1982); (2) plan a study using a quasi-experimental design with matched groups or pseudogroups and a statistic such as analysis of variance (item-by-group interaction), arcsin differences, delta-decrement analysis, delta-plot method, item difficulty performance differences, or item-group correlation (see Angoff, 1982); (3) plan a study with a statistical method that accounts for ability differences such as a chi-square type technique, contingency table analysis (e.g., log-linear model), or one- or three-parameter logistic model (see Ironson, 1982). The first two strategies control the variable of ability differences in the design, whereas the third strategy adjusts for it statistically.

The research evidence clearly indicates that the different statistics yield different results (Burrill, 1982). The choice of a particular strategy and statistic should be governed by a balance of precision with practical constraints.

Table 5.8. Evaluation of Item Homogeneity Measures
(In order of increasing overall complexity)

Statistic	Definition	Source	Comments
Chi-square	Difficulty index of each item measuring an instructional objective is compared with the median difficulty of the set of items using chi-square	Pettie and Oosterhof (1976)	Modification of Popham's (1971) chi-square method for the case of one test administration (pretest only). *Advantage:* Method requires only one test administration. *Disadvantages:* Same as Popham's (1971) measure.
Chi-square	Pretest-posttest item frequencies are compared with median (expected) frequencies of a prototypic item using chi-square	Popham (1971)	Median values are derived from the frequencies of items measuring the same instructional objective. Items that behave differently from the prototype are considered for revision. *Disadvantages:* No critical value has been established for identifying abnormal items. Method is insensitive to the direction of the abnormality (Henrysson & Wedman, 1974).
—	Modification of Long's (1934) index of item homogeneity	Engel and LaDuca (1977)	Accounts for the relationship between item and total score. Conceptually similar to traditional index of item discrimination. *Disadvantages:* Interpretation of a zero index is unclear. Sampling distribution of statistic is unknown; therefore, no significance level can be determined. Item-total score phi coefficient has been the preferred approach (White & Saltz, 1957).
—	Average squared discrepancy index identifies items that yield inconsistent response patterns	Epstein (1977)	Based on the individual discrepancies of item scores from a student × item matrix. *Advantage:* Interpretation of index values seems meaningful. *Disadvantages:* Computation is more complicated than preceding measures. No critical value has been established for identifying "bad" items.

The recommendations of Angoff (1982) and Ironson (1982) can help guide this balancing and the final decision.

Judgmental Review

All of the preceding data gathering and analyses are conducted for one reason—to determine the quality or effectiveness of the test items. The characteristics that have been described are simply indicants of item quality. They must now be used to decide whether the items have functioned consistently with the purposes for which they were constructed. The decision regarding the status of an item may take three forms: (1) *accept* the item for inclusion in the final test; (2) *revise* the item before including it in the final test; or (3) *discard* the item and develop a new item to take its place. Criteria for assigning the items to these mutually exclusive categories have been proposed by Berk (1980). They are intended to guide the judgmental analysis of the statistical results.

Item selection criteria. The item characteristics that weigh most heavily in the item selection process are item-objective congruence, item difficulty, and item discrimination. They may be considered separately or jointly in arriving at one of the item status decisions. Guidelines for selecting items according to the three characteristics are outlined in Table 5.9. In general, an item that satisfies the criteria should be accepted. When an item does not meet one or more of the criteria, however, should it be retained, revised, or discarded? The decision depends largely upon the criterion and the degree to which it is not being met. A detailed discussion of the factors that influence each item decision follows.

Item-objective congruence. The role of item-objective congruence in item selection was clearly defined at the beginning of this chapter. It cannot be overemphasized that this characteristic is crucial to the effectiveness of the total test and the usefulness of the results. Irrespective of all other characteristics *an item that is not congruent with its objective should not be included on the test.* It would contribute nothing to the measurement of the objective.

Table 5.9. Guidelines for Selecting Criterion-referenced Test Items

Item Characteristic	Criterion	Index Value
Item-objective congruence	Matches objective being assessed	None[a]
Difficulty	Difficult for uninstructed group Easy for instructed group	0–50 70–100
Discrimination	Positively discriminates between criterion groups[b]	High positive[b]

[a] There is no index of item-objective congruence for teacher-made tests. An index of agreement among content specialists for tests developed at the district and state levels can be used (Rovinelli & Hambleton, 1977). For those applications the index values should be high positive.

[b] The actual value will vary according to the method used to compute discrimination.

In addition to accounting for the degree of correspondence between an item and an objective, two other factors related to the objective itself need to be considered in the item selection process: (1) the content of the objective and (2) the importance of the objective.

The level of cognition being assessed will frequently dictate the magnitude of the item statistics. Items that measure behavioral objectives requiring simple recall of factual content may exhibit large performance differences between the criterion groups. Such differences or gains should be anticipated. On the other hand, it would also be reasonable to expect that items that measure complex concepts or skills at the upper levels of the cognitive hierarchy may not demonstrate pronounced changes in individual or group performance as a result of the specific instructional treatment. The content of an objective, therefore, is often the primary determinant of the values one might expect for the statistical characteristics.

At this stage in test construction it might seem contradictory to perceive the importance of an objective as a factor. After all, if a teacher wrote the objective as part of the content domain specification, he or she must have deemed it important and worthy of appraisal. It has been recommended, however, that as long as an item reflects an *important attribute* it need not be discarded (Popham & Husek, 1969). While strictly following this advice would diminish the importance of the item statistics, there are a few instances where the ultimate selection decision might rest with this factor. It becomes an issue when an item is judged valid in relation to its objective, yet appears to be invalid according to the item statistics. What weight should be attached to the statistical evidence? Ideally the item should be valid in terms of both characteristics. If an item fails to discriminate between the criterion groups, it should be retained when one or both of the following conditions exist: (1) due to the specificity of the behavioral objective no other item could be written to measure it and (2) the low or zero discrimination index suggests that the item may validly measure the absence of an instructional effect (Cronbach, 1975). Alternatively, the item should be either revised or replaced with a new item.

Difficulty and discrimination indices. As item-objective congruence builds into the test the property of content validity, item discrimination builds into the test the property of decision validity (see Hambleton, chapter 8). This type of validity is reflected in the *accuracy* with which students are classified as masters and nonmasters of an instructional objective. Items with high positive discrimination indices improve the accuracy of these decisions. The relationship between the magnitude of the indices and classification decision accuracy is substantiated by the literature on personality test construction (Edwards, 1970, chap. 4; Wiggins, 1973, chap. 6). The research evidence suggests that selecting only the best discriminating items would produce the best test in terms of decision making. This approach, however, tends to maximize decision validity at the expense of content validity. Items associated with particular behavioral objectives would be discarded systematically if their discrimination indices were low or zero. Given the extent to which the content of an objective governs the values of the statistical characteristics, it would be inappropriate to evaluate item effectiveness purely on statistical grounds. A more comprehensive interpretation of index values should be considered. The interpretation that follows takes into account the objective being measured, the students being tested, and the instructional program that has occurred.

The difficulty and discrimination indices should represent at minimum a logical trend—the difficulty index should be lower for the uninstructed (or incompetent) students than for the instructed (or competent) students; this should be reflected in a positive discrimination index. The range of values shown in Table 5.9 should be viewed from the perspective of *what seems reasonable* relative to the content and importance of the behavioral objective, the abilities and background characteristics of the students, and the actual instruction to which the students were exposed. In each case a test maker needs to answer the question: Does this index express the performance on the item that was expected?

All items judged *acceptable* according to these criteria should be identified first. Those items that remain will require further analyses to determine their status. Pending the outcomes of those analyses, the items may be retained, revised, or discarded.

Where *minimum competencies* are being assessed, the preceding guidelines need to be modified. It is implicit in the measurement of minimum skills essential for success in a particular program or in life that the students in the criterion success group (competents) perform 100% on each item ($DIFF =$ 100%). Allowing for some margin of error (e.g., 5%) in the estimation of the difficulty index, *DIFF* values between 95 and 100% should be expected to validate adequately the items for this group. Students in the second criterion group (incompetents) chosen on the basis of their inability to demonstrate success on the objectives should perform less than 100% on each item ($DIFF <$ 100%). These *DIFF* values might be expected to vary between 0 and 94%. Given that possible range, the magnitude of the discrimination indices could also be expected to exhibit wide variability. This characteristic suggests that item discrimination may not be as meaningful a statistic in this application as it is in the typical uninstructed-instructed group comparison. Only a positive index is required. A restriction on the magnitude of the index would be inappropriate. In effect, the specific difficulty indices for each group provide sufficient information to judge whether the items function as they were intended.

The simplest analysis for determining acceptable items occurs in content domains where *no prior knowledge* on the objectives is possible. No uninstructed group data are gathered. This automatically reduces the interpretation of three indices down to one. Since $DIFF_U$ can be set equal to zero for each item, DIS_{UIGD} is computed only from the instructed group performance. It is, in fact, equivalent to $DIFF_I$. This index is all that a teacher needs to evaluate item quality. It should fall within the range of values specified in Table 5.9.

Item revision or elimination. Difficulty and discrimination indices that deviate from the prespecified criteria may be explained in terms of the item, the objective, or the instruction. While the first inclination is to revise or discard an item that does not meet the specifications, the most common explanation for a difficulty index that is higher or lower than expected relates to the objective being measured. Possible explanations for the different index values are presented in Table 5.10. The actions that are most appropriate for these conditions involve changes in the objectives and/or the instructional program, not in the item. The item would be *retained* until the changes were completed.

If the inconsistency between the expected and the actual index value is not attributable to the objective or instruction, the item itself must be scrutinized. The most conspicuous "flag" of a faulty item is a *negative discrimination index*. It may indicate ambiguity, two correct answers, or ineffective distractors. An examination of the internal structure of the item coupled with the information obtained from the students' reviews will often reveal the part(s) that should be *revised*. When the item is in multiple-choice format, a quantitative analysis of each response choice should be considered. This type of analysis is described in the next section.

In the case of an item that possesses no visible flaws yet fails to yield statistical indices that are acceptable, it is recommended that the item be *discarded* and that a new item be written to replace it. However, this procedure should be viewed as a last resort. It is generally much easier to revise an item than to construct a new one. The new item will also be "untested." It is imperative that an item that must be eliminated be replaced. If it is not, the measure-

Table 5.10. Explanations and Actions for Items with Unexpected Statistical Outcomes

Index	Index Value	Possible Explanation	Suggested Action
$DIFF_{U/PRE}$	Much higher than expected (e.g., expected = 20%; actual = 45%)	Objective may have been taught previously	Write a higher level objective/relocate objective earlier in program
$DIFF_{I/POST}$	Much lower than expected (e.g., expected = 80%; actual = 50%)	Objective may be too difficult or complex	Write a lower level objective/relocate objective later in program
		Instruction may have been ineffective	Correct deficiencies in the instruction with different emphases, new materials, or other modifications
DIS	Much lower than expected	One or a combination of the above explanations	One or a combination of the above actions

ment of the respective instructional objective as well as the overall content validity of the test are weakened.

Items with difficulty and discrimination indices that do not conform to the "guidelines" may occur in the development of teacher-made tests due to the imprecision of the results. The objectives, students, and instructional techniques vary from one classroom to another. In addition, the relatively small number of students commonly available for the item analysis affects the stability of the indices. An analysis conducted on one occasion may yield data quite different from an analysis conducted on another occasion.

In view of these factors it would be not only unrealistic but also rather imperceptive to recommend that teachers strive for items with 0% (uninstructed) and 100% (instructed) difficulty levels and +1.00 discrimination indices. The sources of variability noted herein will generally preclude attainment of these statistical properties. Furthermore, it is incorrect to assume that the students' performance on items measuring objectives at varying levels of complexity should be the same. *The ideal or desired statistical outcomes need not be similar for all items.*

For criterion-referenced tests constructed at the district or state level, the larger sample sizes typically selected for the criterion groups permit the computation of reliable estimates of difficulty and discrimination. The interpretation of the indices, however, may be similar to that of teacher-made tests, depending on the purpose of the test and the decisions for which the scores will be used. For example, the item analysis results of a minimum competency test that is to be used in deciding which students are to receive a high school diploma should be evaluated according to the guidelines given previously for interpreting the item statistics of teacher-made minimum competency tests. For other competency test item data, test makers can use the rules of thumb presented in Table 5.9 or, if the items were calibrated based on the one- or three-parameter logistic model, the criteria suggested by van der Linden (1981).

Choice Response Analyses

All of the reviews and procedures described thus far in the item analysis process have been based on whole-item statistics such as *DIFF* and *DIS* indices. In order to provide specific directions for item revision and other types of analysis, however, it is necessary to break down an item into its component parts. For multiple-choice items, the responses to the choices by different groups of students can be especially informative. Patterns of responses to the correct answer and to the distractors are valuable for three purposes: (1) to guide the revision of faulty items, (2) to assess the sensitivity of the distractors to instruction, and (3) to discern whether true item bias is present and, if it is, to identify the distractors that may be the source of that bias.

Item revision or elimination. When the informal student feedback and/or statistical analyses suggest that a multiple-choice format item is faulty, an analysis of its internal structure can provide insight into what needs to be revised. The most common types of error in the stem and answer choices are often detected by the students and others who review the items. In order to identify flaws that may not readily be apparent a more rigorous analysis based on the student performance data is required. This analysis is particularly appropriate for items yielding low positive, zero, or negative discrimination indices.

The analysis involves the visual inspection of the students' responses to each choice. Both criterion groups are employed to determine whether the distractors are functioning properly. The criteria for evaluating a choice response pattern are as follows:

1. Each distractor should be selected by more students in the uninstructed (or incompetent) group than in the instructed (or competent) group.
2. At least a few uninstructed (or incompetent) students (5–10%) should choose each distractor.
3. No distractor should receive as many responses by the instructed (or competent) group as the correct answer.

If any of these patterns is not observed, it is likely that particular distractors are ambiguous or implausible. Within a given item one or more flaws may be identified. Depending upon the nature of the error(s), either revision or replacement of the specific part is generally indicated. A judgment concerning the amount of modification may also dictate that a completely new item be written. As noted previously, this should be considered only as a last resort. Data would than have to be gathered on the new item to assure that it functions properly.

The procedures described here are applicable to most test items expressed in a multiple-choice format, including multiple-choice cloze and matching items as well as the traditional three- to five-choice item. The data formats for the analyses presented in the tables can easily be adapted to matching items.

The process of analyzing the choice response patterns of multiple-choice items is illustrated for preinstruction-postinstruction measurements, uninstructed-instructed groups, and competent-incompetent groups. Three different sets of item data from two mastery tests and one minimum competency test are presented.

The pretest and posttest responses of 20 tenth-grade students to one item from a criterion-referenced biology test are displayed in Table 5.11. The item has a DIS_{PPD} index of +.05. The teacher felt this value was inadequate in terms of the objective being measured. Of the 20 students tested, essentially just as many answered the item correctly (B) before the instruction as after the instruction. An examination of the three distractors (A, C, and D) indicates that the desired response pattern is not consistently occurring. Distractor A appears to be marginally effective, since only one more student selected it prior to instruction than after instruction. More conspicuous is the fact that so many students in each group chose distractor C. This response suggests that the instructed students may have misread the question or that C is possi-

Table 5.11. Illustrative Preinstruction-Postinstruction Item Data for Choice Response Analysis

Item	Group	Response Choice				Omits	Total
		A	B[a]	C	D		
10	Postinstruction	2	10	8	0	0	20
	Preinstruction	3	9	8	0	0	20
	Total	5	19	16	0	0	40

[a] Correct answer.

bly a second correct answer. The latter would seem most likely. Therefore, distractor C should be revised. Distractor D is completely ineffective since it attracted no one. Consequently the original four-choice item reduces to a three-choice item. Distractor D should be replaced with a distractor that will be plausible to the preinstruction students. In summary, the response analysis of this item indicates that the item can be improved by revising distractor C and replacing distractor D.

In the next example, 20 fifth-grade students serve as the uninstructed group and 15 sixth-grade students served as the instructed group. The item has been selected from a vocabulary test. The choice responses are presented in Table 5.12. The item has a DIS_{UIGD} index of $-.15$. This negative value is evident from the proportionately greater number of students in the uninstructed group than in the instructed group who answered correctly (D). Both distractors B and C appear to be functioning effectively. However, more students in each group chose C than any other choice, including the correct answer. This response pattern along with the negative trend characteristic of choices A and D suggest that the item stem may be ambiguous. Inconsistent responses to three of the four choices indicate that a new item should be written to measure the objective.

A third example of choice response analysis is the response data for a life skills item on a minimum competency test. These data, given in Table 5.13,

Table 5.12. Illustrative Uninstructed-Instructed Groups Item Data for Choice Response Analysis

Item	Group	Response Choice				Omits	Total
		A	B	C	D[a]		
14	Instructed	4	2	6	3	0	15
	Uninstructed	1	4	8	7	0	20
	Total	5	6	14	10	0	35

[a] Correct answer.

represent the performances of 95 service workers (e.g., custodians, cooks, truck drivers) who comprised the occupational group of adults judged to possess survival-level skills in reading and mathematics (competents) and of 47 unemployed adults who were considered to be nonsurvivors (incompetents). The item has a *DIS* index of +.31 and *DIFF* indices of 93% and 62% for the competent and incompetent groups, respectively. The performance of the competents was judged to be less than desirable according to the criteria for acceptable minimum competency test items. An examination of the responses in the table indicates that distractors C and E are ineffective for the incompetents. One or both distractors should be replaced with plausible ones. Although better distractors will probably not affect markedly the responses of the competents, it is inefficient and psychometrically unsound to use nonfunctioning choices in an item. Depending on the structural quality of the revised item, a decision can then be made to retain or discard the item. The current item statistics point toward including the item in the final version of the test.

Error-shift analysis. The choice responses to another item on the biology test mentioned in the first example are presented in Table 5.14. However, only the distribution of *wrong answers* is given for each measurement, and the numbers are the percentages of students picking the distractors. These data furnish the information necessary to perform an error-shift analysis. Accord-

Table 5.13. Illustrative Competent-Incompetent Groups Item Data for Choice Response Analysis

		Response Choice						
Item	Group	A[a]	B	C	D	E	Omits	Total
56	Competent	88	3	0	4	0	0	95
	Incompetent	29	8	1	6	3	0	47
	Total	117	11	1	10	3	0	142

[a] Correct answer.

Table 5.14. Illustrative Preinstruction-Postinstruction Item Data (percentage form) for Error-shift Analysis

		Response Choice			
Item	Group	A	B	C[a]	D
26	Preinstruction	31	23	—	46
	Postinstruction	24	58	—	18

[a] Correct answer.

ing to Donlon (1982), the purpose of this analysis to determine whether a shift in the patterns of wrong answers between pretesting and posttesting is related to the intervening instruction and/or to learner problems. In other words, do the different distractors chosen on the two occasions indicate consequences of instruction not revealed by the whole-item instructional sensitivity index (*DIS*)? For example, the percentage responses for item 26 in the table show that there has been a shift in the most popular wrong answer, from distractor D with 46% response on the pretest to distractor B with 58% response on the posttest (i.e., error shift). This shift suggests that the instruction on the corresponding objective diminished the likelihood of A and D responses, while increasing the relative likelihood of a B response. Considering a DIS_{PPD} index of +.43, it can be inferred that distractors B and D are just as sensitive to instruction as the correct answer (C). The popularity of choice B, in particular, may be attributed either to some aspect of the instruction that is actually encouraging students to make that response or to some aspect that fails to reach those students who enter instruction believing in B.

To conduct an error-shift analysis the distractor response data from preinstruction-postinstruction measurements must first be collected in frequency form for all of the items on a criterion-referenced test. Second, it is recommended that district or state level tests makers apply an appropriate test of significance such as chi-square or another index (see Harris & Pearlman, 1977) to confirm that any identified error shift is not a chance occurrence. Finally, the frequencies should be converted to percentages and displayed in a format similar to Table 5.14. As the preceding example illustrates, the percentage patterns can be quite informative to classroom teachers. However, teachers should not attempt to compute manually the frequencies and percentages. Their role should be to interpret the output in terms of instruction. If the data are readily available from school-based microcomputer programs or other tools, then the wrong answer responses can be studied.

The value of error-shift analysis should be evident. It provides insight into the parts of the item, beyond the correct answer, that are affected by instruction. The consequences deduced can be used to modify the instruction or to revise the distractors so that they are consistent with those consequences.

A posteriori analysis for bias. As a follow-up analysis to an item bias study, it is necessary to examine each item detected by the statistical procedure. The statistical methods suggested in a previous section of the chapter are intended to flag items that exhibit performance discrepancies between the sexes and between racial or ethnic subgroups. Further item scrutiny is required to answer these questions: What contributed to the performance discrepancy? Why did the discrepancy occur? Is the item or some part of it truly biased against one group or was the discrepancy in performance a statistical artifact? Can the source of the bias be eliminated?

These questions indicate that "bias" can only be inferred from the statistical results and a subsequent judgmental or logical analysis of the items. It is not an objectively measured component of an item. Scheuneman (1982) has hypothesized four features of items or tests that can produce performance discrepancies in an item bias study: "(1) Flaws that may result from inadequacies or ambiguities of the test instructions, the item stem, the keyed response, or one of the distractors; (2) flaws that cause one or more of the options of an item (correct or incorrect) to be differentially attractive to members of different groups; (3) item features that reflect real differences between groups other than ethnicity; and (4) item features that directly reflect group differences in cultural characteristics or values" (p. 195).

The first category of flaws was addressed earlier in the item analysis process by eliciting student feedback on the items and test structure and by the choice response analysis to guide item revision. The second category, however, is derived from a different data base, the choice responses of the sexes or of ethnic subgroups, not of the criterion mastery groups. A distractor analysis using groups of, for example, males and females or blacks and whites can reveal whether one group is attracted to a particular distractor and another group is drawn to other distractors.

Several statistical procedures for the analysis of distractors have been proposed in an attempt to identify not only biased items, but also the source of the bias, so that the item may be revised to eliminate the bias, instead of being discarded. Since the procedures have been described in detail by Scheuneman (1982), only one method recommended by Veale and Foreman (1983) is presented here. The response data structure and statistical analysis for their method are analogous to those of the error-shift analysis. An example is shown in Table 5.15.

For the two items in the table, choice response frequencies were tallied for each group, a chi-square test of significance was computed for the group × response choice (2 × 3) contingency table, and then the frequencies were expressed as percentages of individuals choosing each wrong answer. An additional statistic, Cramer's *V*, could also be used to provide a measure of effect

Table 5.15. Illustrative Racial Group Item Data (percentage form) for Distractor Analysis of Bias

		Response Choice				
Item	Group	A	B	C	D[a]	*DIFF*
17 (*unbiased*)[b]	black	11	14	75	—	45
	white	13	7	80	—	60
32 (*biased*)[c]	black	21	61	18	—	33
	white	40	57	3	—	70

Source: Adapted from Scheuneman (1982, p. 190, Table 7.2).
[a] Correct answer.
[b] $\chi^2 = 4.92$ (*n.s.*).
[c] $\chi^2 = 28.73$ ($p < .01$).

size or "degree of cultural variation" (Scheuneman, 1982, p. 190). The percentage response patterns along with the chi-square values are reported in Table 5.15. The results for item 17 indicate relatively consistent distractor attractiveness for both blacks and whites, which is confirmed by a nonsignificant chi-square. In contrast to this apparently unbiased item are the differing patterns of distractor attractiveness in item 32. These patterns yielded a significant chi-square. Distractor C seems to be considerably more attractive to blacks than to whites, although distractor B is pulling more blacks away from the correct answer (D). An examination of these choices in conjunction with the correct responses should suggest the specific type of item revision needed.

The other item features mentioned by Scheuneman (1982) that can reflect group differences can be identified only by a carefully planned, systematic item review. She even cautions against too great a reliance on distractor data because they *can* be misleading. The complex and time-consuming tasks involved in an a posteriori analysis should not be underestimated. Scheuneman's (1982) nuts-and-bolts description of one phase of the analysis illustrates this complexity:

> Examine the items, singly or in groups, looking for item flaws and clues suggesting plausible explanations for the differences found and using the conventional item statistics where they may be helpful. Try to find patterns of differences that may support or disprove some of the possible explanations or that may suggest new hypotheses concerning the differences. Do not expect to find an explanation or hypothesis to account for all items. Remember that it is almost certain that some items have been incorrectly classified as biased, and the proportion of such items can be quite high depending on sample size and the decision rule(s) used for selecting biased items. (p. 196)

SUGGESTIONS FOR FUTURE RESEARCH

The preceding review of the judgmental and statistical procedures that can be used in the item analysis process indicates that the technology for assessing the quality/effectiveness/validity of criterion-referenced test items has been established. It is applicable to tests developed at the classroom, district, and state levels. While there is a need for further research on a few technical issues, a firm conceptual foundation and substantial evidence exist to support the use of the various methodologies for current practices.

The specific aspects of item analysis that require additional study are delineated as follows:

1. *Statistical validation of items for the special case of "no prior knowledge."* One of the most obvious limitations of the criterion-groups validation model is where no uninstructed group data can be obtained due to the nature of the content domain. When a group of students cannot be expected to have any prior knowledge related to a particular set of objectives, the computation and interpretation of item discrimination lose

meaning. The application of item discrimination indices and item selection criteria under those circumstances requires clarification.

2. *Relationship between preinstruction-postinstruction discrimination indices*. The numerous indices based on preinstruction-postinstruction measurements (see Tables 5.5 and 5.7) should be compared to determine how they ultimately affect the final selection of items. An empirical evaluation of the simple and complex statistics would also be of value in assessing their relative sensitivity to performance gains and instructional treatments (e.g., Subkoviak & Harris, 1984).
3. *Relationship between DIS_{PPD} and DIS based on independent samples*. The relationship between the item discrimination indices estimated from the alternative criterion-group selection procedures (i.e., preinstruction-postinstruction, uninstructed-instructed, contrasting groups) needs to be investigated. The conflicting results of the few previous studies suggest that the indices may be very different, depending on the composition of the mastery group.
4. *Use of occupational groups of adults to validate minimum competency test items*. When survival or life skills in reading, mathematics, and writing are measured, occupational groups of "survivors" could be chosen to study the validity of the items. This population has rarely been considered in this context. Research should be conducted to explore the utility and meaningfulness of selecting occupational groups to validate minimum competency tests.
5. *Relationship between item discrimination and classification accuracy and consistency*. There is no evidence using criterion-referenced item and test data regarding the relationship between item discrimination and the selection and validation of a cut-off score based on the criterion groups model. Only studies by Subkoviak and Harwell (1983) and Smith (1978) have examined the effect of item selection on one type of reliability. It is important to appraise how the magnitude of the discrimination indices affects the accuracy and consistency of mastery-nonmastery classification decisions.
6. *Role of item homogeneity indices in item analysis*. The homogeneity of items constructed from domain specifications is often perceived as a highly desirable characteristic. It is, in fact, claimed to be one of the major benefits to result from operationally defining a content domain. Two basic statistical approaches are recommended: (1) compute an item statistic from among those listed in Table 5.8 and compare performance on one item with performance on the set of items, and (2) analyze the performance on the set of items using analysis of variance procedures to determine whether the set is homogeneous (e.g., Hively, Patterson, & Page, 1968; Macready & Merwin, 1973). The use of the former approach in an item analysis, however, is not clear. The magnitude of the proposed indices tends to fluctuate from item to item as a function of the generality-

specificity of the objective from which the items were generated. How should a homogeneity index be incorporated into the item selection process? Should item validity be assessed in terms of three statistics: difficulty, discrimination, and homogeneity? While further insight in an attempt to resolve this confusion might accompany additional research efforts, it is also important to question whether that line of research is productive and meaningful. Perhaps Nitko's (1974) reflections on this point are worth pondering:

> The insistence on homogeneity . . . is too sweeping and is poor psychology. It leads to statistical techniques being used to drive the definition of performance domains. There is no logical basis for contending *a priori* that any domain of performance identified as instructionally relevant ought to be homogeneous (cf. Cronbach, 1971). Homogeneity should be viewed as a question for empirical experimentation and item performance theory (cf. Bormuth, 1970) and would probably vary with the target population and the class of behaviors under consideration. (p. 66)

7. *Item analysis computer programs*. There are no item analysis programs available that compute the indices appropriate for criterion-referenced tests. Comprehensive programs for large computer machines as well as microcomputers are essential to facilitate the proper construction of mastery and minimum competency tests. Two types of programs should be considered: one would compute difficulty indices for criterion groups, a variety of discrimination indices, and choice response tables for item revision, error-shift analysis, and distractor analysis of bias; a second type would compute the statistics for a latent trait item analysis, including difficulty and discrimination indices, bias statistics, and distractor analysis data. Special attention should be given to reporting the statistical indices in a form that is interpretable to teachers and other practitioners who will be using the results.

GUIDELINES FOR PRACTITIONERS

The framework for executing a criterion-referenced test item analysis proposed in this chapter consisted of four phases: (1) a judgmental review, (2) statistical analyses, (3) a judgmental review (of the statistical results), and (4) choice response analyses. The specific procedures that need to be considered in each phase differ according to the type of test being developed and the decisions for which the scores will be used. A basic distinction was drawn between mastery tests used for classroom level instructional decisions and competency tests used for grade level decisions of promotion and graduation. The test makers involved tend to be teachers and district/state level specialists, respectively. A summary of the guidelines offered throughout the chapter is presented next for each of these categories of practitioner. A section directed at test publishers and consulting firms who have been active in the production of criterion-referenced tests concludes the chapter.

Classroom Teachers

The following is the step-by-step procedure by which a teacher should conduct an item analysis for a mastery test:

1. Review the items in relation to their instructional and behavioral objectives to determine whether they are valid measures of these objectives. Item-objective congruence should be evaluated according to three criteria: (1) behavior, (2) content, and (3) hierarchical classification. The greatest emphasis should be placed on the third criterion. Any discrepancies that occur in the course of the review should be corrected.
2. Review the items for content bias using a checklist such as the one in Table 5.1. Any language in an item that is stereotypic, culture specific, or offensive to a particular sex or a racial or ethnic subpopulation should be removed. Attention should also be given to the characteristics of the persons and the situations described in the items to assure fair representation in the work roles and life styles of various groups, especially females and minorities.
3. Define the criterion of success for the set of items constructed. A teacher should select one class for preinstruction-postinstruction measurements or one uninstructed and one instructed class.
4. Administer the test to the criterion groups.
5. Immediately following the administration to the instructed group, conduct a class discussion of the items and test structure. Use the student feedback to improve the test.
6. Score the items (0, 1) for each student in the two groups and assemble the data into two student × item matrices (see Tables 5.2 and 5.3).
7. Compute the difficulty index of each item for both uninstructed and instructed groups.
8. Compute the discrimination index for each item. DIS_{PPD}, DIS_{IG}, or DIS_{NG} can be used for preinstruction-postinstruction measurements; DIS_{UIGD} can be used for uninstructed-instructed groups (see Table 5.4).
9. Summarize the three item statistics for each item into three lists. A numerical scheme identifying the behavioral objectives to which the items are coded should also be included. An exemplary format is given in Table 5.16.
10. Evaluate the extent to which the items discriminate between masters and nonmasters of each instructional objective. This assessment of item validity should be based on the "guidelines" presented in Table 5.9. Good judgment and common sense are an integral part of the assessment in interpreting the item difficulty and discrimination indices in terms of the objective being measured, the students for whom the test was designed, and the instructional program that has occurred. If the statistical item characteristics seem reasonable in view of these considerations, select the item. Items that are questionable should be sub-

Table 5.16. Exemplary Format for Assembling Item Analysis Results

Objective	Item	$DIFF_I$	$DIFF_U$	DIS_{UIGD}
1.1	1	100	58	.42
1.1	2	100	54	.46
1.2	3	91	58	.33
1.2	4	86	33	.53
1.3	5	100	33	.67
1.3	6	96	17	.79
1.3	7	86	21	.65
1.3	8	82	8	.74
2.2	9	100	13	.87
2.2	10	100	8	.92
.	.	.	.	.
.	.	.	.	.

jected to further analysis. This may result in their retention, revision, or elimination.

11. Conduct a choice response analysis of those questionable items in multiple-choice format that are suspected of having internal flaws (see Tables 5.11 and 5.12). This analysis can reveal the specific defects and guide the item revision process.
12. Assemble the items into the final test. All improvements and changes undertaken as a result of the item validation should be incorporated into this version.

District and State Level Test Makers

Certain modifications in the proceding 12 steps are required for criterion-referenced tests constructed at the district and state levels. They are a function of the skills being measured, the decisions to be made with the scores, and the expertise and development resources (e.g., computer support) that may be available. The modifications described next are applicable to competency tests used for decisions about grade level promotion and high school graduation:

1. The judgmental review of the items for item-objective congruence and content bias should be performed by specially formed panels. Appropriate content specialists should serve on the panel that assesses congruence; professional educators and lay persons representative of the different subpopulations (e.g., males, females, blacks, whites, Hispanics) should compose the panel that evaluates the items for bias.
2. In defining the criterion of competence for the measurement of academic and life skills, the contrasting-groups approach should be employed. Attention should be given to sample size requirements and the base rate for mastery of the skills.

3. The item statistics of difficulty and discrimination may be the same as those used for classroom level mastery tests, or the latent trait (one- or three-parameter) indices for preinstruction-postinstruction measurements can be computed (see Table 5.7). The latter choice presumes that the test items are being calibrated according to one of the logistic models and that the necessary computer programs are available.
4. An item bias study should be planned using a true experimental design, quasi-experimental design, or a statistical method that accounts for ability differences between groups (see Angoff, 1982; Ironson, 1982; Schmeiser, 1982).
5. Choice response analyses should be considered for both competency groups and for the sexes and/or the ethnic groups involved in the statistical item bias study. The analyses should focus on the revision or elimination of faulty and biased items. If preinstruction-postinstruction measurement data were collected for the academic skills items, then an error-shift analysis should also be performed and the results should be compared with the whole-item instructional sensitivity statistics (e.g., DIS_{PPD}).

Test Publishers

Given the role that test publishers and educational consulting firms have assumed in recent years in the development of criterion-referenced tests, all of the recommendations in the preceding two sections are just as applicable to their technical staff members. A critical review of published mastery testing programs by Hambleton and Eignor (1978) indicated that the item analysis procedures described in this chapter were virtually ignored in the construction of the tests. Attention must be devoted to these procedures in order to provide evidence that the items are technically adequate. In addition, publishers and consulting firms that contract with school districts and state departments of education to build competency tests are urged to consider seriously the various judgmental and statistical procedures, particularly those that relate to item bias.

REFERENCES

Angoff, W. H. Use of difficulty and discrimination indices for detecting item bias. In R. A. Berk (Ed.), *Handbook of methods for detecting test bias*. Baltimore, MD: Johns Hopkins University Press, 1982. Pp. 96–116.

Berk, R. A. Determination of optimal cutting scores in criterion-referenced measurement. *Journal of Experimental Education*, 1976, *45*, 4–9.

Berk, R. A. A consumers' guide to criterion-referenced test item statistics. *NCME Measurement in Education*, 1978, *9*, 1–8.

Berk, R. A. Item analysis. In R. A. Berk (Ed.), *Criterion-referenced measurement: The state of the art*. Baltimore, MD: Johns Hopkins University Press, 1980. Pp. 49–79.

Berk, R. A. Minimum competency testing: Status and potential. In B. S. Plake & J.

C. Witt (Eds.), *Future directions of testing and assessment*. Hillsdale, NJ: Erlbaum, in press.

Berk, R. A., & DeGangi, G. A. *DeGangi-Berk Test of Sensory Integration: Manual.* Los Angeles: Western Psychological Services, 1983.

Berk, R. A., & Griesemer, H. A. ITEMAN: An item analysis program for tests, questionnaires, and scales. *Educational and Psychological Measurement*, 1976, *36*, 189-191.

Berk, R. A., & Griesemer, H. A. Change-score item and reliability analyses program. *Applied Psychological Measurement*, 1977, *1*, 40.

Bernknopf, S., & Bashaw, W. L. *An investigation of criterion-referenced tests under different conditions of sample variability and item homogeneity.* Paper presented at the annual meeting of the American Educational Research Association, San Francisco, April 1976.

Birnbaum, A. Some latent trait models and their use in inferring an examinee's ability. In F. M. Lord & M. R. Novick, *Statistical theories of mental test scores*. Reading, MA: Addison-Wesley, 1968. Pp. 397-422.

Block, J. H. (Ed.). *Mastery learning: Theory and practice.* New York: Holt, Rinehart and Winston, 1971.

Block, J. H., & Burns, R. B. Mastery learning. In L. S. Shulman (Ed.), *Review of Research in Education* (Vol. 4). Itasca, IL: Peacock, 1976.

Bormuth, J. R. *On the theory of achievement test items.* Chicago: University of Chicago Press, 1970.

Brennan, R. L. A generalized upper-lower item discrimination index. *Educational and Psychological Measurement*, 1972, *32*, 289-303.

Brennan, R. L. *The evaluation of mastery test items* (Final Report, Project No. 2B118). Washington, DC: National Center for Educational Research and Development, U.S. Office of Education, 1974.

Brennan, R. L., & Stolurow, L. M. *An empirical decision process for formative evaluation.* Paper presented at the annual meeting of the American Educational Research Association, New York, February 1971.

Brown, S. *What do they know? A review of criterion-referenced assessment.* Edinburgh, Scotland: Scottish Education Department, 1980.

Burrill, L. E. Comparative studies of item bias methods. In R. A. Berk (Ed.), *Handbook of methods for detecting test bias.* Baltimore, MD: Johns Hopkins University Press, 1982. Pp. 161-179.

Carroll, J. B. A model of school learning. *Teachers College Record*, 1963, *64*, 723-733.

Carroll, J. B. Problems of measurement related to the concept of learning for mastery. *Educational Horizons*, 1970, *48*, 71-80.

Christie, S. G., & Casey, J. A. Heading off legal challenges to local minimum competency programs. *Educational Evaluation and Policy Analysis*, 1983, *5*, 31-42.

Cox, R. C., & Vargas, J. S. *A comparison of item selection techniques for norm-referenced and criterion-referenced tests.* Paper presented at the annual meeting of the National Council on Measurement in Education, Chicago, February 1966.

Crehan, K. D. Item analysis for teacher-made mastery tests. *Journal of Educational Measurement*, 1974, *11*, 255-262.

Cronbach, L. J. Test validation. In R. L. Thorndike (Ed.), *Educational measurement* (2nd ed). Washington, DC: American Council on Education, 1971. Pp. 443-507.

Cronbach, L. J. Comment: Dissent from Carver. *American Psychologist*, 1975, *30*, 602-603.

Cronbach, L. J., & Meehl, P. E. Construct validity in psychological tests. *Psychological Bulletin*, 1955, *52*, 281-302.

Dahl, T. A. *The measurement of congruence between learning objectives and test items.* Unpublished doctoral dissertation, University of California, Los Angeles, 1971.

Darlington, R. B., & Bishop, C. H. Increasing test validity by considering inter-item correlations. *Journal of Applied Psychology*, 1966, *50*, 322-330.

Donlon, T. F. *"Error-shift" measures of sensitivity to instruction.* Paper presented at the annual meeting of the National Council on Measurement in Education, New York, March 1982.

Edwards, A. L. *The measurement of personality traits by scales and inventories.* New York: Holt, Rinehart and Winston, 1970.

Engel, J. D., & LaDuca, A. *Validity issues in the development of criterion-referenced tests.* Paper presented at the annual meeting of the National Council on Measurement in Education, New York, April 1977.

Epstein, K. I. *Predictive sample reuse and application for criterion-referenced test item analysis.* Paper presented at the annual meeting of the American Educational Research Association, New York, April 1977.

Glaser, R. Instructional technology and the measurement of learning outcomes: Some questions. *American Psychologist*, 1963, *18*, 519-521.

Glaser, R., & Nitko, A. J. Measurement in learning and instruction. In R. L. Thorndike (Ed.), *Educational measurement* (2nd ed.). Washington, DC: American Council on Education, 1971. Pp. 625-670.

Green, D. R., Coffman, W. E., Lenke, J. M., Raju, N. S., Handrick, F. A., Loyd, B. H., Carlton, S. T., & Marco, G. L. Methods used by test publishers to "debias" standardized tests. In R. A. Berk (Ed.), *Handbook of methods for detecting test bias*. Baltimore, MD: Johns Hopkins University Press, 1982. Pp. 228-313.

Haladyna, T. M. Effects of different samples on item and test characteristics of criterion-referenced tests. *Journal of Educational Measurement*, 1974, *11*, 93-99.

Haladyna, T. M., & Roid, G. H. The role of instructional sensitivity in the empirical review of criterion-referenced test items. *Journal of Educational Measurement*, 1981, *18*, 39-53.

Haladyna, T. M., & Roid, G. H. A comparison of two approaches to criterion-referenced test construction. *Journal of Educational Measurement*, 1983, *20*, 271-282.

Hambleton, R. K. *Review methods for criterion-referenced test items.* Paper presented at the annual meeting of the American Educational Research Association, Boston, April 1980. (a)

Hambleton, R. K. Test score validity and standard-setting methods. In R. A. Berk (Ed.), *Criterion-referenced measurement: The state of the art.* Baltimore, MD: Johns Hopkins University Press, 1980. Pp. 80-123. (b)

Hambleton, R. K., & de Gruijter, D. N. M. Application of item response models to criterion-referenced test item selection. *Journal of Educational Measurement*, 1983, *20*, 355-367.

Hambleton, R. K., & Eignor, D. R. Guidelines for evaluating criterion-referenced tests and test manuals. *Journal of Educational Measurement*, 1978, *15*, 321-327.

Hambleton, R. K., Swaminathan, H., Algina, J., & Coulson, D. B. Criterion-referenced testing and measurement: A review of technical issues and developments. *Review of Educational Research*, 1978, *48*, 1-47.

Harris, C. W., & Pearlman, A. P. Conventional significance tests and indices of agreement or association. In C. W. Harris, A. P. Pearlman, & R. R. Wilcox (Eds.), *Achievement test items: Methods of study* (CSE Monograph Series in Evaluation, No. 6). Los Angeles: Center for the Study of Evaluation, University of California, 1977. Pp. 17-44.

Harris, C. W., & Wilcox, R. R. Brennan's B is Peirce's theta. *Educational and Psychological Measurement*, 1980, *40*, 307-311.

Helmstadter, G. C. *Comparison of traditional item analysis selection procedures with those recommended for tests designed to measure achievement following performance-oriented instruction.* Paper presented at the annual meeting of the American Psychological Association, Honolulu, September 1972.

Helmstadter, G. C. *A comparison of Bayesian and traditional indexes of test item effectiveness.* Paper presented at the annual meeting of the National Council on Measurement in Education, Chicago, April 1974.

Hemphill, J., & Westie, C. M. The measurement of group dimensions. *Journal of Psychology*, 1950, *29*, 325-342.

Henrysson, S., & Wedman, I. Some problems in construction and evaluation of criterion-referenced tests. *Scandinavian Journal of Educational Research*, 1974, *18*, 1-12.

Herbig, M. Zur vortest-nachtest-validierung lehrzielorientierter tests. *Zeitschrift für Erziehungswissenschaftliche Forschung*, 1975, *9*, 112-126.

Herbig, M. Item analysis by use in pretests and posttests: A comparison of different coefficients. *Programmed Learning and Educational Technology*, 1976, *13*, 49-54.

Hively, W., Patterson, H. L., & Page, S. A. A "universe-defined" system of arithmetic achievement tests. *Journal of Educational Measurement*, 1968, *5*, 275-290.

Hsu, T. C. *Empirical data on criterion-referenced tests.* Paper presented at the annual meeting of the American Educational Research Association, New York, February 1971.

Ironson, G. H. Use of chi-square and latent trait approaches for detecting item bias. In R. A. Berk (Ed.), *Handbook of methods for detecting test bias.* Baltimore, MD: Johns Hopkins University Press, 1982. Pp. 117-160.

Jackson, R. *Developing criterion-referenced tests* (TM Reports, No. 1). Princeton, NJ: Educational Testing Service, 1970.

Klein, S. P., & Kosecoff, J. B. Issues and procedures in the development of criterion-referenced tests. In W. A. Mehrens (Ed.), *Readings in measurement and evaluation in education and psychology.* New York: Holt, Rinehart and Winston, 1976. Pp. 276-293.

Kosecoff, J. B., & Klein, S. P. *Instructional sensitivity statistics appropriate for objectives-based test items* (CSE Report No. 91). Los Angeles: Center for the Study of Evaluation, University of California, 1974.

Larry P. et al. v. Wilson Riles, Superintendent of Public Instruction for the State of California, et al., No. C-71-2270 (N.D. Cal., Oct. 11, 1979), aff'd, Appeal No. 80-4027 (9th Cir. Jan. 28, 1984).

Levin, L., & Marton, F. *Provteori och provkonstruktion.* Stockholm, Sweden: Almqvist & Wiksell, 1971.

Livingston, S. A., & Zieky, M. J. *Passing scores: A manual for setting standards of performance on educational and occupational tests.* Princeton, NJ: Educational Testing Service, 1982.

Long, J. A. Improved overlapping methods for determining the validities of test items. *Journal of Experimental Education*, 1934, *2*, 264–268.

Lord, F. M. *Applications of item response theory to practical testing problems.* Hillsdale, NJ: Erlbaum, 1980.

Macready, G. B., & Merwin, J. C. Homogeneity within item forms in domain-referenced testing. *Educational and Psychological Measurement*, 1973, *33*, 351–360.

Marks, E., & Noll, G. A. Procedures and criteria for evaluating reading and listening comprehension tests. *Educational and Psychological Measurement*, 1967, *27*, 335–348.

Marton, F. Evalueringsteori och metodik. In G. Handal, L. G. Holmström, & O. B. Thomson (Eds.), *Universitetsundervisning.* Malmö, Sweden: Studentlitterature, 1973.

Millman, J. Criterion-referenced measurement. In W. J. Popham (Ed.), *Evaluation in education: Current applications.* Berkeley: CA: McCutchan, 1974. Pp. 311–397.

Nitko, A. J. Problems in the development of criterion-referenced tests: The IPI Pittsburgh experience. In C. W. Harris, M. C. Alkin, & W. J. Popham (Eds.), *Problems in criterion-referenced measurement* (CSE Monograph Series in Evaluation, No. 3). Los Angeles: Center for the Study of Evaluation, University of California, 1974. Pp. 59–82.

Pettie, A. A., & Oosterhof, A. C. *Indices of item adequacy for individually administered mastery tests.* Paper presented at the annual meeting of the National Council on Measurement in Education, San Francisco, April 1976.

Pine, S. M. Applications of item characteristic curve theory to the problem of test bias. In D. J. Weiss (Ed.), *Applications of computerized adaptive testing* (RR 77-1). Minneapolis: Department of Psychology, Psychometric Methods Program, University of Minnesota, March 1977. Pp. 37–43.

Popham, W. J. Indices of adequacy for criterion-referenced test items. In W. J. Popham (Ed.), *Criterion-referenced measurement: An introduction.* Englewood Cliffs, NJ: Educational Technology Publications, 1971. Pp. 79–98.

Popham, W. J., & Husek, T. R. Implications of criterion-referenced measurement. *Journal of Educational Measurement*, 1969, *6*, 1–9.

Roid, G. H., & Haladyna, T. M. *A technology for test-item writing.* New York: Academic Press, 1982.

Roudabush, G. E. *Item selection for criterion-referenced tests.* Paper presented at the annual meeting of the American Educational Research Association, New Orleans, February 1973.

Rovinelli, R. J., & Hambleton, R. K. On the use of content specialists in the assessment of criterion-referenced test item validity. *Dutch Journal of Educational Research*, 1977, *2*, 49–60.

Saupe, J. L. Selecting items to measure change. *Journal of Educational Measurement*, 1966, *3*, 223–228.

Scheuneman, J. D. A new method of assessing bias in test items. *Journal of Educational Measurement*, 1979, *16*, 143–152.

Scheuneman, J. D. A posteriori analyses of biased items. In R. A. Berk (Ed.), *Handbook of methods for detecting test bias.* Baltimore, MD: Johns Hopkins University Press, 1982. Pp. 180–198.

Schmeiser, C. B. Use of experimental design in statistical item bias studies. In R. A. Berk (Ed.), *Handbook of methods for detecting test bias*. Baltimore, MD: Johns Hopkins University Press, 1982. Pp. 64-95.

Shepard, L. A. Standard setting issues and methods. *Applied Psychological Measurement*, 1980, *4*, 447-467.

Smith, D. U. *The effects of various item selection methods on the classification accuracy and classification consistency of criterion-referenced instruments.* Paper presented at the annual meeting of the American Educational Research Association, Toronto, March 1978.

Stanley, J. C. General and special formulas for reliability of differences. *Journal of Educational Measurement*, 1967, *4*, 249-252.

Subkoviak, M. J., & Harris, D. J. *A short-cut statistic for item analysis of mastery tests*. Paper presented at the annual meeting of the American Educational Research Association, New Orleans, April 1984.

Subkoviak, M. J., & Harwell, M. R. *The effect of item selection method on the reliability of mastery tests.* Manuscript submitted for publication, 1983.

Tittle, C. K. Use of judgmental methods in item bias studies. In R. A. Berk (Ed.), *Handbook of methods for detecting test bias.* Baltimore, MD: Johns Hopkins University Press, 1982. Pp. 31-63.

Tucker, S. B., & Vargas, J. S. *Item analysis of criterion-referenced tests for a large individualized course.* Paper presented at the annual meeting of the National Council on Measurement in Education, Chicago, April 1974.

van der Linden, W. J. A latent trait look at pretest-posttest validation of criterion-referenced test items. *Review of Educational Research*, 1981, *51*, 379-402.

van Naerssen, R. F. Grafieken voor de schatting van de helling van itemkarakteristieken. *Tijdschrift voor Onderwijsresearch*, 1977, *2*, 193-201.

Vargas, J. S. *Item selection techniques for norm-referenced and criterion-referenced tests.* Unpublished doctoral dissertation, University of Pittsburgh, 1969.

Veale, J. R., & Foreman, D. I. Assessing cultural bias using foil response data: Cultural variation. *Journal of Educational Measurement*, 1983, *20*, 249-258.

Webster, H. Maximizing test validity by item selection. *Psychometrika*, 1956, *21*, 153-164.

Webster, H. Item selection methods for increasing test homogeneity. *Psychometrika*, 1957, *22*, 395-403.

Wedman, I. *Theoretical problems in construction of criterion-referenced tests* (Educational Reports, Umea No. 3). Umea, Sweden: School of Education, Umea University, 1973.

Wedman, I. On the evaluation of criterion-referenced tests. In H. F. Crombag & D. N. M. de Gruijter (Eds.), *Contemporary issues in educational testing.* The Hague, The Netherlands: Mouton, 1974. (a)

Wedman, I. *Reliability, validity and discrimination measures for criterion-referenced tests* (Educational Reports, Umea No. 4). Umea, Sweden: School of Education, Umea University, 1974. (b)

White, B. W., & Saltz, E. The measurement of reproducibility. *Psychological Bulletin*, 1957, *54*, 81-99.

Wiggins, J. S. *Personality and prediction: Principles of personality assessment.* Reading, MA: Addison-Wesley, 1973.

Wilcox, R. R. New methods for studying equivalence. In C. W. Harris, A. P. Pearlman, & R. R. Wilcox (Eds.), *Achievement test items: Methods of study* (CSE

Monograph Series in Evaluation, No. 6). Los Angeles: Center for the Study of Evaluation, University of California, 1977. Pp. 66–76. (a)

Wilcox, R. R. New methods for studying stability. In C. W. Harris, A. P. Pearlman, & R. R. Wilcox (Eds.), *Achievement test items: Methods of study* (CSE Monograph Series in Evaluation, No. 6). Los Angeles: Center for the Study of Evaluation, University of California, 1977. Pp. 45–65. (b)

Wood, RL, Wingersky, M. S., & Lord, F. M. *LOGIST: A computer program for estimating examinee ability and item characteristic curve parameters* (ETS Research Memorandum 76-6). Princeton, NJ: Educational Testing Service, 1976.

Wright, B. D., & Mead, R. J. *BICAL: Calibrating items and scales with the Rasch model* (Research Memorandum No. 23A). Chicago: Statistical Laboratory, Department of Education, University of Chicago, 1978.

Zieky, M. J. *Methods of setting standards for criterion-referenced item sets.* Princeton, NJ: Educational Testing Service, 1973.

6 DETERMINING TEST LENGTH

RONALD K. HAMBLETON

INTRODUCTION

THE TECHNICAL PROBLEM of determining the length of a criterion-referenced test or, more commonly, of determining the number of test items measuring each objective to include in a test, is important because the answer to the problem directly relates to the usefulness of the criterion-referenced test scores obtained from the test. Short tests often result in imprecise domain score estimates and lead to mastery classifications that are (1) inconsistent across parallel-form administrations (or retest administrations) and (2) *not* indicative of the true mastery states of examinees; that is, mastery classifications based on scores obtained from short tests are often both *unreliable* and *invalid*. Therefore, criterion-referenced test scores obtained from short tests often have limited value. Short tests should not be used for making important decisions such as who will receive diplomas, licenses, and certificates.

Hambleton, Swaminathan, Algina, and Coulson (1978) described two principal uses for criterion-referenced tests: estimation of domain scores, and assignment to mastery states. When the intended application involves estimating domain scores, the relationships among domain scores, errors of measurement, and test length, as summarized in the item-sampling model, are well known (Lord & Novick, 1968), and provide a basis for determining test length.

When using criterion-referenced tests to assign examinees to mastery states, the technical matter of determining a test length is directly related to the number of classification errors that are tolerable to test users. Low probabilities of misclassification can usually be assured when tests are very long. However, very long tests are not usually feasible because of limits on the available testing time. Currently, there are at least two ways to reduce classification errors *without* lengthening a criterion-referenced test: (1) utilize Bayesian procedures, which incorporate prior and collateral information into the

I am grateful to Daniel Eignor for help in organizing some of the material in this chapter and for preparing the examples.

domain score estimation process (see for example, Novick & Jackson, 1974), and (2) implement an adaptive testing scheme especially designed for hierarchically structured objectives (see, for example, Hambleton & Eignor, 1978; Spineti & Hambleton, 1977). Neither of these two methods is discussed further in this chapter.

The purposes of this chapter are to review several of the available practical methods for determining test length and to offer a set of procedures for practitioners. Since mastery classifications are often made for each objective measured in a test, for the purposes of this chapter *test length* is defined as the number of test items measuring an objective included in a criterion-referenced test. A *unique* test length must be determined for *each* objective, and any of the methods described in this chapter can be applied successively to the objectives measured in the test. Of course, if a test measures several objectives but central interest is focused on the *total* test score for describing examinee performance and/or decision making, then *test length* refers to the total length of the test. Two other terms are used frequently in the chapter: a *cut-off score* is a point on the domain score which is used to separate "true masters" and "true nonmasters"; an *advancement score* is the number of items an examinee must successfully answer to be classified as a "master." An examinee who does not achieve the advancement score is classified as a "nonmaster."

Readers are referred to Wilcox (1980) for a more technical review of several of the methods considered. The methods considered in this chapter are organized into five sections: (1) Millman's (1972, 1973) use of the binomial test model, (2) Novick and Lewis's (1974) Bayesian approach, (3) Wilcox's (1976) use of an "indifference zone," (4) use of computer simulation methods (Eignor & Hambleton, 1979; Hambleton, Mills, & Simon, 1983), and (5) the methods by Birnbaum (1968) and Lord (1980) based on the use of item response theory.

REVIEW OF TEST LENGTH METHODS

Introduction

In the typical criterion-referenced testing situation, a domain or population of test items is available (it may be real or it may have to be hypothesized). These items measure a particular objective or competency and vary (sometimes substantially) in their levels of difficulty. The expected or true proportion of items that an examinee can answer correctly from the whole domain or population of items is called the examinee's *domain score*. Practical constraints, such as time, often force the test developer to estimate the domain score by drawing (usually) a *random* or *stratified random* sample of items from the domain. The *test score* is not likely to coincide with the *domain score* because of measurement errors due to examinee guessing, problems in test administration, ambiguous items, and/or nonrepresentative sampling of test items.

Any differences between examinee test scores and domain scores can result in classification errors. That is, mastery classifications made on the basis of test scores will not completely agree with the correct classifications based on the use of the domain scores. Of course, the latter classifications cannot be made in practice, but they can be closely approximated, in general, with longer tests. In general, the longer a test, the less the chance there is of making classification errors. However, problems such as time limits, item construction difficulties, and so on dictate against having long tests. Thus, the concern usually becomes one of determining a minimal test length that is sufficient to achieve some desirable level of quality, often called the "criterion" or "criterion function." There are many possible criteria or criterion functions that may be chosen or developed. For example, a test developer may adopt the following criterion: choose a test length so that the probability of misclassifying examinees who are below or above the cut-off score by an amount of (say) 10% does not exceed 20%.

Millman's Use of the Binomial Test Model

Millman (1973) considered the probabilities of classification errors which result when decisions are made by comparing domain score estimates to an advancement score. The use of the binomial test model makes it simple to determine the probability of misclassification, conditional upon an examinee's domain score, an advancement score, a cut-off score, and the number of items in the test. By varying test length and advancement score, a test developer can determine the test length and advancement score that produces a desired probability of misclassification for a *given* domain score. Millman's method is based upon four assumptions:

1. the test consists of a random sample of dichotomously scored test items,
2. the likelihood of a correct response is a constant for all test items for an examinee,
3. responses to test items are independent, and
4. errors fit the binomial test model.

No assumptions involving item content or difficulty are necessary, and no group-based reliability or validity indices are used.

Table 6.1, which is similar to several tables prepared by Millman (1972), can be used to obtain the probability that an examinee with a *particular* domain score will be incorrectly passed or failed with a particular advancement score applied to a particular number of items. Other tables like Table 6.1 for different test parameters can easily be constructed by using the binomial test model:

$$\text{Prob}(x \mid \pi) = \binom{n}{x} \pi^x (1 - \pi)^{n-x},$$

Table 6.1. Number of Times (Out of 100) an Examinee Is Expected to Be Incorrectly Passed or Failed (Cut-off Score = 80%)

Advance-ment Score	Number of Test Items	Domain Score Level[a]									
		50	55	60	65	70	75	80	85	90	95
6	7	6	10	16	23	33	45	42	28	15	4
7	8	4	7	11	17	26	37	50	34	19	6
8	9	2	4	7	12	20	30	56	40	23	7
8	10	6	10	17	26	38	53	32	18	7	1
9	11	3	7	12	20	31	46	38	22	9	2
10	12	2	4	8	15	25	39	44	26	11	1
11	13	1	3	6	11	20	33	50	31	13	2
12	15	2	4	9	17	30	46	35	18	6	—
17	20	—	1	2	4	11	23	59	35	13	2
19	22	—	—	1	3	7	16	67	42	17	2

[a] A domain score is the expected proportion of items an examinee can answer correctly in the entire pool of items measuring an objective.

where Prob$(x \mid \pi)$ is the probability of an examinee with domain score π answering x items correctly from an n-item test. For example, suppose $\pi = .60$, $n = 10$, the advancement score of interest $= 8$, and the cut-off score $(\pi_o) = .70$. The examinee in the example is clearly a nonmaster since $\pi < \pi_o$. Therefore the probability of interest is the one associated with making a false positive error for the examinee. It is equal to the sum of probabilities associated with the examinee answering 8, 9, or 10 items correctly. An examinee with a score of 8 or higher would pass the test and be identified incorrectly as a master. The probability associated with a false positive error, therefore, is

$$\text{Prob}(x \geq 8 \mid \pi = .60, n = 10) = \sum_{x=8}^{10} \binom{10}{x} .60^{x} (.40)^{10-x} .$$

Other probabilities can be computed in a similar fashion.

Two points about the results in Table 6.1 need to be made:

1. Examinees to the left of the broken line have domain scores below the cut-off score, while examinees to the right have domain scores equal to or above the cut-off score. Therefore, only false positive errors can result for examinees below the cut-off score, and only false negative errors can result for examinees above the cut-off score.
2. More examinees with domain scores close to or at the cut-off score will be incorrectly classified than examinees at a greater distance from the cut-off score.

Example

For a cut-off score of 80%, suppose a 25% misclassification error can be tolerated for examinees with domain scores at 70% or 90%. What is the shortest acceptable test length, and what value should be chosen for the advancement score?

Answer: It can be seen from Table 6.1 that a test of 9 items with an advancement score of 8 is the shortest test that meets the criterion: only 20% of the examinees at the 70% level, and 23% at the 90% level, will be misclassified.

In practical settings, it is common for test developers to set a cut-off score and specify (1) the maximum acceptable probability for a false positive error at a particular domain score below the cut-off score or (2) the maximum acceptable probability for a false negative error at a particular domain score above the cut-off score, or both (1) and (2), and then choose a test length and advancement score to meet the required specifications.

Novick and Lewis's Bayesian Method*

Novick and Lewis (1974) argued that instead of considering the probability that an examinee will attain a test score, given his or her domain score (an unknown), it would be more useful to consider the probability that an examinee's domain score exceeds a given cut-off score, given the test score. Clearly, the second probability statement is usually the one of interest. An examinee can then be passed if there is a sufficiently high probability that his or her domain score exceeds the cut-off score. Procedures offered by Novick and Lewis allow such a probability to be estimated and used in assigning examinees to mastery states. According to Novick and Lewis (1974):

> To obtain the necessary probability an application of Bayes' theorem is required. In such an analysis prior knowledge (expressed in probabilistic terms) of the student's true level of functioning [domain score] is combined with the (binomial) model information relating the observed test score to true level; the result is a posterior probability for true level of functioning [domain score], given the test score. The probability this distribution assigns to levels above the [cut-off score] is the quantity of interest. (p. 143)

Novick and Lewis, like Millman, sought to select appropriate test lengths and advancement scores. Unlike Millman, Novick and Lewis chose the following criterion: select a test length and advancement score so that for examinees who achieve the advancement score, the probability of their domain scores exceeding the cut-off score is above a specified value (e.g., .60).

*For readers unfamiliar with Bayesian methods, Novick and Jackson (1974) provide an excellent introduction.

Novick and Lewis (1974) produced data reproduced here in Table 6.2 reporting values of Prob($\pi \geq \pi_o |x, n$); i.e., the probability of an examinee having a domain score greater than or equal to the cut-off score, with a score of x on an n-item test, for typical values of the cut-off score, x, and n used with many criterion-referenced tests. No prior information about examinee domain scores is assumed. In Table 6.2, the cut-off score takes on values ranging from .50 to .95 (in increments of .05), test scores vary from 6 to 11, and test lengths vary from 8 to 12. Their table can be used to select both an advancement score and a test length to ensure that Prob($\pi \geq \pi_o$) is larger than some desired value. To use Table 6.2 to select a test length, a test developer must set (1) a cut-off score and (2) the *minimum* acceptable probability that an examinee's domain score exceeds this cut-off score.

Example

Suppose the cut-off score is 80% and the minimum acceptable probability is .50 (e.g., Prob[$\pi \geq \pi_o |x, n$] = .50, where x = test score, n is test length). What is the minimum number of test items that can be used, and what is the minimum advancement score?

Answer: 8 items with an advancement score of 7, because Prob($\pi \geq \pi_o |7, 8$) = .56. An 8-item test with an advancement score of 7 is the shortest test for achieving the desired probability level.

Novick and Lewis (1974) chose the two-parameter beta distribution as the family of curves for specifying prior beliefs about domain scores. Such a choice was desirable for several reasons. First, beta distributions are defined on the same interval as domain scores (0 to 1). Second, through judicious choice of distribution parameters, a very wide range of prior distributions can be represented. Third, beta distributions are convenient to work with and have several desirable properties. Readers are referred to Novick and Jackson (1974) for a detailed discussion of beta distributions. Table 6.3 provides 20 pairs of parameters and the associated beta distributions. These examples of different beta distributions will often be useful for specifying prior beliefs about domain scores.

In compiling Table 6.2, Novick and Lewis (1974) made the assumption that no prior information was available about the location of the examinee's domain score. This prior distribution is given as β (1, 1).

Next, suppose that information is available to suggest that there is a 75% chance that the examinee's domain score exceeds the cut-off score. The information may be based on previous test performance. Novick and Lewis (1974) note that this belief can be characterized by a beta prior distribution denoted

Table 6.2. Probability of an Examinee Having a Domain Score Greater Than the Cut-off Score Given He/She Obtains the Advancement Score for the Test (Based on a Uniform Prior Distribution)

Advance-ment Score	Number of Test Items	Posterior Distribution	Cut-off Score									
			50	55	60	65	70	75	80	85	90	95
6	8	$\beta(7,3)$	91	85	77	66	54	40	26	14	5	1
7	8	$\beta(8,2)$	98	96	93	88	80	70	56	40	23	7
8	8	$\beta(9,1)$	100	100	99	98	96	92	87	77	61	37
7	9	$\beta(8,3)$	95	90	83	74	62	47	32	18	7	1
8	9	$\beta(9,2)$	99	98	95	91	85	76	62	46	26	9
9	9	$\beta(10,1)$	100	100	99	99	97	94	89	80	65	40
7	10	$\beta(8,4)$	89	81	70	57	43	29	16	7	2	—
8	10	$\beta(9,3)$	97	93	88	80	69	54	38	22	9	2
9	10	$\beta(10,2)$	99	99	97	94	89	80	68	51	30	10
8	11	$\beta(9,4)$	93	87	77	65	51	35	21	9	3	—
9	11	$\beta(10,3)$	98	96	92	85	75	61	44	26	11	2
10	11	$\beta(11,2)$	100	99	98	96	92	84	73	56	34	12
9	12	$\beta(10,4)$	95	91	83	72	58	42	25	12	3	—
10	12	$\beta(11,3)$	99	97	94	89	80	67	50	31	13	2
11	12	$\beta(12,2)$	100	100	99	97	94	87	77	60	38	14

Source: Adapted from Novick and Lewis (1974, p. 143) with permission of the Center for the Study of Evaluation, University of California, Los Angeles.

Note: For examinees scoring above the advancement score, associated probabilities of correct classification exceed the values reported above.

β (10.254, 1.746). Table 6.4 gives the same kind of information as Table 6.2, but it is based upon a new prior distribution about the unknown domain score. To use Table 6.4 a test developer must again set a cut-off score and decide on a minimum acceptable probability that an examinee's domain score exceeds this cut-off score.

Example

Suppose the cut-off score is 90% and a Prob$(\pi \geq .90 \mid x, n) = .5$ is desired. What is the minimum number of test items that can be used, and what is the minimum advancement score? (Assume the prior is given by β [10.254, 1.746].)

Answer: For 12 items with an advancement score of 11, the Prob$(\pi \geq .90 \mid 11, 12) = .48$, which is sufficiently close to .50. Shorter test lengths can be chosen—8 and 9 test items—if the advancement score is set at 100%.

Table 6.3. Selected Prior Distributions for Mastery Decisions

No.	Prior Distribution	Effective Prior Sample Size	Mean	Prob $(\pi_1 \leqslant \pi \leqslant \pi_u)^a$					
				.00–.70	.70–.75	.75–.80	.80–.85	.85–.90	.90–1.00
1	$\beta(5.6, 2.4)$	8	.70	.46	.12	.12	.12	.10	.08
2	$\beta(6, 2)$	8	.75	.33	.12	.13	.14	.13	.15
3	$\beta(6.4, 1.6)$	8	.80	.21	.10	.12	.15	.16	.26
4	$\beta(6.8, 1.2)$	8	.85	.12	.07	.09	.13	.17	.42
5	$\beta(7.2, .8)$	8	.90	.05	.04	.06	.09	.14	.62
6	$\beta(7, 3)$	10	.70	.46	.14	.14	.12	.09	.05
7	$\beta(7.5, 2.5)$	10	.75	.32	.13	.15	.15	.13	.12
8	$\beta(8, 2)$	10	.80	.20	.10	.14	.16	.17	.23
9	$\beta(8.5, 1.5)$	10	.85	.10	.07	.10	.14	.19	.40
10	$\beta(9, 1)$	10	.90	.04	.03	.06	.10	.16	.61
11	$\beta(8.4, 3.6)$	12	.70	.47	.15	.15	.12	.08	.03
12	$\beta(9, 3)$	12	.75	.32	.14	.16	.16	.13	.09
13	$\beta(9.6, 2.4)$	12	.80	.18	.11	.15	.18	.18	.20
14	$\beta(10.2, 1.8)$	12	.85	.09	.07	.11	.16	.20	.37
15	$\beta(10.8, 1.2)$	12	.90	.03	.03	.06	.11	.17	.60
16	$\beta(10.5, 4.5)$	15	.70	.47	.17	.16	.12	.06	.02
17	$\beta(11.25, 3.75)$	15	.75	.30	.16	.18	.17	.13	.06
18	$\beta(12.3)$	15	.80	.16	.12	.17	.20	.19	.16
19	$\beta(12.75, 2.25)$	15	.85	.07	.07	.12	.18	.23	.33
20	$\beta(13.5, 1.5)$	15	.90	.02	.03	.06	.11	.19	.59

Source: Adapted from Novick and Lewis (1974, p. 150) with permission of the Center for the Study of Evaluation, University of California, Los Angeles.
[a] All entries have been rounded to two decimal places and smoothed so that the row totals add to 1.00.

Table 6.4. Probability of an Examinee Having a Domain Score Greater Than the Cut-off Score Given a $\beta(10.254, 1.746)$ Prior Distribution

Advancement Score	Number of Test Items	Posterior Distribution	Cut-off Score									
			50	55	60	65	70	75	80	85	90	95
6	8	$\beta(16.254, 3.746)$	100	100	98	96	90	78	60	37	15	2
7	8	$\beta(17.254, 2.746)$	100	100	100	99	97	92	81	62	36	10
8	8	$\beta(18.254, 1.746)$	100	100	100	100	99	98	94	85	66	32
7	9	$\beta(17.254, 3.746)$	100	100	99	97	92	82	65	41	17	2
8	9	$\beta(18.254, 2.746)$	100	100	100	99	98	93	84	66	39	11
9	9	$\beta(19.254, 1.746)$	100	100	100	100	100	98	95	87	69	34
7	10	$\beta(17.254, 4.746)$	100	99	97	93	84	68	47	24	7	1
8	10	$\beta(18.254, 3.746)$	100	100	99	98	93	84	68	45	19	3
9	10	$\beta(19.254, 2.746)$	100	100	100	99	98	95	86	69	42	12
8	11	$\beta(18.254, 4.746)$	100	99	98	94	87	72	51	27	8	1
9	11	$\beta(19.254, 3.746)$	100	100	100	98	95	87	72	48	22	3
10	11	$\beta(20.254, 2.746)$	100	100	100	100	99	96	88	72	45	13
9	12	$\beta(19.254, 4.746)$	100	100	99	96	89	76	55	30	10	1
10	12	$\beta(20.254, 3.746)$	100	100	100	99	96	89	75	52	24	4
11	12	$\beta(21.254, 2.746)$	100	100	100	100	99	96	90	75	48	14

Source: Adapted from Novick and Lewis (1974, p. 145) with permission of the Center for the Study of Evaluation, University of California, Los Angeles.

The effect of prior information about domain scores can be assessed by looking at some representative situations and associated probabilities.

Situation	Uniform Prior	β (10.254, 1.746) Prior
Prob($\pi \geq .70 \mid 7, 9$)	.62	.92
Prob($\pi \geq .70 \mid 9, 11$)	.75	.95
Prob($\pi \geq .80 \mid 6, 8$)	.26	.60
Prob($\pi \geq .80 \mid 10, 12$)	.50	.75
Prob($\pi \geq .90 \mid 6, 8$)	.05	.15
Prob($\pi \geq .90 \mid 10, 12$)	.13	.24

These six situations show clearly that specifying a prior belief about the mastery status of an examinee results in a much higher probability statement about an examinee's domain score exceeding the cut-off score. Alternatively, if the prior belief had been that the examinee was a "nonmaster," the probability statement about the examinee being a "master" would have been lower than the probability statement associated with a "uniform" or "no-information" prior belief about examinee mastery status.

The assumption has been made up to this point in the chapter that false positive and false negative errors are equally serious. But such an assumption is not always reasonable. Consider the table of losses associated with binary decisions in Table 6.5. For example, when hiring physicians or airline pilots, false positive errors are often substantially more serious (the associated losses are higher) than false negative errors. One consequence of unequal losses associated with the two types of error in this example is that a higher advancement score must be set so as to reduce the number of false positive errors. Of course, such an action will also increase the number of false negative errors,

Table 6.5. Table of Losses Associated with Binary Functions

		Domain Score	
		$\pi \geq \pi_o$	$\pi < \pi_o$
Decision	Advance	o	a
	Retain	b	o

Note: π_o = Cut-off score for the domain of items;
a = Loss associated with advancing an examinee with true level $\pi < \pi_o$ (false positive error);
b = Loss associated with retaining an examinee with true level $\pi \geq \pi_o$ (false negative error).

but such a result is tolerable because of the less serious consequences of this type of error. The use of unequal errors is not discussed further here. Novick and Lewis go on to determine test lengths and advancement scores for cases when the losses are unequal.

Tables like Tables 6.2 and 6.4 for other choices of parameters can be produced very quickly and cheaply.

Wilcox's Use of an "Indifference Zone"

The *binomial distribution* can be used to estimate the probability of an examinee whose domain score is π obtaining a test score of x items out of n items:

$$\text{Prob}(x\,|\pi) = \binom{n}{x} \pi^x (1 - \pi)^{n-x} .$$

To separate examinees into mastery states, a cut-off score, π_o, is established such that if $\pi < \pi_o$ the examinee is a nonmaster; if $\pi \geq \pi_o$, the examinee is a master. But a criterion-referenced test user has only the fallible test score x to work with, not π, and needs to decide if $\pi < \pi_o$ or $\pi \geq \pi_o$. Hence, there is the risk of both false positive and false negative errors. Let α be the probability of a false positive error and β be the probability of a false negative error. According to Wilcox (1976), an advancement score, n_o, needs to be set such that

$$\begin{aligned} &\text{Prob}(x \geq n_o\,|\pi) \leq \alpha \text{ for all } \pi < \pi_o \text{ and} \\ &\text{Prob}(x < n_o\,|\pi) \leq \beta \text{ for all } \pi \geq \pi_o . \end{aligned}$$

But, since $\alpha = 1 - \beta$, it is *not* always possible to keep both probabilities at acceptably low levels. An explicit solution to the criterion function chosen by Wilcox (1976) can be generated by establishing an indifference zone (π_ℓ to π_u where $\pi_\ell = \pi_o - c$ and $\pi_u = \pi_o + c$) (Wilcox, 1976). For individuals with domain scores close to π_o (within the interval from π_ℓ to π_u), the test user can be "indifferent" as to how examinees are classified. The assumption is that there is negligible loss in misclassification of such examinees. For examinees with domain scores greater than π_u or less than π_ℓ, one wants to be reasonably certain (probabilities to be specified) that the correct decisions are made. Schematically, the situation can be seen in Figure 6.1. The minimum acceptable probability for correctly classifying examinees at the end points of the indifference zone can be specified, and then a test length and an advancement score to satisfy the chosen criterion can be found. If the test length is suitable for examinees at the ends of the indifference zone, it is also suitable for examinees with domain scores in excess of π_u or lower than π_ℓ.

Let n_o = advancement score on the test. If $x \geq n_o$, the examinee is advanced; if $x < n_o$, the examinee is retained. A correct decision is made for the examinee if $x < n_o$ and $\pi < \pi_o$ or $x \geq n_o$ and $\pi \geq \pi_o$. Suppose P^* is set, for convenience, to the minimum acceptable probability of correct classification for examinees at π_ℓ and π_u. Then the task is to determine the number of test

Figure 6.1. Domain score scale with an indifference zone

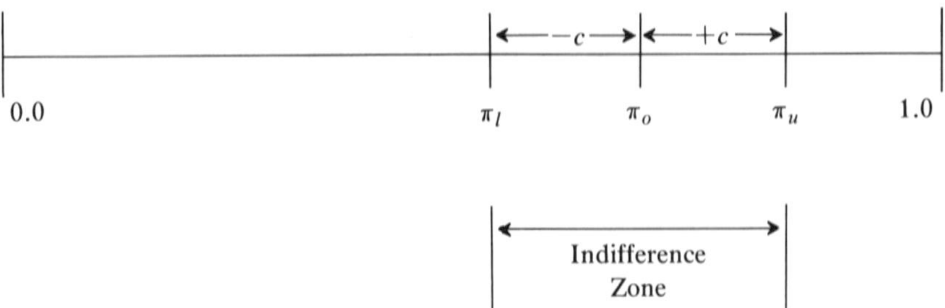

items, n, as small as possible so that for values of π not in the indifference zone, the probability of a correct decision is at least P^*.

For values of $\pi \leq \pi_\ell$, the minimum probability of a correct decision occurs at the point π_ℓ and is given by:

$$\alpha = \sum_{x=0}^{n_o - 1} \binom{n}{x} (\pi_\ell)^x (1 - \pi_\ell)^{n-x} .$$

For values of $\pi \geq \pi_u$, the minimum probability of a correct decision occurs at the point π_u and is given by:

$$\beta = \sum_{x=n_o}^{n} \binom{n}{x} (\pi_u)^x (1 - \pi_u)^{n-x} .$$

Now, to choose n, Wilcox (1976) specifies: "We choose the smallest integer n so that α and β are greater than or equal to P^* which implies that the probability of a correct decision is at least P^* at π_u and π_ℓ" (p. 361).

Wilcox (1976) provided tables (see, for example, Table 6.6) for various combinations of the variables involved in his approach. In order to use these tables, three pieces of information must be specified:

1. the cut-off score for the domain of items (Wilcox uses values .70, .75, .80, and .85);
2. the positive constant, denoted c, that forms the indifference zone (Wilcox uses $c = .05$ and $c = .10$); and
3. the minimum probability of a correct decision for scores not included in the indifference region (Wilcox uses $P^* = .75$).

By specifying these values, Wilcox's (1976) table provides n and n_o, along with the minimum probability of correctly classifying an examinee with a

Table 6.6. Cut-off Scores and the Minimum Probability of a Correct Decision for Values of π Not in the Indifference Zone

Test Items	$\pi_o = .70$		$\pi_o = .75$		$\pi_o = .80$		$\pi_o = .85$	
	$c = .05$	$c = .10$	$c = .05$	$c = .10$	$c = .05$	$c = .10$	$c = .05$	$c = .10$
8	6/.5722	6/.6846	7/.5033	7/.6572	7/.6329	7/.7447	7/.4967	7/.6329
9	7/.6007	7/.7382	7/.5372	7/.6627	8/.5995	8/.7748	8/.5683	8/.6997
10	8/.5256	8/.6778	8/.6172	8/.7384	9/.5443	9/.7361	9/.6242	9/.7560
11	8/.5744	8/.7037	9/.6174	9/.7788	9/.5448	10/.6974	10/.6779	10/.8029
12	9/.6488	9/.7747	10/.5583	10/.7358	10/.6093	10/.7472	11/.6590	11/.8416
13	10/.5843	10/.7473	10/.5794	11/.7296	11/.6674	11/.7975	12/.6213	12/.8646
14	10/.5733	10/.7207	11/.6488	11/.7795	12/.6479	12/.8392	13/.5846	13/.8470
15	11/.6481	11/.7827	12/.6482	12/.8227	13/.6042	13/.8159	13/.6020	14/.8290
16	12/.6302	12/.7982	13/.5981	13/.7899	13/.5950	14/.7892	14/.6482	15/.8108
17	12/.5803	13/.7582	13/.6113	13/.7652	14/.6470	14/.7981	15/.6904	15/.8363
18	13/.6450	13/.7912	14/.6673	14/.8114	15/.6943	15/.8354	16/.7287	16/.8647
19	14/.6678	14/.8369	15/.6733	15/.8500	16/.6841	16/.8668	17/.7054	17/.8887
20	14/.6172	15/.8042	16/.6296	16/.8298	17/.6477	17/.8670	18/.6769	18/.9087

Source: Adapted from Wilcox (1976, p. 362) with permission of the American Educational Research Association, Washington, DC.

domain score $\pi_\ell \geq \pi \geq \pi_u$. Extending Wilcox's tables would be a simple matter.

> *Example*
>
> Suppose the cut-off score = 80% and $c = .1$. What is the least number of items, and the advancement score, that can be used to have greater than an 80% chance of correctly classifying examinees with domain scores greater than .90 or less than .70?
>
> *Answer:* For $\pi_o = .80$ and $c = .1$, the least number of items is 14 with an advancement score of 12.

In conclusion, two points should be noted:

1. When $c = 0$, that is, when there is no indifference region, it is *not* always possible to choose n such that the probability of a correct decision is at least P^*. For this situation, the probability of a correct decision approaches .50 (an unacceptable level) as n increases. Hence, Millman's solution may not be adequate for certain situations.
2. The user may desire to specify two probabilities P_ℓ^* and P_u^* and choose the smallest n so that $\alpha \geq P_\ell^*$ and $\beta \geq P_u^*$.

Unfortunately the Wilcox approach, while it has considerable appeal, is not without problems. It can produce a single test length, but it leads to the selection of highly conservative test lengths. That is, for many examinees in the group of interest, considerably longer tests can result than are actually needed to achieve the desired probabilities of correct classifications.

Use of Computer Simulation Methods

Eignor-Hambleton method. Eignor and Hambleton (1979) offered another method for determining test lengths utilizing computer simulation techniques. Users can simulate examinee item performance data and investigate the effects of test length, cut-off score, advancement score, the shape of the domain score distribution, and other factors, on important criterion measures such as decision consistency and decision accuracy.

The Eignor-Hambleton solution is based upon the compound-binomial test model—a somewhat more plausible test model than the binomial test model that is used in applying the Millman method. Also, in the Eignor-Hambleton method, test lengths are determined to achieve a desired level of decision consistency or accuracy in the *examinee group of interest*, and so the resulting test lengths are typically shorter than those obtained using the Wilcox method.

The Eignor-Hambleton method also has several shortcomings. For one, the heterogeneity of the item pool used in test development is *not* considered. Item pool heterogeneity is high when the range of p-values is wide and the average size of the item intercorrelations is low. Heterogeneity of the item pool will have a direct impact on the required test length. Longer tests are needed when the item pool is heterogeneous. Also, Eignor and Hambleton did not consider in their method the approach chosen for building parallel forms: it is likely that in order to achieve a specified level of decision consistency, longer tests will be required when parallel forms are constructed by randomly sampling items from a pool than when classically parallel forms are constructed by the careful matching of item statistics.

Hambleton, Mills, and Simon method. In view of these shortcomings and those of the methods previously reviewed, Hambleton et al. (1983) offered another approach using computer simulation methods and concepts and models from the field of item response theory (Hambleton, 1979; Lord, 1980; Wright & Stone, 1979). There are three principal advantages to their approach: (1) a variety of item pools can be described quickly and easily, (2) one of two desirable item selection methods can be used to build tests, and (3) examinee performance consistent with the compound binomial test model can be simulated. Of course, the appropriateness of the test lengths identified by the Hambleton et al. method will depend upon the match between the situations simulated and the actual performance of the desired examinee population.

The Hambleton et al. (1983) method utilizes five factors that impact on the reliability and validity of binary decisions (e.g., identifying examinees as masters and nonmasters) emanating from the use of criterion-referenced test scores:

1. Test length
2. Statistical characteristics of the item pool
3. Method of item selection
4. Choice of cut-off score
5. Domain score distribution

Their method is implemented with TESTLEN (Mills & Simon, 1981), a computer program prepared to simulate examinee criterion-referenced test scores via the use of item response theory. TESTLEN provides the user with the option to manipulate the preceding five factors (and several others). Complete information for using the computer simulation program is described by Mills and Simon (1981). Only a few of the more important features are described here:

1. *Test length.* Test lengths of any size can be requested.
2. *Statistical characteristics of the item pool.* The user must describe the statistical characteristics of the items in the pool from which the items will be drawn. The statistical information is often obtained from the item statistics obtained in field tests.
3. *Method of item selection.* It is common to build parallel forms of a criterion-referenced test by drawing two random samples of test items from a pool. This "randomly parallel" method is unlikely to work well when the

test of interest is short and the item pool is heterogeneous. In a second method, the first form of a test is formed by drawing items randomly from the pool, and the second form is constructed by matching items statistically to the corresponding items in the first form. Both methods for selecting test items are available in the simulation program.

4. *Choice of cut-off score.* Any cut-off score can be selected.
5. *Domain score distribution.* Even short tests can be effective when the distribution of examinee domain scores is not too close to the chosen cut-off score or advancement score. The shape and characteristics of the specified domain score distribution in relation to the chosen cut-off score and advancement score have a substantial influence on the test lengths needed to achieve desirable levels for reliability and validity indices.

The computer simulation program requires the user to provide the following information:

1. the test length of interest and the item pool size;
2. the statistical characteristics of the item pool;
3. the preferred method of item selection;
4. the cut-off score of interest in relation to the item pool;
5. an expected distribution of domain scores for the examinee population of interest in the content domain of interest;
6. the number of examinees (when the number is large, the sampling error associated with the three criterion measures [decision consistency, kappa, decision accuracy] will be small [Hambleton et al., 1981]); and
7. the number of replications of interest to determine the variation in one or more of the three criterion measures for the particular set of conditions.

Hambleton et al. (1981, 1983) described a number of applications of their computer program. For example, Hambleton et al. (1983) addressed these two questions using TESTLEN:

1. What is the impact of item pool heterogeneity on the choice of desirable test lengths?
2. What is the impact of the choice of item selection method on decision consistency for tests of different lengths drawn from item pools which differ substantially in item heterogeneity?

Table 6.7 shows the mean level of decision consistency (across 10 replications) for 10 test lengths, 6 item pools and 2 item selection methods. The general trend toward improved consistency with longer tests and homogeneous item pools is evident. (In practice, some of the minor fluctuations in the results can be removed by fitting a curve to the plot of decision consistency values for tests of different length. See, for example, Hambleton et al. [1983].) The advantage of using classically parallel tests can be clearly seen for heterogeneous item pools at all test lengths. As expected, the improvements were less with homogeneous item pools.

Table 6.7. Relationships among Item Pool Characteristics, Item Selection Methods, Test Length, and Decision Consistency (*Number of Replications* = 10)

Item Selection Method	Range of Item Parameters			Range of *P*-values	Test Length									
	b	*a*	*c*		2	4	6	8	10	12	14	16	18	20
Randomly Parallel	−2.00 to +2.00	.40 to 2.00	.00	.83	.61	.64	.69	.73	.71	.78	.73	.76	.81	.80
	−1.00 to +1.00	.40 to 2.00	.00	.53	.70	.74	.77	.81	.81	.83	.84	.86	.87	.88
	.00	.40 to 2.00	.00	.09	.74	.78	.82	.86	.86	.88	.89	.89	.89	.91
Strictly Parallel	−2.00 to +2.00	.40 to 2.00	.00	.84	.73	.75	.81	.79	.83	.84	.85	.84	.85	.86
	−1.00 to +1.00	.40 to 2.00	.00	.54	.75	.76	.82	.82	.84	.87	.87	.86	.87	.89
	.00	.40 to 2.00	.00	.09	.73	.78	.83	.87	.86	.88	.88	.89	.90	.90
Randomly Parallel	−2.00 to +2.00	.40 to 2.00	.15 to .25	.66	.77	.70	.75	.75	.77	.81	.81	.77	.80	.78
	−1.00 to +1.00	.40 to 2.00	.15 to .25	.45	.75	.72	.77	.79	.79	.81	.83	.82	.76	.83
	.00	.40 to 2.00	.15 to .25	.09	.73	.75	.76	.80	.81	.81	.85	.85	.86	.86
Strictly Parallel	−2.00 to +2.00	.40 to 2.00	.15 to .25	.70	.80	.75	.76	.80	.80	.81	.83	.81	.83	.84
	−1.00 to +1.00	.40 to 2.00	.15 to .25	.42	.75	.74	.77	.79	.82	.81	.83	.83	.86	.84
	.00	.40 to 2.00	.15 to .25	.10	.73	.75	.77	.80	.81	.81	.85	.85	.86	.86

Source: Reprinted with permission from Hambleton, Ronald K., Mills, Craig N., and Simon, Robert "Determining the Lengths for Criterion-Referenced Tests," *Journal of Educational Measurement*, 1983, *20*, 27–38, Table 1 (p. 35). Copyright 1983, National Council on Measurement in Education, Washington, DC.

Note: Ability scores were normally distributed with $\mu = 0$, $\sigma = 1$; $N = 300$. The cut-off score was set at $\theta = 0.0$.

Simulation studies similar to the one described here which address the impact of several test lengths on decision consistency and decision accuracy for different testing conditions can be quickly and easily carried out and used to influence the final decision concerning desirable test lengths. The results provided by TESTLEN will be very accurate when the choice of parameters and the model used in TESTLEN closely reflect the situation in which the test of interest is to be used. One major drawback of the Hambleton-Mills-Simon method is that realistic input is needed. When it is not available, the results may be very misleading. A second problem is that the method does not insure high probabilities of correct classifications for examinees near the cut-off score. Instead, the test length selected insures that a desired level of decision consistency and/or decision accuracy is obtained (at least when the simulations are approximately reflective of reality).

In the conclusion of their paper, Hambleton, Mills, and Simon (1983) offer nine steps for using their method:

1. Choose a cut-off score of interest using one of the acceptable standard-setting methods (see Shepard, chapter 7).
2. Describe a likely distribution of domain scores on the objective or test of interest.
3. Specify the test lengths that are under consideration.
4. Describe the statistical characteristics of the item pool.
5. Choose a sample size that will be close to the size of the sample of examinees who are expected to take the final test.
6. Specify the method that will be used to select the items.
7. Generate the examinee response data and associated criterion measures and report the results in tables and figures (see, for example, Table 6.7 herein or fig. 1 in the article by Hambleton et al. [1983]).
8. Carry out additional simulations by revising the choice of parameters in steps 1 to 6.
9. In interpreting the test length results, usually it is best to have a desirable level for decision consistency and accuracy in mind. Choose a test length to obtain the desired values for these statistics.

Use of Item Response Theory

In the four methods reviewed so far, no substantial use is made of item statistics such as item difficulty and discrimination. Once the number of test items to measure an objective is determined, items are normally selected at random from the available pool of acceptable (valid) test items measuring the objective or competency of interest. Alternatively, sometimes a stratified random sample of test items is drawn to enhance the content validity of the chosen item sample. Random (or stratified random) selection of test items is a satisfactory method when an item pool matched to an objective is statistically homogeneous, since, for all practical purposes, the test items are interchangeable. The test items have similar item statistics. When items are similar statistically, the choice of test items has only a minimal impact on the decision consistency and accuracy of the test scores. When item pools are statistically heterogeneous, a random selection of test items will not be the most appropriate for separating examinees into mastery states. For example, test items that may be very easy or very difficult or have low discriminating power are as likely to be selected with the "random selection method" as are other, more suitable, items in the pool. For a fixed test length, the most valid test for separating examinees into mastery states on an objective will consist of test items that are discriminating effectively near the cut-off score on the domain score scale (Lord & Novick, 1968). With a randomly selected set of test items from a heterogeneous pool, the accuracy of the resulting classifications will generally be lower, since not all of the test items will be optimally functioning near the cut-off score.

When constructing tests to separate examinees into two or more mastery states in relation to an objective of interest, the selection of items that are most discriminating within the region of the cut-off score is desirable (Birnbaum, 1968). But criterion-referenced measurement specialists seldom take advantage of optimal items for a test, even though test developers commonly assume that the item pools from which their items will be drawn are heterogeneous. A satisfactory item selection method can be obtained within the framework of item response theory (IRT). The basic IRT item selection method was introduced by Birnbaum (1968). The method has also been studied by Lord (1980). It should be recognized that the problem of interest is no longer determining a test length, but rather finding the best test items within an item pool measuring an objective of interest to achieve a stated criterion (e.g., insuring that the probabilities of correct classification for examinees at the ends of an indifference zone exceed specified minimum values).

Item response models are useful to the problem of item selection because they lead, unlike classical models, to item statistics that are reported on the same scale as examinee abilities and the chosen cut-off score. Thus, it becomes possible to select test items that are maximally discriminating in the region of the cut-off score. Readers are referred to Hambleton (1979), Hambleton and Swaminathan (1984), Lord (1980), and Wright and Stone (1979) for introductions to item response models and their assumptions. It suffices to say here that, in the three-parameter logistic model, an item characteristic curve, $P_i(\theta)$, takes the mathematical form of a cumulative logistic function:

$$P_i(\theta) = c_i + (1 - c_i)\,[1 + \exp(-Da_i(\theta - b_i)]^{-1}\ . \qquad (1)$$

$P_i(\theta)$ represents the probability of an examinee at ability level θ answering item i correctly. Item i parameters, denoted, b_i, a_i, and c_i, are often referred to as item difficulty, discrimination, and pseudo-chance level, respectively. D is a scaling factor typically set equal to 1.7. In the two-parameter model, $c_i = 0, i = 1, 2, \ldots, n$; and in the one-parameter model, $c_i = 0$, and $a_i = a, i = 1, 2, \ldots, n$, where n is the number of test items.

The contribution of each test item to measurement precision, referred to as the *item information function*, is approximately given as

$$I_i(\theta) = \frac{[P_i'(\theta)]^2}{P_i(\theta)Q_i(\theta)} , \tag{2}$$

where $P_i'(\theta)$ is the first derivative of $P_i(\theta)$ and $Q_i(\theta) = 1 - P_i(\theta)$. $I_i(\theta)$ has its maximum at the point θ_i^* where

$$\theta_i^* = b_i + \frac{1}{Da_i} \text{Log}_e \cdot 5(1 + \sqrt{1 + 8c_i}) . \tag{3}$$

When $c_i = 0$, it can be seen from equation 3 that item i makes its biggest contribution to measurement precision at the point b_i on the ability scale. Once the item parameters are estimated and it can be determined that the chosen item response model provides an accurate account of the examinee performance data, θ_i^* and $I_i(\theta)$ provide the necessary statistics for optimal item selection.

When item parameter estimates are available for a large representative sample of items from the domain of items measuring an objective, the estimated relationship between domain scores, π, and latent ability scores, θ, is

$$\pi = \frac{1}{m} \sum_{i=1}^{m} P_i(\theta) , \tag{4}$$

where m is the total number of test items in the representative sample (Lord, 1980; Lord & Novick, 1968). The cut-off score, π_o, usually set on the π-scale, can be transformed to the θ-scale and vice versa using equation 4. For a given value of π_o, θ_o is the value of θ that satisfies equation 5, i.e.,

$$\pi_o = \frac{1}{m} \sum_{i=1}^{m} P_i(\theta_o) . \tag{5}$$

Thus, it is easy to find the value of θ_o on the ability scale which corresponds to the value of π_o on the domain score scale.

According to Hambleton and de Gruijter (1983), the method of optimal item selection utilizing an item response model proceeds in the following manner:

1. Prepare a large bank of valid test items.
2. Obtain item response model parameter estimates with a large examinee sample.
3. Determine the fit between the item response model and the response data. Do not proceed if the fit is poor.
4. Choose a cut-off score and an indifference zone on the domain score scale.
5. Transform π_1, π_o, and π_u to θ_1, θ_o, and θ_u, respectively, with equation 4.
6. Set the value of P^* (see Wilcox's approach).
7. Identify the test item for selection providing the most information at θ_o with the aid of equation 2.

8. Transform θ_1, θ_o, and θ_u to π_1^*, π_o^* and π_u^*, respectively, using the test characteristic curve consisting of the k selected test items. Calculate the probability of candidates at the lower and higher ends of the indifference zone (denoted P_ℓ and P_u, respectively) being correctly classified, and designate the lower of the two probabilities, P_m, for several cut-off scores. Consider integers close to

$$\sum_{i=1}^{k} P_i(\theta_o)$$

as possible cut-off scores.

9a. If $P_m < P^*$, select the next test item providing the most information at θ_o. Repeat the calculations required in step 8.

9b. If $P_m > P^*$, the item selection process can be stopped. The test at this point meets the required specifications.

Through several examples, Hambleton and de Gruijter (1983) demonstrated the theoretical advantages of optimal item selection over one of the most common alternative strategies, random item selection. The method is similar to the Wilcox method except that optimally functioning test items at the cut-off score rather than randomly selected test items are selected. Shorter tests can be used to achieve acceptable levels of misclassification when optimal items, identified through item response theory, are selected. De Gruijter and Hambleton (1983) were able to show advantages even in the more typical case when item parameter estimates rather than the item parameters themselves are used, although their research addressed only some special cases.

SUGGESTIONS FOR FUTURE RESEARCH

At this point, what appears to be more important than additional research studies on the most promising methods, or research to generate new methods, are applications of the existing methods. These applications could be useful in preparing guidelines for practitioners. Surprisingly, there is little evidence that any of the promising methods are being used in practice, let alone being used correctly. For example, often the choice of test lengths seems to be most related to practical constraints imposed on the testing situation, such as the amount of available time. Certainly practical constraints must be considered, but they should not always be the only factor considered.

Second, a research effort is needed on factors associated with (1) determining the width and location of indifference zones, (2) setting minimum probabilities for assigning examinees to mastery states, and (3) choosing a criterion function to maximize (or minimize). While considerable attention is being focused on setting cut-off scores and advancement scores in the literature, these other three parameters are being set or chosen, often, with little or no prior considerations.

Table 6.8. Test Length Methods: Advantages and Disadvantages

Method	Advantages	Disadvantages
Millman	Straightforward to apply Tables are available and others can be produced quickly and inexpensively Can be applied with individual examinees or groups of examinees Can control the probability with which examinees at selected domain scores are correctly classified	Based upon the restrictive binomial test model Test lengths are typically excessive for (at least) some examinees (those examinees with domain scores far away from the indifference zone)
Novick-Lewis	Has intuitive appeal. Users can choose test lengths and advancement scores to achieve desired probabilities for correctly classifying "true masters" Opportunity to include both prior information about examinee domain score performance and seriousness of false positive and false negative errors into the decision-making process Generally results in shorter tests than the other methods. The size of the reduction will depend on the amount of prior information available	Based upon the restrictive binomial test model More complicated to apply than several of the other methods A computer program to produce new tables of probability levels is not readily available Limited to determining test lengths for individual examinees The advantage of this method will depend upon the appropriateness of the priors chosen. Poorly chosen priors with short tests especially will yield misleading results
Wilcox	Straightforward to apply One useful table is available and others can be produced quickly and inexpensively Can be applied to individual examinees or groups of examinees	Based upon the restrictive binomial test model Test lengths are typically excessive for (at least) some examinees (those examinees with domain scores far away from the indifference zone)
Hambleton-Mills-Simon	Straightforward to apply Reliability and validity indices for decisions resulting from the use of the test scores can be controlled for the total group of examinees Computer program is available to produce relationships among test length and reliability and validity indices for specified test and examinee conditions	Input parameters to the program (item statistics and domain score distributions) must be realistic or the test length recommendations will be inaccurate Focus is on a *group* of examinees

Table 6.8. *(continued)*

Method	Advantages	Disadvantages
Item response theory	Generally results in shorter tests than either the Millman or Wilcox method (improvements result from the use of item statistics in the item selection process) Can be applied to individual examinees or groups of examinees	Substantial group sizes are needed to obtain satisfactory item parameter estimates Validity of the method depends on the fit between the chosen model and the test data Method requires a working knowledge of item response theory Relatively large diverse pools of test items are needed so that "optimal" items can be identified for each application Effort must be made to ensure the content validity of the test

Finally, a "test length" is determined either at the objective level or at the test level. When the former applies, there is the likelihood that the total available time is exceeded. In the latter case, there are no well-established procedures for allocating the available testing time to the objectives that must be measured in the total test. A method for optimally allocating testing time to objectives is needed. Berk (1980) has addressed this point, but considerably more research is needed.

GUIDELINES FOR PRACTITIONERS

The five methods introduced earlier in the chapter can easily be implemented in practice, and all of them will provide useful information for selecting test lengths. Of course, the methods have both advantages and disadvantages, and these are highlighted in Table 6.8.

Prior to selecting and implementing one of the methods described in this chapter, several factors described by Berk (1980) should be considered: (1) importance and types of decisions to be made, (2) importance and emphases assigned to the objectives, (3) number of objectives, and (4) practical constraints such as the amount of available testing time. These factors should influence (depending, of course, upon the choice of method) (1) the setting of cut-off scores needed when determining test lengths, (2) the determination of the minimally acceptable probability levels of correct examinee classifications (these probabilities must be higher on important tests), (3) the locations and widths of indifference zones on the domain score scale, (4) the attachment of values to the two types of classification errors, (5) the setting of minimally acceptable levels for reliability and validity indices, and (6) the establishment of prior distributions for examinee and group domain scores.

None of the test length determination methods reviewed in this chapter is without shortcomings. But any one of them, when applied correctly by test developers, can be helpful in determining desirable test lengths. Almost any method would be better than the common practice of choosing a test length to fit the available amount of testing time.

REFERENCES

Berk, R. A. Practical guidelines for determining the length of objectives-based, criterion-referenced tests. *Educational Technology*, 1980, *20*, 36–41.

Birnbaum, A. Some latent trait models and their use in inferring an examinee's ability. In F. M. Lord & M. R. Novick, *Statistical theories of mental test scores*. Reading, MA: Addison-Wesley, 1968. Pp. 397–479.

de Gruijter, D. N. M., & Hambleton, R. K. Using item response models in criterion-referenced test item selection. In R. K. Hambleton (Ed.), *Applications of item response theory*. Vancouver, BC: Educational Research Institute of British Columbia, 1983. Pp. 142–154.

Eignor, D. R., & Hambleton, R. K. *Effects of test length and advancement score on several criterion-referenced test reliability and validity indices* (Report No. 86). Amherst: Laboratory of Psychometric and Evaluative Research, School of Education, University of Massachusetts, 1979.

Hambleton, R. K. Latent trait models and their applications. In R. E. Traub (Ed.), *New directions for testing and measurement* (No. 4): *Methodological developments.* San Francisco: Jossey-Bass, 1979. Pp. 13–32.

Hambleton, R. K., & de Gruijter, D. N. M. Application of item response models to criterion-referenced test item selection. *Journal of Educational Measurement*, 1983, *20*, 355–367.

Hambleton, R. K., & Eignor, D. R. Adaptive testing applied to hierarchically-structured objectives-based curricula. In D. J. Weiss (Ed.), *Proceedings of the Second Computerized Adaptive Testing Conference*. Minneapolis: Computerized Adaptive Testing Laboratory, University of Minnesota, 1978. Pp. 290–311.

Hambleton, R. K., Mills, C. N., & Simon, R. *Determining the optimal length of a criterion-referenced test* (Report No. 111a). Amherst: Laboratory of Psychometric and Evaluative Research, School of Education, University of Massachusetts, 1981.

Hambleton, R. K., Mills, C. N., & Simon, R. Determining the lengths for criterion-referenced tests. *Journal of Educational Measurement*, 1983, *20*, 27–38.

Hambleton, R. K., & Swaminathan, H. *Item response theory: Principles and applications.* Hingham, MA: Kluwer-Nijhoff, 1984.

Hambleton, R. K., Swaminathan, H., Algina, J., & Coulson, D. B. Criterion-referenced testing and measurement: A review of technical issues and developments. *Review of Educational Research*, 1978, *48*, 1–47.

Lord, F. M. *Applications of item response theory to practical testing problems.* Hillsdale, NJ: Erlbaum, 1980.

Lord, F. M., & Novick, M. R. *Statistical theories of mental test scores.* Reading, MA: Addison-Wesley, 1968.

Millman, J. *Tables for determining number of items needed on domain-referenced tests and number of students to be tested* (Technical Report No. 5). Los Angeles: Instructional Objectives Exchange, 1972.

Millman, J. Passing scores and test lengths for domain-referenced measures. *Review of Educational Research*, 1973, *43*, 205–216.

Mills, C. N., & Simon, R. *A method for determining the length of criterion-referenced tests using reliability and validity indices* (Report No. 110). Amherst: Laboratory of Psychometric and Evaluative Research, School of Education, University of Massachusetts, 1981.

Novick, M. R., & Jackson, P. H. *Statistical methods for educational and psychological research.* New York: McGraw-Hill, 1974.

Novick, M. R., & Lewis, C. Prescribing test length for criterion-referenced measurement. In C. W. Harris, M. C. Alkin, & W. J. Popham (Eds.), *Problems in criterion-referenced measurement* (CSE Monograph Series in Evaluation, No. 3). Los Angeles: Center for the Study of Evaluation, University of California, 1974. Pp. 139–158.

Spineti, J. P., & Hambleton, R. K. A computer simulation study of tailored testing strategies for objectives-based instructional programs. *Educational and Psychological Measurement*, 1977, *37*, 139–158.

Wilcox, R. R. A note on the length and passing score of a mastery test. *Journal of Educational Statistics*, 1976, *1*, 359–364.

Wilcox, R. R. Determining the length of a criterion-referenced test. *Applied Psychological Measurement*, 1980, *4*, 425–446.

Wright, B. D., & Stone, M. H. *Best test design: Rasch measurement.* Chicago: MESA Press, 1979.

7 SETTING PERFORMANCE STANDARDS

LORRIE A. SHEPARD

INTRODUCTION

STANDARDS CONNOTE EXCELLENCE. They are used to separate the good from the bad, to sort goats from sheep. As with any other psychological construct that cannot be embodied exactly by concrete test scores, performance standards pose special problems for measurement experts.

When criterion-referenced tests are used to distinguish between masters and nonmasters, the competent and incompetent, a cut-off point is essential. The validity of the final classification decisions will depend as much upon the validity of the standard as upon the validity of the test content. The specification of a content domain, however, and representative sampling from the domain is a fundamentally more tractable problem than determining cut-off points. Therefore, standard setting is the Achilles heel of criterion-referenced testing. The most elaborate domain specifications in the world cannot compensate for invalid standards.

In developing this chapter, I have adopted a stance of constructive pessimism. The problems inherent in trying to dichotomize a continuum of performance are reiterated. But in deference to the editor's importuning, practical advice is also given for those instances when standards must be set. For example, state officials required by law to implement a minimum competency testing program can hardly refuse to set passing scores on the grounds that it is bad psychology and insupportable psychometrically. Standards must be set, so what is the most defensible procedure?

The negativism before the practical advice serves two purposes: (1) the limitations of specific standard-setting methods will be better understood, and (2) alternatives to mastery-nonmastery classifications will be sought more actively in those contexts where dichotomous decisions are neither educationally nor politically mandatory. Hambleton, Swaminathan, Algina, and Coulson (1978) distinguished two uses for criterion-referenced tests: (1) to estimate examinee domain scores and (2) to assign examinees to mastery states. The first use involves locating examinees along a performance continuum but does not require that a standard be invoked.

Numerous reviews of standard-setting methods have already been written (Glass, 1978b; Hambleton, 1980; Hambleton & Eignor, 1979; Hambleton et al., 1978; Hambleton, Powell, & Eignor, 1979; Jaeger, 1976, 1979; Meskauskas, 1976; Millman, 1973), including Shepard (1979, 1980a, 1980b, 1983). To justify yet another review and avoid redundancy, I have aimed in this chapter for a higher level of synthesis and summary. Borrowing from the collective wisdom of previous reviewers, major categories of standard-setting methods are presented, but an exhaustive cataloging of specific techniques is not repeated. Instead, in keeping with the need for practical advice, the best methods of each type are described along with a rationale for their preference in particular applications.

The Arbitrariness Debate

Glass (1978b) analyzed existing standard-setting methods and concluded that all methods are arbitrary or rest on arbitrary premises. For example, when judges set standards, the choice of judges, the choice of procedure, and the decision to average the judgments or accept the lowest one will each lead to different standards. When seemingly more empirical measures are used, the choice of criterion indicators of success, choice of examinees, and the weighting of errors still rest on human judgments that can produce a variety of standards. Glass did not imply that licensing or personnel selection tests were uncorrelated with valid criteria; he merely stated that such tests do not permit "sensible, nonarbitrary demarcation of scores into two categories described by words and ideas like 'competent and incompetent,' 'skilled and unskilled,' 'knowledgeable and ignorant'" (p 246). Glass concluded that standard-setting methods were so fundamentally flawed that other means should be sought to interpret test scores and to make educational decisions.

Popham (1978a) and others (Block, 1978; Hambleton, 1978) objected to Glass's conclusion. They pointed out that there are two dictionary definitions for *arbitrary* and only one denotes capriciousness; the other definition permits that arbitrary decisions can be made with careful deliberation. They conceded that all standard-setting methods require human judgment, but declared that they are not thereby arbitrary in the more pejorative sense. Furthermore, they argued that since classification decisions are often unavoidable, the judgments should be made as defensibly and as reasonably as possible.

The exchange between Glass and Popham is so important that it has been recapitulated in almost every article on standard setting since. Because the central proposition was conceded (all standards are arbitrary) before whimsy was debated, many practitioners overlook the significance of the point won by Glass. It should be remembered that no matter how judicious the procedures are for arriving at a standard, the cut-off point still imposes a false dichotomy on a continuum of proficiency. Just because excellence can be distinguished from incompetence at the extremes does not mean excellence and incompetence can be unambiguously separated at the cut-off. The fallacy in the standard-setting enterprise is characterized in a parody by Rowley (1982):

> It was only when the need for a decision arose that we were forced to impose an artificial dichotomy on the distribution of beardedness scores. Prior to doing this, it had been obvious that there were as many degrees of beardedness as there were beards. After the dichotomy had been made, we found ourselves referring to people as if there were simply two kinds—bearded and unbearded—forgetting the oversimplification which this involved. We began to ask ourselves: "I wonder to what category that person *really* belongs," as though bearded and non-bearded were pre-ordained categories, and our task was merely to discover the truth. But beardedness, like height, beauty, competence, and most human characteristics, is a matter of degree, even if our use of language sometimes makes it appear otherwise. (p. 94)

The reification of two categories of persons can create a much bigger distortion than individual measurement error. In this chapter, when standards are called arbitrary, the intended connotation is not that they are capricious, but that they impose an artificial dichotomy. The problem of how to treat grey areas between recognizable black and white is addressed in the review of standard-setting methods. Furthermore, the guidelines for practitioners include advice about which test uses warrant the imposition of cut-offs and which do not, given the distortion in the dichotomized results.

A Standard-setting Vignette

The standards problem is not new. Teachers face the same dilemma each time they assign grades. How excellent should a student be to receive an A? Where should the cut-off be between a C and a D?* With somewhat the air of a confession, I thought it might be instructive to review what considerations influence my decisions when I determine grades for an introductory graduate-level statistics course. This, in microcosm, is how I grapple with the standards problem.

First, because it is a graduate level course, it is understood that most of the grades will be A's and B's, with only those students who are not performing acceptably as graduate students receiving C's. (On very rare occasions a student with below-chance performance will be given a D.) The problem is to determine how many test questions "right" constitutes acceptable performance and, further, how many represent excellence. Both normative and absolute conventions are available. Because of administrative directives to hold the line on grade inflation and a personal desire for high standards, a starting point in the deliberation is to draw the line that will produce half A's and half

*Teachers who believe they have escaped the subjectivity of grading by contracting with students for grades have merely substituted *amount* of work for any judgment of the *quality* of that work, e.g., one 25-page term paper with footnotes and three book reports equal an A. If they intend to judge the content of the work in any way, teachers will still face the problem of deciding how good is good enough.

B's. This norm can be overriddden, but only if some evidence is available that the class is unusually able to unusually weak. Those who protest this allegiance to norms without knowing what level of statistics the students have actually mastered would certainly be convinced by the foolishness of specific cases that deviated significantly from this norm. The instructor who gave all A's would have, upon inspection, called a student excellent who could not read data from a table or graph. The instructor who imposed a lower distribution of grades (one-third C's perhaps) would have ignored that some selection occurs in the admission to graduate school and would have assigned the equivalent of a failing grade (C) to students who answered all of the terminology questions correctly and could do simple computations. It turns out, then, that the norm was not created in a vacuum; the expected percentage of A's and B's is linked somehow with experience about actual skills that students typically possess. In fact, the content of the course has evolved (in universities across the country) so as to make it possible for some students to be excellent and most to be satisfactory. The tailoring of reasonable instructional expectations to student capabilities is similar to grading practices 30 years ago, when 70% correct was always the passing mark. The content was adjusted so that 70% was always the standard (see Shepard, 1980b); but 70% would not automatically be a valid standard if the content had not been appropriately tailored.

The risk of having normative standards is that students will be misjudged if they are, by chance, in an unusually strong (or weak) class. Some allowance could be made subjectively for the strength of the class. Ebel (1979) suggested collecting independent data on ability level. After many years of experience with tests of roughly parallel content and difficulty, I am willing to promise students an absolute standard of 85% correct being an A and 65% being a B. Note that these absolute cut-offs are nearly always higher than the actual cut-offs, i.e., 80% may turn out to be an A after other considerations are brought to bear. But students are assured that outstanding performance will be recognized, even if everyone achieves at the same high level. These absolute cut-offs can be defended in terms of the actual test content they reflect. A student who receives a no-passing C missed 40% or 35% of the test content, which, on closer scrutiny, means that they could not label a graph correctly, recognize paraphrased definitions of terms, or perform simple algebraic substitutions. The absolute standards proposed here would of course be meaningless with a different test. The absolute standards were derived only after years of experience with the same or parallel test content. Interestingly, these standards are consistent in the long run with the normative standard (half A's and half B's), and only serve to mediate year-to-year fluctuations in the caliber of specific classes.

When normative and absolute criteria suggest different cut-off points, I will often study individual test papers in the region of dispute. Examining the kinds of errors students make could have the effect of lowering the cut-off, if the mistakes were all on esoteric or ambiguous items or on those I felt were poorly instructed. Because the test was already constructed to sample essential bits of knowledge, it is more often the case that looking at the items missed will make me choose the higher cut-off. Conversely, too few students receiving A's in a seemingly typical class will make me suspect the test and the teacher rather than the students' knowledge, and therefore I would lower the standard. Occasionally I am struck that students who clearly seem outstanding in class would not get an A by one of the cut-offs and am moved to choose the more generous standard. Of course, this personal favoritism is passed along to all students with similar scores.

Several lessons may be derived from this example. First, standards are implicitly normative. In any context our sense of what is outstanding (worthy of a Nobel prize or an A+) and what is ordinary but acceptable comes from our experience with typical performance. Second, normative and content-based standards are more likely to converge when instructional material and grading criteria have evolved together over a period of time. This situation is, of course, not likely to pertain when standards are created de novo for minimum competency tests. Finally, normatively based standards can be adjusted if there is a compelling rationale based on either inspection of the test content or on nontest evidence of student knowledge.

REVIEW OF STANDARD-SETTING METHODS

State Mastery Models

Throughout this chapter the standard-setting dilemma is characterized by having to locate a point on a continuum where unacceptable performance switches to acceptable. The learning being assessed is viewed as incremental and continuous, hence the artificiality of dichotomous scores. A quite different model of learning is possible, however. State models as distinct from continuum models have been nurtured in the literature on criterion-referenced testing. According to the mastery-state paradigm, learning is "all or nothing." Either you have mastered the skill or you have not. Conceptualizing learning in this way is consistent with the emphasis in criterion-referenced testing with carefully defining discrete homogeneous bits of a content domain.

If traits were truly dichotomous, the standard-setting problem would not be so fundamentally difficult. Dichotomous test scores would mirror the dichotomous true states, and standard setters would only have to make allowance for measurement error in the observed scores. Indeed, advocates of state models assert that they hold the solution to the arbitrariness problem. The most up-to-date review of the arguments underlying state models and development of less restrictive mathematical paradigms has been provided by Macready and Dayton (1980).

In this chapter I virtually ignore state model standard-setting methods and proceed unconvinced by Macready and Dayton (1980). An explanation is called for and may be helpful to practitioners. State models will be of little use in most real testing situations because neither their logical nor their mathematical assumptions can be satisfied. Although the more general models developed by Macready and Dayton have eliminated some of the most restrictive assumptions, e.g., that all items in the test must be equally difficult, state models still require that each "test" cover highly specific homogeneous content domains. An example of how narrow the domains must be comes from Macready's (1975) research on model fit. The domain for the sample test was defined by an item form that required that "all items have a three-digit multiplier and a three-digit multiplicand, and may require one or more 'carry' operations for a correct solution" (p. 511). Livingston (1980) has noted that this type of specificity in skill acquisition is not likely to exist for subject areas outside of mathematics. Berk (1980) likewise concluded that state models rest on assumptions that make them incompatible with actual testing situations.

Old state models (Emrick, 1971; Macready & Dayton, 1977; Roudabush, 1974) required that no other trait could be predictive of a correct response except the underlying mastery states. This meant, for example, that all nonmasters had to have a uniform probability of success rather than some guessing at random and some benefiting from partial knowledge. Interestingly, Macready and Dayton (1980) have gotten around this restriction by introducing a covariate into the mathematical model to account for differential probabilities of success. If the covariate is continuous, it can be dichotomized to facilitate parameter estimation. Nothing has been gained at this point over the arbitrariness of continuum models. Something may be lost, in fact, if practitioners are distracted by the mathematical modeling too much to notice the judgments involved in selecting a covariate and imposing a dichotomy on it.

My advice would be not to use state models in applied testing programs such as state assessments or district-administered criterion-referenced testing programs. State models are obviously too complicated for classroom use. The only area where state models should be applied is in research designed to test that which the models assume. Are some cognitive skills "all or nothing"? Are there learning hierarchies? Are Piagetian abilities acquired in giant steps or incrementally? Can a stair-step model of learning be demonstrated by manipulating prerequisite training? For research of this type, it is important to have a well developed theoretical model as an alternative to the continuous, linear model that thus far characterizes most learning data.

Judgments of Test Content

All standard-setting methods rely on human judgment (Hambleton, 1980; Jaeger, 1976; Shepard, 1979) and are, in this sense, arbitrary. Methods may, in fact, be categorized by the different ways in which judgments enter the standard-setting process. The category of method that has received the greatest attention involves judgments of test content. That is, standard setters look at items on the test and decide how many should be passed to reflect minimal proficiency. Livingston (1980) referred to this as the conjectural approach because it involves decisions about a hypothetical minimally competent examinee rather than judgments about real test takers.

Historically, standards based on test content have been sought because this is the only way to go about setting standards that are *absolute*. In the early writing on criterion-referenced testing, careful definition of criterion behaviors associated with a test score was contrasted with the *relative* information provided by norm-referenced tests (Glaser, 1963; Popham & Husek, 1969). Therefore, it was implied that any kind of normative data would be antithetical to the purpose of criterion-referenced testing. Later, it was acknowledged that test scores could be both criterion-referenced (content domain-referenced) and norm-referenced, so as to tell not only *what* pupils were doing but *how well* they were doing (Popham, 1976). Similarly, authors reviewing standard-setting procedures have sanctioned the supplemental use of normative data (Conaway, 1979; Hambleton et al., 1979; Jaeger, 1978; Shepard 1979, 1980b). After all, the experience that standard setters use to determine what constitutes acceptable performance is nothing more than imperfect norms (Shepard, 1976). Still, the most important aspect of test content methods is that they are relatively absolute; that is, standards are derived from judgments about what examinees *should* be able to do.

Standard-setting procedures based on judgments of test content include the Angoff (1971), Ebel (1979), Jaeger (1978), and Nedelsky (1954) methods. My advice is to use the Angoff procedure because it is the most straightforward. Ultimately judges must determine a cut-off score on the test, e.g., 31 right out of 50 is a passing mark. It is more helpful if judges can see directly how their judgments of individual test items will be aggregated to comprise the final standard. With some methods, the Nedelsky technique particularly, the treatment of individual items is so complex or mysterious that judges do not see the direct link between item ratings and the final test standard.

All of the test content methods first require that judges have some conception of minimally acceptable performance on the trait being assessed. Depending on the nature of the test, this may mean envisioning a minimally competent doctor, a high school graduate, or a third-grade reader. Livingston and Zieky (1982) have written a very clear manual on steps to follow in setting passing scores. They provide advice for eliciting an agreed-upon definition of borderline performance. These training activities can help eliminate those differences of opinion that *can be stated*, e.g., the judge who confuses college entrance requirements with high school exit requirements. The definitional phase is essential, but it will not eliminate subjective differences of opinion as the construct is translated into concrete test scores.

Using the Angoff procedure, a judge reads each item on the test and assigns a probability to it. The probability is the likelihood that a minimally competent test taker will answer the item correctly. Because the examinee is hypothetical, the judge is expressing what *should* be true. Angoff (1971) suggested that the probabilities might be easier to estimate if judges imagined a large number of minimally competent individuals and then stated what proportion of this group would answer each item correctly. An alternative way to think about the task would be to imagine sets of items of similar difficulty and then state what proportion of such items should be answered correctly. As we will see, this reasoning borrows a little from the Ebel (1979) and Jaeger (1978) methods.

All of the methods for judging test content establish a standard by summing the probabilities assigned to individual test items. The techniques differ only in how the rating task is posed to the judges. Ebel (1979) had judges sort items into a matrix defined by three levels of difficulty and four levels of relevance. The judges then had to decide on a fixed probability of success for each cell in the matrix, e.g., easy-essential items should be answered correctly 95% of the time, but easy items of questionable relevance might only be assigned a 75% probability. The drawback to the Ebel method is that judges do not seem to be able to keep the two dimensions distinct.* However, grouping items and then assigning a common probability does facilitate the judges' task.

A modified version of the Angoff method using groupings of items is somewhere between the Ebel and Jaeger approaches in complexity. Jaeger (1978) made the judges' task even simpler and more concrete by asking for each item, "Should every high school graduate be able to answer this item correctly?" "__Yes, __No," and "If a student *does not* answer this item correctly should he/she be denied a high school diploma?" "__Yes, __No" (p. 10). Because of the Yes-No format, the allowable item probabilities are only 0% and 100%. Judges might be frustrated by the absence of a "maybe" choice. My preference for the Angoff method comes from the feeling that in most knowledge areas there are very few 100% essential items; ignorance on one point can usually be compensated for by success on other points. The grouped item Angoff strategy allows a continuum of probabilities, with the judge making only as many distinctions as seem meaningful. Each judge comprises a cut-off by saying, for example, a minimally competent individual should be able to answer so many (say 90%) of these really important items plus 75% of these next important items and only 50% of the so-so important items. In this example, if there were 25, 15, and 10 items, respectively, the final cut-off score would be 39 out of 50 [or $(.90 \times 25) + (.75 \times 15) + (.50 \times 10)$].

The Nedelsky (1954) method is the oldest of the procedures designed to set absolute standards. It has been widely used with minimum competency tests and on certification examinations in the health professions. Nedelsky's method requires judges to imagine a minimally competent candidate. Then, for each multiple-choice item, the judge is to say what answer choices the minimally competent person could eliminate as clearly not true. Finally, a

*It is also worrisome to have a test containing items that are easy but are of questionable relevance. Once the cut-off is set, there is no control over which easy items the examinee actually gets right, the relevant or the irrelevant.

probability of success is derived for each item by *assuming that the minimally competent examinee guesses at random* from among the remaining answer choices.

Unfortunately, the Nedelsky approach has serious conceptual and technical flaws that have only recently received attention (Brennan & Lockwood, 1980; van der Linden, 1982). The method is conceptually flawed because there is no good reason or evidence to support the idea that examinees who do not know the answer guess at random. Test theory has changed considerably since the 1940s when the Nedelsky method was first used. Examinees seldom guess at random; in fact test items are specifically written so that distractors will be attractive to examinees who have not mastered the concept. Technically, the Nedelsky method is limited because it only allows a discrete set of probability values, depending on the number of answer choices (Brennan & Lockwood, 1980; van der Linden, 1982). More importantly, it does not permit probabilities between 1 and .5. Because judges are rarely willing to assign probabilities of 1 (equivalent to 100% standard), judges may be forced to assign a value of .5 to many items. This may explain why standards set with the Nedelsky method tend to be systematically lower than with other judgmental methods (Shepard, 1980b). Practically, the Nedelsky method is more trouble than it is worth since it requires more training of judges than the other methods. Ironically, it may be the complexity of the Nedelsky method which continues to make it attractive. That is, because judges are led through more elaborate steps, they may feel that the standard has been more scientifically and objectively determined. In fact, the Nedelsky method is not more scientific and should not be preferred to methods where judges are more self-conscious about their deliberations.

In addition to choosing a standard-setting technique, there are several other procedural matters that influence the determination of the final cut-off. Shepard (1976) and Jaeger (1978) suggested that various constituencies should be represented in the standard-setting process. Furthermore, the independent judgments of different "experts" should be preserved to prevent the judges with the most status (e.g., principals) from determining the standard. Even when a single method is used, the standards produced by different judges are usually highly variable (Brennan & Lockwood, 1980; Koffler, 1980; Skakun & Kling, 1980). This is not surprising given the arbitrariness of the task, the subjectivity in the definition of minimal competence, and differences in value positions. Jaeger (1978) used a Delphi technique and Brennan & Lockwood (1980) proposed a reconciliation procedure to try to bring judges to some kind of consensus. In my opinion, seeking consensus may be misplaced precision at this stage of the standard-setting process. It could be that the range of individual judges' standards spans a reasonable range on the performance continuum; it could also be that all of the judges have proposed unrealistic standards. The various judgmentally recommended standards should be arrayed along the score continuum. Then, insights from entirely different types of methods should be sought. Especially, the empirical and normative approaches discussed in the next section are akin to gathering validity evidence to corroborate the absolute judgments.

Judgments of Test Takers: Validation Groups

When judges look only at test questions and not at examinees they sometimes set standards that are demonstrably invalid. Schoon, Gullion, and Ferrara (1979) reported that using the Ebel and Nedelsky techniques, experts would have failed more than half of the candidates seeking certification in the health professions. Given extensive knowledge of the candidates in supervised field settings, the experts were inclined to believe that most of the candidates were competent and that the cut-off score was wrong. Similarly, when 38% of the high school students in Florida failed the minimum competency test (MCT) in mathematics, Glass (1978a) concluded that the standard was in error; on norm-referenced tests, Florida students do not look worse in math than in other subject areas (in reading the MCT failure rate was only 10%).

Indeed, experienced test developers recognize that it is sometimes difficult to tell by inspection how examinees will respond to test questions. Consider, for example, the New Jersey (1976, p. 179) assessment items where 86% of the seventh graders answered an addition problem correctly when it was presented in vertical format, but only 46% knew the answer when the problem was in horizontal format. (A parallel discrepancy occurred for subtraction problems.) It is because we cannot always anticipate the meaning of items to examinees that construct validity evidence is now considered essential for criterion-referenced tests (Hambleton, 1980; Linn, 1980; Messick, 1975).

The examples given suggest that the validity criterion for evaluating a standard can be found by obtaining more in-depth assessment of the examinees themselves. When we already have substantial evidence of which students are masters and which are nonmasters (leaving out the uncertain cases), we will judge the test and its passing score by how closely it replicates this prior classification. Zieky and Livingston (1977) proposed a standard-setting method whereby this validity data would be used directly to establish a cut-off score. Their Contrasting Groups method requires that teachers or experts judge examinees. Their judgments of who is a master and who is a nonmaster are presumably based on a much more thorough familiarity with what the students can do than is represented on the test. Although this kind of in-depth investigation would not be feasible on a regular basis, it is worthwhile to conduct a single study to establish how good the test is as a surrogate for better-informed evaluations. The Contrasting Groups method is analogous to known-groups validation whereby the diagnostic validity of a test is established with known cases (see also Berk, chapter 5).

After masters and nonmasters have been identified apart from the test, a cut-off score on the test is selected which best discriminates between the two groups. In Figure 7.1, a hypothetical cut-off score is illustrated; in this case the standard was selected to equate the two types of error, that is, "true" masters would fail the test as often as "true" nonmasters would pass. The

Figure 7.1. Simple illustration of the contrasting groups standard-setting method with one sample, one judge, one rule for treating uncertain cases

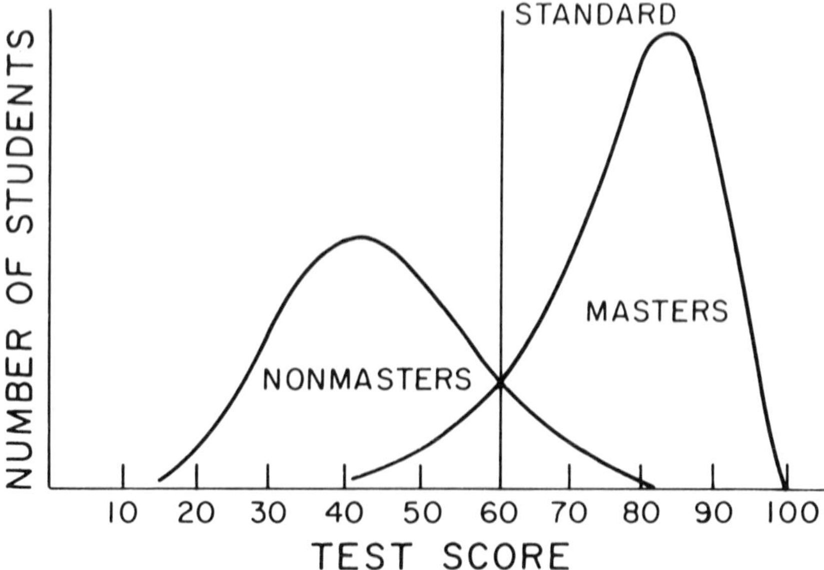

question of whether the two types of error should be weighted equally is discussed in a later section.

At this point the reader may believe that since the Contrasting Groups method can provide validity evidence to discredit the test content methods, this is the true standard-setting procedure. Unfortunately, the Contrasting Groups method can produce a variety of different standards, none of which is certifiably more valid than another. The illustration of the method in Figure 7.1 is misleadingly simple. The region of overlap between the two groups can be altered by numerous factors, including the proportion of nonmasters in the sample, judges' stringency in defining mastery, and how uncertain cases are classified (are they cast out, called nonmasters, or called masters?). Figure 7.2 better illustrates the vagaries of choosing a standard, even by the empirical method. Although it can surely be argued that an absolutely determined standard could be so far out of bounds that known-groups data would invalidate it, it does not follow that the Contrasting Groups method will find the "true" standard with precision. At best this procedure serves to identify the region on the performance continuum where masters and nonmasters are virtually indistinguishable. Somewhere in this range a credible cut-off point can be drawn.

Refinements of the Contrasting Groups method have been proposed. Livingston and Zieky (1982) offer a smoothing technique to pinpoint the line of demarcation between the groups. Koffler (1980) used a quadratic discrimi-

Figure 7.2. Complex illustration of the contrasting groups standard-setting method with multiple samples and multiple judges

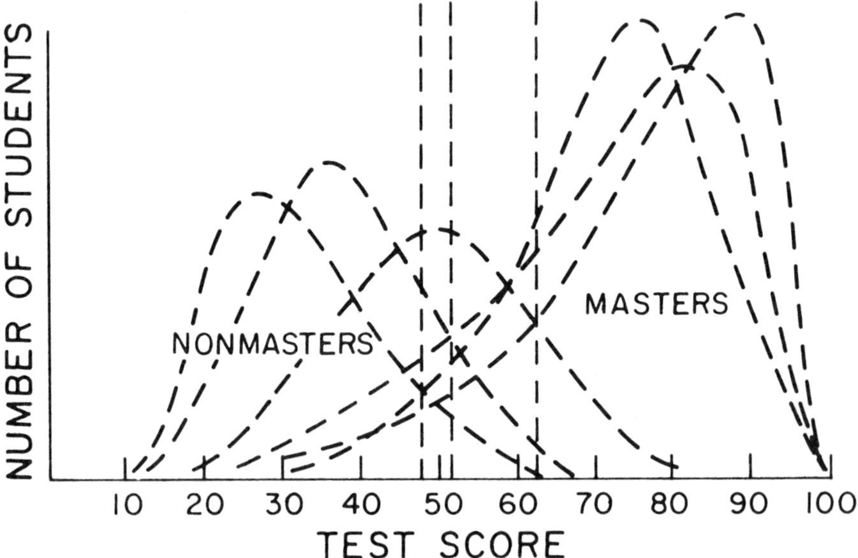

nant function to select a point that minimized the classification errors. Again, it may be misplaced precision to use elegant statistical techniques to refine a cut-off point when greater sources of error are ignored. At least the statistical techniques reveal when the test is expected to make a discrimination that cannot be verified. For example, on the New Jersey eleventh-grade mathematics competency test, Koffler (1980) found that the distribution of judged masters and nonmasters overlapped so much that a cut-off could not be set. In addition to accounting for random error, however, it might also be helpful to preserve information about systematic sources of variation such as the range of cut-offs that would have resulted from the separate judges and samples before the data were aggregated. A logical "confidence interval" of this type again reminds decision makers that the cut-off point is arbitrary and that a range of values can be rationalized.

An alternative standard-setting method proposed by Zieky and Livingston (1977) also involves judgments about groups. They call it the Borderline Group method. Using the same judgmental procedure already described, borderline cases are identified and the median test score for the group is set as the standard. Because it would require larger sample sizes to get an adequate number of borderline cases and because the definitional problems would be even greater than with masters and nonmasters, there is no compelling reason ever to use this method instead of the Contrasting Groups procedure.

Norms and Quotas

Glass (1978b) argued that since any differences in passing rates would be attributable to arbitrariness in the standard-setting methods, standards should be set directly by deciding upon an acceptable proportion to fail. Passing rates associated with potential cut-off scores serve two important purposes: (1) they supply meaning and (2) they anticipate the practical consequences of test-based decisions.

Passing rates, normative percentiles corresponding to a cut-off score, are a form of validity evidence. Just as a cut-off score is supported if it discriminates between known masters and nonmasters, validity is enhanced if the proportion failing the test is in keeping with the proportion of known nonmasters. For example, we would consider a passing score on a high school equivalency exam to be too high if fewer than half of high school seniors could pass the exam. Using the same reasoning, cut-off scores on C.L.E.P. tests, the college credit-by-examination program, are usually set such that B students are separated from C students in comparable college courses (Shea, 1980).

In the minds of many criterion-referenced test advocates, there remains a lingering aversion to normative standards because they are *relative*. In California, for example, a school official in a large urban school district lamented, "Our students have learned more but the norms keep moving up so our percentile rank stays the same." Norms can also appear as a foolish standard when every school district in the country sets as its goal "to be above the national norms." Such an accomplishment (however unlikely) would of course be defined away by computing a new median.

This lack of mooring could be eliminated by setting up a comparison to a fixed benchmark as well as to a changing norm, just as when costs are expressed in standardized 1967 dollars as well as in current dollars. But suggesting that passing rates be considered directly when setting standards is not the same as saying that standards should always be dictated by "the norm" (indeed, the median score would be too high a cut-off for MCT programs), nor does it mean that the cut-off is free floating, changing with the vagaries of examinee samples. Rather, considering plausible passing rates as a source of validity evidence is merely to acknowledge that even seemingly absolute standards are implicitly normative. In Shepard (1980a), I argued that Einstein was a genius because what he could do was *rare*. If everyone had Einstein's capabilities, what he could do would be incorporated into our "absolute" expectations for high school graduates. Thus, in the grading vignette offered earlier, the cut-off between a B and a C in introductory statistics is rationalized in terms of students being able to read graphs and make algebraic substitutions; but if none of the students had been able to demonstrate these skills, it is more likely that the course content would change than that all of the students would fail. Similarly, aspiring physicians are not failed on certification exams if they have not mastered a surgical procedure that only one senior physician in the world can do. Standards and expectations evolve from experience with typical rather than exceptional performance. Popham (1978b) has made the point that normative data should not be considered heretical to criterion-referenced testers. Moreover, specifically regarding performance standards, he has said, "One fairly standard strategy for deciding upon reasonable performance expectations involves the use of an assessment device over a period of time until a sufficient amount of information has been accumulated to indicate how a group of students will typically perform" (p. 165).

Given that absolute standards can always be challenged as invalid if they seriously violate normative expectations, it may be that standards based directly on a selected passing rate are relatively less arbitrary and more defensible than methods based only on test content. Glass (1978b) argued that passing scores on certification exams are most often governed by marketplace considerations such as the number of available positions. Specific cases reported by Kleinke (1980) and Rentz (1980) (see Shepard, 1980a) suggest that professional licensure committees will "adjust" a judgmentally set standard to achieve a credible passing rate. In many universities, the "standards" in freshmen English composition courses happen to correct very closely for the overadmission of first-year students.

The call for absolute standards assumes that most testing situations are quota-free, that is, it is possible that everyone or no one could pass the test. In fact, there are usually implicit quotas (the acceptable passing rates), and these may be more useful than inspection of test content in selecting cut-offs. Millman (1973) suggested, for example, that the amount of resources available for providing remediation should be considered in setting standards. Shepard (1983) noted that most test-based decisions are neither strictly fixed quota nor quota free. Just as in the grading example, norms or quotas set the plausible boundaries for cut-offs. Then minor adjustments can be made to allow for a particularly able or deficient class or to add something for educational aspirations.

If passing rates are selected, or at least considered, directly, there is the additional benefit that neither the standard setters nor the public will be fooled into thinking that the number of students passing the test is a measure of the quality of schooling. The tautology always exists that if standard setters choose a lenient standard, many students will pass (and schools will look good); if they set a stringent standard, fewer students will pass (and schools will look bad). If standard setters choose the passing rate, everyone sees the tautology; if they look at test content, the direct link between the stringency of the standard and passing rates is obscured. In the Florida example (Glass, 1978a), panels of experts set a 70% cut-off score on both the math and the reading test without looking at the test questions. When the test was administered 38% failed in math and 10% in reading. The best explanation for the difference was that the math test was harder (i.e., the standard was higher). Because politicians and educators *believed* that the standards were comparable, however, enormous resources were poured into improving math instruction.

Other Empirical Methods

As proposed in the introduction, this review of standard-setting methods has been selective; not all techniques have been treated with the same level of detail. Several other empirical methods deserve mention. They have been given short shrift in this chapter largely on practical grounds. That is, they are conceptually intriguing, but turn out not to help in resolving the standard setters' dilemma.

Berk (1976) proposed a procedure identical to the Contrasting Groups method except that criterion groups would be instructed and uninstructed groups rather than judged masters and nonmasters. Although this method may seem to avoid the need for judgment, in fact, choices would have to be made about how long the instructional period should be and whether to eliminate "instructed" students who had not yet learned the material. For high school competency programs, Berk's method would not be applicable because an uninstructed group could not be identified. (Recent court decisions would make it illegal for tests to cover what some examinees have not been taught.) Berk's method would be more appropriate for classroom uses of criterion-referenced tests, as originally intended. Clearly, the ability to distinguish between instructed and uninstructed examinees as well as judged masters and nonmasters is essential for test validity. It is unlikely, however, that this procedure will pinpoint a particular cut-off score.

Block (1972) developed a standard-setting model called "educational consequences." It was intended to locate the point on the test score continuum which maximized performance on some later learning outcome dimension. Data would be required to determine the functional relationship between test scores and criterion performance. Block expected that the graph relating these two variables would be an "S" shaped learning curve,* that is, low scores on the test would be associated with low scores on the criterion and high scores on the test would be associated with high scores on the criterion, and in some region of the curve there would be a dramatic rise in criterion performance for a small increase in test score (also called a step function). It would be in this region of the graph, presumably leading to acceptable criterion performance, that the cut-off score would be drawn. Unfortunately, these thresholds or step functions do not often materialize in real data. Rather, as Block (1972) found in his own research, the relationship between test scores and a subsequent valued outcome measure is usually linear; the relationship is described by a straight line with no dramatic increments sug-

*Although learning curves are sometimes said to be "S" shaped, the printed letter does not properly depict the mathematical function which is a monotonic increasing curve like this.

gesting an optimization point. The inadequacy of this model with real data is explained further in Glass (1978b) and Shepard (1980a).

Numerous other "empirical" standard-setting procedures exist. They are treated in the next section on false positive and false negative errors. The remaining methods assume not only that a functional relationship exists between the test continuum and an intended criterion, but also that a cut-off has already been specified on the criterion. These remaining procedures, then, are not standard-setting methods per se, but rather are methods to minimize test classification errors given the "true" dichotomy on the criterion.

Classification Errors

When a test is used to classify examinees into *two* groups, "pass or fail," "competent or incompetent," there are really *four* outcome possibilities, depending upon examinees' true level of mastery. Correct classification decisions are made by the test when the test-based classifications correspond to the true level of mastery, that is, masters are called masters and nonmasters are identified as nonmasters. Given, however, that there is error associated with the test, it is also possible to make two types of incorrect decisions. False positive errors occur where incompetents are passed by the test; false negative errors occur when true masters are mistakenly failed by the test.

Early in the development of criterion-referenced tests it was recognized that differential costs associated with the two types of error should be taken into account when setting the passing score. Millman (1973) suggested, for example, that standards should be set relatively low if the psychological and financial costs associated with remedial instruction were judged to be high. Adjustments to the final cut-off score could be informal and crude, reflecting only a general sense that one type of error is more serious in a given situation. For example, Jaeger (1978) recommended that the lowest of several standards recommended by panels of judges be adopted, presumably because false negative errors are the more serious in the context of minimum competency testing. Sometimes cut-offs on state high school exams or teacher certification tests are adjusted downwards by one or two standard errors of measurement (using classical formulas) "just to be safe." It is also possible to use fairly elegant mathematical models to describe the relationship of the test to the intended criterion and to reflect differential utilities associated with the two types of error.

The very best and up-to-date review of mathematical models for optimizing cut-off scores is found in van der Linden (1980). It should be emphasized that these models are not intended to set standards; rather they are used to select a cut-off on the observed score continuum to minimize classification errors, given that a standard has already been determined on the true score scale. Glass (1978b) called methods of this type "bootstrapping on other criterion scores"; he debunked them because they accepted without question the validity of the criterion cut-offs. Obviously, the methods do not obviate the arbitrariness dilemma and cannot be substituted for the judgmental standard-setting approaches discussed earlier. In his review, van der Linden (1980) makes it clear that the decision-theoretic approach is not a standard-setting technique, "but a technique to minimize the consequences of measurement and sampling error, which, as a part of the normal routine, ought to follow each time a standard-setting technique is used" (p. 470). It should also be noted that the decision-theoretic models reviewed by van der Linden are distinct from the state mastery models reviewed earlier, which also follow a decision theory formulation. The state models assume that two distinct latent states exist in nature, whereas the decision theory models considered here assume a continuous latent variable, but with a standard predetermined on that continuum.

Many readers may find the mathematical presentation of van der Linden's article too difficult. Indeed, for many applications of criterion-referenced tests, especially for classroom use, the methods are too complex to be practical. Even with computer programs available to implement particular models (Isaacs & Novick, 1978; Koppelaar, van der Linden, & Mellenbergh, 1977), considerable sophistication is required to choose the correct model and assign utilities. The amount of investment required to master these procedures would probably only be warranted in large-scale assessment programs, e.g., state minimum competency testing programs or district-developed criterion-referenced tests. The novice may wish to start by reading Livingston's (1980) conceptual summary of decision theory used to weight errors. Then, van der Linden's (1980) review should be consulted. It is the single best source inasmuch as the differences among many models are laid out. Previous contributions from individual authors differ as to the nature of the presumed criterion (internal or external), the psychometric model for the data (e.g., classical or latent trait), and the form of the loss function. These distinctions leading to the final choice among models are well explicated by van der Linden.

It is especially important that practitioners be aware of recent developments in the specification of loss functions. Originally, threshold loss was deemed appropriate for criterion-referenced tests (Hambleton & Novick, 1973); that is, classification errors of one type were considered to be equally serious regardless of how *far* the examinee's true score was from the cut-off. So, a false negative whose true score was one point above the true standard was given the same weight as a false negative whose true score was markedly above the true standard. More recent work in identifying loss functions allows for "more serious" errors (i.e., more clearly above or below the true standard) to be weighted more heavily. For example, van der Linden and Mellenbergh (1977) proposed a linear loss function, and Novick and Lindley (1978) demonstrated that normal ogive functions can be realistic in describing the losses that decision makers assign to classification errors.

It should be reiterated that several procedures heretofore called standard-setting methods are better understood as techniques for adjusting standards. In Berk's (1980) review of continuum methods, for example, he notes that the models are either for setting cut-off scores *or* for estimating error rates. These adjustment methods, which take unreliability into account and allow for the weighting of two types of error, include well-known procedures by Huynh (1976; Huynh & Saunders, 1979) using the beta-binomial model, the Bayesian decision-theoretic model (Novick & Lewis, 1974), and linear loss models (Livingston, 1975; van der Linden & Mellenbergh, 1977). Allowing for measurement error is similar to using discriminant function procedures to find the optimum cut-off score between contrasting groups. It may sometimes have the effect of setting a cut-off on the test of 95% correct to correspond to a standard on the underlying continuum of 85% correct. The goal is to make the fewest classification errors. Moreover, unlike the discriminant function approach, these decision models make it possible to treat one type of classification error as more serious than the other. Although decision makers often find it difficult to choose specific numeric utilities, a conceptually simpler task would be to state a loss ratio, e.g., errors of one type are *two or three times* as serious as errors of the other type.

As with previous methods, a caution should be issued. It may be misplaced precision to try to fine tune a cut-off score using error models when a range of defensible values could still be entertained for the "true" standard. Decision makers may wish to implement an "adjustment" procedure as one way to reflect on the choice of a final standard. Van der Linden (1980) expects that the techniques will be used sequentially, i.e., the best judgmental standard will be chosen, then the decision-theoretic adjustment will be applied. Given the arbitrariness of the first decision, however, decision makers may wish to gain some experience with the effect of measurement error on the observed score cut-off before deciding on the final standard. It may even be that what is technically defensible is not logically defensible, as in the case where Koffler (1980) found that the statistically determined cut-off score was 0. Instances like this may occur especially when the test is either too hard or too easy relative to the standard so that it does not discriminate in the region of the cut-off. This condition suggests it may be better to revise the test rather than adjust the cut-off score. In the following section, compromise procedures are considered for combining the insights provided by different standard-setting approaches.

Compromise Procedures

In the preceding sections I have argued against premature closure in trying to resolve a final standard. The various approaches to standard setting are all arbitrary; none of the methods will lead to a "true" standard. Why attempt to reconcile judges' standards based on judgments of test questions if these are out of bounds of what would be defensible normatively? Although the Contrasting Groups strategy is based directly on known-groups validity data, there is still considerable subjectivity involved in choosing the actual cut-off. Should this choice be made statistically or judgmentally? Finally, there are formal models for specifying utilities and weighting errors, but little is known about how the choice of a psychometric model (seemingly a technical decision) can be translated into a strict or lenient policy.

Previously I have suggested (Shepard, 1980b) that since all of the methods are fallible, some insight should be sought from each of the major approaches. This is merely common-sense advice. One should try to build into the standard-setting procedure the kinds of evidence that would be compelling (and perhaps embarrassing) if produced after the fact. Both normative and absolute comparisons establish the boundaries within which plausible standards can be set.

Hofstee (1980, 1983) developed several "compromise models" for psychometric problems; one model addressed the issue of standards. Hofstee's procedure involves composing a graph of the empirical cumulative test score distribution. Then it is possible to see the corresponding failure rate (percentage of examinees falling below that point) for every test score (percentage of items correct). Hofstee asked decision makers to specify the following values:

k_{max} is the maximum percentage correct score. This is the cut-off score set high enough so that you would believe it signified mastery even if every student taking the test attained this score.

k_{min} is the minimal percentage correct score. This score is set low enough so that every student scoring below it should surely fail, even if every student scored below it.

f_{max} is the maximum acceptable percentage of failures.

f_{min} is the minimum acceptable percentage of failures.

Finally, Hofstee offered a formula for arriving at a midpoint in the range delimited by these constraints. The particular formula is not important. Rather, the model helps to make any discrepancies between the perspectives explicit so that a compromise can be reached between absolute and relative standards.

SUGGESTIONS FOR FUTURE RESEARCH

The focus of this chapter has been on practical advice for those situations where test standards must be set despite the arbitrariness of artificially dichotomizing a performance continuum. No hint has been made that these problems will eventually be solved by a vigorous program of research. It is important to see that it is the nature of the problem rather than lack of effort which prevents us from finding the preferred model for standard setting. Searching for a theoretical solution would be like the alchemists' quest to turn base metal into gold rather than like researchers conducting a reasonable series of experiments to find the cause of cancer.

At the time of Glass's (1978b) review, only one study could be cited that provided an empirical comparison of standard-setting methods (Andrew & Hecht, 1976). Recently, numerous studies of this type have been reported, including Kleinke (1980), Koffler (1980), Poggio, Glasnapp, and Eros (1981), and Skakun and Kling (1980). Although it was important that studies of this type be undertaken to see how great the differences in standards could be, this line of inquiry will not uncover the true standard-setting method. Moreover, the studies are a little misguided to the extent that they treat the methods like sacrosanct entities that are to be applied by rote (like a statistical algorithm) to arrive at a standard. The methods are strategies to try to elicit both the absolute and the normative standard *in the judges*. The standard we are groping to express is a psychological construct in the judges' minds rather than *in the methods*. When the judges' gestalt impression of what the standard should be differs from the cut-off score they themselves derive from a step-by-step procedure, the question should be: How have the mechanics of this method distorted the judges' perceptions? Studies intended to refine the instructions to judges or in other ways bring the judgments into line seem to imply that the truth is in the method, not in the judges. My own preference would be for more anecdotal information from the judges about the effect of the techniques on their formulation of a standard.

In the future, applied research on standard setting would be most helpful if the focus were on not only how absolute and empirical standards differ, but also how they are reconciled in particular situations. In the Kleinke (1980) example, decision makers chose the lower absolute standard because the passing rate was more acceptable. Does it help to array the standards based on test content and those based on judged masters before arriving at a final decision? Studies of this type will not lead to a theory of standard setting, but they may furnish more useful information for practical applications.

In the following section, guidelines for practitioners are suggested for several different testing situations. Although the complexity of standard-setting procedures will differ with testing purpose, the rationale for a composite approach is consistent. Normative expectations are always the starting point, because norms are the source of validity evidence and ultimately determine our psychological absolutes. Allowance can be made, however, for departures from what is typical and for measurement error.

GUIDELINES FOR PRACTITIONERS

Specific advice about what standard-setting procedures to use in particular situations will depend primarily on the amount of time and money that should be spent (see Hambleton, 1980). Classroom teachers should not spend more time on test development (including standard setting) than they spend on teaching. For large-scale minimum competency testing programs or professional licensure exams, the consequences of incorrect decisions are much more serious. Hence, more investment is warranted to gather the judgments and the data to arrive at a defensible passing score.

In Shepard (1980a), I distinguished three uses of criterion-referenced tests: pupil diagnosis, pupil certification, and program evaluation. When diagnostic or instructional-planning decisions are made about individual pupils, the purpose of mastery-nonmastery classifications is to decide whether a pupil needs more instruction or knows enough to go on to the next topic. Pupil diagnosis and pupil certification uses of tests are similar in that both require dichotomous mastery-nonmastery classification of examinees. They differ, however, in that certification test uses, e.g., high school graduation tests, are intended more to serve an external accountability purpose. Unlike day-to-day instructional decisions, where faulty diagnosis has low cost and is easily redressed, certification tests have more serious costs associated with invalid classifications. When criterion-referenced tests are used for program evaluation, the performance of individual pupils is not of interest. Program evaluation uses include evaluations of specific programs like Title I reading and state assessments designed to track academic achievement in local school districts. As we will see, when dichotomous classifications are not required, there are other, more appropriate comparisons one can make to evaluate the attained level of performance. In the next section, I further differentiate between two types of classroom diagnostic tests, those developed by individual teachers and those developed on a large scale by either a school district or a test publisher, but still intended for use in day-to-day instructional decisions. In each of the following cases, the use of the test determines the standard-setting procedure.

Teacher-made Classroom Tests

It is inappropriate to invoke elaborate technical procedures to set cut-off scores on teacher-made tests. Hambleton (1980) has suggested a thorough procedure whereby classroom teachers could solicit and aggregate parent judgments about passing scores. Although this level of effort may be appropriate if a school undertakes end-of-year competency testing, I believe it is bad advice for individual teachers. First, complex procedures are inappropriate because they steal a teacher's time. Even when test development also serves an instructional-planning purpose, it is indefensible to spend more time on testing procedures than on teaching. Second, numerous research studies on standard setting have shown that judges' standards are usually highly divergent from one another. Furthermore, the average of all of the judges' separate standards does not have any particular psychometric validity and can be widely discrepant from empirically derived standards based on known masters and nonmasters. Unfortunately, both parents and teachers may believe that the cut-offs have some intrinsic meaning because of the formal procedures used to set them. Therefore, they may try to "live with" indefensible standards where none of the students pass or all of the students pass or, more likely, where some of the standards seem unusually easy and some unusually hard.

At present, very few classroom teachers use even rudimentary item analysis procedures to see if test questions function as intended. It is, therefore, inappropriate to ask them to implement standard-setting procedures that rest on an understanding of test validity and item difficulty.

Faced with the problem of setting passing scores, teachers might ask these questions about the test: Is the test highly homogeneous? (That is, are the items all parallel versions of one another? For example, are they all one-digit multiplications by nines?) Is the purpose for testing to decide on the next day's instruction or to assign grades? Only when the tests are highly homogeneous do insights derive from state mastery models. With math mastery tests, for example, it is possible to imagine that a child has either mastered his nines table or not. (Note that partial knowledge is simply defined as nonmastery.) On highly homogeneous tests, mastery is defined as 100%, with some allowance for measurement error. There are no magical or particularly scientific ratios here. The conventional 80% may be too high or too low. The teacher simply tries to judge how many careless errors to expect typically from pupils who are clearly masters.

For subject areas other than math, content cannot be divided into homogeneous bits. Furthermore, test questions covering identical instructional objectives can be either hard or easy. Therefore, standards should not exist independent of a test. We should be suspicious of testing programs where the standard is a fixed value, always 80% or 70%. When standards are highly arbitrary (set without regard to the test), apparent successes and failures may merely be the result of changes in the strictness of the standard.

Norms and experience are acceptable sources for testing and grading practices (Popham, 1976, 1978b). For instructional-planning purposes, the overriding consideration is not to go on and on to new material as a student falls further and further behind. Except in math, however, there are no verifiable learning hierarchies to guide passing requirements. There is no evidence that bringing students to level X on task one will facilitate their learning of task two. Although it makes good sense not to start working on multiplying by four until a student knows his or her threes table, teachers will have to weight factors such as motivation and boredom to decide whether a student should persevere with a social studies topic poorly mastered or go on to the next (for which the first is not a prerequisite).

Large-scale Diagnostic Tests

Sometimes the development of criterion-referenced tests for pupil diagnosis is undertaken on a larger scale than individual classroom teachers can manage. Examples include district-developed criterion-referenced tests and those developed by test publishers to accompany specific curriculum materials. The collective effort and the scale of these projects makes it possible to be more rigorous in the development and try-out of individual test questions; it also makes it possible to be more formal about standard-setting procedures. Notice that a key feature of the projects is the *size* of the enterprise, yet the *purpose* of testing is still presumed to be day-to-day assessment for instructional planning. If the purpose of the test is certification (end-of-year promotion, high school graduation), regardless of who develops the test, issues of fairness and problems of misclassification become much more salient. A certification example is considered in the next section.

Instructional uses of tests differ from certification uses (see National Academy of Education, 1978) not only because errors are less serious, but also because faulty test results can be immediately observed in the classroom and corrected. When district-wide criterion-referenced tests are administered, in fact, teachers should be encouraged to investigate discrepancies between their own judgments of what students have mastered and test-based conclusions.

When a committee of teachers or teachers and parents is convened to set standards, the general rule should be to try to set a score on the test that distinguishes between known masters and nonmasters (a restatement of the Contrasting Groups method). When content domains are highly homogeneous, this may mean expecting 100% (with some allowance for the typical marking errors of known masters). For subject areas other than math number facts, the percentage of questions answered correctly can vary considerably. Although judges may wish to start by reviewing test items and establishing an absolute cut-off, this should always be subject to revision after trying the test with real students. In addition to empirical validation using a representative sample, it may also be useful to ask classroom teachers for anecdotal reports on the congruence between test results and typical classroom performance. When discrepancies occur, are they the result of a child's test anxiety or a systematic difference between classroom instruction and the content of the test, or is the teacher faced with a shy student who seemed like a master but who was not?

Although collective standard-setting efforts may make it more feasible to go through formal steps, large-scale diagnostic tests may also make the purpose of standards more confused. The empirical and judgmental procedures suggested here would allow a committee to establish cut-off scores on each of 30 first-grade reading tests representing the curricular domain. Thus students who scored above the cut-offs can be said to have mastered particular decoding or comprehension skills. These are like the checklists that come home from beginning swimming classes stating, for example, that your child can "blow bubbles under water" or "float on his back." Notice that other very crucial issues are not resolved by these standards. For example, how many of the objectives should be mastered (at the specified level) to be excellent in first grade? To pass first grade? These questions are fundamentally normative (see Popham 1976, 1978a). The standard-setting process also does not answer the question of whether students should start learning a new skill before they have "mastered" the old. This is an old problem that has not been solved by cognitive psychology or instructional science. Sometimes the inclination is to set low standards when the subject matter is not hierarchical (i.e., when it is possible to benefit from instruction on a subsequent topic without having mastered an earlier skill). An alternative is to set standards that denote full "mastery" but not to make mastery of one subdomain prerequisite to the next.

Certification Tests

Certification tests are used to make crucial decisions about individuals, for example, to grant them a high school diploma. Although state and local competency tests may look more like diagnostic tests in content, for standard-setting purposes they more resemble professional licensure examinations because of the seriousness of the test-based classifications. It is reasonable that the full artillery, all of the insights from various standard-setting techniques, be called upon to tackle this problem.

A composite model for setting standards would include the following elements (corresponding to the major categories of methods):

1. absolute judgments based on inspection of test questions,
2. empirical validation data based on judged masters and nonmasters,
3. decisions about acceptable passing rates, and
4. adjustments for unreliability to minimize the costs of classification errors.

Specifically, the process could include using the Angoff method with appropriate panels of experts, the Contrasting Groups method with experts who know the examinees, estimation of passing rates by decision makers or politically constituted committees, and statistical refinement of the cut-off score. The committee or individual who is ultimately responsible for choosing the passing score is likely to be confronted with an array of different possible cut-off scores suggested by these methods. There is no best way to reconcile them. Clearly, it has been emphasized in this review that the normative methods (Contrasting Groups and passing rates) should take precedence over widely discrepant absolute standards, since the former methods make it possible to gather validity evidence. This recommendation does not help, however, when the ranges of suggested values overlap and the question becomes: "Should we set a tough or a lenient standard?" It is possible, for example, that a range of values from the Angoff and the Contrasting Groups data would suggest that the cut-off be somewhere between 70% and 75% correct. Suppose that for a test with these cut-off score differences failure rates are 10% and 30%. Which of these rates is acceptable? Usually posing the question will help resolve the dilemma even though the same relevant insights were captured in the initial standard-setting procedures. A committee of professionals can say, for example, that it is unacceptable to fail as many as 30% of the candidates; or a chief state school officer may say that a test is too easy if only 10% fail the first time it is given.

Logically, there should not be a discrepancy between a Contrasting Groups standard and an expected passing rate. Both come from the same empirical validity data; the proportion of judged masters is the same as the expected passing rate. When the two approaches appear to differ, it can be attributable to one of two factors: either the judgments come from different sources or the test is not an efficient measure in the region of the cut-off. If teachers are the experts who implement the Contrasting Groups method but a politically constituted committee suggests the acceptable passing rates, the resulting standards can differ sharply. Knowing the source of the difference may help to decide which standard to uphold. For example, if most of the parents participating on voluntary committees expected their own children to attend college, it may be that their standards are considered to be too high. Conversely, a decision maker may decide that teachers from inner city schools were too generous in identifying masters and, therefore, discrepancies should be resolved in the more stringent direction.

Statistical procedures used to find the optimum cut-off between contrasting groups are similar to the decision-theoretic error models. Because of measurement error, the observed score cut-off will not always equal the intended true score cut-off. It is also the case that the observed proportion passing may not equal the expected true passing rate. Unfortunately, the credibility of the test depends on the observed results. If the test cannot discriminate in the region of the intended cut-off score, statistical adjustments may lead to a bizarre policy (e.g., 100% passing). When this happens, the test should be revised rather than juggling the standard.

Program Evaluation

When a newspaper report carries the news that only 60% of the local high school students could pass a functional literacy test or when a school principal announces that 95% of our students have mastered all of their math facts, educational *programs* are being evaluated in terms of a standard. Throughout this chapter the arbitrariness of locating standards on a performance continuum has been stressed. Nevertheless, because it is often necessary to make concrete categorical decisions about individuals, suggestions have been made for setting standards as wisely as possible. For program evaluation purposes, however, it is not necessary to categorize individuals in order to summarize the school or school district's accomplishment. Doing so erroneously assumes that the standards have more intrinsic meaning than they do. A principal can easily make a program look successful by setting low standards (incidentally, this deception does not have to be done consciously). When a mean score is reported for a school, the errors of measurement in individual pupil scores "balance out." But when a percent passing is the summary statistic, classification errors on either side of the cut-off are locked in. These errors may not be serious when school A is compared to school B on the same standard. However, if a school or state tries to compare its attainments in different curricular areas or subdomains, differences in the stringency of the standards will be mistaken for program strengths and weaknesses.

In other work (Shepard 1980a, 1980b), I have urged that for program evaluation purposes criterion-referenced test results should be summarized for the full continuum, i.e., mean scores, quartile scores, and perhaps 10th and 90th percentile points. To *evaluate* whether the obtained distribution of scores is indicative of a good or bad educational accomplishment requires that it be compared to normative data (see Popham, 1976, 1978b). Livingston (1980), in criticizing my position, said:

> Shepard, taking an extreme position on the use of standards in program evaluation, states that "because standards impose an artificial dichotomy, they obscure performance information about individuals along the full performance continuum. Therefore, standards should not be used to interpret test data regarding the worth of educational programs." The first assertion is true, but the second does not follow. Any time data are summarized, information is lost. A statement such as "30% of the city's students scored below the level that a committee of teachers had selected as representing the minimum arithmetic ability acceptable for a high school graduate," is meaningful. It does not tell the whole story, but it tells an important part of the story. True, it focuses attention on achievement gains near the cutoff. In doing so, it may cause more educational resources to be directed at those students who have an acute need for them and the ability to benefit from them. (p. 577)

Perhaps it will make the difficulties clearer if I respond to Livingston specifically. He asserts that using a percent passing as a summary statistic is like using any other aggregate indicator (e.g., the arithmetic mean); some individual information is lost to achieve a summary picture. But in the case of a mean, errors of measurement are averaged out and the final number is evaluated to see if it is good or bad. With percent passing, each score is evaluated in relation to an arbitrary cut-off without regard to measurement error. The sum of these evaluations is believed to be an indicator of the quality of the program, but the pupil achievements and the validity of the standard are inextricably mixed. The city with 30% below the minimum math level will lose nothing by redoubling math instruction for that 30% (an individual placement decision). The mistake would come when teachers made judgments about program strengths and weaknesses based on differential passing rates. For example, math concepts may be emphasized over computation because the failure rates were 40% and 20%, or citizenship courses may be required over basic math because the failure rates were 30% and 10%. Vagaries in the arbitrarily set standards will be mistaken for program effects. Apparent strengths and weaknesses should never be interpreted from standards alone, without confirmation from normative comparisons.

REFERENCES

Andrew, B. J., & Hecht, J. T. A preliminary investigation of two procedures for setting examination standards. *Educational and Psychological Measurement*, 1976, *36*, 35–50.

Angoff, W. H. Scales, norms, and equivalent scores. In R. L. Thorndike (Ed.), *Educational measurement* (2nd ed.). Washington, DC: American Council on Education, 1971. Pp. 508–600.

Berk, R. A. Determination of optimal cutting scores in criterion-referenced measurement. *Journal of Experimental Education*, 1976, *45*, 4–9.

Berk, R. A. A framework for methodological advances in criterion-referenced testing. *Applied Psychological Measurement*, 1980, *4*, 563–573.

Block, J. H. Student learning and the setting of mastery performance standards. *Educational Horizons*, 1972, *50*, 183–190.

Block, J. H. Standards and criteria: A response. *Journal of Educational Measurement*, 1978, *15*, 291–295.

Brennan, R. L., & Lockwood, R. E. A comparison of the Nedelsky and Angoff cutting score procedures using generalizability theory. *Applied Psychological Measurement*, 1980, *4*, 219–240.

Conaway, L. E. Setting standards in competency-based education: Some current practices and concerns. In M. A. Bunda & J. R. Sanders (Eds.), *Practices and problems in competency-based measurement*. Washington, DC: National Council on Measurement in Education, 1979. Pp. 72–88.

Ebel, R. L. *Essentials of educational measurement* (3rd ed.). Englewood Cliffs, NJ: Prentice-Hall, 1979.

Emrick, J. A. An evaluation model for mastery testing. *Journal of Educational Measurement*, 1971, *8*, 321–326.

Glaser, R. Instructional technology and the measurement of learning outcomes: Some questions. *American Psychologist*, 1963, *18*, 519–521.

Glass, G. V. Minimum competence and incompetence in Florida. *Phi Delta Kappan*, 1978, *59*, 602–605. (a)

Glass, G. V. Standards and criteria. *Journal of Educational Measurement*, 1978, *15*, 237–261. (b)

Hambleton, R. K. On the use of cutoff scores with criterion-referenced tests in instructional settings. *Journal of Educational Measurement*, 1978, *15*, 277–290.

Hambleton, R. K. Test score validity and standard-setting methods. In R. A. Berk (Ed.), *Criterion-referenced measurement: The state of the art.* Baltimore, MD: Johns Hopkins University Press, 1980. Pp. 80–123.

Hambleton, R. K., & Eignor, D. R. Competency test development, validation, and standard setting. In R. M. Jaeger & C. K. Tittle (Eds.), *Minimum competency testing: Motives, models, measures, and consequences*. Berkeley, CA: McCutchan, 1979. Pp. 367–396.

Hambleton, R. K. & Novick, M. R. Toward an integration of theory and method for criterion-referenced tests. *Journal of Educational Measurement*, 1973, *10*, 159–170.

Hambleton, R. K., Powell, S., & Eignor, D. R. Issues and methods for standard setting. In R. K. Hambleton & D. R. Eignor, *A practitioner's guide to criterion-referenced test development, validation, and test score usage* (Report No. 70). Amherst: Laboratory of Psychometric and Evaluative Research, School of Education, University of Massachusetts, 1979.

Hambleton, R. K., Swaminathan, H., Algina, J., & Coulson, D. B. Criterion-referenced testing and measurement: A review of technical issues and developments. *Review of Educational Research*, 1978, *48*, 1–47.

Hofstee, W. K. B. *Policies of educational selection and grading: The case for compromise models.* Paper presented at the Fourth International Symposium on Educational Testing, Antwerp, Belgium, June 1980.

Hofstee, W. K. B. The case for compromise in educational selection and grading. In

S. B. Anderson & J. S. Helmick (Eds.), *On educational testing.* San Francisco: Jossey-Bass, 1983. Pp. 109-127.

Huynh, H. Statistical consideration of mastery scores. *Psychometrika*, 1976, *41*, 65-78.

Huynh, H., & Saunders, J. C. *Bayesian and empirical Bayes approaches to setting passing scores on mastery tests.* Paper presented at the annual meeting of the National Council on Measurement in Education, San Francisco, April 1979.

Isaacs, G. L., & Novick, M. R. *Computer-assisted data analysis—1978, Manual for the Computer-Assisted Data Analysis (CADA) Monitor.* Iowa City: University of Iowa, 1978.

Jaeger, R. M. *Measurement consequences of selected standard-setting models.* Paper presented at the annual meeting of the National Council on Measurement in Education, San Francisco, April 1976.

Jaeger, R. M. *A proposal for setting a standard on the North Carolina High School Competency Test.* Paper presented at the spring meeting of the North Carolina Association for Research in Education, Chapel Hill, 1978.

Jaeger, R. M. Measurement consequences of selected standard-setting models. In M. A. Bunda & J. R. Sanders (Eds.), *Practices and problems in competency-based measurement.* Washington, DC: National Council on Measurement in Education, 1979. Pp. 48-58.

Kleinke, D. J. *Applying the Angoff and Nedelsky techniques to the National Licensing Examinations in Landscape Architecture.* Paper presented at the annual meeting of the National Council on Measurement in Education, Boston, April 1980.

Koffler, S. L. A comparison of approaches for setting proficiency standards. *Journal of Educational Measurement*, 1980, *17*, 167-178.

Koppelaar, H., van der Linden, W. J., & Mellenbergh, G. J. A computer program for classifications in dichotomous decisions based on dichotomously scored items. *Tijdschrift voor Onderwijsrearch*, 1977, *2*, 32-37.

Linn, R. L. Issues of validity for criterion-referenced measures. *Applied Psychological Measurement*, 1980, *4*, 547-561.

Livingston, S. A. *A utility-based approach to the evaluation of pass/fail testing decision procedures* (Report No. COPA-75-01). Princeton, NJ: Educational Testing Service, 1975.

Livingston, S. A. Comments on criterion-referenced testing. *Applied Psychological Measurement*, 1980, *4*, 575-581.

Livingston, S. A. & Zieky, M. J. *Passing scores: A manual for setting standards of performance on educational and occupational tests.* Princeton, NJ: Educational Testing Service, 1982.

Macready, G. B. The structure of domain hierarchies found within a domain-referenced testing system. *Educational and Psychological Measurement*, 1975, *35*, 583-598.

Macready, G. B. & Dayton, C. M. The use of probabilistic models in the assessment of mastery. *Journal of Educational Statistics*, 1977, *2*, 99-120.

Macready, G. B. & Dayton, C. M. The nature and use of state mastery models. *Applied Psychological Measurement*, 1980, *4*, 493-516.

Meskauskas, J. A. Evaluation models for criterion-referenced testing: Views regarding mastery and standard-setting. *Review of Educational Research*, 1976, *45*, 133-158.

Messick, S. A. The standard problem: Meaning and values in measurement and evaluation. *American Psychologist*, 1975, *30*, 955-966.

Millman, J. Passing scores and test lengths for domain-referenced measures. *Review of Educational Research*, 1973, *43*, 205–216.

National Academy of Education. *Improving educational achievement*. Washington, DC: Author, 1978.

Nedelsky, L. Absolute grading standards for objective tests. *Educational and Psychological Measurement*, 1954, *14*, 3–19.

New Jersey Department of Education, *Educational Assessment Program: State report 1975–1976*. Trenton, NJ: Author, 1976.

Novick, M. R., & Lewis, C. Prescribing test length for criterion-referenced measurement. In C. W. Harris, M. C. Alkin, & W. J. Popham (Eds.), *Problems in criterion-referenced measurement* (CSE Monograph Series in Evaluation, No. 3). Los Angeles: Center for the Study of Evaluation, University of California, 1974. Pp. 139–158.

Novick, M. R. & Lindley, D. V. The use of more realistic utility functions in educational applications. *Journal of Educational Measurement*, 1978, *15*, 181–191.

Poggio, J. P., Glasnapp, D. R., Eros, D. S. *An empirical investigation of the Angoff, Ebel, and Nedelsky standard setting methods.* Paper presented at the annual meeting of the American Educational Research Association, Los Angeles, April 1981.

Popham, W. J. Normative data for criterion-referenced tests? *Phi Delta Kappan*, 1976, *58*, 593–594.

Popham, W. J. As always, provocative. *Journal of Educational Measurement*, 1978, *15*, 297–300. (a)

Popham, W. J. *Criterion-referenced measurement.* Englewood Cliffs, NJ: Prentice-Hall, 1978. (b)

Popham, W. J. & Husek, T. R. Implications of criterion-referenced measurement. *Journal of Educational Measurement*, 1969, *6*, 1–9.

Rentz, R. R. *Discussion*. Presented at the annual meeting of the National Council on Measurement in Education, Boston, April 1980.

Roudabush, G. E. *Models for a beginning theory of criterion-referenced tests.* Paper presented at the annual meeting of the National Council on Measurement in Education, Chicago, April 1974.

Rowley, G. L. Historical antecedents of the standard-setting debate: An inside account of the minimal-beardedness controversy. *Journal of Educational Measurement*, 1982, *19*, 87–95.

Schoon, C. G., Gullion, C. M., & Ferrara, P. Bayesian statistics, credentialing examinations, and the determination of passing points. *Evaluation and the Health Professions*, 1979, *2*, 181–201.

Shea, W. M. *Selection of cutting scores: The CLEP experience.* Paper presented at the annual meeting of the National Council on Measurement in Education, Boston, April 1980.

Shepard, L. A. Setting standards and living with them. *Florida Journal of Educational Research*, 1976, *18*, 23–32.

Shepard, L. A. Setting standards. In M. A. Bunda & J. R. Sanders (Eds.), *Practices and problems in competency-based measurement.* Washington, DC: National Council on Measurement in Education, 1979. Pp. 59–71.

Shepard, L. A. Standard setting issues and methods. *Applied Psychological Measurement*, 1980, *4*, 447–467. (a)

Shepard, L. A. Technical issues in minimum competency testing. In D. C. Berliner (Ed.), *Review of research in education* (Vol. 8). Washington, DC: American Educational Research Association, 1980. Pp. 30–82. (b)

Shepard, L. A. Standards for placement and certification. In S. B. Anderson & J. S. Helmick (Eds.), *On educational testing.* San Francisco: Jossey-Bass, 1983. Pp. 61–90.

Skakun, E. N., & Kling, S. Comparability of methods for setting standards. *Journal of Educational Measurement*, 1980, *17*, 229–235.

van der Linden, W. J. Decision models for use with criterion-referenced tests. *Applied Psychological Measurement*, 1980, *4*, 469–492.

van der Linden, W. J. A latent trait method for determining intrajudge inconsistency in the Angoff and Nedelsky techniques of standard setting. *Journal of Educational Measurement*, 1982, *19*, 295–308.

van der Linden, W. J., & Mellenbergh, G. J. Optimal cutting scores using a linear loss function. *Applied Psychological Measurement*, 1977, *1*, 593–599.

Zieky, M. J., & Livingston, S. A. *Manual for setting standards on the Basic Skills Assessment Tests.* Princeton, NJ: Educational Testing Service, 1977.

8 VALIDATING THE TEST SCORES

RONALD K. HAMBLETON

INTRODUCTION

CRITERION-REFERENCED tests are constructed to permit test score users to assess examinee performance in relation to one or more well-defined objectives, sometimes called competencies (Popham, 1978). The scores on each objective or competency measured by the test can be used (1) to describe examinee performance, (2) to assign examinees to mastery states, and (3) to describe the performance of specific groups of examinees in program evaluation studies. These three principal uses of criterion-referenced tests are of limited value unless the test scores themselves and/or the decisions resulting from the uses of the scores serve their intended purposes, that is, unless they have validity for some intended use. Test score validity can be defined as the accuracy with which the scores from the test can be used to achieve a stated purpose (such as making inferences about examinee domain score performance or assigning examinees to mastery states). It is important to recognize that validity refers to the appropriateness of particular uses of scores obtained from a test and not specifically to the test itself (Linn, 1979, 1980).

While many contributions to the criterion-referenced testing literature have been made since the late 1960s (for reviews, see Berk, 1980; Hambleton, Swaminathan, Algina, & Coulson, 1978; Millman, 1974; Popham, 1978), the important topic of criterion-referenced test score validity has received limited attention from researchers. Only a few researchers have attempted to define the nature of validity questions with criterion-referenced tests, to identify special problems encountered when validating the uses of the tests (for example, restricted ranges of scores are common), or to offer guidelines for validating criterion-referenced test scores (Hambleton, 1980; Linn, 1979, 1980; Madaus, 1983; Messick, 1975; Millman, 1974, 1979; Popham, 1978).

Very often, measurement specialists assume the validity of criterion-referenced test scores rather than make a special effort to establish the validity of

I am grateful to Anne Fitzpatrick for providing extensive comments on an earlier draft of this chapter.

the scores in any formal way. The argument seems to be that if the appropriate test development steps are carried out, a valid criterion-referenced test will necessarily result. But the validity of the resulting scores will depend on their intended use in addition to the care and sophistication with which the test was constructed. A review of 12 commercially prepared criterion-referenced tests was conducted by Hambleton and Eignor (1978). Not one of the test manuals reviewed included a discussion of what the authors felt was a satisfactory test score validity investigation. Evidence that the items matched the objectives they were intended to measure was the only evidence publishers reported concerning test score validity. No evidence of the accuracy of the domain scores or of the "mastery" and "nonmastery" classifications was presented.

With respect to criterion-referenced tests (or, alternatively, competency tests, basic skills tests, licensure exams, or certification exams), validity questions may take a variety of forms, such as:

1. Is the test appropriate for its intended uses with specific groups of examinees?
2. Does the test measure what the test developers claim their test measures?

But it should be noted that the validity of a set of test scores and/or related mastery-nonmastery decisions can never be demonstrated conclusively; instead, evidence is accumulated to determine if the test scores and/or resulting decisions appear to be serving their intended purpose. Eventually, when a sufficient amount of evidence is collected (to fit the importance of the intended use of the test), a judgment can be made about the validity of the test scores and/or decisions for the intended application. Of course, researchers will need to validate the use of the test scores with each new examinee group (Millman, 1979).

The purposes of this chapter are (1) to review several criterion-referenced test score validity issues and (2) to describe a set of methods for conducting validation studies of criterion-referenced test scores. The next section provides a framework for the material that is considered in the remainder of the chapter.

Criterion-referenced Test Development

It is essential to specify in as clear a form as possible the domain of content or behaviors defining the objectives that are measured by a criterion-referenced test. The mechanism through which the objectives are identified will vary from one application to the next. With high school graduation exams, the process might involve district educational leaders meeting to review school curricula and identify a relatively small set of important broad objectives (e.g., study skills, mathematics concepts). On the other hand, within an objective-based instructional program, it is common for developers first to divide a curriculum into broad areas known as "strands" and difficulty levels (which usually correspond roughly to grade levels). Next, for each strand-difficulty level combination, the sets of relevant objectives, often stated in behavioral form, are specified, reviewed, revised, and finalized. Finally, with certification or licensure exams, it is common to conduct a "role delineation study" or "job-study" first, with individuals working in the area identifying the responsibilities, subresponsibilities, and activities which serve to define the role. Next, the knowledge and skills which are needed to carry out the role are identified, and later they are validated. The validated or approved list of knowledge and skills comprises the objectives that need to be measured in the test.

Many of the steps in test development are aimed at making the test scores valid, but there are no guarantees that the test scores will be valid or that the scores will be used in valid ways, and so validity investigations must be carried out. Attention in this chapter is focused on steps 4, 6, 10, and 12 in the 12-item list of steps for constructing criterion-referenced tests that follows (adapted from Hambleton [1982a, 1984]).

1. Preliminary considerations
    a. Specify test purposes
    b. Specify groups to be measured and (any) special testing requirements (due to examinee age, race, sex, socioeconomic status, handicaps, etc.)
    c. Determine the time and money available to produce the test
    d. Identify qualified staff
    e. Specify an initial estimate of test length
2. Review of objectives
    a. Review the descriptions of the objectives to determine their acceptability
    b. Make necessary revisions to the objectives to improve their clarity
3. Item writing
    a. Draft a sufficient number of items for pilot testing
    b. Carry out item editing
4. Assessment of content validity
    a. Identify a sufficient pool of judges and measurement specialists
    b. Review the test items to determine their match to the objectives, their representativeness, and their freedom from bias and stereotyping
    c. Review the test items to determine their technical adequacy
5. Revisions to test items
    a. Based upon data from 4b and 4c, revise test items (when possible) or delete them
    b. Write additional test items (if needed) and repeat step 4
6. Field test administration
    a. Organize the test items into forms for pilot testing
    b. Administer the test forms to appropriately chosen groups of examinees
    c. Conduct item analyses and item bias studies

7. Revisions to test items
   a. Revise test items when necessary or delete them using the results from 6c
8. Test assembly
   a. Determine the test length and the number of forms needed and the number of items per objective
   b. Select test items from the available pool of valid test items
   c. Prepare test directions, practice questions, test booklet layout, scoring keys, answer sheets, etc.
9. Selection of a standard
   a. Initiate a process to determine the standard to separate "masters" and "nonmasters"
10. Pilot test administration
   a. Design the test administration to collect score reliability and validity information
   b. Administer the test form(s) to appropriately chosen groups of examinees
   c. Evaluate the test administration procedures, test items, and score reliability and validity
   d. Make final revisions based on data from 10c.
11. Preparation of manuals
   a. Prepare a test administrator's manual
   b. Prepare a technical manual
12. Additional technical data collection
   a. Conduct reliability and validity investigations

REVIEW OF SELECTED VALIDITY ISSUES

Many criterion-referenced test developers have argued that in order to "validate" their tests and test scores it is sufficient to assess "content validity." This argument usually means that judgments are obtained from persons with content expertise concerning the match between test content and the objectives a test is designed to measure. Since these judgments focus on test content, the expression "content validity" is used to describe the nature of the activities carried out by the content specialists; but it should be clear that content validity refers to certain characteristics of the test content. The content validity of a test does not vary from one sample of examinees to the next, nor does the content validity of a test vary over time. However, any use of a test (whether *norm-referenced* or *criterion-referenced*) is ultimately dependent on the scores obtained from a test administration, and the validity of the scores depends upon many factors (most especially, the intended use of the scores) in addition to test content. It is possible that examinee item responses and resulting test scores do not adequately reflect or address the skills of interest, even though the test itself is judged to be content valid. For example, consider the situation where a criterion-referenced test is administered, perhaps by mistake, under highly speeded testing conditions. The validity of any descriptions or decisions based on test scores obtained from the test administration will be lower than if the test had been administered with a suitable time limit. The content validity of the test does not depend on the speed of test administrations, but the validity of any use of the scores does. Clearly, content validity evidence is not sufficient to establish the validity of intended uses of the test scores with particular groups of examinees.

As obvious and important as the point about the necessity of validating criterion-referenced test score uses is, the point has been neglected or missed by many criterion-referenced test developers. Cronbach (1971) made the same point more than a decade ago, but because his chapter was not in the mainstream of the criterion-referenced testing literature, its relevance was not recognized. Perhaps the importance of validating scores and desired uses rather than test content alone was most clearly brought to the attention of educators by Messick (1975) and Linn (1979, 1980). Messick (1975) wrote:

> The major problem...is that content validity...is focused upon test *forms* rather than test *scores*, upon *instruments* rather than *measurements*. Inferences in educational and psychological measurement are made from scores, and scores are a function of subject responses. Any concept of validity of measurement must include reference to empirical consistency. Content coverage is an important consideration in test construction and interpretation, to be sure, but in itself it does not provide validity. (pp. 960–961)

Linn (1979) made a similar point:

> Questions of validity are questions for the soundness of the interpretations of a measure.... Thus, it is the interpretation rather than the measure that is validated. Measurement results may have many interpretations which differ in their degree of validity and in the type of evidence required for the validation process. (p. 109)

Both Messick and Linn stressed the need for evidence of the validity of the intended interpretation and use of any set of test scores. Fortunately, there is a wide assortment of methods (see Table 8.1 for a sample) that can be used to gather validity evidence relevant to the intended uses of a set of test scores:

1. *intra-objective methods*, which include item analyses and the evaluation of test content (determination of item and content validity) and score reliability;
2. *inter-objective methods*, which include what are often called "convergent" and "divergent" validity studies—studies to determine whether test scores correlate with variables they might reasonably be expected to relate to, and studies to determine if test scores are uncorrelated with variables they should not be related to;
3. *criterion-related methods*, which include prediction studies and studies of the relationships between test scores and independent measures of performance such as those that might be obtained from teachers, instructors, or supervisors;

Table 8.1. Approaches for Assessing Validity

Approach	Description
Intra-objective	Measure of internal consistency at the objective level (e.g., KR-20) Item analyses Content specialists' ratings of item-objective congruence, bias, technical quality, and representativeness (content validity) Confirmatory factor analysis (do the items fit a hypothesized structure?) Distractor analysis (for example, do many of the high performers choose an incorrect answer choice?)
Inter-objective	Confirmatory factor analysis Scalogram analysis Convergent validity studies (includes studies of relationships between test scores and other tests that measure the same objectives or measure traits that should correlate with the objectives) Divergent validity studies (includes studies of relationships between tests that purport to measure different skills or traits)
Criterion-related (continuous or dichotomous criterion variable)	Correlation between domain score estimates obtained from "actual" and the "lengthened" test (called "domain validity") Correlation of test scores with instructor ratings, on-the-job measures (or simulated on-the-job measures), self-ratings, or peer-ratings Comparison of examinee performance on the test before and after instruction Comparison of the score distributions or percentage of masters for (1) "masters" and "nonmasters" (as identified by means other than the test itself), or, for example, (2) "uninstructed" and "instructed" groups of examinees Correlation between test scores and the number of years of preparation Correlation between test scores and examinee performance in real or simulated situations representing the same or similar content Bias studies to determine if unexpected differences arise due to race, ethnic background, sex, etc.
Experimental	Studies to investigate sources of possible invalidity such as degree of speededness (for example, administer test with and without time limits to compare performance), clarity of directions, answer sheets, race and sex of test examiner Study of pretest and posttest performance with treatment and control groups Study of the influence of response sets and personality on test performance
Multitrait-multimethod	Simultaneous investigation of construct validity of several objectives utilizing two or more methods for assessing each objective

4. *experimental methods*, which include determining the sensitivity of test scores to the effects of instruction on test content; and
5. *multitrait-multimethod studies*, which address what it is that a test actually measures.

Of course, accumulating validation evidence is a never-ending process. The amount of time and energy that is expended in the direction of validation of test scores must be consistent with the importance of the testing program. Criterion-referenced tests that are being used to monitor student progress in a curriculum on a day-to-day basis should demand less attention and resources, obviously, than tests that will be used to determine whether or not students graduate from high school or tests used to certify or license professionals such as physicians, insurance salespersons, and clinical care nurses.

Messick (1975, 1980) not only challenged the sufficiency of content validity evidence to establish the validity of test score uses and interpretations, but along with Guion (1977) and most recently Fitzpatrick (1983), he also argued that content validity is *not* validity at all. In essence, these authors feel that the term *validity* should be used only in conjunction with test scores. They would prefer to see the expression *content representativeness* substituted for *content validity*. But whatever the soundness of the logic for discontinuing the use of the term *content validity*, in the publication of the new *Joint Technical Standards for Educational and Psychological Testing* (AERA/APA/NCME Joint Committee, in preparation), *content validity* is described as one of the three main components of validity (the other two are construct validity and criterion-related); therefore the term will be with us for a long time to come.

Consistent with the new *Technical Standards*, the validity of any uses of the test scores will need to be established within a general framework that contains three components: content, criterion-related, and construct validity. Evidence addressing all three components will often be important, although in some situations one or two of the components may be more important or desirable.

REVIEW OF VALIDATION METHODS

Background

In this section, material addressing validation methods is organized around four categories: item validity, content validity, construct validity, and criterion-related validity. Item validity studies can provide important information about item-objective congruence and the technical soundness of test items. Content validation studies will be necessary to address the content relevance of a test (i.e., the match between item content and the objectives the items are intended to measure). Construct validation studies are required to address questions related to what the test is measuring. Finally, when criterion-referenced test scores are used to make decisions (i.e., to assign examinees to "mastery states"), as they are, for example, with high school proficiency tests, the validity of these classifications or decisions must also be established. Within the category of criterion-related validity studies, the method for establishing a standard must also be evaluated, and meaningful criterion groups must be defined and the performance of these groups on the test in relation to the standard must be studied.

Two relatively new types of validity, *curricular* and *instructional*, for criterion-referenced tests used in awarding high school diplomas, have recently been discussed and recommended in the psychometric literature and the courts (Madaus, 1983; McClung, 1978). The reader is warned, however, that there exists some semantic confusion surrounding the use of the terms to describe these two new types of validity. In addition, Yalow and Popham (1983) argue that *instructional validity* is not a valid term at all. *Curricular validity* refers to the degree to which the items in a test match the objectives that define the school curriculum that students are being held accountable for. When the same set of objectives are used to define a school curriculum and to build a test, the concepts of content validity and curricular validity are identical. When the two sets are different, curricular validity studies can be carried out separately. Methods for doing this involve reviewing curriculum objectives, curriculum materials, textbooks, communications of expectations to students, time allocated to segments of courses, and so on. These and other methods are described in Madaus (1983). (See, for example, Schmidt, Porter, Schwille, Floden, & Freeman, 1983.)

Instructional validity refers to the degree of match between the objectives measured in a test and the objectives that were actually taught to students in the schools. Linn (1983) and Yalow and Popham (1983) describe a number of useful techniques for addressing instructional validity, although Yalow and Popham are adamant about preferring the term *adequacy of preparation* to *instructional validity*. Their techniques include classroom observations, review of instructional materials, self-reports of instructors, and interviews with students. For our purposes, it seems reasonable to include studies that address the match between test content and what was actually taught in a curriculum under the category of criterion-related validity. Such a placement seems reasonable since the types of evidence collected in instructional validity or adequacy of preparation studies are essential for assessing the validity of the use of a criterion-referenced test for awarding high school diplomas.

Domain Specifications

Because of its central role in criterion-referenced test development and validation, perhaps first it is necessary to define what is meant by a domain specification and to explain how the concept of a domain specification differs from that of a behavioral objective. Since the early 1960s, it has been popular to write expected learner outcomes in "behavioral" terms. However, while behavioral objectives have some desirable features (for example, they are relatively easy to produce), they often lack sufficient clarity to permit a clear determination of the relevant domains of test items. If the proper domain of test items measuring an objective is not clear, it is impossible to select a representative sample of test items from *that* domain. A representative sample of test items measuring an objective included in a test is necessary in order to obtain an unbiased estimate of examinee performance in the full domain of behaviors measuring the objective.

The importance of having well-written domain specifications cannot be overemphasized. Examples of such specifications are presented in chapters 2, 3, and 4. Popham (1974) described the problem clearly. When the domain of items measuring an objective is unclear (or unspecified, as with objectives-referenced tests), only the weakest form of a criterion-referenced test score interpretation is possible: Test performance must be interpreted in terms of the *particular* items included in the test. A generalization of examinee performance to a larger class of behaviors (a "strong" interpretation) is *not* warranted. This situation is analogous to drawing nonrepresentative samples of respondents in survey research studies. Any statistics based upon data provided by the sample can be used to describe the sample, but inferences to a larger population of respondents are not warranted because of the difficulty of assessing the representativeness of the sample of an unspecified population.

Item Validity

Determination of item validity involves a consideration of three item features: (1) item-objective congruence (i.e., an assessment of the extent to which an item actually measures some aspect of the content included in the domain specification), (2) technical quality, and (3) bias. The first two features are considered next. Judgmental assessment of bias is addressed in chapter 5, and by Shepard (1981) and Tittle (1982).

Item-objective congruence. Generally speaking, the quality of criterion-referenced test items can be determined by the extent to which they reflect, in terms of their content, the domains from which they were derived. Unless it can be said with a high degree of confidence that the items in a criterion-referenced test measure the intended objectives, any use of the test score information will be questionable.

When item generation rules are used (for details, see chapters 3 and 4), a high degree of confidence in terms of items measuring intended objectives is derived through the direct relationship between the items and the domain from which they were generated. This might be called an a priori approach to item-objective congruence; the approach itself assures essentially that the items are valid indicators of the domains.

On the other hand, when domain specifications (or similar approaches) are utilized (see chapter 2), the domain definitions are never precise enough to assume, a priori, that the items are valid. Also, item writers may differ in their interpretations and applications of the domain specifications. Thus the degree of item-objective congruence in a context independent of the process by which the items were generated must be determined. This is an a posteriori approach to item-objective congruence (see also Berk, chapter 5).

There are at least two general methods that can be used to establish item-objective congruence, although the first is far less desirable than the second. The first method entails using empirical techniques in much the same way as empirical techniques are applied in norm-referenced test development. In fact, along with some recently developed empirical procedures for criterion-referenced tests, several norm-referenced test item statistics are commonly used in the context of criterion-referenced test development. But there are at least four problems with empirical techniques. First, nearly all of the techniques are dependent upon the characteristics of the group of examinees and are influenced by the impact of instruction. Second, few computer programs for estimating new criterion-referenced test item statistics are available to practitioners. Third, when item statistics derived from empirical analyses of test data are used to select items for a criterion-referenced test, the test developer runs the risk of obtaining a nonrepresentative set of items from the domains measuring the objectives included in the test. Finally, some empirical procedures require pretest and posttest data on the same items (see Berk, chapter 5). Pretest data are rarely collected in school settings because there is a reluctance on the part of administrators and teachers to administer tests to examinees when there is little chance of moderate or high levels of test performance.

Empirical techniques do have one important use in the item validation process. According to Rovinelli and Hambleton (1977), "In situations where the test constructor is interested in identifying aberrant items, not for elimination from the item pool but for correction, the use of an empirical approach to item validation should provide important information with regard to the assessment of item validity" (p. 51). A review of available item statistics for use with criterion-referenced tests is given in chapter 5.

A second method for addressing item-objective congruence involves collecting judgments from content specialists. Content specialists are individuals who have the experience to determine the appropriate breadths of content areas of interest from reading a set of domain specifications or similar approaches for defining objectives or competencies. While the parameters of the domains are often well delineated, usually some experience is required with curricula to use them correctly. Also, content specialists need to be capable of determining the content match between items and the objectives they are intended to measure. To do this task effectively, in addition to having some experience with the relevant content, knowledge of the examinees is often very useful.

Rovinelli and Hambleton (1977) described one procedure in which content specialists evaluate the match between sets of test items and objectives. The content specialists' task is to make a judgment about whether or not each test item reflects the content defined by each domain specification. With, for example, 10 objectives and 5 test items/domain specification, a content specialist is required to make 500 judgments. An item rating of "+1" indicates a definite feeling on the part of the content specialist that the item is a measure of the objective; "0" shows that the specialist is undecided about whether the item is a measure of the objective; and "−1" shows a definite feeling that an item is not a measure of the objective.

Rovinelli and Hambleton also developed a statistic for providing a numerical summary of the ratings data. They called their statistic the *index of item-objective congruence*. The assumptions under which this index was developed are: (1) that perfect item-objective congruence should be represented by a value of "+1" and will occur when all the specialists assign a "+1" to the item for the appropriate objective and a "−1" to the item for the inappropriate objectives; (2) that the worst value of the index an item can receive should be represented by a value of "−1" and will occur when all the specialists assign a "−1" to the item for the appropriate objective and a "+1" to the item for all the other objectives; and (3) that the value of the index should not depend on the number of content specialists or the number of objectives.

The index of item-objective congruence is given by

$$I_{ik} = \frac{(N-1)\sum_{j=1}^{n} X_{ijk} - \sum_{i=1}^{N}\sum_{j=1}^{n} X_{ijk} + \sum_{j=1}^{n} X_{ijk}}{2(N-1)n}, \qquad (1)$$

where:

I_{ik} is the index of item-objective congruence for item k on objective i,
N is the number of objectives ($i = 1, 2, \ldots, N$),
n is the number of content specialists ($j = 1, 2, \ldots, n$), and
X_{ijk} is the rating ($-1, 0, +1$) of item k as a measure of objective i by content specialist j.

A cut-off score for the index can be chosen to separate "valid" from "nonvalid" items. This is best done after some experience is gained with content specialists' ratings and with the index itself. When we feel it is desirable to set a cut-off score, we create the poorest set of content specialists' ratings that we would willingly accept as evidence that an item was in the content domain of interest. The value of the index for this set of minimally acceptable ratings can then serve as the cut-off score for judging the item-objective congruence of each of the test items. For example, suppose that there are 20 content specialists and 10 objectives. We might desire that at least 15 of the content specialists match the item to the intended objective and that they indicate that the item is not a measure of the other 9 objectives. In this example, the index of item-objective congruence would be .75, and so .75 would serve as the criterion against which we would judge the congruence of items from the content specialists' ratings. With large-scale and/or important test development projects, it is desirable to involve a group of individuals in the process for setting a cut-off score.

There are several problems with the Rovinelli-Hambleton procedure. One is that it is very time consuming to implement. A possible solution is to assign content specialists only a portion of the domain specifications and test items to review. A second problem arises when the set of available domain specifications is very heterogeneous. Content specialists can waste considerable time reading domain specifications before making the obvious determination that many items are unrelated. This difficulty can be overcome by organizing the domain specifications into reasonably homogeneous clusters and limiting the rating task to assessing the match between the domain specifications and only test items that were written to measure domain specifications in the cluster. Secolsky (1983) described two additional problems that seem relevant. First, the Rovinelli-Hambleton index is of very limited value unless multiple reviewers are available. Therefore, for many classroom tests produced by individual teachers, other approaches must be found for assessing item-objective congruence. Second, the reviewers' directions should be revised to reduce some ambiguity concerning the nature of the review task. Some emphasis should be given in the review task as to how candidates are expected to interpret the test items. For classroom tests, at least, Secolsky (1983) described a new procedure for addressing item-objective congruence in which students, through their judgments about the items and their performance on the same test items, provide information that can be used. The success of his procedure, however, has not been established at this time.

A second procedure for assessing item-objective congruence requires content specialists to rate an item-objective match on, say, a 5-point scale that ranges from poor (1) to excellent (5). This procedure requires less time to complete than the first procedure because items are only rated in relation to the domain specifications they were intended to measure. A sample of a judge's rating form is presented in Appendix A.

The ratings data may be analyzed without employing elaborate statistical procedures. Therefore, the rating form with the 5-point rating scale can easily be used in practical settings, such as by teachers in the classroom. The information needed is the mean and/or median rating assigned to the items by a group of content specialists. However, more elaborate statistical analyses, when they are desired, can be carried out. An examination of the range of ratings given each item provides an indication of the extent of disagreement among the content specialists.

It is also possible to determine the "closeness" of each judge's ratings to the median responses from the judges. When a judge's rating differs substantially from the ratings of the other judges, and there is evidence of carelessness or incompetence on his or her part, the validity of the statistics will be enhanced if the "deviant" judge's responses are removed from the analysis.

For a summary and analysis of the hypothetical ratings of 9 judges on 14 test items measuring 4 objectives, see Table 8.2.

A third procedure that can be used to obtain the judgments of content specialists involves the use of a *matching task*. Content specialists are presented with two lists, one with test items and the other with objectives or domain specifications. The content specialist's task is to indicate which objective he or she thinks each test item measures (if any). A contingency table can then be constructed by calculating the number of content specialists matching each item to each objective in the sets of items and objectives being studied. The chi-square test for independence is commonly used to analyze data that are presented in a contingency table format. Also, a visual analysis of the contingency table will reveal the amount of agreement among the specialists and the type and location of disagreements. A sample of a judge's summary sheet for the items/objectives matching task is presented in Appendix B. Some hypothetical results are reported in Table 8.3.

The "accuracy" of the ratings of each content specialist can be checked if a specified number of "bad" items (i.e., items not measuring any of the objectives) is introduced into the matching task. A content specialist's effectiveness can be measured by the number of such items he or she detects. However, this method of evaluation does tend to favor the overly critical content specialist. The item ratings of content specialists who do not achieve some minimum level of performance in detecting "bad" test items can be removed from the analysis. While not discussed with the first two procedures, the notion of

Table 8.2. Summary of Judges' Ratings of Fourteen Test Items

		Judges' Ratings									Summary Statistics		
Objective	Test Item	1	2	3	4	5	6	7	8	9	Mean	Median	Range
1	2	4	3	5	5	4	5	5	5	4	4.4	5	3
	7	4	2	5	5	5	5	5	4	5	4.4	5	4
	14	4	5	5	5	4	5	5	5	5	4.8	5	2
2	1	3	5	3	2	1	4	5	2	4	3.2	3	5
	3	3	1	4	4	3	4	4	3	3	3.2	3	4
	8	1	3	1	2	1	1	1	1	1	1.3	1	3
	13	1	3	2	1	1	2	1	2	3	1.8	2	3
3	4	4	5	5	4	5	5	5	5	5	4.8	5	2
	6	4	2	4	4	4	4	4	4	4	3.8	4	3
	12	5	3	5	5	5	5	5	5	5	4.8	5	3
4	5	4	3	5	5	4	5	5	4	5	4.4	5	3
	9	2	2	4	1	4	2	4	4	4	3.0	4	4
	10	1	3	1	2	1	1	1	1	1	1.3	1	3
	11	4	3	4	4	5	5	5	5	5	4.6	5	3
Judges' discrepancies from median responses		9	24	2	10	6	4	4	3	3			

Table 8.3. Summary of Judges' Item/Objective Matching Task

Objective	Test Item	Judges' Matches 1	2	3	4	5	6	7	8	9	Percentage of Matches for Each Test Item
1	2	1[a]	0	1	0	1	1	1	1	1	78
	7	1	1	1	0	1	1	1	1	1	89
	14	0	1	1	1	1	1	1	1	1	89
2	1	0	0	1	1	1	1	1	1	1	78
	3	1	1	1	1	1	1	1	1	0	89
	8	1	0	1	0	0	0	0	1	0	33
	13	0	0	1	0	0	0	0	0	0	11
3	4	1	0	1	1	1	1	1	1	1	89
	6	0	0	1	0	1	0	1	1	0	44
	12	1	1	1	1	1	1	1	1	1	100
4	5	1	0	1	1	1	1	1	1	1	89
	9	1	1	1	1	0	0	1	1	1	78
	10	0	0	1	0	0	0	0	0	0	11
	11	1	1	1	1	1	1	1	1	0	89
Percentage of matches for each judge		64	43	100	64	71	64	79	86	57	
"Lemons"	1	0[b]	1	0	0	1	0	0	0	0	
	2	1	1	0	1	0	0	0	0	0	
	3	1	1	0	0	0	0	0	0	0	
Number of "lemons" not identified		2	3	0	1	1	0	0	0	0	

[a]A score of "0" means that the judge did not match the test item to the objective it was developed to measure. A score of "1" means that the judge did make the expected match.

[b]A score of "0" means that the judge did not match the "lemon" item to any of the objectives. A score of "1" means that the judge did match the "lemon" item to one of the objectives.

"marker" or "lemon" items for evaluating the expertise of content specialists and/or the care with which they complete their ratings can easily be incorporated there. In a recently completed study for the Louisiana Department of Education, we found it necessary to eliminate one reviewer out of a total of 20 from our analysis because this reviewer detected only 2 of 19 "bad" items inserted into the review task.

An interesting question that needs to be answered concerns whether or not content specialists should be informed about the existence of "marker items" in the pool of items they are reviewing. How would the information impact on their ratings? On the surface it appears that they might be more attentive, but on the other hand, many reviewers may be reluctant to participate if they themselves are being judged.

In summary, data from all of the procedures sketched out in this section are useful for addressing item-objective congruence. The data derived from any of the procedures can be used to address the important question of which items failed to "match" the domain specification they were prepared to measure. Other important questions can also be addressed. How successful were the test item writers? That is, how many acceptable test items did each writer produce? How can the item ratings' data be used to rewrite the domain specifications? For example, an analysis of the "invalid" items may reveal areas of shortcoming and ambiguity in the domain specifications. Needed, however, are more guidelines for (1) setting cut-off scores for identifying faulty items and poor reviewers, and (2) using "lemon" or "marker" items in the item review process.

Technical quality of test items. The technical quality of test items can be established at the same time as test items are reviewed for item-objective congruence and freedom from bias. Examples of item review directions and a technical review form for multiple-choice test items are presented in Appendices C and D, respectively. Many other forms are reported by Hambleton (in press) and Hambleton and Eignor (1979). The form in Appendix D has been well received in the many settings where it has been used, including school districts, provincial and state departments of education, the armed services, and certification exam boards. Question 16 concerns item-objective congruence, but it is included on the technical review form for the convenience of reviewers. It is often convenient to have both content and technical review questions included in a single form.

Content Validity

The content validity of a test is determined by judging the representativeness of the test items of a specified domain of content. Two requirements for assessing content validity are (1) a clear statement of the content domain, and (2) details about the sampling plan used in item selection. Note that when test scores are reported at the objective level, the content validity of each sample of items measuring an objective must be assessed.

It is usually desirable to have items in a criterion-referenced test that are representative of the content specified in a domain specification. In fact, the set of items should be *broadly* representative of the content domain of interest. However, to date only in some highly special cases has it been possible to specify completely a pool of valid test items. For example, there have been some successes in the areas of reading, mathematics, and spelling. But these examples are far removed from the more complex content domains in the areas of geography, world history, and English.

Descriptions of content domains can range from broad areas of relevant content to tightly defined domains where every appropriate test item in the domain could be delineated. The former is unacceptable for criterion-referenced tests and the latter is impractical in most instances. Somewhere in between falls Popham's notion of a domain specification (see chapter 2), which is both more reasonable and more practical than other methods presently available for specifying domains of content. If relevant content is described clearly, then it will be obvious to content specialists what domain a set of items is intended to represent. Categories or multidimensional classification schemes can often be developed to delineate further the content in a domain specification, and then content specialists can make judgments about the representativeness of the selected test items. When representativeness has not been achieved, new test items can often be added to a test, and perhaps others can be removed.

With respect to certification and licensure exams, content validity is often assessed by evaluating the test items in terms of their representativeness in relation to a set of responsibilities, subresponsibilities, and activities that define a professional role based on a role delineation study. The following is a small section from the role definition for family physicians (Hambleton, 1982b).

I. Helping patients and their families plan for maintenance of good health
   A. Providing basic health information
      1. Offering growth and nutritional information
      2. Advising on prescribed and nonprescribed drugs, alcohol, tobacco, and substance abuse
   B. Providing families with realistic expectations regarding health problems and health care results
      1. Counseling and educating patients/families regarding health care and illness

II. Collecting and organizing history, physical, and family information for the purpose of providing health care for patients and their families
   A. Conducting a medical history, a family medical history, and a history of the patient's chief complaints
      1. Defining the origin and progression of a patient's complaints
      2. Assessing how a patient perceives his/her own complaints
   B. Conducting a physical examination
      1. Determining the scope of examination indicated
   C. Generating an initial potential problem list, which includes a differential diagnosis (sometimes called assessments)
      1. Recording all of the patient's pertinent subjective data
      2. Recording all appropriate objective findings on physical examinations
      3. Recording a problem list and differential diagnosis

Many certification and licensure exams are constructed to reflect candidate competence in relation to a role definition. The set of test items can be reviewed to determine how well they sample the responsibilities, subresponsibilities, and activities identified in the role. It is also common to substitute "importance," "frequency," or "criticality" for "representativeness" in many content validity investigations with certification and licensure examinations.

Another procedure for assessing content validity is to carry out Cronbach's duplication experiment. This experiment requires two teams of equally competent item writers and reviewers to work independently in developing a criterion-referenced test. Cronbach (1971) stated that: "they would be aided by the same definition of relevant content, sampling rules, instructions to reviewers, and specifications for tryout and interpretation of the data" (p. 456). If the domain specifications are clear, and if item sampling is representative, the two tests should be equivalent. Equivalence of forms can be checked by administering both forms to the same group of examinees and by comparing the two sets of examinee test scores. A feature of the procedure is that content validity can be described by a statistic. One problem with the procedure is that "a common blind spot is almost impossible to detect" (Cronbach, 1971, p. 456). That is, obscure or unclear parts of the domain specifications may be by-passed by both teams and result in an overestimate of content validity. Another problem is that this procedure may double the cost of producing the test. On the other hand, such a procedure for assessing content validity may be more feasible when a second form of the test is needed.

Construct Validity

Messick (1975) offered a useful definition of construct validation: "Construct validation is the process of marshaling evidence in the form of theoretically relevant empirical relations to support the inference that an observed response consistency has a particular meaning ' (p. 955).

Construct validation studies have not been common in criterion-referenced measurement. This may be because criterion-referenced test score distributions are often homogeneous (for example, it often happens that before instruction most individuals do poorly on a test and after instruction most individuals do well). Correlational methods do not work very well with homogeneous score distributions because of problems due to score range restrictions. But, as Messick (1975) has noted, "Construct validation is by no means limited to correlation coefficients, even though it may seem that way from the prevalence of correlation matrices, internal consistency indices, and factor analysis" (p. 958).

Construct validation studies should begin with a statement of the proposed use of the test scores. A clearly stated use will provide direction for the kind of evidence that is worth collecting. Cronbach (1971) stated, "Investigations to be used for construct validation, then, should be purposeful rather than haphazard" (p. 483). Later, when all of the data are collected and analyzed, a final judgment as to the validity of the intended use (or uses) of the test scores can be made. Unlike criterion-related validity evidence, construct validity evidence cannot be reported in the form of a single statistic; instead, it is a judgment based upon a consideration of (usually) a substantial amount of evidence.

Kirsch and Guthrie (1980) reported a construct validation investigation of functional literacy test scores. In view of the importance being accorded this type of examination, such investigations are overdue. Their study is an outstanding example of what can and should be done to validate the intended uses of criterion-referenced test scores. Kirsch and Guthrie studied the effects of six cognitive processes on test performance and investigated the significance of the effects across groups with different educational backgrounds and family income levels. They concluded their paper with the following comment:

> Understanding the requisite abilities needed for completing tasks relating to personal, social, and occupational reading demands is an important step toward developing functional literacy tests that are valid with respect to psychological processes, as well as content coverages. We suggest that construct, as well as content validity is required for measurement and program development in functional literacy. (p. 44)

One hopes there will be many more studies like the one by Kirsch and Guthrie.

Some of the investigations that could be undertaken to estimate the construct validity of a set of criterion-referenced test scores are described next. Others are listed in Table 8.1 and are reviewed by Cronbach (1971).

Guttman scalogram analysis. It frequently occurs that objectives can be arranged linearly or hierarchically on the basis of a logical analysis. Guttman scaling is a relevant procedure for the construct validation of criterion-referenced test scores in situations where the objectives can be organized into either a linear or a hierarchical sequence. To use Guttman's scalogram analysis as a technique in a test score validation methodology, one would first need to

Figure 8.1. Sample hierarchy of five objectives

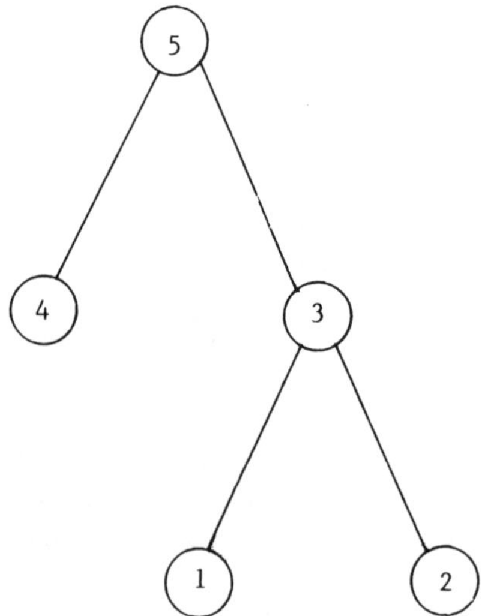

Note: Objectives 1 to 4 are prerequisite skills to terminal objective 5.

specify the hierarchical structure of a set of objectives. Figure 8.1 provides an example of a hierarchy involving 5 objectives. To the extent that examinee mastery/nonmastery status on the objectives in the hierarchy is predictable from a knowledge of the hierarchy, one would have evidence to support the construct validity of the objective scores. On the other hand, in situations where examinee mastery-nonmastery status is not predictable, one of three situations has occurred: the hierarchy is incorrectly specified, the objective scores are not valid measures of the intended objectives, or a combination of the two explanations is true. Assuming the correctness of the hierarchy in Figure 8.1, only 11 patterns of mastery-nonmastery across the 5 objectives would be predicted, where "1" and "0" designate "mastery" and "nonmastery" of an objective, respectively:

Pattern No.	Objective				
	1	2	3	4	5
1	1	1	1	1	1
2	1	1	1	1	0
3	1	1	1	0	0
4	1	1	0	1	0
5	1	0	0	1	0
6	0	1	0	1	0
7	1	1	0	0	0
8	1	0	0	0	0
9	0	1	0	0	0
10	0	0	0	1	0
11	0	0	0	0	0

Any frequent occurrence of patterns other than those listed here would suggest problems in the assessment of objectives or flaws in the hierarchy (or both). By substituting item scores for objective scores, Guttman scaling can also be used to assess item validity.

More precise specifications for the utilization of Guttman scaling will, of course, be needed before the method can be fully implemented in the validation process for criterion-referenced test scores. Research by White (1974) on the investigations of learning hierarchies seems especially promising.

Factor analysis. While factor analysis is a commonly employed procedure for the dimensional analysis of items in a norm-referenced test, or of scores derived from different norm-referenced tests, it has rarely, if ever, been used in construct validation studies of criterion-referenced test scores. Perhaps one reason for its lack of use is that the usual input for factor analytic studies are correlations, and correlations are often low between items on a criterion-referenced test or between criterion-referenced test scores and other variables, because score variability is often not very great. Also, interitem correlations are often low because of the unreliability of item scores. However, the problem due to limited score variability can be reduced to some extent by choosing a sample of examinees with a wide range of performance, for example, a group including both masters and nonmasters.

The research problem in the language of factor analysis becomes a problem of determining whether or not the factor pattern matrix has a prescribed form. The prescribed form is set by the researchers and is based upon a logical analysis of the objectives and other research evidence concerning the structure of the objectives measured in the test. Alternatively, additional cognitive variables can be introduced into the analysis with the resulting expanded structure being compared to some structure specifying the theoretical relationships among the expanded set of variables. Evidence that the estimated structure among the variables matches the prescribed form will support both the research hypotheses and the validity of the scores as measures of the desired variables. A study by Ward, Frederiksen, and Carlson (1980) provides an excellent example of the use of factor analysis in construct validation investigations.

Experimental studies. There are many sources of error that reduce the validity of an intended use of a set of criterion-referenced test scores. Suppose, for example, that an examinee was estimated to have a 40% level of performance on a test measuring "ability to identify the main idea in paragraphs." Is the test providing valid information about the student's level of proficiency? Is it reasonable to infer that the student has a skill deficiency? The answers to these questions depend on the answers to several other questions:

1. Were the test directions clear to the student?
2. Did the student have a problem using the answer sheet?
3. Was the test administered under speeded testing conditions?
4. Was the student motivated to perform to the best of his or her ability?
5. Was the content of the paragraph interesting to the student?
6. Was the choice of vocabulary suitable?
7. Did test-taking skills play any role in the student's test performance?
8. Was the item format suitable for measuring the desired skill?
9. Was the test scheduled at a suitable time during the day?

To the extent that any of these nine factors or other factors influence test scores, the validity of the test scores is reduced.

Experimental studies of potential sources of error to determine their effect on test scores are an important way to assess the construct validity of a set of test scores. Logical analyses and observations of testing methods and procedures can also be used to detect sources of invalidity in a set of test scores.

Other types of experiments to assess the construct validity of criterion-referenced test scores can also be designed. For example, individuals can be randomly assigned to one of two groups: one group receives instruction on content contained in a domain specification, the second group receives no instruction. If the instruction is effective, and this could be inferred from the instructor's past teaching experiences, higher test scores by the experimental group would provide evidence for the validity of the test scores. In studies of this type, it is especially important to have evidence that the objectives of interest were actually addressed in the instruction. Numerous experiments could be conducted, alternating control and experimental groups, so that no single group of examinees would be denied instruction. With more broadly defined objectives, the test performance of individuals assumed to have mastery of the objectives can be compared with the test performance of those individuals who are assumed to be nonmasters of the objectives.

Multitrait-multimethod approach. The category of construct validation would also include "multitrait-multimethod" validation of objective scores (Campbell & Fiske, 1959). Multitrait-multimethod validation includes any techniques addressing the questions of how much examinee responses to items reflect the "trait" (objective) of interest, and of how much they reflect methodological effects. To give a concrete example, one might ask if an item assessing knowledge of proper health care would elicit the same or different results when asked as an open-ended question, a multiple-choice question, or a true-false question. Ideally, experimental administrations would be given in which the same questions would be presented in different formats to groups of examinees formed by random assignment. Item format characteristics supposed to be irrelevant would be varied across groups of examinees, and the performance of these groups would then be compared to determine whether the "irrelevant" factors affected responses.

Criterion-related Validity

Even if scores derived from criterion-referenced tests are descriptive of the objectives they are supposed to reflect, the usefulness of the scores as predictors of, say, "job success" or "success in the next unit of instruction" cannot be assured. For example, sometimes in instructional settings the criterion-related validity of a set of decisions from a test can be investigated by comparing the mastery-nonmastery decisions to the resulting mastery-nonmastery decisions in a subsequent unit of instruction. This type of comparison is reasonable when it is appropriate to assume that the initial set of test scores and decisions will predict future performance. (Such a prediction is not always appropriate, however.) This type of investigation requires that examinees be assigned to future units without regard for their past performance.

Criterion-related validity studies of criterion-referenced test scores are not different in procedure from studies conducted with norm-referenced tests. Correlational, group separation, and decision accuracy methods are commonly used (Cronbach, 1971). Also, selection of reasonable and practical criterion measures that do not themselves require extensive validation efforts remains as serious a problem for conducting validation studies with criterion-referenced tests as it is for norm-referenced tests. There are, however, two important differences: first, test scores are usually dichotomized (examinees above a cut-off score are described as masters, and, otherwise, nonmasters); second, and related to the first, instead of reporting correlational measures, as is commonly done in criterion-related validity investigations with norm-referenced tests, readily interpretable validity indices reflecting the agreement between decisions based on the test and an external dichotomous criterion measure are reported.

Decision validity. Criterion-referenced test scores are commonly used to make decisions. In instructional settings, an examinee is assumed to be a "master" when his or her test performance exceeds a minimum level of performance (often referred to as a standard). Decision validity, which is simply a particular kind of criterion-related validity, involves (1) setting a standard of test performance, and (2) comparing the test performance of two or more criterion groups in relation to the specified standard. Instructional decisions based on the classroom criterion-referenced test scores can be evaluated, in part, by comparing the test performance and mastery status of two criterion groups, groups consisting of those who have received instruction and those who have not. An example is given in Figure 8.2. Alternatively, two criterion groups might be formed by asking teachers to identify students who they are certain have an excellent grasp of the skills measured by the test and students who do not. Decision validity on each objective may be assessed by summing the percentage of "competent" students who pass and the percentage of "incompetent" students who do not.

For high school graduation examinations, it may be possible for teachers to identify two extreme groups, one group consisting of students they are certain have the required competencies to graduate from high school and a second group of students who do not. Borderline students would not be included in a study of this type. Again, the test is administered and the percentage of

Figure 8.2. Frequency polygons of criterion-referenced test scores for two groups (an instructed group and an uninstructed group on the content measured by the test)

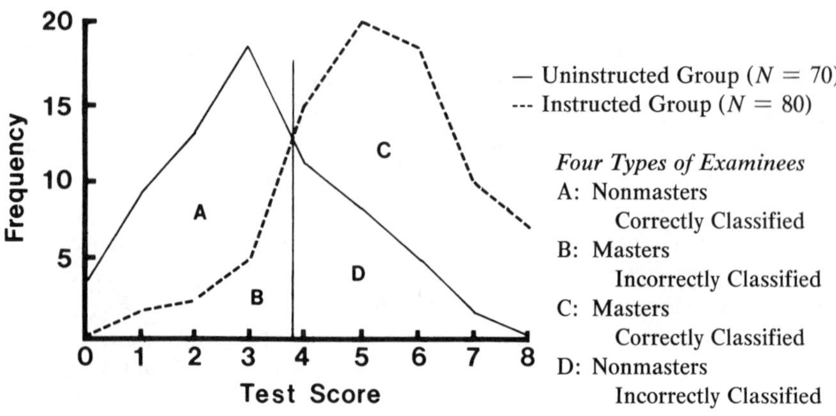

students who are correctly classified by the testing procedure is calculated and used as an estimate of decision validity. Also, *instructional validity* investigations, which were described briefly earlier in the chapter, ought to be included here. Evidence addressing the match between test content and instruction is essential information for determining the appropriateness or validity of using test scores to award high school diplomas.

One advantage of decision validity studies is that the results can be reported in a readily interpretable way (percentage of correct decisions). Alternatively, the correlation between two dichotomous variables (group membership and the mastery decision) can be reported and used as an index of decision validity. Other statistics are reported by Berk (1976), Hambleton (in press), and Popham (1978). Finally, the validity of a set of decisions will depend on four important factors: (1) the quality of the test under investigation, (2) the appropriateness and size of the criterion groups, (3) the characteristics of the examinee sample, and (4) the minimum level of performance required for mastery. All four factors will impact on decision validity. Clearly, since a number of factors substantially influence the level of decision validity, it must be recognized that what is being described through a summary statistic of interest is *not the test*, but the *use of the test* in a particular way with a specified group of examinees. The same point applies equally well when interpreting norm-referenced reliability and validity indices.

SUGGESTIONS FOR FUTURE RESEARCH

What is needed in the future is not so much new methodological studies (although additional methodological developments, for assessing content validity, for example, would be helpful), but more experience on the part of test developers in designing and carrying out validation studies with criterion-referenced tests. For example, the rating forms presented in Appendices A, B, C, and D need to receive more use so that their strengths and weaknesses can be assessed in a variety of settings with many types of reviewers. Also, work is needed on the problem of integrating validity evidence from content specialists, logical analyses of the test, and empirical analyses with the test scores. Guidelines for making judgments about the validity of intended uses of the scores in the midst of various kinds of evidence, some of which may be in conflict, are needed.

Perhaps in time experience will provide answers to the problems described here as well as answers to a number of other implementation questions:

1. How many judges are normally useful in conducting item reviews, and what criteria should be used in selecting them?
2. When is it legitimate to discard judges' ratings from an analysis?
3. What types of item review training should be given to judges?
4. What kinds of evidence and how much evidence should be collected to support an intended use of a criterion-referenced test?

Of course these questions and many others do not have simple answers; appropriate answers depend upon many situational factors, such as the previous training and experience of judges, the importance of the test use, and the availability of resources. But with more experience and some exemplary validity studies, the situation will improve considerably. The work of Kane (1982), Kirsch and Guthrie (1980), Linn (1980), and Ward et al. (1980) seems to be especially helpful at this time in shaping validity studies, either by providing guidelines or by describing exemplary studies.

GUIDELINES FOR PRACTITIONERS

Papers by Cronbach (1971, 1980), Kane (1982), Messick (1975), and Linn (1979, 1980) have enhanced my understanding and views of criterion-referenced test score validity. Perhaps I can now be absolved of my sin, committed in 1973, of saying, "Above all else, a criterion-referenced test must have content validity" (Hambleton & Novick, 1973, p. 168). Certainly, any good criterion-referenced test must have content validity, but content validity evidence will not be sufficient to ensure the validity of the many different uses of criterion-referenced test scores.

Here are a few guidelines for improving the development, validation, and uses of criterion-referenced tests:

1. Prepare domain specifications (or something similar) to provide clear statements about the desired content and behaviors to be measured by a criterion-referenced test. Domain specifications are invaluable to item writers and they are essential for assessing both item validity and content validity.
2. Follow the criterion-referenced test development steps listed early in this chapter. Each step is an integral part of the test development process. Technically sound tests can be produced if the steps are followed carefully. Hambleton (1982a, 1984, in press), Popham (1978), and the other chapters in this volume provide implementation strategies for the steps.
3. All of the criterion-referenced test development steps listed are important, although only steps 4, 6, 10, and 12 were emphasized in this chapter. Let the size and importance of the test development project influence the scope and depth of the validation investigation. Carry out the validity investigation within a broad framework that includes evidence pertaining to the three components of validity: content, construct, criterion-related.
4. Content reviews can be very time consuming when specifications are complicated (e.g., see Popham, 1978) and the number of test items requiring review is large. Be sure to allow sufficient time to have the review task completed properly. Also, have content reviewers work independently to the extent possible. Later in the review process have the reviewers consider their areas of agreement and disagreement (Lindheim, 1982). Very often the areas of disagreement can be resolved quickly because they re-

flect carelessness or misinformation on the part of one or more of the reviewers.

5. In describing the available validity evidence, it is highly desirable to report score means and standard deviations, sample sizes, pass rates, standards, correlations between items and between objective scores, reliability of the objective scores, complete descriptions of criterion measures, etc. The reader should have sufficient data available to determine the worth of an investigation and the correctness of the interpretations.

In summary, validating criterion-referenced test scores and/or decisions based upon the test scores is an ongoing process of collecting evidence addressing the three components of validity (content, construct, and criterion-related) and integrating and interpreting many kinds of evidence in relation to a specific intended use of the test. While the total validation process can be both time consuming and (occasionally) expensive, without evidence of score validity, test score users place themselves in the precarious position of being ignorant of the soundness of their actions.

APPENDIX A: JUDGE'S ITEM RATING FORM (SAMPLE)

Item Content Review Form

Reviewer: ______________________ Date: ________ Content Area: ________

First, read carefully through the lists of domain specifications and test items. Next, please indicate how well you feel each item reflects the domain specification it was written to measure. Judge a test item solely on the basis of the match between its content and the content defined by the domain specification that the test item was prepared to measure. Please use the five-point rating scale shown below:

Poor	Fair	Good	Very Good	Excellent
1	2	3	4	5

Circle the number corresponding to your rating beside the test item number.

Objective	Test Item	Item Rating	Comments
1	2	1 2 3 4 5	
	7	1 2 3 4 5	
	14	1 2 3 4 5	
2	1	1 2 3 4 5	
	3	1 2 3 4 5	
	8	1 2 3 4 5	
	13	1 2 3 4 5	
3	4	1 2 3 4 5	
	6	1 2 3 4 5	
	12	1 2 3 4 5	
4	5	1 2 3 4 5	
	9	1 2 3 4 5	
	10	1 2 3 4 5	
	11	1 2 3 4 5	

APPENDIX B: JUDGE'S SUMMARY SHEET FOR THE ITEMS/OBJECTIVES MATCHING TASK (SAMPLE)

Items/Objectives Matching Task

Reviewer: ______________________ Date: ________ Content Area: ________

First, read carefully through the lists of domain specifications and test items. Your task is to indicate whether or not you feel each test item is a measure of *one* of the domain specifications. It is, if you feel examinee performance on the test item would provide an indication of an examinee's level of performance in a pool of test items measuring the domain specification. Beside each objective, write in the test item numbers corresponding to the test items that you feel measure the objective. In some instances, you may feel that items do not measure any of the available domain specifications. Write these test item numbers in the space provided at the bottom of the rating form.

Objective	Matching Test Items
1	
2	
3	
4	
No Matches	

APPENDIX C: INSTRUCTIONS FOR USING THE MULTIPLE-CHOICE ITEM REVIEW FORM (SAMPLE)

1. Obtain a copy of the objective and the test items written to measure it.
2. Place the objective number, your name, and today's date in the space provided at the top of the Item Review Form.
3. Place the numbers corresponding to the test items you will evaluate in the spaces provided near the top of the Item Review Form. The numbers should be in ascending order as you read from left to right. (This must be done if the processing of your data along with the data from many other reviewers is to be done quickly and with a minimum number of errors.)
4. Read the objective statement carefully.
5. Read the first test item carefully and answer the first 15 questions. Mark "✓" for "yes"; mark "X" for "no"; and mark "?" if you are "unsure." The last question requires you to provide an overall evaluation of the test item as an indicator of the objective it was written to measure. There are five possible ratings:

   5—Excellent
   4—Very Good
   3—Good
   2—Fair
   1—Poor

6. Write any comments or suggested wording changes on or beside the test item.
7. Repeat the rating task for each of the test items.
8. Staple your Item Review Form, objective, and copy of the test items together, and return them to the coordinator.

APPENDIX D: TECHNICAL REVIEW FORM FOR ITEMS (SAMPLE)

Item Review Form
(Multiple-Choice)

Objective No.: ______ Reviewer: ______________________________ Date: ______

Test Item Characteristics (Mark "✓" for "yes," "X" for "no," and "?" for "unsure")	Test Item Numbers					
1. Is the readability level of the test item stem and answer choices suitable for the examinees being tested?						
2. Does the item stem describe a single problem for an examinee?						
3. Is the item stem free of ambiguities and/or irrelevant material?						
4. Is the content of the test item matched closely to the goal statement, objective, or task?						
5. Are all negatives underlined?						
6. Do the item stem and answer choices follow standard rules of punctuation, capitalization, and grammar?						
7. Are the answer choices arranged logically (if such an arrangement exists)?						
8. Is there *one* correct or *clearly best* answer?						
9. Is the placement of the correct answer made on a random basis?						
10. Are the answer choices free of irrelevant material?						
11. Are numbers or letters used to label the answer choices?						
12. Is any material provided in another test item that will provide a clue to the correct answer?						
13. When pictorials, tables, or figures are used, are they printed clearly and labeled correctly?						
14. Can the test item be answered by simple logic or common sense?						
15. a. Have words that give verbal clues to the correct answer such as: "always," "may," "none," "never," "all," "sometimes," "usually," "generally," "typically," etc., been avoided?						
b. Have repetitious words or expressions been removed from the answer choices?						
c. Will the distractors be plausible and appealing to examinees who do not know the correct answer?						
d. Are the answer choices of approximately the same length?						
e. Has the use of "all of the above" or "none of the above" as answer choices been avoided?						
f. Are four or five answer choices used?						
g. Have double negatives been avoided?						
h. Have "clang" associations with the stem been avoided for the correct answer?						
i. Have distractors that mean the same thing or are opposites been avoided?						
j. Are the answer choices for an item similar in type, concept, and focus so that they are as homogeneous as possible?						
k. Is the correct answer stated at the same level of detail as the other answer choices?						
16. Disregarding any technical flaws which may exist in the test item (addressed by the first 25 questions), how well do you think the content of the test item matches with some part of the content defined by the objective? (Remember the possible ratings: 1 = poor, 2 = fair, 3 = good, 4 = very good, 5 = excellent.)						

REFERENCES

AERA/APA/NCME Joint Committee. *Joint technical standards for educational and psychological testing.* Washington, DC: American Psychological Association, in preparation.

Berk, R. A. Determination of optimal cutting scores in criterion-referenced measurement. *Journal of Experimental Education*, 1976, *45*, 4-9.

Berk, R. A. (Ed.). *Criterion-referenced measurement: The state of the art.* Baltimore, MD: Johns Hopkins University Press, 1980.

Campbell, D. T., & Fiske, D. W. Convergent and discriminant validation by the multitrait-multimethod matrix. *Psychological Bulletin*, 1959, *56*, 81-105.

Cronbach, L. J. Test validation. In R. L. Thorndike (Ed.), *Educational measurement* (2nd ed.). Washington, DC: American Council on Education, 1971. Pp. 443-507.

Cronbach, L. J. Validity on parole: How can we go straight? In W. B. Schrader (Ed.), *New directions for testing and measurement* (No. 5): *Measuring achievement—Progress over a decade*. San Francisco: Jossey-Bass, 1980. Pp. 99-108.

Fitzpatrick, A. R. The meaning of content validity. *Applied Psychological Measurement*, 1983, *7*, 3-13.

Guion, R. M. Content validity: The source of my discontent. *Applied Psychological Measurement*, 1977, *1*, 1-10.

Hambleton, R. K. Test score validity and standard-setting methods. In R. A. Berk (Ed.), *Criterion-referenced measurement: The state of the art*. Baltimore, MD: Johns Hopkins University Press, 1980. Pp. 80-123.

Hambleton, R. K. Advances in criterion-referenced testing technology. In C. R. Reynolds & T. B. Gutkin (Eds.), *The handbook of school psychology*. New York: Wiley, 1982. Pp. 351-379. (a)

Hambleton, R. K. *Validity investigation of the American Board of Family Practice Certification Exam.* Unpublished Research Report. Lexington, KY: American Board of Family Practice, 1982. (b)

Hambleton, R. K. Criterion-referenced measurement. In T. Husén & T. N. Postlethwaite (Eds.), *International encyclopedia of education: Research and studies.* Oxford, England: Pergamon Press, 1984.

Hambleton, R. K. *Advances in criterion-referenced testing methods*. Hingham, MA: Kluwer-Nijhoff, in press.

Hambleton, R. K., & Eignor, D. R. Guidelines for evaluating criterion-referenced tests and test manuals. *Journal of Educational Measurement*, 1978, *15*, 321-327.

Hambleton, R. K., & Eignor, D. R. *A practitioner's guide to criterion-referenced test development, validation, and test score usage* (Report No. 70). Amherst: Laboratory of Psychometric and Evaluative Research, School of Education, University of Massachusetts, 1979.

Hambleton, R. K., & Novick, M. R. Toward an integration of theory and method for criterion-referenced tests. *Journal of Educational Measurement*, 1973, *10*, 159-170.

Hambleton, R. K., Swaminathan, H., Algina, J., & Coulson, D. B. Criterion-referenced testing and measurement: A review of technical issues and developments. *Review of Educational Research*, 1978, *48*, 1-47.

Kane, M. T. The validity of licensure examinations. *American Psychologist*, 1982, *37*, 911-918.

Kirsch, I., & Guthrie, J. T. Construct validity of functional reading tests. *Journal of Educational Measurement*, 1980, *17*, 81–93.

Lindheim, E. *Content validation of criterion-referenced tests.* Paper presented at the annual meeting of the American Educational Research Association, New York, March 1982.

Linn, R. L. Issues of validity in measurement for competency-based programs. In M. A. Bunda & J. R. Sanders (Eds.), *Practices and problems in competency-based measurement.* Washington, DC: National Council on Measurement in Education, 1979. Pp. 108–123.

Linn, R. L. Issues of validity for criterion-referenced measures. *Applied Psychological Measurement*, 1980, *4*, 547–561.

Linn, R. L. Curriculum validity: Convincing the court that it was taught without precluding the possibility of measuring it. In G. F. Madaus (Ed.), *The courts, validity, and minimum competency testing.* Hingham, MA: Kluwer-Nijhoff, 1983. Pp. 115–132.

Madaus, G. F. (Ed.) *The courts, validity, and minimum competency testing.* Hingham, MA: Kluwer-Nijhoff, 1983.

McClung, M. S. *Developing proficiency programs in California public schools: Some legal implications and a suggested implementation schedule.* Sacramento, CA: California Department of Education, 1978.

Messick, S. A. The standard problem: Meaning and values in measurement and evaluation. *American Psychologist*, 1975, *30*, 955–966.

Messick, S. A. Test validity and the ethics of assessment. *American Psychologist*, 1980, *35*, 1012–1027.

Millman, J. Criterion-referenced measurement. In W. J. Popham (Ed.), *Evaluation in education: Current applications.* Berkeley, CA: McCutchan, 1974. Pp. 311–397.

Millman, J. Reliability and validity of criterion-referenced test scores. In R. E. Traub (Ed.), *New directions for testing and measurement* (No. 4): *Methodological developments*. San Francisco: Jossey-Bass, 1979. Pp. 75–92.

Popham, W. J. An approaching peril: Cloud referenced tests. *Phi Delta Kappan*, 1974, *56*, 614–615.

Popham, W. J. *Criterion-referenced measurement.* Englewood Cliffs, NJ: Prentice-Hall, 1978.

Rovinelli, R. J., & Hambleton, R. K. On the use of content specialists in the assessment of criterion-referenced test item validity. *Dutch Journal of Educational Research*, 1977, *2*, 49–60.

Schmidt, W. H., Porter, A. C., Schwille, J. R., Floden, R. E., & Freeman, D. J. Validity as a variable: Can the same certification test be valid for all students? In G. F. Madaus (Ed.), *The courts, validity, and minimum competency testing.* Hingham, MA: Kluwer-Nijhoff, 1983. Pp. 133–151.

Secolsky, C. Using examinee judgments to detect ambiguity on teacher-made criterion-referenced tests. *Journal of Educational Measurement*, 1983, *20*, 51–63; Erratum, 1983, *20*, 303.

Shepard, L. A. Identifying bias in test items. In B. F. Green (Ed.), *New directions for testing and measurement* (No. 11): *Issues in testing—Coaching, disclosure, and ethnic bias.* San Francisco: Jossey-Bass, 1981. Pp. 79–104.

Tittle, C. K. Use of judgmental methods in item bias studies. In R. A. Berk (Ed.), *Handbook of methods for detecting test bias.* Baltimore, MD: Johns Hopkins University Press, 1982. Pp. 31–63.

Ward, W. C., Frederiksen, N., & Carlson, S. B. Construct validity of free-response and machine-scorable forms of a test. *Journal of Educational Measurement*, 1980, *17*, 11–29.

White, R. T. The validation of a learning hierarchy. *American Educational Research Journal*, 1974, *11*, 121–136.

Yalow, E. S., & Popham, W. J. Content validity at the crossroads. *Educational Researcher*, 1983, *12*, 10–14, 21.

9 SELECTING THE INDEX OF RELIABILITY

RONALD A. BERK

INTRODUCTION

OVER THE PAST decade more than a dozen different statistics have been devised for measuring the reliability of criterion-referenced tests. Recent summaries and critiques of those measures have been conducted by Hambleton, Swaminathan, Algina, and Coulson (1978), Linn (1979), Millman (1979), Shepard (1980), and Traub and Rowley (1980). Hambleton et al. (1978, pp. 15–23) defined three major categories of reliability: (1) reliability of mastery classification decisions—consistency of mastery-nonmastery classification decision making across repeated measures with one test form or parallel test forms; (2) reliability of criterion-referenced test scores—consistency of squared deviations of individual scores from the cut-off score across parallel or randomly parallel test forms; (3) reliability of domain score estimates—consistency of individual scores across parallel or randomly parallel test forms. Subsequently, in-depth analyses of the indices that fall into the first category, which are based on a threshold loss function, and the indices that fall into the second category, which are based on a squared-error loss function, have been presented by Subkoviak (1980, also chapter 10) and Brennan (1980, also chapter 11), respectively. These sets of indices are appropriate for criterion-referenced tests where mastery-nonmastery decisions are made on the basis of a cut-off score. The indices that fall into the last category which are used to estimate the stability of an individual's domain score or proportion correct have received the least attention.

Despite the number of indices and the available sources, a reliability index is rarely reported for criterion-referenced and minimum competency tests. When an index is reported, it is usually the Kuder-Richardson Formula 20 or 21. In order to facilitate increased and proper use of the reliability indices by teachers, district and state level test makers, and test publishers, Berk (1980a) compiled and evaluated the indices in the form of a "consumers' guide." This chapter is an extension of that guide. It is intended to provide a framework for selecting the appropriate reliability index in a given test application.

A dozen different approaches that yield 13 reliability indices for criterion-referenced tests are identified and grouped into three categories: threshold loss function, squared-error loss function, and domain score estimation. Selection of a reliability index for a specific application is conceived as a two-stage decision process: (1) choose the appropriate category of reliability and (2) choose a specific index within that category.

The initial choice of a reliability category is based on certain preliminary considerations related to the assumptions, interpretations, and uses of the indices. These considerations include: a clarification of terminology, test forms assumption, setting the cut-off score, and test score interpretation and decision making.

The choice of a specific index is based on the characteristics, precision, and practicability of each index. Practicability pertains to the ease with which an index can be computed and interpreted. A critical review of the dozen approaches and corresponding indices according to these factors is presented.

A Clarification of Terminology

The use of the term *reliability coefficient* to characterize the indices recommended for criterion-referenced tests is inappropriate. That term is, in fact, a misnomer since neither the threshold loss nor the squared-error loss function approach is defined or interpreted in the language of the standard psychometric reliability components of observed score and true score variance (cf. APA/AERA/NCME Joint Committee, 1974). It is certainly possible to relate many of the indices to classical reliability theory or to describe them within a broad framework of variance components. However, their properties suggest that the term *agreement index* provides a more accurate label (see also Kane & Brennan, 1980). The threshold loss function indices are measures of agreement between categorical data sets based on mastery-nonmastery classifications; the squared-error loss function indices are measures of agreement between the scores on two test forms.

Unfortunately, the domain score estimation procedures cannot be explained as easily in terms of an agreement function. Four of the procedures involve a consideration of different types of standard error, while the other consists of a reliability-like index. Therefore, the statistics in this last category will not be relabeled.

Test Forms Assumption

All of the statistics reviewed in this chapter require an assumption about test forms. It is assumed that two or more forms of a criterion-referenced test are either classically parallel or randomly parallel. The assumption is related to the characteristics of the item domain from which the item samples are generated and to how the item sample that defines one test form and the samples that define alternate forms are selected.

Classically parallel test forms. When items are written from objectives-based specifications using traditional item construction rules, those items viewed collectively constitute a sample from a theoretical domain of "all possible items" that could be written for the objective. When two or more samples are developed for the same objective and domain, those samples should contain content and yield means, variances, and item intercorrelations identical to the first sample. Item samples or alternate test forms with these properties are said to be classically parallel or equivalent. The statistical equivalence imposes restrictions on the domain. Very often when a test maker does not actually produce parallel forms, the alternate form(s) and its statistical properties are simply "assumed." All of the agreement indices except Brennan's (1980, chapter 11) index and one domain score estimation statistic (Lord & Novick, 1968) are based on this assumption.

Randomly parallel test forms. In contrast, the recent technological advances in the specification of behavioral domains offer alternative strategies that can generate "all possible items" in a domain. The progress that has been made over the past decade is reflected in the methodologies of amplified objectives, IOX test specifications, mapping sentences (facet theory), item transformations, item forms, and algorithms (for details, see chapters 2, 3, and 4). Proponents of the last three strategies, in particular, claim that generating an item domain is an objective, mechanical process. While the precision of the different strategies varies markedly and much more research lies ahead, the strategies do provide some evidence to refute the skepticism expressed by Thorndike in 1967: "As soon as we try to conceptualize a test score as a sample from some universe, we are brought face to face with the very knotty problem of defining the universe from which we are sampling. . . . The universe is considerably restricted, is hard to define, and the sampling from it is hardly to be considered random" (pp. 285, 288).

When one of the item-generating strategies is employed in test construction, the items to be included on one test form or alternate test forms are selected from the item domain using a random or stratified random sampling plan. The resulting test forms are said to be randomly parallel. None of the statistical properties mentioned previously applies to these forms. When the test maker cannot actually build test forms by randomly sampling from the domain, the alternate form(s) and its characteristics can more reasonably be "assumed" (cf. Cardinet, Tourneur, & Allal, 1976). Only one agreement index (Brennan & Kane, 1977a) and four domain score estimation statistics (Berk, 1980b; Brennan, 1980; Lord, 1957) assume randomly parallel test forms.

Setting the Cut-off Score

Computation of the threshold loss and squared-error loss function indices presumes that a cut-off score for mastery of an objective has been selected. All of the indices are affected by the position of the cut-off score in the score distribution. The relationship between an agreement index and the cut-off score makes it essential that the cut-off be included in the interpretation of the index.

Setting the cut-off score is a crucial step prior to the consideration of an agreement index. In fact, without decision validity evidence related to the cut-off score (see Hambleton, chapter 8) or a sound justification for setting the score (see Shepard, chapter 7), it seems pointless even to compute an agreement index. Certainly one can compute an index based on any performance standard. However, if it is not known whether the decisions based on the cut-off score will be accurate, then one possible interpretation of a high index of decision consistency might be that the *test can consistently classify students into the wrong groups*. Consistent decision making without accurate decision making has questionable value.

In addition, a priori decisions regarding the relative seriousness of the losses related to the probabilities of false mastery and false nonmastery errors must be reached before choosing a loss function. Those decisions are contingent upon whether such losses are perceived to be equally serious (threshold loss function) or to vary as a function of how far above or below the cut-off score the misclassified students' scores are located (squared-error loss function).

Test Score Interpretation and Decision Making

The scores on a criterion-referenced test can be used for decision making about individuals and programs at the classroom, school, district, state, and national levels. The decisions made by the classroom teacher within the context of mastery learning theory and diagnostic-prescriptive teaching have best demonstrated the utility of criterion-referenced test scores. Typically, those decisions are derived from an objectives-based assessment of individual strengths (mastery) and weaknesses (nonmastery). They involve placing students at the appropriate points in the instructional sequence, monitoring students' successes and failures as they progress through the program, and assigning letter grades/pass-fail to certify competencies in a subject area or course. Recently the last type of summative evaluation has been extended in the form of minimum competency certification for grade-to-grade promotion and high school graduation. Even outside the public school arena, similar score interpretations are being contemplated for the certification and/or licensing of professionals in medicine and the allied health fields, social work, psychology, law, and engineering.

In addition to making assessments for these different types of individual decisions, test scores may be used to assess program effectiveness at the decision levels mentioned previously. These evaluation decisions usually focus on the effectiveness of curricular materials or instructional methods. The actual decisions may be to continue, to modify, or to terminate a given program. In order to supply information that will be meaningful for these decisions, it is often necessary to summarize the test score results into various forms, such as: (a) percentage of students demonstrating mastery of each objective, (b) percentage of students demonstrating mastery of sets of objectives, (c) estimated mean performance on the total test, and (d) estimated mean performance based on the matrix sampling of students and items from their respective populations or domains. The appropriateness of these summaries will vary as a function of the level of the decision maker, from classroom teacher to state superintendent, and the nature of the decision. The summary that is needed for a particular decision is composed by aggregating the individual test scores at the appropriate decision level. Examples of several report formats have been assembled by Mills and Hambleton (1980) and Berk (1984, chap. 3).

The initial choice of a "reliability" category is contingent upon the intended interpretation of the test scores, type of decision to be made with those scores, and the consequences or losses associated with false mastery and false nonmastery decision errors. Table 9.1 is a brief list of score and decision characteristics related to the three categories of "reliability." Since the score interpretations for the numerous levels of program evaluation decisions are derived from aggregates of individual scores and their corresponding uses and interpretations, only individual score and decision characteristics are specified in the table.

REVIEW OF RELIABILITY INDICES

Threshold Loss Agreement Indices

The concept of classification decision consistency using a threshold loss function was first proposed by Hambleton and Novick (1973, p. 168). The use of the threshold loss function assumes that (a) a dichotomous, qualitative classification of students as masters and nonmasters of an objective based on a threshold or cut-off score exists, and (b) the losses associated with all false mastery and false nonmastery classification errors are equally serious regardless of their size.

The characteristics and evaluation of the six approaches in this category are outlined in Table 9.2. The various approaches actually involve only two agreement indices: p_o, proportion of individuals consistently classified as masters and nonmasters across (classically) parallel test forms, and κ, proportion of individuals consistently classified beyond that expected by chance (for computational examples, see Subkoviak, chapter 10). While two other indices developed by Carver (1970) might be considered in this review, they are omitted because they are insensitive to the consistency of individual classification decisions and only reflect whether the group percentage of masters stays the same.

The choice between p_o and κ as indices of classification consistency depends upon how consistency is defined in a given decision context and how the properties of the statistics are evaluated. This section of the chapter will concentrate on the appropriateness of the indices for tests used for individual decisions at the classroom level, individual certification decisions at the

Table 9.1. Score and Decision Characteristics for Three Categories of "Reliability"

Characteristic	Category of "Reliability"		
	Threshold Loss	Squared-error Loss	Domain Score Estimation
Score interpretation	Individual score is referenced to cut-off score	Individual score is referenced to cut-off score	Individual score is used to estimate domain score
Type of decision or information required for decision	Mastery or nonmastery classification	Degree of mastery or nonmastery along score continuum	Level of competency in content domain
Losses associated with decision errors	Losses are equally serious	Losses related to misclassified students who are far above or below cut-off score are more serious than losses related to other misclassified students	Consideration of losses varies with the estimation procedures

Source: Reprinted with permission from Berk, Ronald A. "A Consumers' Guide to Criterion-Referenced Test Reliability." *Journal of Educational Measurement*, 1980, *17*, 323–349, Table 1 (p. 326). Copyright 1980, National Council on Measurement in Education, Washington, DC.

Table 9.2. Evaluation of Threshold Loss Function Indices
(In order of increasing overall complexity)

Index	Definition	Source	Number of Administrations	Test Forms Assumption	Distribution Assumptions	Correction for Chance Agreement	Comments
$\hat{p}_o$	Proportion of individuals consistently classified as masters and nonmasters on repeated measurements of one form or parallel forms	Hambleton and Novick (1973)	2	1 Form or classically parallel forms	None	No	*Advantages:* Provides unbiased estimate of p_o. Hand calculable and easily interpretable. *Disadvantages:* Requires two test administrations. When only one test form is used, testing effect can spuriously deflate estimates. $\hat{p}_o$ has comparatively large standard errors for classroom size samples (Subkoviak, 1978, 1980, chapter 10)
$\hat{\kappa}$	Proportion of individuals consistently classified, as above, beyond that expected by chance	Swaminathan, Hambleton, and Algina (1974) based on Cohen (1960)	2	1 Form or classically parallel forms	None	Yes[a]	*Advantages:* Hand calculable; computer programs are also available (e.g., Antonak, 1977; Berk & Campbell, 1976; Wixon, 1979). $\hat{\kappa}$ and ϕ coefficients are virtually identical (Marshall & Serlin, 1979; Reid & Roberts, 1978). *Disadvantages:* Yields biased estimate of κ. Sensitivity to test length and variance may restrict range of values. Requires two test administrations. Testing effect based on test-retest design can spuriously deflate estimates. Dependence of index values on cut-off score, marginal frequencies, test length, and score variance complicates index interpretation.

Table 9.2. *(continued)*

Index	Definition	Source	Number of Adminis- trations	Test Forms Assumption	Distribution Assumptions	Correction for Chance Agreement	Comments
$\hat{p}_o$; $\hat{\kappa}$	Same as $\hat{p}_o$ and $\hat{\kappa}$ defined previously	Huynh (1976)	1	Classically parallel[b]	Binomial distribution of observed scores over repeated measurements; Beta distribution of true scores	No; Yes	Indices computed from the univariate and bivariate distributions. Under similar distribution assumptions for double length tests $\hat{p}_o$ equals $\beta(\hat{p}_o)$ (Marshall & Serlin, 1979). *Advantages:* Requires only one test administration. Comparatively small standard errors for classroom-sized samples (Subkoviak, 1978). $\hat{p}_o$ is easily interpretable. Based on the mathematically elegant Keats and Lord (1962) model (see Gross & Shulman, 1980). Provides most accurate estimates of p_o for unimodal distributions. Violation of equal item difficulty assumption seems to have negligible effect on estimates (Huynh & Saunders, 1980; Subkoviak, 1978). Tabled values of $\hat{p}_o$ and $\hat{\kappa}$ for tests with 5 to 10 items per objective as well as a computer program are currently available (Huynh, 1979; Subkoviak, 1980). A simple normal approximation method that is hand calculable has also been recommended (Peng & Subkoviak, 1980).

							Disadvantages: Yields biased (slightly conservative) estimates of p_o and κ for short tests (Huynh & Saunders, 1980; Subkoviak, 1978). Sensitivity of κ to test length and variance may restrict range of values. Most conceptually and mathematically complex approach.
$\beta(\hat{p}_o)$	Same as $\hat{p}_o$ defined previously	Marshall (1976)	1	Classically parallel	Binomial distribution of observed scores over repeated measurements (assumes 0–1 items, statistical independence of items, and equal item difficulties)	No	Average p_o across all possible split-halves of a single test, extended to a full-length (double-length test) estimate with Spearman-Brown type prophecy formula. *Advantages:* Requires only one test administration. Comparatively small standard errors for classroom-sized samples (Subkoviak, 1978). Easily interpretable. *Disadvantages:* Yields biased estimates for short tests (Subkoviak, 1978, 1980). Provides no estimate of κ. Computationally complex with no readily available computer program.
$\hat{p}_o$; $\hat{\kappa}$	Same as $\hat{p}_o$ and $\hat{\kappa}$ defined previously	Subkoviak (1976, 1980, chapter 10)	1	Classically parallel	Binomial or compound binomial distribution of observed scores over repeated measurements	No; Yes	Observed proportion correct scores and KR-20 coefficient are used to obtain linear regression approximations to the compound binomial p_o. Relies on the estimation of the true score for each person. Consistency index for each person is averaged over the population to produce $\hat{p}_o$. *Advantages:* Same as $\beta(\hat{p}_o)$ (see also Scheetz & vonFraunhofer, 1980).

Table 9.2. (continued)

Index	Definition	Source	Number of Adminis-trations	Test Forms Assumption	Distribution Assumptions	Correction for Chance Agreement	Comments
							Disadvantages: Yields biased estimates of p_o for short tests (Algina & Noe, 1978; Subkoviak, 1978). Sensitivity of $\hat{\kappa}$ to test length and variance may restrict range of values. Computationally complex with no readily available computer program.
KM	Kappamax (maximum value of $\hat{\kappa}$)	Huynh (1977)	1	Classically parallel[b]	Same as Huynh's (1976) $\hat{\kappa}$	Yes	Upperbound of $\hat{\kappa}$ is usually reached at a cut-off score near the mean, although *KM* is not a function of the cut-off score. It reflects the situation in which a test functions best in terms of decision consistency. *Advantages:* Same as Huynh's (1976) $\hat{\kappa}$. *Disadvantages:* Same as Huynh's (1976) $\hat{\kappa}$. Interpretation and utility of *KM* by itself or in conjunction with $\hat{\kappa}$ are unclear (see also Brennan & Prediger, 1981).

Source: Adapted from Berk (1980a, pp. 328–331) with permission of the National Council on Measurement in Education, Washington, DC.

[a] The κ index is corrected for chance according to the marginal frequencies of the particular contingency table data set under consideration. This constraint may be viewed as a disadvantage of using κ for tests intended for individual decisions at the classroom level.

[b] Huynh (1976, pp. 254–255, 1977, p. 1) defined two equivalent test forms as two independent random samples of items drawn from a specified item universe. While these test forms *could be* randomly parallel, the author indicates that they possess the properties of classically parallel forms essential for the assumptions of the beta-binomial model (Huynh, personal communication, November 1979).

school level (e.g., minimum competency testing), and program evaluation decisions at the district level.

p_0 index. The p_0 index measures the overall consistency of mastery-nonmastery classifications. Subkoviak (1980, p. 152) noted two factors that contribute to that consistency: the master-nonmastery composition of the group tested and the measurement precision or accuracy of the test itself. The index is sensitive to the selected cut-off score, test length, and score variability. However, the position of the cut-off score tends to have a much more profound effect upon the magnitude of the index than either of the other two characteristics. Higher values of p_0 are associated with cut-off scores at the tails of a unimodal score distribution, and lower values occur with cut-off scores near the mean. This trend may not follow for bimodal distributions. The index values can also increase as the number of test items increases and the score variance increases. In practice, however, it is possible to obtain $\hat{p}_0$ values of .75 or higher with subtests containing fewer than 10 items and exhibiting relatively little score variance.* These properties are especially important in view of the structure and uses of most teacher-made criterion-referenced tests.

κ index. Although these advantages indicate why p_0 might be the preferred index of agreement for tests intended for individualized instructional decisions at the classroom level, the disadvantages associated with the uses of κ will demonstrate more dramatically why κ may *not* be the preferred index for such tests. The rejection of p_0 in favor of Cohen's (1960) κ coefficient was advanced originally by Swaminathan, Hambleton, and Algina (1974, p. 264). They felt that κ was somewhat more appropriate since it took into account the agreement that could be expected by chance alone. The κ index measures the test's contribution to the overall proportion of consistent classifications, that is, test consistency. It is calculated by subtracting from p_0 the proportion of consistency expected from the particular mastery-nonmastery composition of the group. The properties of κ that stem from this "correction for chance agreement" are what make this index problematic.

There are three properties of the κ index that render it undesirable for criterion-referenced tests used for classroom decision making: the correction for chance is constrained by the marginal frequencies, and κ's sensitivity to test length and test score variability may restrict the range of values. All three properties complicate the interpretation of κ.

First, the correction for chance agreement is constrained by the marginal frequencies of the particular 2×2 contingency table data set under consideration. An index of $+1.00$ can be obtained only when the marginals on both forms or measurements are equal. Livingston and Wingersky's (1979) arguments on this issue are most persuasive:

> Applying such a correction to a pass/fail contingency table is equivalent to assuming that the proportion of examinees passing the test could not have been anything but

*All estimates of indices cited throughout the chapter and the tables will be distinguished from the parameters with the symbol "^".

> what it happened to be. For example, if 87% of the examinees passed the test, kappa will "correct for chance" under the assumption that "chance" would result in exactly 87% of the examinees passing the test. This assumption makes sense when the pass/fail cutoff is chosen on the basis of the scores to which it will be applied, so as to pass a specified proportion of the examinees. It does *not* make sense when the pass/fail cutoff represents an absolute standard that is to be applied individually to each examinee. (p. 250)

For a technical discussion of the chance correction and the consequences of using κ when the marginals are unequal and free to vary (i.e., not fixed a priori), the reader is referred to Brennan and Prediger (1981).

One condition under which the correction for chance could be justified is where the selection of the cut-off score is determined, in part, by the consequences (losses) of passing or failing a particular proportion or segment of the population. In this case, the marginals are fixed a priori. Also, the cut-off score is relative rather than absolute. Exemplary of this type of cut-off score are the performance standards for many minimum competency tests that are set by district or state level decision makers. When these tests are used for individual certification decisions, the cut-off score is usually adjusted according to the political, economic, social, and/or instructional consequences of not passing or certifying a certain proportion of the students in the school district.

Second, the values of κ increase with test length. Since this is a characteristic of most reliability statistics, it should not be viewed necessarily as a disadvantage of κ. It is the consequences of this sensitivity that are troublesome. In criterion-referenced testing an item sample or subtest designed to assess mastery of an instructional objective generally consists of between 3 and 10 items on tests developed for classroom usage, and rarely of more than 20 items on tests developed for district or state level usage (see chapter 6). For the majority of test applications at these levels, then, the values of κ may be restricted in range due to short subtest lengths. Short tests could be expected to provide less reliable information and, hence, yield lower indices. This restriction would not be of concern in large-scale minimum competency testing programs where the items are often aggregated across objectives to apply a single cut-off score to the total test and, subsequently, to estimate classification consistency based on that score.

Third, the values of κ increase with score variability. A restriction in variance that would be accompanied by a restriction in the range of κ will occur frequently in criterion-referenced testing due to short subtests as discussed here and to the homogeneous composition of the group that is tested (cf. Divgi, 1980). In many cases the test results tend to yield a large proportion of masters or nonmasters. This composition is especially evident when classroom test scores are used for individual placement, formative, and summative decisions. The former two types of decisions are typically diagnostic in nature and are made prior to instruction. At that point in instruction, the results usually indicate disproportionately large numbers of nonmasters. Conversely, summative decisions that are made at the conclusion of instruction are often based on results with disproportionately large numbers of masters.

In addition to these properties of κ, there are other characteristics worthy of consideration: (a) κ's sensitivity to the cut-off score is just the inverse of p_o, such that higher values of κ correspond to cut-off scores near the mean score and lower values correspond to cut-off scores at the tails of the distribution (Huynh & Saunders, 1980; Subkoviak, 1980, chapter 10); $\hat{\kappa}$ is a biased estimator (Harris & Pearlman, 1977, p. 35); (c) one of the single administration approaches (Huynh, 1976) provides less accurate estimates of κ (about 10% error) than of p_o; and (d) the interpretation and usefulness of the κ index in practice is not clear (see, for example, Brennan & Prediger, 1981; Safrit & Stamm, 1979).

Recommendations. The foregoing comparison of p_o and κ as indices of classification consistency suggests that p_o should be the index of agreement for criterion-referenced tests where an absolute cut-off score is chosen and for other tests that may contain short subtests and/or yield low score variance. While κ may be the preferred index of agreement for tests where relative cut-off scores are set according to the consequences of passing or failing a particular proportion of the students, the problems associated with κ render it less useful than p_o. Caution should be observed in the use and interpretation of κ. Given the dependence of both indices on the cut-off score, test length, score variability, and the cell frequencies of the 2×2 contingency table, it is recommended that the test maker report all of this information along with the agreement index to facilitate perceptive and correct index interpretations (cf. Livingston & Wingersky, 1979; Millman, 1974a).

One- versus two-administration approaches. Once an initial decision has been made to estimate p_o or κ, a second decision about whether to use a one- or two-administration approach must be made. Among the six classification consistency approaches, the Hambleton and Novick (1973) two-administration method appears to have the greatest utility for classroom test construction. For tests developed at the district and state levels and by commercial publishers, either the Hambleton and Novick (1973) or Swaminathan et al. (1974) two-administration method or the Huynh (1976) one-administration method should be used.

The Hambleton and Novick (1973) and Swaminathan et al. (1974) two-administration methods require two sets of scores from *testing one group of students twice*, with a one- to two-week interval between the first and second testing. This is the same test-retest procedure used traditionally to estimate a stability coefficient for norm-referenced tests. The two test administrations should occur near the point in the instruction when the decisions are to be made. For example, for placement decisions the tests might be given during the first couple of weeks of instruction, or soon thereafter. Feedback on the results of the first testing should be deferred until after the second testing has been completed. Giving students the correct answers to the items prior to the second test administration can greatly improve their performance on that testing. Although such improvement may be desirable for instructional purposes, it will confound the estimation of p_o and κ. In addition, no formal instruction on the specific instructional objectives being measured should be conducted during the intervening period between the two testings for the same reason. These problems are discussed later in terms of testing effect.

The simplest testing procedure is to administer the *same test* to the *same students* on the *two occasions*. This framework produces a measure of *stability*. However, although the stability of the test scores over time is being assessed, the p_o or κ index for a criterion-referenced test focuses on the stability of the mastery-nonmastery *decisions* based on those scores.

Alternatively, a classically parallel test form can be used on the second administration. The two test forms will then make it possible to measure both *stability and equivalence*. That is, p_o and κ will reflect the stability of the decisions over time *and* the equivalence of the scores for two item samples. Since two sources of error are being measured, the stability-equivalence estimate will typically be lower than the stability estimate.

Whichever method is selected, the structure of the information that results is identical. Repeated measurements with one test or parallel tests yield two sets of scores on the same objectives. Since it is usually quite difficult and very time consuming for teachers to build parallel forms that are matched on both content and statistical characteristics, the single test approach may be preferable.

When one test is administered twice in close succession, the problem of *testing effect* associated with the test-retest method must be addressed. If the specific content being tested is not easily remembered (e.g., algebraic equations, phonics) or both testings occur near the end of instruction and the retest data are collected for review purposes, the effect will be negligible. On the other hand, a significant testing effect could be expected when (a) some items can be easily recognized on the retest, (b) teaching of the test content occurs during the intervening period between the two testings, or (c) errors on the first testing are corrected prior to the second testing.

Inasmuch as the knowledge gained from the initial testing tends to inflate the scores on the retest, typically only the status of nonmasters on measurement 1 will be altered on measurement 2. How does this affect the p_o or κ index? Certainly if several nonmasters become masters, thereby reducing the total number of *consistent* decisions, the index will be deflated. In other words, when a testing effect is suspected, the value of p_o or κ will usually be lower than it would be without that effect (i.e., a conservative bias). The teacher should be cognizant of this possible bias in interpreting the index.

In addition to possible testing effect, the two-administration estimate of p_o has comparatively large standard errors (6 to 8%) for classroom-sized samples of 30 students or fewer. Consequently, if $\hat{p}_o$ is computed from data gathered on only a few students, caution should be observed in attaching undue weight to the resultant value, for example, a high value could be very misleading. A consideration of about 6% error in evaluating classification consistency based on mastery standards at or above 80% seems advisable. (*Note*: This recommendation is derived from preliminary evidence indicating that the magnitude of the error decreases as the cut-off score increases on short subtests.) The accuracy of $\hat{p}_o$ can be improved by administering the test to several classes at a given grade level. A teacher would then be able to place greater confidence in the estimate and, if it happens to be in the .80s or above, in his or her decisions.

Despite these disadvantages of testing effect and the imprecision of the estimate based on two test administrations, there are several advantages to using the test-retest method for computing the p_o index. First, the Hambleton and Novick (1973) method provides the only unbiased estimate of p_o. Second, it is easy to understand, to use, to compute, and to interpret. Third, the method can be applied to most types of items and tests, including: (a) dichotomous or multipoint items, (b) short or long subtests and tests, (c) paper-and-pencil tests or performance tests, and (d) tests and scales measuring cognitive, affective, or psychomotor behaviors. Finally, the testing procedure can be employed with samples representing virtually any population of students for which a criterion-referenced test can be designed.

Weighing these advantages against the previously stated disadvantages suggests that, depending on whether p_o or κ is selected, the Hambleton and Novick (1973) or Swaminathan et al. (1974) method should be employed by test makers at the district and state levels and by test publishers. If parallel test forms are constructed for test security or other reasons, the two-administration estimate is recommended over the one-administration estimate (discussed next). The two-administration estimate is more accurate and is simpler to compute and to interpret.

When it is not possible to develop parallel forms, the more sophisticated test maker should seriously consider the one-administration estimate using Huynh's (1976) procedure. Subkoviak (1980) has recommended this approach on statistical as well as practical grounds. It provides relatively precise though conservatively biased estimates of p_o and κ. However, since the estimates are based on only one test administration, they do not reflect all sources of instability across repeated testings. Huynh's (1976) method, as well as the other one-administration approaches, assume that a student's knowledge and all of the test administration conditions remain unchanged from one testing to the next. This assumption would never be upheld in practice. Consequently, the method may overestimate decision consistency even though the estimates of the parameters are conservatively biased.

Huynh's (1976) beta-binomial model is one of the most conceptually, mathematically, and computationally complex threshold loss function approaches. Despite this complexity, it has several distinct advantages compared to the alternatives (see Table 9.2). In addition, a simple normal approximation of the beta-binomial distributions tested by Peng and Subkoviak (1980) provides relatively accurate estimates of p_o and κ. This finding should be particularly meaningful to test makers without computer facilities, since the approximation procedures can be hand calculated (for details, see chapter 10).

Squared-error Loss Agreement Indices

In contrast to the threshold loss function, which focuses on the consistency of classifications, the squared-error loss approach to measurement error deals with the consistency of measurements or scores. It is based on the squared deviations of individual scores from the cut-off score. This builds in a sensitivity to degrees of mastery and nonmastery along the score continuum in addition to the qualitative master-nonmaster classification assumed by the threshold loss function. The losses associated with false mastery and false nonmastery errors are not assumed to be equally serious. The consequences of misclassifying students who are far above or below the cut-off score are considered more serious than the consequences of misclassifying those who are close to the cut-off score. The sensitivity to degree of mastery also means that a squared-error loss agreement index reflects the magnitude of all errors of measurement, including those that do not lead to misclassification (Brennan & Kane, 1977a, p. 287). This is one fundamental problem with this loss function.

Table 9.3 is an evaluation of the two agreement indices in this category. The indices are quite similar in regard to what they are measuring, although the actual formulations are very different. The primary distinctions between the indices pertain to their assumptions about test forms (classically parallel or randomly parallel) and, based on these assumptions, their definitions of error variance or squared-error loss.

Brennan (1980) defined two types of *error variance* in terms of analysis of variance components: $\sigma^2(\delta)$, person $\times$ item interaction, and $\sigma^2(\Delta)$, item effect plus person $\times$ item interaction. The former, which is derived from the assumption of classically parallel test forms, is part of Livingston's (1972a) $k^2(X, T_x)$ index; the latter, which is derived from the assumption of randomly parallel test forms, is incorporated in Brennan's (1980, chapter 11) $\Phi(\lambda)$ index.

There are several technical features common to both indices that should be mentioned: (a) no distribution assumptions are necessary, (b) as agreement indices, they are uncorrected for chance agreement (see Kane & Brennan, 1980), (c) index values can change, independent of their standard errors of measurement, (d) index values increase as the cut-off score is set farther and farther from the mean (similar to values of $\hat{p}_o$), (e) index values increase as test length (number of items sampled) increases due to decreases in error variance, and (f) when there is no true or universe score variance, the indices can still have positive values as long as the true score mean does not equal the cut-off score. It is also interesting to note that when the cut-off score equals the sample mean, $\hat{k}^2(X, T_x)$ reduces to the KR-20 coefficient and $\hat{\Phi}(\lambda = \bar{X})$ is identical to the KR-21 coefficient.

Criticisms of $k^2(X, T_x)$. Criticisms of some of these technical features of Livingston's (1972a) index have been expressed by Harris (1972), Shavelson,

Block, and Ravitch (1972), and Hambleton and Novick (1973). Since the criticisms may also be directed at Brennan's (1980, chapter 11) index, the responses that follow apply to both k^2 and $\Phi(\lambda)$.

Harris (1972) argued that "*although Livingston's reliability coefficient is (generally) larger than the conventional one, the standard error of measurement is the same*, and consequently this larger coefficient does *not* imply a more dependable determination of whether or not a true score falls below (or exceeds) a given criterion value" (p. 29). Brennan and Kane (1977a, p. 286) felt that this criticism was primarily a matter of "form rather than substance." Livingston's k^2 index and the standard error of measurement are different statistics that provide different information for different purposes. The k^2 index as well as the $\Phi(\lambda)$ index measure the consistency of scores in relation to the cut-off score on repeated testings; the standard errors of measurement $\sigma(\delta)$, which is identical to that derived from classical reliability theory, and $\sigma(\Delta)$, respectively, measure the inconsistency or average imprecision of an individual's scores independent of the cut-off score on repeated testings. These standard errors could be used as domain score estimation statistics for setting up confidence intervals around individual scores. Those statistics do not diminish the meaningfulness and utility of k^2 and $\Phi(\lambda)$. As Livingston (1972b) pointed out in his reply to Harris, "reliability is not a characteristic of a single score, but of a group of scores ... the larger criterion-referenced reliability coefficient *does* imply a more dependable overall determination of whether each true score falls above or below the criterion level, when this decision is to be made for every individual score in the distribution" (p. 31).

Shavelson et al. (1972) cited three problems with k^2: (a) it is "a function of the criterion as well as a function of individuals' responses to items.... [Consequently, it] is not directly related to the repeatability of the measure" (p. 134); (b) "this theory is applicable to situations where there may be no differences among true scores of individuals.... This seems unnecessary" (pp. 134–135); and (c) $\hat{k}^2$ "does not estimate the ratio of true score variance over observed score variance alone; $k^2(X, T_x)$ cannot be used or interpreted like conventional reliabilities.... We suggest that this statistic be given some other name than 'reliability'" (p. 135).

The first charge pertains to the *sensitivity of the indices to the cut-off score*, specified previously as technical feature (d). Livingston (1972c) argued, "It is entirely appropriate that [k^2] ... should depend heavily on the difference between the group mean score and the criterion score.... [This] difference ... can be considered 'true variance' for criterion-referenced purposes" (p. 139). Brennan (1979) contended, "As an examinee's observed score gets farther away from the cutting score, it becomes less likely that the examinee will be misclassified.... Since 'most' examinee scores are concentrated around the mean, it seems intuitively reasonable that $\Phi(\lambda)$ should increase as the cutting score moves away from the mean" (p. 38). Both researchers perceive the characteristic as desirable rather than as a limitation. However, it is essential that the test maker report the cut-off score upon which a particular index value is based along with other information so that the

Table 9.3. Evaluation of Squared-error Loss Function Indices
(*Both indices are rated equal in overall complexity*)

Index	Definition	Source	Number of Adminis-trations	Test Forms Assumption	Distribution Assumptions	Correction for Chance Agreement	Comments
$k^2(X, T_x)$	Ratio of true score to expected observed score mean squared deviations from the cut-off score—error variance $\sigma^2(\delta)$ based on person × item interaction	Livingston (1972a, 1977)	1	Classically parallel	None	No	A generalization of the classical reliability coefficient, where the expected mean squared deviation about the cut-off score is substituted for the variance about the mean score. When the cut-off score equals the mean, $\hat{k}^2$ reduces to the KR-20 coefficient. *Advantages:* Requires only one test administration. Hand calculable. *Disadvantage:* Dependence of index values on cut-off score, test length, and the estimated true or universe score variance and error variance complicates index interpretation.

$\Phi(\lambda)$	Ratio of universe score to expected observed score mean squared deviations from the cut-off score—error variance $\sigma^2(\Delta)$ based on item effect plus person $\times$ item interaction	Brennan (1980, chapter 11) Brennan and Kane (1977a, 1977b)	1	Randomly parallel	None	No	Measures the dependability of mastery-nonmastery decisions based on the testing procedure.[a] Derived from generalizability theory (Cronbach, Gleser, Nanda, & Rajaratnam, 1972). When the cut-off score (λ) equals the mean, $\hat{\Phi}(\lambda)$ is identical to the KR-21 coefficient (Brennan, 1977). *Advantages:* Same as k^2. Computer programs especially useful for more complex analysis of variance designs and the estimation of variance components are available (e.g., Brennan, 1979; Crick & Brennan, 1983; Erlich & Shavelson, 1976). Estimation procedures are very flexible to accommodate different test structures and score uses. *Disadvantage:* Same as k^2.

Source: Adapted from Berk (1980a, p. 336) with permission of the National Council on Measurement in Education, Washington, DC.

[a] Brennan (1980, pp. 204–213) also defined another index of dependability Φ that is independent of any cut-off score. It estimates the contribution of the testing procedure to the dependability of the decisions, over what would be expected on the basis of chance agreement. Unlike the above indices, the Φ index is most useful as a domain score estimation statistic (see Table 9.4).

relationship is considered in interpreting the magnitude of $\hat{k}^2$ and $\hat{\Phi}(\lambda)$. Brennan (1980, p. 228) also suggests that it might even be better to report a "curve" of index values as a function of several possible cut-off scores. Furthermore, the Shavelson et al. (1972) assertion regarding the concept of repeatability does not appear to follow from the dependence of the index on the cut-off score. Both k^2 and $\Phi(\lambda)$ are defined in terms of the repeatability of squared deviations of scores from the cut-off score rather than from the mean score.

Shavelson et al.'s second charge focuses on the circumstances whereby the *indices may yield positive values when there may be no true score variance*, specified previously as technical feature (f). Livingston (1972a, p. 19) noted that even if a group of students randomly guessed at all items and the resultant set of scores produced a high index, that index would be meaningful; the test user could be quite confident that all of the students had true scores below the cut-off score (Livingston, 1972c, p. 139). Brennan (1980) offered an explanation for the situation where the error variance is positive and all students have identical high universe scores compared to the cut-off score. He indicated, "In this case, $\Phi(\lambda)$ will be positive, reflecting the fact that it is relatively easy to determine correctly whether or not examinees are above the cut-off score" (p. 203).

The third charge relates to the *appropriateness of the term "reliability"* for describing and interpreting the indices. Livingston's (1972c) position on this issue is clear: "[k^2] deserves to be called a reliability coefficient because it represents the ratio of 'true' to 'observed' mean squared deviations from the criterion score, *and* the criterion-referenced correlation between alternate forms of the same test, *and* the squared criterion-referenced correlation between true scores and observed scores" (p. 139). Brennan and Kane (1977a, p. 285), however, have rejected the term *reliability coefficient* in favor of another term, *dependability coefficient*, for three reasons: (a) $\Phi(\lambda)$ is defined in terms of expected squared deviations rather than variances, (b) $\Phi(\lambda)$ entails definitions of error and parallel tests not usually associated with reliability coefficients, and (c) the magnitude of $\Phi(\lambda)$ depends upon a constant (λ), while the magnitude of the error variance is independent of λ. At the beginning of this chapter a rationale was given for the term *agreement index* which is similar, in part, to Brennan and Kane's first reason (see also Kane & Brennan, 1980).

Unlike the foregoing criticisms by Harris (1972) and Shavelson et al. (1972), which concentrate on technical characteristics of the indices, Hambleton and Novick's (1973) comments address the more fundamental issue of whether the squared-error loss approach to estimating reliability should be employed at all in criterion-referenced measurement. They stated emphatically that "Livingston misses the point for much of criterion-referenced testing. . . . The problem is one of deciding whether a student's true performance level is above or below some cutting score. . . . Livingston's choice of a loss function . . . is wrong" (p. 168). Recently Hambleton et al.

(1978, p. 17) admitted that their position was based on conjecture, and only time will tell if they are correct. Given the numerous decision applications and interpretations of criterion-referenced test scores in practice at the outset of the 1980s, Hambleton and Novick's (1973) earlier comments would appear to have become outdated.

Advantages of $k^2(X, T_x)$ and $\Phi(\lambda)$. On the positive side, both indices have certain advantages that deserve serious attention by test makers at the classroom, district, and state levels. First, the estimates $\hat{k}^2$ and $\hat{\Phi}(\lambda)$ require only one test administration. Second, the indices have particular utility for criterion-referenced tests used by teachers to place students into instructional treatments. Once an initial assessment of mastery-nonmastery status has been completed based on the cut-off score, the information typically of greatest value to teachers prior to instruction is the degree of mastery or nonmastery of each student along the score continuum. The detailed diagnosis of how much and what content a student does or does not know can assist the teacher in planning and assigning individualized prescriptions. Third, from a practical standpoint, the ease with which both indices could be hand calculated is comparable to that of the KR-20. The formula and computational examples for $\hat{\Phi}(\lambda)$ prepared especially for practitioners by Brennan (chapter 11) should contribute greatly to that ease. For test makers with computer resources, computer programs with extensive documentation are also available (e.g., Brennan, 1979; Crick & Brennan, 1983; Erlich & Shavelson, 1976).

In addition to these advantages, Brennan's (1980) approach has the advantage of *flexibility* in the analysis of different test structures corresponding to different test score uses. Brennan's application of generalizability theory to criterion-referenced measurement makes it possible to estimate $\Phi(\lambda)$ and universe score variance and error variance components so that they reflect the various facets of interest in a given situation.

Recommendations. With regard to the interpretation of the indices, it is strongly recommended that the cut-off score, test length, and estimated error variance [either $\hat{\sigma}^2(\delta)$ or $\hat{\sigma}^2(\Delta)$] be reported to test users. This information should furnish an adequate base for index interpretation given the number and diversity of factors that affect the values of $\hat{k}^2$ and $\hat{\Phi}(\lambda)$. Brennan (1980, chapter 11) also urged test makers to report estimates of universe score variance and the squared deviation of the grand mean from the cut-off score and, whenever possible, to estimate $\Phi(\lambda)$ in terms of variance components. This emphasis on variance components is consistent with the guidelines set forth in *Standards for Educational and Psychological Tests* (APA/AERA/NCME Joint Committee, 1974) and in the latest revision of these standards* (see also Kane, 1980).

*A new edition of the *Standards* titled *Joint Technical Standards for Educational and Psychological Testing* was being developed as this chapter was being written. The fourth draft of the document prepared for professional review in February 1984 suggests that it will place greater emphasis on the reporting of variance components in reliability studies than did the 1974 edition of the *Standards*. Expected publication date is 1985.

The choice between $k^2(X, T_x)$ and $\Phi(\lambda)$ is reduced to the simple decision of whether the assumption of classically parallel test forms or randomly parallel test forms, respectively, is appropriate for the test that was constructed. The advantages and disadvantages of the squared-error loss function should also be considered in that choice.

The guidelines presented previously for determining the appropriate loss function dealt with the type of decision to be made with the scores and the losses associated with the two types of decision error. There are some contexts where the threshold loss or squared-error loss function may be preferable and other contexts where neither may be preferable. Shepard (1980) suggested an "ideal index" that implies another loss function; it would reflect only false mastery and false nonmastery classification errors and it would weight those errors by degree. Unfortunately, at present such an index and loss function do not exist.

Domain Score Estimation Statistics

Unlike the agreement indices reviewed in the previous sections, the domain score estimation statistics are concerned generally with estimating the stability of an individual's score or proportion correct in the item domain, independent of any mastery standard. Five statistics in this category are described in this section. All of them have meaning for individual decision making at the classroom or school level. Program evaluation decisions would require estimates of the average domain score and the standard error of that average. These estimates vary as a function of the multiple matrix sampling design that is used in the school district. A discussion of the different estimates corresponding to the different matrix sampling designs is beyond the scope of this chapter. Interested readers should consult Sirotnik's (1974) chapter, which is oriented especially toward the practicing evaluator. More technical treatments of the topic include Lord and Novick's (1968, chap. 11) chapter and Shoemaker's (1973) monograph.

The domain score estimation statistics are evaluated in Table 9.4. They are organized into two subcategories, individual specific and group specific. The characteristics of these subcategories are examined first.

The *individual specific* statistics are defined, computed, and interpreted separately for each individual. They consist of two estimates of standard error that can be used to set up a confidence interval around each individual's observed proportion correct score. The *group specific* statistics represent averages of particular individual specific statistics over persons. Two of those statistics consist of estimates of the standard error of measurement based on assumptions of classically parallel and randomly parallel test forms. The third statistic is an agreement index devised exclusively for domain-referenced interpretations.

Distribution assumptions. The four standard errors ϵ_p, $S.E._{meas.}(x_a)$, σ_E, and $\sigma(\Delta)$ can be estimated without any distribution assumptions. However, some assumptions are necessary when those errors are used to provide interval estimates of the domain score. A distribution assumption is essential for

Table 9.4. Evaluation of Domain Score Estimation Statistics
(*Statistics within each category are listed in order of increasing overall complexity*)

Statistic	Definition	Source	Number of Adminis-trations	Test Forms Assumption	Comments
Individual Specific					
$\hat{\epsilon}_p$	Standard error of a proportion—binomial formula for sampling error	Berk (1980b); Cochran (1963, pp. 49–59); Millman (1974a, 1974b)	1	Randomly parallel	*Advantages:* Provides unbiased estimate of error based on infinite or finite item domain; latter might require finite population correction (*fpc*) if item sample is large relative to item domain. Hand calculable and easily interpretable; tabled values are also widely available (e.g., Marascuilo, 1971). Standard error remains the same for all tests of the same length irrespective of item format (Lord, 1957). Error can be used to set up a confidence interval or Uncertainty Band (UB) around an individual's $\hat{P}$ or the $\hat{P}$ standard for mastery. *Disadvantages:* Computed using only $\hat{P}$ and the number of items; estimate does not depend on the content, form, or statistical characteristics of the items. Therefore, estimates of error for a given test length will be lower for extreme values of $\hat{P}$ and higher for moderate values. Hand computation is tedious because the error must be computed for each individual $\hat{P}$.

Table 9.4. *(continued)*

Statistic	Definition	Source	Number of Adminis-trations	Test Forms Assumption	Comments
$S.E._{meas.}(x_a)$	Standard error of measurement—binomial formula for sampling error	Lord (1955, 1957, 1959)	1	Randomly parallel	Equivalent to the unbiased estimate of ϵ_p based on an infinite item domain (see Cochran, 1963, p. 51). *Advantages:* Same as $\hat{\epsilon}_p$. *Disadvantages:* Same as $\hat{\epsilon}_p$.
Group Specific					
$\hat{\sigma}_E$	Standard error of measurement—average of individual-specific errors of measurement $\hat{\sigma}(E_{ga})$	Lord and Novick (1968, pp. 60, 153-160) (See also Brennan, 1980, chapter 11)	1	Classically parallel	Conventional estimate of error derived from classical reliability theory. Equivalent to $\hat{\sigma}(\delta)$ in the context of generalizability theory, which is based on person × item interaction. *Advantages:* Hand calculable and easily interpretable. Error can be used to set up a confidence interval around an individual's $\hat{P}$. *Disadvantages:* Yields biased estimate of error (see Lord & Novick, 1968, p. 192). Due to the fluctuation of the individual specific standard errors with different values of $\hat{P}$, the average of those errors will tend to be lowest when there is a large number of extremely high and/or extremely low scores in the distribution (e.g., skewed or bimodal distribution); that low estimate can be very misleading.

$\hat{\sigma}(\Delta)$	Standard error of measurement—average of individual-specific errors of measurement $S.E._{meas.}(x_a)$	Brennan (1980, chapter 11)	1	Randomly parallel	Incorporates the effect due to item sampling along with the person × item interaction into the estimate. Derived from generalizability theory (Cronbach et al., 1972). *Advantages:* Same as $\hat{\sigma}_E$. For the simple matrix sampling of persons and items, $\hat{\sigma}(\Delta)$ is equivalent to the square root of Lord and Novick's (1968, p. 251) unbiased estimate $\hat{\sigma}_I^2(\eta^*)$; therefore, it can be computed easily from the mean and variance using formula (11.9.4). *Disadvantages:* Same as $\hat{\sigma}_E$, except for first statement.
Φ	Ratio of universe score variance to expected observed score variance—error variance $\hat{\sigma}^2(\Delta)$ based on item effect plus person × item interaction	Brennan (1980, chapter 11)	1	Randomly parallel	Measures the contribution of the testing procedure to the dependability of the decisions. Derived from generalizability theory (Cronbach et al., 1972). $\hat{\Phi}$ has an upper limit equal to the KR-20 coefficient and a lower limit equal to the KR-21 coefficient (Brennan, 1980, p. 213). *Advantages:* Hand calculable; computer programs are also available (e.g., Brennan, 1979). Estimation procedures are very flexible to accommodate different test structures and score uses. *Disadvantages:* Dependence of index values on test length and the estimated universe score and error variance complicates index interpretation. Specific application of the index in practice is unclear.

Source: Reprinted with permission from Berk, Ronald A. "A Consumers' Guide to Criterion-Referenced Test Reliability." *Journal of Educational Measurement*, 1980, *17*, 323–349, Table 4 (pp. 340–341). Copyright 1980, National Council on Measurement in Education, Washington, DC.

each standard error of measurement in this application so that a probability level can be assigned to the established confidence interval (e.g., 68%, 95%). Therefore, it is recommended that the binomial distribution be assumed for the two individual specific standard errors, the normal distribution be assumed for the traditional $\hat{\sigma}_E$, and either the binomial or compound binomial distribution may be assumed for $\hat{\sigma}(\Delta)$.

Point estimates of domain score. Although not included in Table 9.4, there are two point estimates of the domain score that have been proposed, $\hat{P}$ and $\hat{\gamma}_i$. Although they do not estimate the degree of error in the measurement process as the other statistics do, a brief description of their properties seems warranted since the interval estimates or standard errors examined in the next section are based on point estimates.

The simplest point estimate is $\hat{P}$, the observed proportion of items answered correctly by an individual. This estimate of the domain score P is unbiased and highly stable for full-length tests. For short subtests that are keyed to instructional objectives, the estimate can be very unstable (Hambleton, Hutton, & Swaminathan, 1976).

The other point estimate is $\hat{\gamma}_i$ (Hambleton et al., 1976). It involves a quasi-Bayesian approach that extends the binomial model underlying $S.E._{meas.}$ (x_a) (see Table 9.4) by incorporating direct ($\hat{P}$), collateral (group performance), and prior information (past test performance) into the estimate of P. This approach yields more precise values than $\hat{P}$ and several alternative classical and Bayesian estimates (Jackson, 1972; Lewis, Wang, & Novick, 1975; Novick, Lewis, & Jackson, 1973), even for subtests with as few as eight items (for details, see Hambleton et al., 1976). The trade-offs the test maker needs to consider to obtain this increase in precision over $\hat{P}$ are the conceptual and computational complexity of the model and some distribution assumptions that may be rather tenuous in many practical applications.

Interval estimates of domain score (standard errors). Four of the five approaches in Table 9.4 consist of different types of standard error that can be used to set up a confidence interval or band within which the domain score P lies. All of the estimates of error measure the degree of imprecision or inconsistency of an individual's scores on repeated testings.

The two individual-specific estimates ϵ_p and $S.E._{meas.}$ (x_a) are identical when the item domain is assumed to be infinite. The former is defined in the language of survey-sampling theory, where an individual's test performance is expressed as a "p value" or the percentage or proportion of items answered correctly (p); the latter is defined in the language of psychometric theory, where an individual's test performance is expressed as a raw score (x_a). Both are based on the binomial formula for the "sampling error of the number of white balls in a sample drawn at random from an urn containing a large number of white and black balls" (Lord, 1957, p. 511). The equivalence of the two unbiased estimates is readily apparent from their computational formulas:

$$\hat{\epsilon}_p = \sqrt{\frac{pq}{n-1}} \tag{1}$$

and

$$S.E._{meas.}\ (x_a) = \sqrt{\frac{x_a(n - x_a)}{n - 1}} \tag{2}$$

The formulas recommended by Berk (1980b) and Millman (1974b) include the finite population correction (*fpc*) that is appropriate for finite item domains. It is:

$$\hat{\epsilon}_p = \sqrt{\frac{(N - n)}{N}\left(\frac{pq}{n - 1}\right)}. \tag{3}$$

In most situations, however, formula 1 can be employed for infinite as well as finite domains as long as the projected or real domain size (N) is large relative to the sample size (n).

The application of this standard error of measurement in the context of an interval estimate can focus on either an individual's $\hat{P}$ or the $\hat{P}$ standard for mastery. Establishing a confidence interval or Uncertainty Band (Millman, 1974b) around the cut-off score is one method for relating the standard error to mastery-nonmastery decisions. Individuals with scores that lie above the error region and those with scores that lie below may be classified as masters and nonmasters, respectively. If a 95% confidence interval is used, the probability of correct mastery and nonmastery decisions will be at least 95% (see Millman, 1974b, for examples). This concept can also be linked to the issue of test length. The standard error could be specified a priori to guide the determination of the number of items to be randomly sampled from a finite item domain (see Berk, 1980b).

Probably the most distinctive feature of the individual-specific estimate is that for any given value of $\hat{P}$, the error remains the same for all tests of the same length irrespective of item content, format, or statistical characteristics (Lord, 1957, 1959; Swineford, 1959). Unfortunately, due to the fact that the estimate is a function only of $\hat{P}$ and the number of items, short subtests, say of 10 items or fewer, measuring particular objectives will predictably yield sizable errors, indicating the instability of $\hat{P}$.

The two group-specific estimates $\hat{\sigma}_E$ and $\hat{\sigma}(\Delta)$ are averages of the individual-specific errors of measurement $\hat{\sigma}\ (E_{ga})$ and $S.E._{meas.}\ (x_a)$, respectively. These relationships have been proven by Lord and Novick (1968) and Brennan and Kane (1977b). Since the single average or "blanket estimate" of the standard error of measurement is applied to each individual score, the ideal level of precision is attained only when each individual has the same error. This condition seldom occurs in practice. Consequently, $\hat{\sigma}_E$ and $\hat{\sigma}(\Delta)$ should be considered as rough approximations of their corresponding individual-specific errors.

These approximations are affected by test length and by the composition of the group tested or the form of the score distribution. Based on the previous discussion, if the individual-specific estimates of error are markedly influenced by the number of items, so are the averages. Therefore, the most stable estimates of group-specific error are obtained with lengthy subtests or the total test. With regard to the score distribution, the best approximations seem to require homogeneous group performance. If the distribution contains a large number of extremely high and/or extremely low scores plus some moderate scores, as in the case of a skewed or bimodal distribution, the estimate of error would be comparatively low. This result could be misleading because the estimate, when applied to each of the scores, would tend to overestimate the standard errors for the extreme scores and underestimate the errors for the moderate scores. One way to minimize and possibly eliminate this bias is to homogenize the data base. That can be accomplished, using Lord and Novick's (1968, p. 155) suggestion, by partitioning a given score distribution (whether it is normal, bimodal, or another shape) into sections that identify subgroups of relatively similar ability and then computing $\hat{\sigma}_E$ or $\hat{\sigma}(\Delta)$ for each subgroup. This strategy assures that each estimated subgroup standard error of measurement will generally be uniform for all points in that part of the distribution to which it is applied.

Selection of a standard error of measurement. The choice among the individual-specific standard error of measurement $S.E._{meas.}\ (x_a)$ and the two group-specific standard errors $\hat{\sigma}_E$ and $\hat{\sigma}(\Delta)$ is contingent upon how *error* is defined in a particular test application. If the imprecision of an individual's scores is measured over a hypothetical set of repeated testings with classically parallel test forms and the test is primarily used to rank order individuals, the appropriate error would be $\hat{\sigma}_E$. In this case the sampling of items does not introduce error into the estimation of an individual's domain score relative to the average domain score for the group (Brennan & Kane, 1977a, p. 283). On the other hand, if the imprecision is measured over a hypothetical set of repeated testings with randomly parallel test forms and the test is used to determine an individual's level of performance in the domain irrespective of the performance of other students, either $S.E._{meas.}\ (x_a)$ or $\hat{\sigma}(\Delta)$ would be appropriate. In that case the sampling of items does introduce error into the estimator of an individual's domain score. The final decision then rests with whether the individual-specific or "blanket estimate" should be employed. Although the estimate of error for each individual P has the several advantages that were mentioned previously, it is also usually subject to excessively large sampling fluctuations (Lord, 1955). Therefore, when the standard error is applied to the cut-off score, the individual-specific estimate $S.E._{meas.}\ (x_a)$ should be computed; otherwise, preference should be given to the estimate $\hat{\sigma}(\Delta)$ averaged over individuals.

Domain-referenced agreement index. The last group-specific statistic, Φ, measures the contribution of the testing procedure to the dependability of the decisions that are made. In contrast to the other domain score estimation statistics, Φ can be viewed as an agreement index corrected for chance. Developed within the framework of generalizability theory, the index has many of the features of its squared-error loss function counterpart $\Phi(\lambda)$. However, since it is not defined in relation to the cut-off score (λ), it furnishes different information and answers a different question. While Φ is recommended as a general-purpose index of dependability for domain-referenced interpretations (Brennan, 1980, p. 204), the specific utility of the index in practice needs further clarification.

Recommendations. All of the foregoing statistics can be computed by hand from just one test administration. This advantage plus their ease of interpretation and application suggest that they could be used by teachers to estimate the precision of an individual's scores on repeated testings with classically parallel or randomly parallel test forms. A teacher need only select one of the estimates of standard error [$S.E._{meas.}$ (x_a), $\hat{\sigma}_E$, or $\hat{\sigma}$ (Δ)] or the agreement index Φ.

There are two problems, however, that appear to restrict the usefulness of those statistics for individual decision making at the classroom or school level. First, as noted in the preceding descriptions of the statistics, a relatively large number of items per objective or the total number of items on the test must be used to obtain stable estimates. This requirement is contrary to the characteristics of most teacher-made and commercially developed criterion-referenced tests. Seldom are there more than 10 items per objective on these tests, and the use of the total score for classroom level decisions about individuals is inconsistent with the intent and structure of the test. (*Note*: Total score decision making about an individual's level of competence in the domain *is* justified for individual certification decisions in the context of minimum competency testing programs.) Second, the actual use of test scores for decision making typically requires some reference point or standard—relative or absolute. Although the estimate of a student's domain score supplies information about how much a student knows or his or her level of skill in a given content domain, it is difficult to make placement, formative, or summative decisions based on that information alone. Once a score is transformed into a normative score (e.g., percentile, stanine) for norm-referenced test score interpretations or a score is referenced to a mastery standard for criterion-referenced test score interpretations, individual decision making becomes considerably easier. The aforementioned statistics must be assessed in light of these practices. Consequently, the meaning of the various errors of measurement might be enhanced if they are related to the cut-off score, as in the application of the Uncertainty Band concept. The Φ index has already received attention from this perspective in the form of the $\Phi(\lambda)$ squared-error loss agreement index.

These issues are not generalizable to estimates of the *average* domain score. The precision and utility of "averages" in the evaluation of competing instructional programs using appropriate units of analysis (individual, class, school, or district) have been demonstrated (see, for example, Sirotnik, 1974). When criterion-referenced tests are employed in program evaluation, the use of various matrix-sampling designs can provide more dependable estimates of average domain scores without any loss in the dependability of estimates of individual domain scores (cf. Brennan, 1980, p. 217).

SUGGESTIONS FOR FUTURE RESEARCH

As the preceding review of reliability indices indicates, the criterion-referenced measurement literature is replete with studies of reliability. Most of the major contributions occurred during the 1970s. Since that period, researchers have refined (e.g., Brennan & Prediger, 1981), simplified (e.g., Peng & Subkoviak, 1980), tested (Scheetz & vonFraunhofer, 1980), extended (e.g., Raju, 1982), and applied (e.g., Berk & DeGangi, 1983, chap. 4; Goodstein, 1982) many of the original approaches.

Despite these efforts, there are still several unresolved problems and areas that require research attention. In the next two chapters, Subkoviak (chapter 10) and Brennan (chapter 11) suggest specific directions for future research on the threshold loss and squared-error loss agreement indices, respectively. Additions to their lists might include investigations of indices and loss functions compatible with the following cut-off score conditions and assumptions:

1. when it is preferable to use two cut-off scores—one to identify masters at the upper end of the score distribution and a second to identify nonmasters at the lower end—with a region of no-decision (indifference zone) between the two cut-offs, as in adaptive testing procedures (see Millman, chapter 4);
2. when the losses related to all false mastery and false nonmastery decision errors are not equally serious, as in instructional decisions where false errors are deemed more serious; and
3. condition (2) where degrees of mastery and nonmastery are also of concern, such as in the diagnosis of specific learning disabilities (e.g., Berk, 1984, chap. 3).

GUIDELINES FOR PRACTITIONERS

The four tables and the accompanying discussion in this chapter were presented to guide the selection of a "reliability" index for a criterion-referenced test used for particular individual or program decision making. The specific recommendations offered in each section were oriented toward teachers, district and state level test makers, and test publishers. A summary of those recommendations organized according to these three types of practitioner follows.

Classroom Teachers

Among all of the indices reviewed, the p_o index appears to have the greatest utility for classroom test construction and decision making. Hambleton and Novick's (1973) two-administration (test-retest) method for estimating p_o is the easiest method to understand, to compute, and to interpret. Essentially, a classroom teacher would only have to count the number of consistent mastery and nonmastery classifications on two test administrations. The disadvantages of the method pertain to satisfying the assumption of equal seriousness of classification errors, the consequences of testing effect, and the imprecision of the estimate with small sample sizes.

For placement decisions where degrees of mastery and nonmastery are of interest and the losses related to misclassified students who are far from the cut-off score are assumed to be the most serious, either Livingston's (1972a) k^2 (X, T_x) or Brennan's (1980) $\Phi(\lambda)$ index should be considered. Although these indices are more difficult to compute manually than $\hat{p}_o$, they do provide meaningful information about the consistency of scores in relation to the cut-off score. The choice between the indices depends upon the assumption about test forms.

The domain score estimation statistics seem to have limited usefulness for classroom decisions unless they are linked to the cut-off score. Even then, the aforementioned indices may be judged more appropriate.

District and State Level Test Makers

There are a variety of individual and program decisions for which the criterion-referenced tests developed by school districts and state departments of education are used. Given the number of different individual decisions, ranging from diagnosis at the classroom level to certification for high school graduation, it would be useless to recommend a single index or approach to determining reliability which could apply to all tests. Instead, the test maker should proceed step by step according to the stages in selecting a "reliability" index described in the chapter: first choosing a "reliability" category that is appropriate for a given test application, and then choosing an appropriate index within that category.

The choice of a category—threshold loss, squared-error loss, or domain score estimation—should be based on the following (see also Table 9.1):

1. test forms assumption (classically parallel or randomly parallel);
2. cut-off score (yes or no);
3. intended score interpretation (score referenced to cut-off score or domain score);
4. type of decision (mastery-nonmastery, degree of mastery-nonmastery, level of competency in domain); and
5. seriousness of losses associated with decision errors (equally serious or not equally serious).

Factors 3, 4, and 5 are the primary determinants of the loss function. When mastery-nonmastery/successful-unsuccessful/competency-incompetency classifications are to be made and the losses related to the decision errors are assumed to be equally serious regardless of how far the misclassified students are from the cut-off score, the threshold loss function should be chosen; when degrees of mastery and nonmastery are to be measured and the seriousness of the losses depends on how far the misclassified students are from the cut-off, the squared-error loss function should be used. Unfortunately, there are decision applications of some criterion-referenced tests (e.g. minimum competency tests) which may indicate that neither of these loss functions is appropriate. When level of competency in the domain, with or without a mastery-nonmastery distinction, is to be assessed, domain score estimation statistics should be considered.

The choice of a "reliability" index and a method for its estimation should be guided by the comments in Tables 9.2 to 9.4. A few of the key recommendations are presented here:

1. *Threshold loss function*: The selection of p_o or κ is a function of the method for setting the cut-off score (relative or absolute) and the conclusions reached from an analysis of the disadvantages of each index. The p_o index should be used where an absolute standard is chosen and for tests that contain short subtests and/or yield low score variance. The κ index may be the preferred index of agreement where relative cut-off scores are set according to the consequences of passing or failing a particular proportion of the students. However, the problems associated with κ render it less useful than p_o. In regard to estimating p_o or κ, Hambleton and Novick's (1973) and Swaminathan et al.'s (1974) two-administration procedures are recommended, using either one test form twice or two classically parallel forms of a test. Alternatively, Huynh's (1976) one-administration approach or Peng and Subkoviak's (1980) approximation can be employed.
2. *Squared-error loss function*: The guidelines for selecting either $k^2(X, T_x)$ or $\Phi(\lambda)$ presented in the preceding section are applicable to tests developed at the district and state levels. One of the indices may be appropriate for a minimum competency test where the degree to which a student fails is important in deciding on proper placement into a remedial program.
3. *Domain score estimation*: Estimates of the average domain score can be especially useful in the context of program evaluation decisions, in which case a standard error statistic must be chosen to reflect both the imprecision of measurement and the sampling error of students. This choice will also be contingent on the particular matrix sampling design that is used.

Test Publishers

Over the past decade, test publishers have become involved in the development of criterion-referenced tests for both individual and program decision making. The bulk of their efforts, however, has concentrated on criterion-referenced testing systems and diagnostic-prescriptive packages for use by classroom teachers. A few years ago, an assessment of the technical adequacy of these tests by Hambleton and Eignor (1978) indicated that the publishers devoted little attention to reliability evidence. Perhaps the guidelines proffered in the previous sections should be considered by those publishers.

In addition, publishers and consulting firms that contract with state departments of education to build minimum competency tests should carefully review the advantages and disadvantages of both the threshold loss and the squared-error loss agreement indices. Although a few state legislatures have mandated competency standards for high school graduation, it is unlikely that they will mandate one of the agreement indices described in this chapter.

REFERENCES

Algina, J., & Noe, M. J. A study of the accuracy of Subkoviak's single-administration estimate of the coefficient of agreement using two true-score estimates. *Journal of Educational Measurement*, 1978, *15*, 101-110.

Antonak, R. F. A computer program to compute measures of response agreement for nominal scale data obtained from two judges. *Behavior Research Methods and Instrumentation*, 1977, *9*, 533.

APA/AERA/NCME Joint Committee. *Standards for educational and psychological tests* (rev. ed.). Washington, DC: American Psychological Association, 1974.

Berk, R. A. A consumers' guide to criterion-referenced test reliability. *Journal of Educational Measurement*, 1980, *17*, 323-349; Erratum, 1981, *18*, 131. (a)

Berk, R. A. Estimation of test length for domain-referenced reading comprehension tests. *Journal of Experimental Education*, 1980, *48*, 188-193. (b)

Berk, R. A. *Screening and diagnosis of children with learning disabilities*. Springfield, IL: Charles C Thomas, 1984.

Berk, R. A., & Campbell, K. L. A FORTRAN program for Cohen's kappa coefficient of observer agreement. *Behavior Research Methods and Instrumentation*, 1976, *8*, 396.

Berk, R. A., & DeGangi, G. A. *DeGangi-Berk Test of Sensory Integration: Manual*. Los Angeles: Western Psychological Services, 1983.

Brennan, R. L. *KR-21 and lower limits of an index of dependability for mastery tests* (ACT Technical Bulletin No. 27). Iowa City, IA: American College Testing Program, December 1977.

Brennan, R. L. *Handbook for GAPID: A FORTRAN IV computer program for generalizability analyses with single-facet designs* (ACT Technical Bulletin No. 34). Iowa City, IA: American College Testing Program, October 1979.

Brennan, R. L. Applications of generalizability theory. In R. A. Berk (Ed.), *Criterion-referenced measurement: The state of the art*. Baltimore, MD: Johns Hopkins University Press, 1980. Pp. 186-232.

Brennan, R. L., & Kane, M. T. An index of dependability for mastery tests. *Journal of Educational Measurement*, 1977, *14*, 277-289. (a)

Brennan, R. L., & Kane, M. T. Signal/noise ratios for domain-referenced tests. *Psychometrika*, 1977, *42*, 609-625; Errata, 1978, *43*, 289. (b)

Brennan, R. L., & Prediger, D. J. Coefficient kappa: Some uses, misuses, and alternatives. *Educational and Psychological Measurement*, 1981, *41*, 687-699.

Cardinet, J., Tourneur, Y., & Allal, L. The symmetry of generalizability theory: Applications to educational measurement. *Journal of Educational Measurement*, 1976, *13*, 119-135.

Carver, R. P. Special problems in measuring change with psychometric devices. In *Evaluative research: Strategies and methods.* Pittsburgh: American Institutes for Research, 1970. Pp. 48-63.

Cochran, W. G. *Sampling techniques* (2nd ed.). New York: Wiley, 1963.

Cohen, J. A. A coefficient of agreement for nominal scales. *Educational and Psychological Measurement*, 1960, *20*, 37-46.

Crick, J. E., & Brennan, R. L. *Manual for GENOVA: A generalized analysis of variance system* (ACT Technical Bulletin No. 43). Iowa City, IA: American College Testing Program, 1983.

Cronbach, L. J., Gleser, G. C., Nanda, H., & Rajaratnam, N. *The dependability of behavioral measurements: Theory of generalizability for scores and profiles.* New York: Wiley, 1972.

Divgi, D. R. Group dependence of some reliability indices for mastery tests. *Applied Psychological Measurement*, 1980, *4*, 213-218.

Erlich, O., & Shavelson, R. J. Generalizability of measures: A computer program for two- and three-facet designs. *Behavior Research Methods and Instrumentation*, 1976, *8*, 407-408.

Goodstein, H. A. The reliability of criterion-referenced tests and special education: Assumed versus demonstrated. *Journal of Special Education*, 1982, *16*, 37-48.

Gross, A. L., & Shulman, V. The applicability of the beta binomial model for criterion referenced testing. *Journal of Educational Measurement*, 1980, *17*, 195-201.

Hambleton, R. K., & Eignor, D. R. Guidelines for evaluating criterion-referenced tests and test manuals. *Journal of Educational Measurement*, 1978, *15*, 321-327.

Hambleton, R. K., Hutton, L. R., & Swaminathan, H. A comparison of several methods for assessing student mastery in objectives-based instructional programs. *Journal of Experimental Education*, 1976, *45*, 57-64.

Hambleton, R. K., & Novick, M. R. Toward an integration of theory and method for criterion-referenced tests. *Journal of Educational Measurement*, 1973, *10*, 159-170.

Hambleton, R. K., Swaminathan, H., Algina, J., & Coulson, D. B. Criterion-referenced testing and measurement: A review of technical issues and developments. *Review of Educational Research*, 1978, *48*, 1-47.

Harris, C. W. An interpretation of Livingston's reliability coefficient for criterion-referenced tests. *Journal of Educational Measurement*, 1972, *9*, 27-29.

Harris, C. W., & Pearlman, A. P. Conventional significance tests and indices of agreement or association. In C. W. Harris, A. P. Pearlman, & R. R. Wilcox (Eds.), *Achievement test items: Methods of study* (CSE Monograph Series in Evaluation, No. 6). Los Angeles: Center for the Study of Evaluation, University of California, 1977. Pp. 17-44.

Huynh, H. On the reliability of decisions in domain-referenced testing. *Journal of Educational Measurement*, 1976, *13*, 253-264.

Huynh, H. *The kappamax reliability index for decisions in domain-referenced testing.* Paper presented at the annual meeting of the American Educational Research Association, New York, April 1977.

Huynh, H. Statistical inference for two reliability indices in mastery testing based on the beta-binomial model. *Journal of Educational Statistics*, 1979, *4*, 231-246.

Huynh, H., & Saunders, J. C. Accuracy of two procedures for estimating reliability of mastery tests. *Journal of Educational Measurement*, 1980, *17*, 351-358.

Jackson, P. H. Simple approximations in the estimation of many parameters. *British Journal of Mathematical and Statistical Psychology*, 1972, *25*, 213-229.

Kane, M. T. *Interpreting variance components as evidence for reliability and validity.* Paper presented at the annual meeting of the American Educational Research Association, Boston, April 1980.

Kane, M. T., & Brennan, R. L. Agreement coefficients as indices of dependability for domain-referenced tests. *Applied Psychological Measurement*, 1980, *4*, 105-126.

Keats, J. A., & Lord, F. M. A theoretical distribution for mental test scores. *Psychometrika*, 1962, *27*, 59-72.

Lewis, C., Wang, M. M., & Novick, M. R. Marginal distributions for the estimation of proportions in *m* groups. *Psychometrika*, 1975, *40*, 63-75.

Linn, R. L. Issues of reliability in measurement for competency-based programs. In M. A. Bunda & J. R. Sanders (Eds.), *Practices and problems in competency-based measurement.* Washington, DC: National Council on Measurement in Education, 1979. Pp. 90-107.

Livingston, S. A. Criterion-referenced applications of classical test theory. *Journal of Educational Measurement*, 1972, *9*, 13-26. (a)

Livingston, S. A. A reply to Harris' "An interpretation of Livingston's reliability coefficient for criterion-referenced tests." *Journal of Educational Measurement*, 1972, *9*, 31. (b)

Livingston, S. A. Reply to Shavelson, Block, and Ravitch's "Criterion referenced testing: Comments on reliability." *Journal of Educational Measurement*, 1972, *9*, 139-140. (c)

Livingston, S. A. Psychometric techniques for criterion-referenced testing and behavioral assessment. In J. D. Cone & R. P. Hawkins (Eds.), *Behavioral assessment: New directions in clinical psychology.* New York: Brunner/Mazel, 1977. Pp. 308-329.

Livingston, S. A., & Wingersky, M. S. Assessing the reliability of tests used to make pass/fail decisions. *Journal of Educational Measurement*, 1979, *16*, 247-260.

Lord, F. M. Sampling fluctuations resulting from the sampling of test items. *Psychometrika*, 1955, *22*, 1-22.

Lord, F. M. Do tests of the same length have the same standard error of measurement? *Educational and Psychological Measurement*, 1957, *17*, 510-521.

Lord, F. M. Tests of the same length do have the same standard error of measurement. *Educational and Psychological Measurement*, 1959, *19*, 233-239.

Lord, F. M., & Novick, M. R. *Statistical theories of mental test scores.* Reading, MA: Addison-Wesley, 1968.

Marascuilo, L. A. *Statistical methods for behavioral science research.* New York: McGraw-Hill, 1971.

Marshall, J. L. *The mean split-half coefficient of agreement and its relation to other test indices: A study based on simulated data* (Technical Report No. 350). Madison: Wisconsin Research and Development Center for Cognitive Learning, 1976.

Marshall, J. L., & Serlin, R. C. *Characteristics of four mastery test reliability indices: Influence of distribution shape and cutting score.* Paper presented at the annual meeting of the American Educational Research Association, San Francisco, April 1979.

Millman, J. Criterion-referenced measurement. In W. J. Popham (Ed.), *Evaluation in education: Current applications.* Berkeley, CA: McCutchan, 1974. Pp. 311-397. (a)

Millman, J. Sampling plans for domain-referenced tests. *Educational Technology*, 1974, *14*, 17-21. (b)

Millman, J. Reliability and validity of criterion-referenced test scores. In R. E. Traub (Ed.), *New directions for testing and measurement* (No. 4): *Methodological developments.* San Francisco: Jossey-Bass, 1979. Pp. 75-92.

Mills, C. N., & Hambleton, R. K. *Guidelines for reporting criterion-referenced test score information.* Paper presented at the annual meeting of the American Educational Research Association, Boston, April 1980.

Novick, M. R., Lewis, C., & Jackson, P. H. The estimation of proportions in *m* groups. *Psychometrika*, 1973, *38*, 19-45.

Peng, C-Y. J., & Subkoviak, M. J. A note on Huynh's normal approximation procedure for estimating criterion-referenced reliability. *Journal of Educational Measurement*, 1980, *17*, 359-368.

Raju, N. S. The reliability of a criterion-referenced composite with the parts of the composite having different cutting scores. *Educational and Psychological Measurement*, 1982, *42*, 113-129.

Reid, J. B., & Roberts, D. M. *A Monte Carlo comparison of phi and kappa as measures of criterion-referenced reliability.* Paper presented at the annual meeting of the American Educational Research Association, Toronto, March 1978.

Safrit, M. J., & Stamm, C. L. *The reliability of criterion-referenced measures of motor behavior: A comparative study.* Paper presented at the annual meeting of the National Council on Measurement in Education, San Francisco, April 1979.

Scheetz, J. P., & vonFraunhofer, J. A. *Measuring criterion-referenced test reliability with a single test administration.* Paper presented at the annual meeting of the National Council on Measurement in Education, Boston, April 1980.

Shavelson, R. J., Block, J. H., & Ravitch, M. M. Criterion-referenced testing: Comments on reliability. *Journal of Educational Measurement*, 1972, *9*, 133-137.

Shepard, L. A. Technical issues in minimum competency testing. In D. C. Berliner (Ed.), *Review of research in education* (Vol. 8). Washington, DC: American Educational Research Association, 1980. Pp. 30-82.

Shoemaker, D. M. *Principles and procedures of multiple matrix sampling.* Cambridge, MA: Ballinger, 1973.

Sirotnik, K. A. Introduction to matrix sampling for the practitioner. In W. J. Popham (Ed.), *Evaluation in education: Current applications.* Berkeley, CA: McCutchan, 1974. Pp. 451-529.

Subkoviak, M. J. Estimating reliability from a single administration of a mastery test. *Journal of Educational Measurement*, 1976, *13*, 265-276.

Subkoviak, M. J. Empirical investigation of procedures for estimating reliability for mastery tests. *Journal of Educational Measurement*, 1978, *15*, 111-116.

Subkoviak, M. J. Decision-consistency approaches. In R. A. Berk (Ed.), *Criterion-referenced measurement: The state of the art.* Baltimore, MD: Johns Hopkins University Press, 1980. Pp. 129-185.

Swaminathan, H., Hambleton, R. K., & Algina, J. Reliability of criterion-referenced tests: A decision-theoretic formulation. *Journal of Educational Measurement*, 1974, *11*, 263-267.

Swineford, F. Note on "Tests of the same length do have the same standard error of measurement." *Educational and Psychological Measurement*, 1959, *19*, 241-242.

Thorndike, R. L. Reliability. In A. Anastasi (Ed.), *Testing problems in perspective.* Washington, DC: American Council on Education, 1967. Pp. 284-291.

Traub, R. E., & Rowley, G. L. Reliability of test scores and decisions. *Applied Psychological Measurement*, 1980, *4*, 517-545.

Wixon, D. R. Cohen's kappa coefficient of observer agreement: A BASIC program for minicomputers. *Behavior Research Methods and Instrumentation*, 1979, *11*, 602.

10 ESTIMATING THE RELIABILITY OF MASTERY-NONMASTERY CLASSIFICATIONS

MICHAEL J. SUBKOVIAK

INTRODUCTION

THIS CHAPTER IS concerned with the *reliability or consistency of mastery and nonmastery classifications* over repeated testing of the same group (cf. Huynh, 1976; Marshall & Haertel, 1976; Subkoviak, 1976, 1980; Swaminathan, Hambleton, & Algina, 1974). For example, Table 10.1 lists the scores of 30 students on two 10-item tests; both the students and the items were drawn from larger pools described elsewhere (Subkoviak, 1978). Let us assume that a student in Table 10.1 must answer correctly 8 or more items on the test to be considered a master, and that otherwise the student is classified as a nonmaster. The reliability of mastery-nonmastery classifications, the topic of the present chapter, refers to the consistency (or lack thereof) with which individuals are designated as masters or nonmasters across both forms 1 and 2 in Table 10.1. Student 2, for instance, is consistently classified as a master on both forms when the cut-off score is set at 8 out of 10 items correct, while students 3 to 30 are consistently classified as nonmasters on both forms. Thus, 29 of the students, or a proportion of $29/30 = .97$, are consistently classified. This value of .97 illustrates one type of reliability coefficient that could be reported for a mastery test, more technically referred to as a threshold loss agreement index in the preceding chapter.

In contrast to chapter 9 and the other reviews of reliability coefficients proposed expressly for criterion-referenced tests, this chapter attempts to provide an in-depth treatment of coefficients that measure the consistency of mastery-nonmastery classifications on two tests administered to the same group.

REVIEW OF CLASSIFICATION CONSISTENCY APPROACHES

At least five separate approaches for assessing the consistency of mastery-nonmastery classifications can be found in the literature: (1) Carver (1970); (2) Swaminathan et al. (1974); (3) Huynh (1976); (4) Subkoviak (1976); and (5) Marshall and Haertel (1976). In the review that follows, each of these ap-

Table 10.1. Performance of 30 Students on Parallel Ten-Item Tests

	Total Score	
Student	Form 1	Form 2
1	9	7
2	8	8
3	7	7
4	7	4
5	7	3
6	6	7
7	6	7
8	6	5
9	6	4
10	5	6
11	5	4
12	5	2
13	5	2
14	4	7
15	4	7
16	4	7
17	4	6
18	4	4
19	4	4
20	4	4
21	4	3
22	4	2
23	3	6
24	3	4
25	3	4
26	3	4
27	3	2
28	3	2
29	2	4
30	1	1

Note: Mastery cut-off score = 8.

proaches is illustrated, discussed, and evaluated. Note that Carver's method is not generally recommended (for reasons outlined in the following) and is noted here primarily for historic purposes.

Carver Method

The first formal proposal for assessing classification consistency seems to be due to Carver (1970), who suggested two possible procedures. One involved the administration of two parallel tests to the same group, followed by a comparison of the percentages of students on each test who were classified as masters. If the two percentages were the same or nearly the same, then the tests were considered reliable. Note, however, that two tests can be quite unreliable and still produce equal percentages of masters. For example, half of the group could be classified as masters on one test, while the other half of the group could be classified as masters on the second test. In each case the percentage is 50%, but the mastery group is totally different. Carver's second procedure involved administration of the same test to two comparable groups, with subsequent comparison of the percentage of masters in each group, but it suffers from the same limitation. As illustrated, the basic problem with Carver's procedures is that they are not sensitive to the consistency of *individual* classifications. However, the methods that follow are sensitive to this key ingredient of reliability.

Swaminathan-Hambleton-Algina Method

Subsequent to Carver's proposal, Hambleton and Novick (1973, p. 168) suggested that the proportion of individuals consistently classified as master/master and nonmaster/nonmaster on two tests be used as an index of reliability. Swaminathan et al. (1974) later expanded upon this notion.

For example, if the criterion is 8 in Table 10.1, the mastery-nonmastery outcomes on forms 1 and 2 can be summarized as in Table 10.2. For instance, student 2 is the only individual classified as master/master on forms 1 and 2, respectively, so 1 is the entry in the first cell of Table 10.2. Students 3 to 30 are classified nonmaster/nonmaster, so 28 is the entry in the fourth cell. The 1 in the off-diagonal cell of Table 10.2 corresponds to the inconsistent mastery/nonmastery outcome for student 1. Thus, the proportion of individuals in Table 10.2 consistently classified on the two tests is

$$\begin{aligned}\hat{p}_o &= \frac{1}{30} + \frac{28}{30} \\ &= \frac{29}{30} \\ &= .97,\end{aligned}$$

Table 10.2. Mastery-Nonmastery Outcomes on Forms 1 and 2 of Table 10.1

	Form 2		
Form 1	Mastery	Nonmastery	Total
Mastery	1	1	2
Nonmastery	0	28	28
Total	1	29	

Note: Mastery cut-off score = 8.

as previously noted. More generally, the proportion of individuals consistently classified into m mastery states (e.g., $m = 2$ in this example: master, nonmaster) is given by

$$\hat{p}_o = \sum_{k=1}^{m} \hat{p}_{kk}, \tag{1}$$

where $\hat{p}_{kk}$ is the proportion of individuals consistently classified in the kth category on both tests. Equation 1 also applies when there are more than two categories (e.g., $m = 3$: high, medium, low).

The upper limit of $\hat{p}_o$ is, of course, 1.00, which occurs only if all individuals are consistently classified. For two equivalent tests, the lower limit of $\hat{p}_o$ is the proportion of consistent classifications on two tests expected by chance alone. In Table 10.2 the proportion of consistent classifications expected by chance is obtained from the product of corresponding row and column totals:

$$\begin{aligned}\hat{p}_c &= \frac{2}{30} \times \frac{1}{30} + \frac{28}{30} \times \frac{29}{30} \\ &= \frac{2}{900} + \frac{812}{900} \\ &= .90,\end{aligned}$$

which is the proportion of consistent outcomes expected for this particular group if the classifications on forms 1 and 2 were statistically independent of one another. In other words, $\hat{p}_c$ can be thought of as the proportion of consistent outcomes expected in two flips of a biased coin whose sides are weighted or "loaded" according to the relative numbers of masters and nonmasters in the group. More generally, the proportion of individuals consistently classified into m categories by chance is

$$\hat{p}_c = \sum_{k=1}^{m} \hat{p}_{k.}\, \hat{p}_{.k}, \tag{2}$$

where $\hat{p}_{k.}$ and $\hat{p}_{.k}$ are the proportions assigned to category k on forms 1 and 2, respectively; for example, in Table 10.2 $\hat{p}_{1.} = 2/30$, $\hat{p}_{.1} = 1/30$, $\hat{p}_{2.} = 28/30$, and $\hat{p}_{.2} = 29/30$.

Swaminathan et al. (1974) suggested that the proportion of consistent decisions expected by chance, $\hat{p}_c = .90$, be deleted from the proportion actually observed, $\hat{p}_o = .97$, in formulating an index of reliability for Table 10.2. Accordingly, they recommended the use of Cohen's (1960) kappa coefficient:

$$\hat{\kappa} = \frac{\hat{p}_o - \hat{p}_c}{1 - \hat{p}_c}$$

$$= \frac{.97 - .90}{1 - .90}$$

$$= .70.$$

$\hat{\kappa}$ can be interpreted as the proportion of consistent classifications beyond that expected by chance or, more precisely, beyond that attributable to the particular proportions ($\hat{p}_{k.}$ and $\hat{p}_{.k}$ in equation 2) of masters and nonmasters in the group tested. The upper limit of $\hat{\kappa}$ is again 1.00, indicating perfect reliability. In the present context, values of $\hat{\kappa}$ less than zero are theoretically impossible, and near-zero values indicate a condition where most of the observed consistency is attributable to chance, as previously defined.

The properties of $\hat{\kappa}$ have been widely discussed (Cohen, 1960, 1968; Fleiss, Cohen, & Everitt, 1969; Hubert, 1977). In fact, in many instances, kappa differs little from the familiar Pearson correlation for dichotomous data, i.e., the phi coefficient (Reid & Roberts, 1978). For the present, it should simply be noted that the two coefficients $\hat{p}_o$ and $\hat{\kappa}$ defined here are sensitive to different aspects of classification consistency, have different lower limits, and, subsequently, require different interpretations. More is said about the properties of $\hat{p}_o$ and $\hat{\kappa}$ after the various methods for estimating these coefficients have been introduced.

The three reliability methods discussed next have the advantage of requiring only *one* test administration (Huynh, 1976; Marshall & Haertel, 1976; Subkoviak, 1976), whereas the Swaminathan-Hambleton-Algina method requires two administrations. However, these one-test procedures are computationally much more difficult than the Swaminathan-Hambleton-Algina approach, although computer programs are available for performing the required computations for each method.

Huynh Method

The reader will recall that the coefficients $\hat{p}_o$ and $\hat{\kappa}$ were based on Table 10.2, which, in turn, was obtained from the joint distribution of scores on forms 1 and 2 in Table 10.1. But suppose form 2 does not exist, so that only the scores on form 1 are available. Keats and Lord (1962) showed that given only the scores on form 1 and granted certain assumptions, scores on the nonexistent form 2 could be simulated. The steps involved in this simulation are as follows (Huynh, 1976, pp. 254–258).

1. Compute the mean ($\hat{\mu}$), variance ($\hat{\sigma}^2$), and Kuder-Richardson 21 coefficient ($\hat{\alpha}_{21}$) of the scores (x) on form 1 of Table 10.1. In the following equations, N represents the number of students and n represents the number of test items. Specifically, $N = 30$ and $n = 10$ for Table 10.1.

$$\hat{\mu} = \frac{\Sigma x}{N} = \frac{139}{30} = 4.63$$

$$\hat{\sigma}^2 = \frac{\Sigma x^2}{N-1} - \frac{(\Sigma x)^2}{N(N-1)}$$

$$= \frac{739}{30-1} - \frac{(139)^2}{30(30-1)} = 3.27$$

$$\hat{\alpha}_{21} = \frac{n}{n-1}\left[1 - \frac{\hat{\mu}(n-\hat{\mu})}{n\hat{\sigma}^2}\right]$$

$$= \frac{10}{10-1}\left[1 - \frac{(4.63)(10-4.63)}{(10)(3.27)}\right] = .27$$

2. Compute parameters $\hat{\alpha}$ and $\hat{\beta}$, which, together with the number of test items (n), determine the particular shape of the joint distribution of scores on forms 1 and 2.

$$\hat{\alpha} = \left(-1 + \frac{1}{\hat{\alpha}_{21}}\right)\hat{\mu} = \left(-1 + \frac{1}{.27}\right)(4.63) = 12.52$$

$$\hat{\beta} = -\hat{\alpha} + \frac{n}{\hat{\alpha}_{21}} - n = \left(-12.52 + \frac{10}{.27} - 10\right) = 14.52$$

3. Using the values of $\hat{\alpha}$ and $\hat{\beta}$ as computed in step 2, and $n = 10$, determine the joint distribution of scores on forms 1 and 2, as shown in Table 10.3. This distribution is symbolized $\hat{f}(x, y)$, which represents the proportion of persons scoring x on form 1 and y on form 2. For example, given $\hat{\alpha} = 12.52$, $\hat{\beta} = 14.52$, and $n = 10$, the value of $\hat{f}(x, y)$ for the scores $x = 0$ and $y = 0$ is obtained as follows:

$$\hat{f}(0, 0) = \prod_{i=1}^{2n} \frac{2n + \hat{\beta} - i}{2n + \hat{\alpha} + \hat{\beta} - i}$$

$$= \frac{20 + 14.52 - 1}{20 + 12.52 + 14.52 - 1}$$

$$\times \frac{20 + 14.52 - 2}{20 + 12.52 + 14.52 - 2} \times \ldots$$

$$\times \frac{20 + 14.52 - 20}{20 + 12.52 + 14.52 - 20}$$

$$= .0002 \text{ (approximately).}$$

Then, given $\hat{f}(0, 0) = .0002$, values of $\hat{f}(x, y)$ for other x and y pairs, like $x = 1$ and $y = 0$, are obtained as follows:

$$\hat{f}(x + 1, y) = \hat{f}(x, y) \cdot \frac{(n - x)(\hat{\alpha} + x + y)}{(x + 1)(2n + \hat{\beta} - x - y - 1)}$$

$$\hat{f}(0 + 1, 0) = \hat{f}(0, 0) \cdot \frac{(10 - 0)(12.52 + 0 + 0)}{(0 + 1)(20 + 14.52 - 0 - 0 - 1)}$$

$$= .0006 \text{ (approximately).}$$

Also, $\hat{f}(x, y)$ is symmetric in the sense that $\hat{f}(x, y) = \hat{f}(y, x)$. Thus, for example, $\hat{f}(0, 1) = \hat{f}(1, 0) = .0006$. Huynh (1976, pp. 254–58) also provides formulas that are somewhat more manageable than those in the preceding discussion for values of x and y near n. In either case, after much computation, the joint distribution of scores on forms 1 and 2 is obtained, as shown in Table 10.3. Each entry of the table represents the proportion of students that would obtain score x on form 1 and score y on form 2. Note that decimal points have been omitted from the table for the sake of readability.

4. Coefficient $\hat{p}_o$, the proportion of consistent classifications, is obtained by summing appropriate entries in Table 10.3. For example, if the mastery cut-off is again set at 8, the proportion of persons consistently classified as masters on both tests is the sum of the 9 entries in the lower right-hand corner of Table 10.3:

$$.0040 + .0014 + .0003 + .0014 + .0006 + .0001 + .0003 + .0001 + .0000 = .0082.$$

Similarly, the proportion of persons consistently classified as nonmasters on both tests is the sum of the 64 entries in the upper left-hand corner of

Table 10.3. Joint Distribution of Scores on Test Forms 1 and 2

	Form 2(y)										
Form 1(x)	0	1	2	3	4	5	6	7	8	9	10
0	0002	0006	0011	0013	0012	0008	0004	0002	0000	0000	0000
1	0006	0024	0050	0069	0068	0050	0028	0012	0004	0001	0000
2	0011	0050	0116	0174	0188	0152	0093	0043	0014	0003	0000
3	0013	0069	0174	0286	0338	0299	0201	0101	0036	0008	0001
4	0012	0068	0188	0338	0436	0421	0308	0169	0066	0017	0002
5	0008	0050	0152	0299	0421	0444	0354	0211	0090	0025	0003
6	0004	0028	0093	0201	0308	0354	0308	0200	0093	0028	0004
7	0002	0012	0043	0101	0169	0211	0200	0142	0072	0024	0004
8	0000	0004	0014	0036	0066	0090	0093	0072	0040	0014	0003
9	0000	0001	0003	0008	0017	0025	0028	0024	0014	0006	0001
10	0000	0000	0000	0001	0002	0003	0004	0004	0003	0001	0000

Note: Each entry in the body of this table represents the proportion of students who would obtain score x on form 1 and y on form 2. Decimal points are omitted.

the table, or .8928. Thus, the total proportion of consistent decisions in Table 10.3, derived solely from form 1, is:

$$\hat{p}_o = .0082 + .8928$$
$$= .90.$$

The previous, two-form, estimate of this quantity, derived from Table 10.2, was $\hat{p}_o = .97$.

5. Coefficient $\hat{\kappa} = (\hat{p}_o - \hat{p}_c)/(1 - \hat{p}_c)$, the proportion of consistent decisions beyond that expected by chance, can also be obtained from Table 10.3 as follows. Proportion $\hat{p}_o = .90$ is given in step 4. The proportion of consistent decisions due to chance, $\hat{p}_c$, is a function of the marginal proportions of masters and nonmasters in Table 10.3. Specifically, the proportion of masters on form 1 (or form 2) is the sum of the last three rows (or columns) of the table, or .0577; the proportion of nonmasters is $1 - .0577 = .9423$. Thus, the proportion of consistent decisions expected by chance is

$$\hat{p}_c = .0577 \times .0577 + .9423 \times .9423$$
$$= .89.$$

The previous, two-form, estimate of this quantity in Table 10.2 was $\hat{p}_c = .90$.

Finally, the proportion of consistent decisions beyond that expected by chance is

$$\hat{\kappa} = \frac{\hat{p}_o - \hat{p}_c}{1 - \hat{p}_c}$$
$$= \frac{.90 - .89}{1 - .89}$$
$$= .09$$

The previous, two-form, estimate of kappa based on Table 10.2 was much larger, $\hat{\kappa} = .70$, because the estimates of $\hat{p}_o = .97$ and $\hat{p}_c = .90$ were different in that case, and kappa is quite sensitive to such differences.

As noted earlier, certain assumptions are implicit in the Huynh procedure outlined here (see Huynh, 1976; Keats & Lord, 1962). The first is that students' true scores on the test are distributed as a beta distribution. Beta distributions can take a variety of different forms—skewed or symmetric, peaked or flat—corresponding to different values of $\hat{\alpha}$, $\hat{\beta}$, and n in step 2. Some examples are bell, rectangular, J, and U shapes (see LaValle, 1970, for more illustrations). Many real data sets meet or closely approximate this first condition (see Keats & Lord, 1962); exceptions would be multihumped distributions, which are uncommon if not rare.

The second assumption is that if n-item tests were repeatedly administered to a fixed individual, the resulting distribution of test scores would be binomial in form. This assumption is most tenable if (a) the test items (or "trials") are scored 0 or 1, (b) the items are statistically independent so that the outcome on one does not determine or affect the outcome on others, and (c) the items are equally difficult. The first requirement does not represent a significant limitation, since most objective items are scored as either right (1) or wrong (0). Similarly, the second can be approximated by insuring, for instance, that incorrect computations on one item do not automatically lead to incorrect computations on others, by including rest periods to minimize fatigue effects on the later items of a long test, and so forth. However, at first glance, the third requirement appears to be restrictive, since in practice test items do vary in difficulty. Yet, a number of studies (Gross & Shulman, 1980; Huynh & Saunders, 1980; Subkoviak, 1978) suggest that the Keats-Lord model may provide reasonable estimates of $\hat{p}_o$ and $\hat{\kappa}$ for a wide variety of test data.

Lord (1965, 1969) has also extended the earlier work of Keats and Lord (1962) by replacing the beta and binomial assumptions used previously with somewhat less simplistic conditions that more closely approximate actual test data. Consequently, reliability procedures like Huynh's (1976) could be based on these later, more sophisticated models (see, for example, Livingston & Wingersky, 1979). However, an advantage of the Huynh procedure is that it involves the estimation of only two parameters, $\hat{\alpha}$ and $\hat{\beta}$ in step 2, which can be accomplished with relatively small samples (e.g., $N > 40$ for very short tests or $N > 2n$ for longer tests [Huynh, personal communication, 1978]); the later models involve more parameters and require much larger samples (e.g., $N > 1{,}000$). More recently, Wilcox (1981a, 1981b) has also considered extensions of and alternatives to the Keats-Lord model which may prove more appropriate for obtaining reliability estimates for certain data sets.

Peng and Subkoviak approximation. The computations involved in steps 1 to 5 obviously become quite tedious, if not prohibitive, unless performed by a computer. However, Huynh (1976) and Peng and Subkoviak (1980) have proposed approximation methods that involve much less computation and still require only one test administration. The methods assume that if both forms 1 and 2 were administered (again, only one form need actually be administered), the joint distribution of scores on the two forms would be approximately normal or bell shaped. Huynh suggests that this may be reasonable if $n > 8$ and if $\hat{\mu}/n$ is between .15 and .85 (see Novick, Lewis, & Jackson, 1973); of course, the shape of the observed score distribution should also shed light on the reasonableness of this normal assumption. Using the scores on form 1 of Table 10.1 as an example, the steps involved in the Peng-Subkoviak approximation are as follows.

1. Compute the mean ($\hat{\mu}$), variance ($\hat{\sigma}^2$), Kuder-Richardson 21 coefficient ($\hat{\alpha}_{21}$), and specify the cut-off score (c), as before.

$$\hat{\mu} = \frac{\Sigma x}{N} = \frac{139}{30} = 4.63$$

$$\hat{\sigma}^2 = \frac{\Sigma x^2}{N-1} - \frac{(\Sigma x)^2}{N(N-1)}$$

$$= \frac{739}{30-1} - \frac{(139)^2}{30(30-1)} = 3.27$$

$$\hat{\alpha}_{21} = \frac{n}{n-1}\left[1 - \frac{\hat{\mu}(n-\hat{\mu})}{n\hat{\sigma}^2}\right]$$

$$= \frac{10}{10-1}\left[1 - \frac{(4.63)(10-4.63)}{10(3.27)}\right] = .27$$

2. Compute the normal deviate corresponding to the cut-off score.

$$z = (c - .5 - \hat{\mu})/\hat{\sigma} = (8 - .5 - 4.63)/\sqrt{3.27} = 1.59$$

3. Using the $\hat{p}_z$ column of Table 10.4 or equivalent tables found in most statistical texts, obtain the probability ($\hat{p}_z$) that a standard normal variable is less than $z = 1.59$: $\hat{p}_z = .94$.
4. Using Table 10.4 or more extensive tables of this type (Gupta, 1963; *Tables of the Bivariate Normal Distribution Function and Related Functions*, 1959), obtain the probability ($\hat{p}_{zz}$) that two standardized normal variables with correlation $\hat{\alpha}_{21} = .27$ are less than $z = 1.59$: $\hat{p}_{zz} = .89$.
5. Finally, compute $\hat{p}_o$ or $\hat{\kappa}$.

$$\hat{p}_o = 1 + 2(\hat{p}_{zz} - \hat{p}_z) = 1 + 2(.89 - .94) = .90$$

$$\hat{\kappa} = \frac{\hat{p}_{zz} - \hat{p}_z^2}{\hat{p}_z - \hat{p}_z^2} = \frac{.89 - (.94)^2}{.94 - (.94)^2} = .11$$

To reduce even further the amount of computation involved, Huynh (1978) has also tabled values of the proportion of consistent classifications ($\hat{p}_o$) and kappa ($\hat{\kappa}$), but only for short tests containing between 5 and 10 items. In order to use Huynh's tables for the example in Table 10.1, the following values are determined: $n = 10$ (items), $c = 8$ (cut-off), $\hat{\mu} = 4.63$ (mean), and $\hat{\alpha}_{21} = .27$ (Kuder-Richardson 21 coefficient). The values $\hat{p}_o = .89$ and $\hat{\kappa} = .09$ can then be obtained from the tables (also reprinted in Subkoviak, 1980).

In summary, Huynh's method (1976) represents a mathematically sophisticated procedure for estimating classification consistency from a single administration of a mastery test. The next method considered is computationally somewhat less complex, but in practice the two procedures generally provide similar results (Subkoviak, 1978). This is not totally unexpected, since the assumptions involved in the two methods are basically equivalent, despite outward appearances.

Table 10.4. Probability That Two Standard Normal Variables with Correlation $\hat{\alpha}_{21}$ Are Less Than or Equal to z

z	$\hat{p}_z$	$\hat{\alpha}_{21}=.10$	.20	.30	.40	.50	.60	.70	.80	.90
−2.00	.0228	.0009	.0014	.0020	.0029	.0041	.0055	.0074	.0098	.0134
−1.90	.0287	.0013	.0020	.0030	.0041	.0056	.0075	.0098	.0129	.0173
−1.80	.0359	.0020	.0030	.0042	.0058	.0077	.0100	.0130	.0168	.0221
−1.70	.0446	.0030	.0043	.0059	.0079	.0104	.0133	.0170	.0216	.0281
−1.60	.0548	.0044	.0061	.0083	.0108	.0139	.0175	.0220	.0276	.0353
−1.50	.0668	.0063	.0086	.0113	.0145	.0183	.0228	.0282	.0349	.0440
−1.40	.0808	.0090	.0119	.0154	.0193	.0239	.0293	.0357	.0436	.0543
−1.30	.0968	.0126	.0163	.0205	.0254	.0309	.0374	.0449	.0541	.0664
−1.20	.1151	.0173	.0219	.0271	.0329	.0396	.0471	.0559	.0665	.0806
−1.10	.1357	.0234	.0291	.0353	.0423	.0500	.0587	.0688	.0809	.0969
−1.00	.1587	.0313	.0381	.0455	.0536	.0625	.0725	.0840	.0976	.1155
−0.90	.1841	.0413	.0492	.0578	.0671	.0773	.0887	.1015	.1167	.1365
−0.80	.2119	.0536	.0628	.0726	.0832	.0947	.1073	.1216	.1383	.1600
−0.70	.2420	.0685	.0791	.0902	.1020	.1147	.1286	.1442	.1625	.1860
−0.60	.2743	.0865	.0983	.1106	.1237	.1376	.1527	.1696	.1893	.2145
−0.50	.3085	.1078	.1207	.1342	.1483	.1633	.1796	.1976	.2186	.2453
−0.40	.3446	.1324	.1464	.1609	.1760	.1920	.2092	.2282	.2503	.2784
−0.30	.3821	.1606	.1755	.1908	.2067	.2235	.2415	.2614	.2843	.3135
−0.20	.4207	.1924	.2079	.2239	.2404	.2577	.2763	.2968	.3204	.3504
−0.10	.4602	.2276	.2435	.2598	.2767	.2944	.3134	.3343	.3583	.3888
0.00	.5000	.2659	.2821	.2985	.3155	.3333	.3524	.3734	.3976	.4282
0.10	.5398	.3072	.3232	.3395	.3564	.3741	.3930	.4139	.4379	.4684
0.20	.5793	.3509	.3664	.3824	.3989	.4162	.4348	.4553	.4789	.5089
0.30	.6179	.3965	.4113	.4266	.4426	.4593	.4773	.4972	.5202	.5493
0.40	.6554	.4433	.4573	.4718	.4869	.5028	.5200	.5391	.5612	.5893
0.50	.6915	.4907	.5036	.5171	.5312	.5462	.5625	.5805	.6015	.6283
0.60	.7258	.5380	.5498	.5621	.5752	.5891	.6042	.6211	.6408	.6660
0.70	.7580	.5846	.5951	.6062	.6181	.6308	.6447	.6603	.6786	.7021
0.80	.7881	.6298	.6391	.6489	.6595	.6710	.6836	.6979	.7146	.7363
0.90	.8159	.6731	.6811	.6897	.6990	.7092	.7205	.7334	.7486	.7684
1.00	.8413	.7140	.7208	.7282	.7363	.7452	.7552	.7667	.7803	.7982
1.10	.8643	.7521	.7577	.7640	.7709	.7787	.7874	.7975	.8096	.8255
1.20	.8849	.7872	.7918	.7970	.8028	.8094	.8169	.8257	.8363	.8504
1.30	.9032	.8190	.8227	.8269	.8318	.8373	.8438	.8513	.8605	.8728
1.40	.9192	.8475	.8504	.8538	.8578	.8624	.8678	.8742	.8821	.8928
1.50	.9332	.8727	.8750	.8777	.8809	.8847	.8892	.8946	.9012	.9103
1.60	.9452	.8948	.8965	.8987	.9012	.9043	.9079	.9124	.9180	.9257
1.70	.9554	.9139	.9152	.9168	.9188	.9212	.9242	.9279	.9325	.9389
1.80	.9641	.9302	.9311	.9324	.9339	.9358	.9382	.9411	.9449	.9503
1.90	.9713	.9439	.9446	.9455	.9467	.9482	.9500	.9524	.9555	.9598

Source: Adapted from Gupta, S. S. Probability integrals of multivariate normal and multivariate *t*. *Annals of Mathematical Statistics*, 1963, *34*, 792–828, with permission of the author and of the Institute of Mathematical Statistics.

Subkoviak Method

Again, suppose that only the scores on form 1 of Table 10.1 are available and that one wishes to estimate either the proportion of consistent classifications ($\hat{p}_o$) or coefficient kappa ($\hat{\kappa}$). The steps involved in Subkoviak's (1975, 1976) procedure are illustrated in Table 10.5

1. The first two columns of the table contain the scores (x) and the frequency of each score (N_x) in the sample of thirty students. The mean and Kuder-Richardson 20 coefficient of the scores are, respectively, $\hat{\mu} = 4.63$ and $\hat{\alpha}_{20} = .47$. These two quantities are used in the next step.
2. The 10-item test in the example can be thought of as a sample of items from an actual or hypothetical universe of such items. The third column of Table 10.5 contains an estimate of the proportion of items in that universe $\hat{p}_x$ that a person with test score x would be expected to answer correctly. Thus, $\hat{p}_x$ can be thought of as the probability of a correct item response. The $\hat{p}_x$ values in Table 10.5 are obtained from the following equation:

$$\hat{p}_x = \hat{\alpha}_{20}(x/n) + (1 - \hat{\alpha}_{20})(\hat{\mu}_x/n)$$
$$= .47(x/10) + (1 - .47)(4.63/10).$$

   For example, if $x = 9$, then $\hat{p}_x = .47(9/10) + (1 - .47)(4.63/10) = .67$. Hambleton, Swaminathan, Algina, and Coulson (1978, pp. 5–10) and Wilcox (1979) also review other methods for estimating $\hat{p}_x$; in fact, the simple estimate $\hat{p}_x = x/n$ provides reasonably accurate results if n is large, e.g., $n > 40$.
3. If a student's probability of a correct response to a single item is $\hat{p}_x = .67$, what is the probability that the student will correctly answer eight or more items on the 10-item test, and thus be classified as a master? If the items can be considered as trials in a binomial process, the probability of 8 or more successes in 10 trials is $\hat{P}_x = .3070$ for such a student, as indi-

Table 10.5. An Illustration of Subkoviak's Estimation Procedure

x	N_x	$\hat{p}_x$	$\hat{P}_x$	$1 - 2(\hat{P}_x - \hat{P}_x^2)$	$N_x[1 - 2(\hat{P}_x - \hat{P}_x^2)]$	$N_x\hat{P}_x$
9	1	.67	.3070	.5745	.5745	.3070
8	1	.62	.2013	.6784	.6784	.2013
7	3	.57	.1236	.7834	2.3502	.3708
6	4	.53	.0791	.8543	3.4172	.3164
5	4	.48	.0420	.9195	3.6780	.1680
4	9	.43	.0202	.9604	8.6436	.1818
3	6	.39	.0103	.9796	5.8776	.0618
2	1	.34	.0039	.9922	.9922	.0039
1	1	.29	.0012	.9976	.9976	.0012
Total	30				27.2093	1.6122

cated in the fourth column of Table 10.5 (see *Tables of the Binomial Probability Distribution*, 1949). The other values in column four were similarly obtained.

4. The probability that this student will be consistently classified as a master on two independent testings is $\hat{P}_x^2$; conversely, the probability that this student will be consistently classified as a nonmaster is $(1 - \hat{P}_x)^2$. Thus, the probability of consistent classification for such an individual is $\hat{P}_x^2 + (1 - \hat{P}_x)^2 = 1 - 2(\hat{P}_x - \hat{P}_x^2) = 1 - 2(.3070 - .3070^2) = .5745$, as indicated in the fifth column of the table; and the number of such individuals scoring x who will be consistently classified is estimated by $N_x[1 - 2(\hat{P}_x - \hat{P}_x^2)] = (1)[.5745] = .5745$, as indicated in the sixth column of the table.
5. The probability of consistent classification across the entire group, $\hat{p}_o$, is then obtained by dividing the total number of consistently classified individuals in column six (27.2093) by the number in the group ($N = 30$).

$$\hat{p}_o = \frac{\Sigma N_x[1 - 2(\hat{P}_x - \hat{P}_x^2)]}{N}$$

$$= \frac{27.2093}{30}$$

$$= .91.$$

6. Finally, the chance probability of consistent classification $\hat{p}_c$ can be obtained from the total number of estimated masters in column seven (1.6122), and, subsequently, coefficient kappa ($\hat{\kappa}$) can be computed:

$$\hat{p}_c = 1 - 2\left[\frac{\Sigma N_x\hat{P}_x}{N} - \left(\frac{\Sigma N_x\hat{P}_x}{N}\right)^2\right]$$

$$= 1 - 2\left[\frac{1.6122}{30} - \left(\frac{1.6122}{30}\right)^2\right]$$

$$= .90$$

$$\hat{\kappa} = \frac{\hat{p}_o - \hat{p}_c}{1 - \hat{p}_c}$$

$$= \frac{.91 - .90}{1 - .90}$$

$$= .10.$$

In short, the estimates of $\hat{p}_o$, $\hat{p}_c$, and $\hat{\kappa}$ derived from Tables 10.3 (Huynh) and 10.5 (Subkoviak) are similar. As noted previously, this is not unexpected, since the two methods involve certain common assumptions. For instance, both posit a binomial distribution of observed scores over repeated testing of an individual. The Marshall-Haertel method, discussed next, involves this same assumption. However, the three methods are not identical; and each leads to somewhat different numerical results.

Marshall-Haertel Method

Like the Huynh and Subkoviak procedures, the Marshall-Haertel (1976) method requires only a single test administration and involves the assumption that if an individual were repeatedly tested, his or her distribution of observed scores would be binomial in form.

Given the scores on an n-item test, like form 1 of Table 10.1, and granted the binomial assumption, Marshall and Haertel estimate the group's scores on a *hypothetical* $2n$-item test. Theoretically, this test could be split into half-tests of n items each; and the proportion of consistent classification on the two half-tests could be estimated as in Table 10.2. Moreover, such an estimate could be obtained for each of the many possible ways that a $2n$-item test can be partitioned into half-tests. Marshall and Haertel take the average of the various split-half estimates as their final estimate of $\hat{p}_o$, the proportion of consistent classifications on two tests. As illustrated in the following, Marshall and Haertel obtained this average via a computing formula.

Given the frequency (N_x) of score (x) on form 1 of Table 10.1, Marshall and Haertel obtain the frequency (N_w) of score (w) on a test twice as long as form 1:

$$N_w = \sum_{x=0}^{n} N_x \binom{2n}{w} \left(\frac{x}{n}\right)^w \left(1 - \frac{x}{n}\right)^{2n-w} \tag{4}$$

For example, the number of students in the example who would receive the score $w = 13$ on a test twice as long as form 1 is estimated to be

$$\begin{aligned} N_{13} &= \sum_{x=0}^{10} N_x \binom{20}{13} \left(\frac{x}{10}\right)^{13} \left(1 - \frac{x}{10}\right)^{20-13} \\ &= (0)\binom{20}{13}\left(\frac{0}{10}\right)^{13}\left(1 - \frac{0}{10}\right)^{7} + (1)\binom{20}{13}\left(\frac{1}{10}\right)^{13}\left(1 - \frac{1}{10}\right)^{7} \\ &\quad + \cdots + (1)\binom{20}{13}\left(\frac{9}{10}\right)^{13}\left(1 - \frac{9}{10}\right)^{7} \\ &\quad + (0)\binom{20}{13}\left(\frac{10}{10}\right)^{13}\left(1 - \frac{10}{10}\right)^{7} \\ &= 1.65. \end{aligned}$$

Frequencies of the other possible scores on a $2n$-item test ($N_0, N_1, \ldots, N_{20}$) are estimated similarly.

Next, the probability of consistent classification on two half-tests for a person with score w on the double-length test is computed. This quantity is symbolized $\Phi_w(a, b)$ and is obtained as follows:

$$\Phi_w(a, b) = \sum_{j=a}^{b} \frac{\binom{w}{i}\binom{2n-w}{n-i}}{\binom{2n}{n}}. \tag{5}$$

In equation 5, values a and b are determined by the particular value of w and the cut-off score (c) on an n-item test. For example, if $w = 13$ and $c = 8$, then $a = w - [c - 1] = 6$ and $b = c - 1 = 7$, and the probability of consistent classification is:

$$\begin{aligned}\Phi_{13}(6, 7) &= \sum_{j=6}^{7} \frac{\binom{13}{i}\binom{20-13}{10-i}}{\binom{20}{10}} \\ &= \frac{\binom{13}{6}\binom{7}{4}}{\binom{20}{10}} + \frac{\binom{13}{7}\binom{7}{3}}{\binom{20}{10}} \\ &= \frac{(1{,}716)(35)}{184{,}756} + \frac{(1{,}716)(35)}{184{,}756} \\ &= .65.\end{aligned}$$

For certain values of w, the probability of consistent classification is either 0 or 1 and need not be calculated via equation 5.

The computational formula for the Marshall-Haertel estimate combines the quantities obtained by equations 4 and 5 as follows:

$$\begin{aligned}\hat{p}_o = \frac{1}{N}\Bigg[&\sum_{w=0}^{c-1} N_w + \sum_{w=c}^{2c-2} N_w \cdot \Phi_w(w - [c - 1], c - 1) \\ &+ \sum_{w=2c}^{n+c-1} N_w \cdot \Phi_w(c, w - c) + \sum_{w=n+c}^{2n} N_w\Bigg],\end{aligned} \tag{6}$$

where:

N = number of persons
n = number of items
c = cut-off score of an n-item test
N_w = frequency of score w given by equation 4
$\Phi_w(a, b)$ = probability of consistent classification given by equation 5.

Thus, the Marshall-Haertel estimate for form 1 of Table 10.1 with $c = 8$ is:*

*Computations provided by Laird Marshall.

$$\hat{p}_o = \frac{1}{30}\left[\sum_{w=0}^{8-1} N_w + \sum_{w=8}^{16-2} N_w \cdot \Phi_w(w - [8-1], 8-1) + \sum_{w=16}^{10+8-1} N_w \cdot \Phi_w(8, w-8) + \sum_{w=18}^{20} N_w\right]$$

$$= .87.$$

Finally, although Marshall and Haertel do not specifically consider the computation of coefficient kappa ($\hat{\kappa}$), it appears possible to estimate a kappa-like coefficient within the framework of their procedure.

Comparison of Four Approaches

A comparative study of the four approaches conducted by Subkoviak (1977a, 1978) illustrates their various properties (see also Huynh, 1981; Huynh & Saunders, 1980). The study involved 1,586 students, each of whom took parallel forms of 10, 30, and 50 items. On each test, four different mastery criteria were considered: 50%, 60%, 70%, and 80% of the items correct.

As indicated in the third column of Table 10.6, the proportion of the students consistently classified as master/master or nonmaster/nonmaster on the two forms was computed for each criterion score and test length, for a total of 12 distinct values of p_o, referred to as parameter values.

Next, 50 classroom-sized samples of 30 students each were randomly drawn with replacement from the population of 1,586; for example, Table 10.1 contains scores for the first such sample on parallel 10-item tests. For each of the 50 samples, the Swaminathan, Huynh, Subkoviak, and Marshall methods were applied, as previously illustrated, to estimate each parameter value. Thus 50 estimates of each parameter value were obtained by each method. The mean and standard error of these 50 estimates were then calculated (see the last four columns of Table 10.6). For example, when the parameter value is .67 in Table 10.6 the mean of 50 Swaminathan estimates is .68 and their standard error is .08; that is, the estimates deviate .08 units on the average from the parameter value of .67.

The same procedure was repeated using 50 samples of 300 persons, and the resulting means and standard errors can be seen in parentheses in Table 10.6. For example, when the parameter is .67, the mean of 50 Swaminathan estimates based on samples of 300 is .67 and the standard error is .02, which is much smaller than the previous standard error due to the larger sample size.

A number of points can be gleaned from Table 10.6 and from the previous discussion of the various methods.

The Swaminathan method is computationally simple (see Table 10.2) and produces unbiased estimates. The latter point can be inferred from the fact that Swaminathan means equal corresponding parameter values in almost all cases in Table 10.6. However, the Swaminathan method also requires two test administrations, and resulting errors of estimation tend to be relatively large

Table 10.6. Means and Standard Errors of Four Reliability Methods

Test Length (n)	Mastery Criterion (c)	Parameter Value (p_o)	Swaminathan		Huynh		Subkoviak		Marshall	
			Mean	St. Error	Mean	St. Error	Mean	St. Error	Mean	St. Error
10	50%	.67	.68(.67)	.08(.02)	.66(.65)	.06(.03)	.66(.64)	.06(.04)	.74(.73)	.08(.06)
	60%	.72	.72(.72)	.07(.02)	.67(.66)	.06(.06)	.69(.66)	.06(.06)	.75(.74)	.05(.03)
	70%	.80	.79(.80)	.08(.02)	.76(.74)	.06(.06)	.79(.77)	.05(.03)	.79(.79)	.03(.01)
	80%	.88	.87(.88)	.06(.02)	.86(.86)	.05(.02)	.90(.90)	.05(.03)	.85(.85)	.04(.03)
30	50%	.79	.79(.79)	.07(.02)	.80(.79)	.03(.01)	.81(.79)	.04(.01)	.82(.81)	.04(.02)
	60%	.84	.83(.84)	.06(.02)	.82(.81)	.03(.03)	.84(.83)	.04(.02)	.84(.84)	.03(.01)
	70%	.88	.88(.88)	.06(.02)	.88(.88)	.03(.01)	.89(.90)	.04(.02)	.88(.89)	.03(.01)
	80%	.94	.93(.94)	.05(.01)	.94(.94)	.02(.01)	.95(.96)	.03(.02)	.93(.94)	.03(.01)
50	50%	.83	.84(.83)	.06(.02)	.83(.82)	.02(.01)	.84(.83)	.03(.01)	.84(.83)	.03(.01)
	60%	.87	.87(.87)	.06(.02)	.86(.85)	.02(.01)	.88(.87)	.03(.01)	.87(.87)	.03(.01)
	70%	.91	.91(.91)	.05(.01)	.91(.91)	.02(.01)	.93(.93)	.03(.01)	.91(.92)	.03(.01)
	80%	.96	.96(.96)	.08(.01)	.96(.97)	.02(.01)	.97(.97)	.02(.01)	.96(.96)	.02(.01)

Note: Means and standard errors based on 50 samples of 30 persons/(300 persons).

for classroom-sized samples. Of course, two test administrations would be desirable if one were interested in studying the effects of nonequivalent test forms or different test occasions on classification consistency; and the comparatively large standard errors observed for the Swaminathan method in Table 10.6 for samples of size 30 are attributable to the varying forms and occasions.

The Huynh, Subkoviak, and Marshall methods are generally similar. All three methods require only one test administration and produce estimates having relatively small standard errors for classroom-sized samples, which can be verified in Table 10.6, and which is attributable to the constancy of forms and occasions. However, the three methods are computationally complex and produce somewhat biased estimates for short tests. Regarding the latter point, each method is characterized by a different type of bias that is most pronounced in the 10-item test of Table 10.6. Specifically, the Huynh procedure tends to produce underestimates for all criterion levels on the 10-item test; and Huynh and Saunders (1980) have shown that this tendency also extends to estimates of kappa. If there must be bias, such conservative estimation may be the most tolerable. On the other hand, for short tests, the Subkoviak procedure seems to produce slight underestimates for criterion levels, like 50%, near the center of the test score distribution and overestimates for criterion levels, like 80%, in the tails. This pattern was also detected by Algina and Noe (1978) in a simulated-data study of the Subkoviak method. Conversely, the Marshall method produces overestimates for criterion levels in the center of the distribution and underestimates for criterion levels in the tails. In the Algina and Noe study, this type of pattern was related to the use of the observed proportion correct (x/n) as an estimate of the binomial probability of success, which is the estimate employed in equation 4 of the Marshall procedure.

All things considered, the Huynh procedure seems worthy of recommendation for standard data sets of the type considered here. It requires only one test administration, tends to produce slightly conservative estimates, has an associated normal approximation method, and is based on the mathematically elegant Keats-Lord model. (On the other hand, the Subkoviak and Marshall methods seem also to produce reasonably accurate estimates in practice, and, of course, Swaminathan appears to be the only totally unbiased method.)

SUGGESTIONS FOR FUTURE RESEARCH

This section attempts to offer specific suggestions for research in the area of test reliability. In this regard, five recommendations come to mind immediately.

1. More work is needed to facilitate the computation of criterion-referenced reliability coefficients, particularly for teachers and other practitioners who do not have direct access to computer facilities. Huynh's (1978) tables (Subkoviak, 1980) are a definite step in the right direction, but, at

present, these tables include coefficients for tests between 5 and 10 items only. Extensions to longer and, perhaps, shorter tests are in order. In the same vein, further study of approximation methods that minimize the computational labor involved in obtaining reliability estimates also seems warranted (cf. Huynh, 1976, p. 258; Peng & Subkoviak, 1980).

2. There is a need for additional studies, such as Huynh and Saunders (1980), Marshall and Serlin (1979), and Subkoviak (1978), comparing the characteristics and properties of the various methods reviewed here. Further discussion of the relative merits of $\hat{p}_o$, $\hat{\kappa}$, and other consistency coefficients would also appear to be worthwhile.
3. A number of authors have recently shown an interest in deriving coefficients that measure the extent to which observed outcomes on mastery tests agree with the outcomes that would occur if students' true scores were known (Huynh, 1980; Livingston & Wingersky, 1979; Subkoviak & Wilcox, 1978, Wilcox, 1977). For example, Subkoviak and Wilcox (1978) proposed a procedure for estimating the proportion of students in a group that is *correctly* classified in the sense that the test classification agrees with the true mastery or nonmastery level of the student. Their approach is based upon the 1962 Keats and Lord model discussed earlier. Livingston and Wingersky's (1979) method is similar, but is based on the 1969 Lord model, also alluded to earlier. In practice it may be more relevant and useful to know the extent to which a test leads to correct outcomes than the extent to which it leads to consistent, but possibly incorrect, outcomes. In any event, this line of research warrants further consideration.
4. There is a need for a comprehensive test analysis computer package for criterion-referenced test users who have access to data-processing equipment. Ideally, such a package would include routines for test scoring and for computing item statistics, reliability coefficients, validity coefficients, and the like, for evaluating and improving criterion-referenced tests of various kinds. Presently, a number of isolated programs exist for particular purposes, such as computing the type of reliability coefficients discussed here, but I am unaware of any panoramic packages specifically designed for criterion-referenced test analysis. Certainly, reasons for the apparent nonexistence of such an inclusive system are the lack of total agreement regarding which procedures and statistics should be computed and the existence of problems for which practical solutions have yet to be proposed. However, theoretical and practical developments may soon be sufficient to support such an undertaking.
5. There is a need for further study of the relative merits of the reliability of mastery classification decisions, reviewed here, and the reliability of criterion-referenced test scores, reviewed by Brennan in chapter 11. The final section of this chapter seeks to introduce some of the relevant distinctions between these two approaches. The interested reader is referred to Kane and Brennan (1980), Mellenbergh and van der Linden (1979), and van der Linden and Mellenbergh (1978) for more on this topic.

GUIDELINES FOR PRACTITIONERS

Coefficient $\hat{p}_o$ versus $\hat{\kappa}$

Having selected a particular reliability method (Huynh, Marshall, Subkoviak, or Swaminathan), the user is next faced with the question of which reliability coefficient to report, $\hat{p}_o$ or $\hat{\kappa}$. The fact that $\hat{p}_o$ and $\hat{\kappa}$ are sensitive to different types of consistency is illustrated in Figure 10.1, which was obtained by computing $\hat{p}_o$ and $\hat{\kappa}$ (à la Subkoviak) at the points $c = 2, 4, 6, 8$ for form 1 of Table 10.1. Also shown at the bottom of the figure is the distribution of test scores for the example. The most obvious conclusion to be drawn from Figure 10.1 is that coefficients $\hat{p}_o$ and $\hat{\kappa}$ do not measure exactly the same thing. In fact, $\hat{p}_o$ assumes its largest values in the tails of the score distribution and smallest values in the center, while $\hat{\kappa}$ does just the opposite.

The converse relationship between $\hat{p}_o$ and $\hat{\kappa}$ depicted in Figure 10.1 occurs because these two coefficients are sensitive to different types of consistency, and *the primary reason for choosing one index over the other should be the desire to measure the type of consistency particular to that coefficient* (see Subkoviak, 1977b). To be specific, coefficient $\hat{p}_o$ represents the total propor-

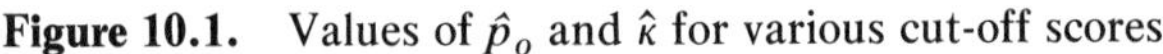

Figure 10.1. Values of $\hat{p}_o$ and $\hat{\kappa}$ for various cut-off scores

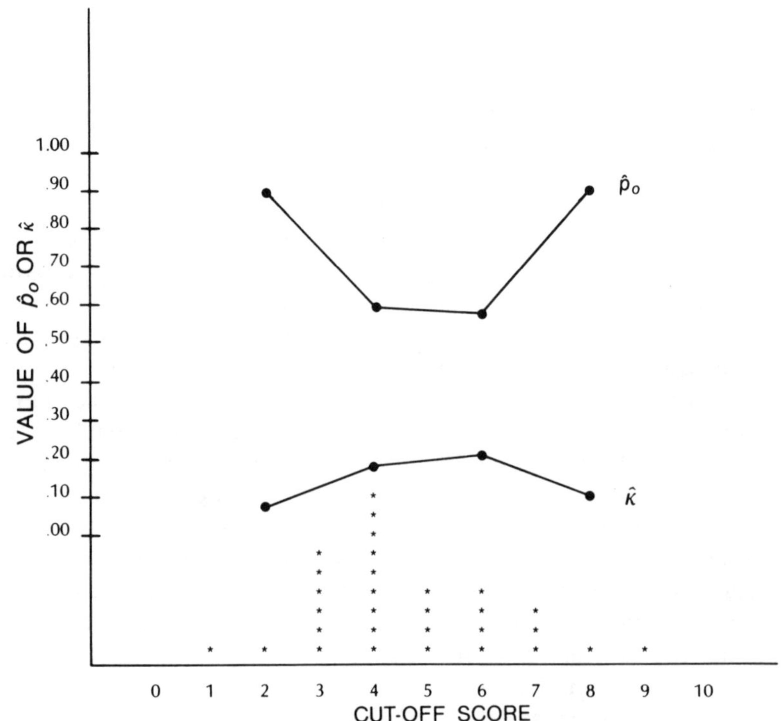

tion of consistent classification that occurs *for whatever reason* on two tests. For example, two of the factors that contribute to overall consistency as measured by $\hat{p}_o$ are the relative numbers of masters and nonmasters in the group tested and the precision or accuracy of the test. The latter point needs no explanation; however, an example may help to clarify the former. If a group is composed entirely or almost entirely of high-ability students, that fact alone tends to assure a large proportion of consistent mastery/mastery outcomes, just as a heavily biased coin tends to produce consistent results on two independent flips.

If one were primarily interested in the test's contribution to the overall proportion ($\hat{p}_o$) of consistent classifications, it might be desirable to extract from $\hat{p}_o$ that proportion of consistency expected from or attributable to the particular mastery-nonmastery composition of the group tested. Coefficient kappa does just that. In the expression for kappa $\hat{\kappa} = (\hat{p}_o - \hat{p}_c)/(1 - \hat{p}_c)$, the quantity $\hat{p}_c$ represents the portion of consistency due to the mastery-nonmastery composition of the group, which is subtracted from the overall proportion $\hat{p}_o$; the difference is then divided by $(1 - \hat{p}_c)$, which simply puts kappa on a scale from 0 to $+1$.

The use of $\hat{p}_o$ or $\hat{\kappa}$ should stem primarily from the desire to measure overall consistency or solely test consistency, respectively. Having made that conscious choice, certain other properties of the coefficients become matters for consideration. For example, the standard errors reported in Table 10.6 for estimates of $\hat{p}_o$ are somewhat smaller than would be observed if estimates of $\hat{\kappa}$ and their standard errors had been computed instead (Huynh, 1977a; Huynh & Saunders, 1980; Subkoviak, 1977b). In other words, for a fixed sample size, like 30 students, $\hat{p}_o$ can generally be estimated with greater precision than $\hat{\kappa}$.

In point of fact, $\hat{p}_o$ and $\hat{\kappa}$ are not the only options open to the user. Huynh (1977b) has also proposed the use of the kappamax coefficient, which is simply the largest value that kappa attains within the range of cut-off scores, and Goodman and Kruskal (1954) discuss a number of others. To date, none of these coefficients has gained universal acceptance. However, as previously indicated, this does not imply that the choice of a coefficient should be made indiscriminately. Rather, a particular coefficient should be selected on the basis of what it measures. For more on this topic, the reader is referred to Brennan and Prediger (1981) and Livingston and Wingersky (1979).

Classification Consistency Approach versus Generalizability Theory Approach

In chapter 9, a distinction was drawn between (a) the reliability of mastery-nonmastery classifications and (b) the reliability of mastery test scores. In the example of Table 10.1 the former refers to the consistency of mastery-nonmastery classifications across forms 1 and 2 when the cut-off score is set at 8, while the latter refers to the consistency of score deviations from the cut-off across forms 1 and 2. In other words, these two approaches are respectively concerned with the reliability of *categories* of mastery and *degrees* of mastery, over repeated testing. Thus, a choice must be made between the type of coefficients discussed here and the type of coefficients discussed in the next chapter.

Support for classification consistency has been advanced by Hambleton and Novick (1973), who argued that the deviation of an examinee's score from the criterion is not as important as whether or not the examinee is consistently assigned to the same side of the criterion on two tests (see also Hambleton, 1974). Harris (1972) and Shavelson, Block, and Ravitch (1972) were also critical of approaches that focus on degree, rather than category, of mastery. However, the objections may be primarily matters of "form rather than substance," as Brennan and Kane phrased it (1977, p. 286).

However, one relevant point worth noting is that approaches concerned with degree of mastery are sensitive to all errors of measurement that occur on a test, including errors that do not lead to inconsistent mastery-nonmastery classifications (see Brennan & Kane, 1977, pp. 286–87). In Table 10.1, for example, reliability coefficients sensitive to degree of mastery are reduced by the fact that student 4's score deviations of -1 and -4 from the cut-off of 8 differ from form 1 to form 2, even though the student is consistently classified as a nonmaster on both forms.

On the other hand, classification consistency approaches are limited in the sense that all inconsistent classifications are regarded as equally serious. Yet the implications in Table 10.1 of misclassifying student 1, whose true ability is close to the cut-off score of 8, may be less serious than the implications of misclassifying a student whose true ability is far below or above the cut-off.

In the final analysis, neither of these reliability approaches is optimal for all applications (Brennan & Kane, 1977, p. 287). Perhaps the simplest recommendation would be to use Brennan's approach (chapter 11) if *degree* of mastery or nonmastery is an important consideration and to use the approach described in this chapter if such distinctions among different levels of mastery or different levels of nonmastery are not important. For a more detailed and technical comparison of reliability approaches, the reader is referred to a paper by Kane and Brennan (1980) that discusses these coefficients.

REFERENCES

Algina, J., & Noe, M. J. A study of the accuracy of Subkoviak's single-administration estimate of the coefficient of agreement using two true-score estimates. *Journal of Educational Measurement*, 1978, *15*, 101–110.

Brennan, R. L., & Kane, M. T. An index of dependability for mastery tests. *Journal of Educational Measurement*, 1977, *14*, 277–289.

Brennan, R. L., & Prediger, D. J. Coefficient kappa: Some uses, misuses, and alternatives. *Educational and Psychological Measurement*, 1981, *41*, 687–699.

Carver, R. P. Special problems in measuring change with psychometric devices. In *Evaluative research: Strategies and methods*. Pittsburgh: American Institutes for Research, 1970. Pp. 48–63.

Cohen, J. A. A coefficient of agreement for nominal scales. *Educational and Psychological Measurement*, 1960, *20*, 37–46.

Cohen, J. A. Weighted kappa: Nominal scale agreement with provision for scaled disagreement of partial credit. *Psychological Bulletin*, 1968, *70*, 213–230.

Fleiss, J. L., Cohen, J., & Everitt, B. S. Large sample standard errors of kappa and weighted kappa. *Psychological Bulletin*, 1969, *72*, 323–327.

Goodman, L. A., & Kruskal, W. H. Measures of association for cross classifications. *Journal of the American Statistical Association*, 1954, *49*, 732–764.

Gross, A. L., & Shulman, V. The applicability of the beta binomial model for criterion referenced testing. *Journal of Educational Measurement*, 1980, *17*, 195–201.

Gupta, S. S. Probability integrals of multivariate normal and multivariate *t*. *Annals of Mathematical Statistics*, 1963, *34*, 792–828.

Hambleton, R. K. Testing and decision-making procedures for selected individualized instruction programs. *Review of Educational Research*, 1974, *44*, 371–400.

Hambleton, R. K., & Novick, M. R. Toward an integration of theory and method for criterion-referenced tests. *Journal of Educational Measurement*, 1973, *10*, 159–170.

Hambleton, R. K., Swaminathan, H., Algina, J., & Coulson, D. B. Criterion-referenced testing and measurement: A review of technical issues and developments. *Review of Educational Research*, 1978, *48*, 1–47.

Harris, C. W. An interpretation of Livingston's reliability coefficient for criterion-referenced tests. *Journal of Educational Measurement*, 1972, *9*, 27–29.

Hubert, L. J. Kappa revisited. *Psychological Bulletin*, 1977, *84*, 289–297.

Huynh, H. On the reliability of decisions in domain-referenced testing. *Journal of Educational Measurement*, 1976, *13*, 253–264.

Huynh, H. *Statistical inference for the kappa and kappamax reliability indices based on the beta-binomial model*. Paper presented at the annual meeting of the Psychometric Society, Chapel Hill, NC, June 1977. (a)

Huynh, H. *The kappamax reliability index for decisions in domain-referenced testing*. Paper presented at the annual meeting of the American Educational Research Association, New York, April 1977. (b)

Huynh, H. *Computation and inference for two reliability indices in mastery testing based on the beta-binomial model* (Research Memorandum 78-1). Columbia: Publication Series in Mastery Testing, College of Education, University of South Carolina, 1978.

Huynh, H. Statistical inference for false positive and false negative error rates in mastery testing. *Psychometrika*, 1980, *45*, 107–120.

Huynh, H. Adequacy of asymptotic normal theory in estimating reliability for mastery tests based on the beta-binomial model. *Journal of Educational Statistics*, 1981, *6*, 257–266.

Huynh, H., & Saunders, J. C. Accuracy of two procedures for estimating reliability of mastery tests. *Journal of Educational Measurement*, 1980, *17*, 351–358.

Kane, M. T., & Brennan, R. L. Agreement coefficients as indices of dependability for domain-referenced tests. *Applied Psychological Measurement*, 1980, *4*, 105–126.

Keats, J. A., & Lord, F. M. A theoretical distribution for mental test scores. *Psychometrika*, 1962, *27*, 59–72.

LaValle, I. H. *An introduction to probability, decision, and inference*. New York: Holt, Rinehart and Winston, 1970.

Livingston, S. A., & Wingersky, M. S. Assessing the reliability of tests used to make pass/fail decisions. *Journal of Educational Measurement*, 1979, *16*, 247–260.

Lord, F. M. A strong true score theory, with applications. *Psychometrika*, 1965, *30*, 239-270.

Lord, F. M. Estimating true score distributions in psychological testing (An empirical Bayes estimation problem). *Psychometrika*, 1969, *34*, 259-299.

Marshall, J. L., & Haertel, E. H. *The mean split-half coefficient of agreement: A single administration index of reliability for mastery tests.* Unpublished manuscript, University of Wisconsin, 1976.

Marshall, J. L., & Serlin, R. C. *Characteristics of four mastery test reliability indices: Influence of distribution shape and cutting score*. Paper presented at the annual meeting of the American Educational Research Association, San Francisco, April 1979.

Mellenbergh, G. J., & van der Linden, W. J. The internal and external optimality of decisions based on tests. *Applied Psychological Measurement*, 1979, *3*, 257-273.

Novick, M. R., Lewis, C., & Jackson, P. H. The estimation of proportions in *m* groups. *Psychometrika*, 1973, *38*, 19-45.

Peng, C-Y. J., & Subkoviak, M. J. A note on Huynh's normal approximation procedure for estimating criterion-referenced reliability. *Journal of Educational Measurement*, 1980, *17*, 359-368.

Reid, J. B., & Roberts, D. M. *A Monte Carlo comparison of phi and kappa as measures of criterion-referenced reliability.* Paper presented at the annual meeting of the American Educational Research Association, Toronto, March 1978.

Shavelson, R. J., Block, J. H., & Ravitch, M. M. Criterion-referenced testing: Comments on reliability. *Journal of Educational Measurement*, 1972, *9*, 133-137.

Subkoviak, M. J. *Estimating reliability from a single administration of a mastery test* (Occasional Paper No. 15). Madison: Laboratory of Experimental Design, University of Wisconsin, 1975.

Subkoviak, M. J. Estimating reliability from a single administration of a mastery test. *Journal of Educational Measurement*, 1976, *13*, 265-276.

Subkoviak, M. J. *Evaluation of criterion-referenced reliability coefficients* (Final Report of Grant NIE-G-76-0088). Washington, DC: National Institute of Education, 1977. (a)

Subkoviak, M. J. *Further comments on reliability for mastery tests*. Unpublished manuscript, University of Wisconsin, 1977. (b)

Subkoviak, M. J. Empirical investigation of procedures for estimating reliability for mastery tests. *Journal of Educational Measurement*, 1978, *15*, 111-116.

Subkoviak, M. J. Decision-consistency approaches. In R. A. Berk (Ed.), *Criterion-referenced measurement: The state of the art.* Baltimore, MD: Johns Hopkins University Press, 1980. Pp. 129-185.

Subkoviak, M. J., & Wilcox, R. R. *Estimating the probability of correct classification in mastery testing*. Paper presented at the annual meeting of the American Educational Research Association, Toronto, March 1978.

Swaminathan, H., Hambleton, R. K., & Algina, J. Reliability of criterion-referenced tests: A decision-theoretic formulation. *Journal of Educational Measurement*, 1974, *11*, 263-267.

Tables of the Binomial Probability Distribution. Washington, DC: U.S. Government Printing Office, 1949.

Tables of the Bivariate Normal Distribution Function and Related Functions. Washington, DC: U.S. Government Printing Office, 1959.

van der Linden, W. J., & Mellenbergh, G. J. Coefficients for tests from a decision theoretic point of view. *Applied Psychological Measurement*, 1978, *2*, 119-134.

Wilcox, R. R. Estimating the likelihood of false-positive and false-negative decisions in mastery testing: An empirical Bayes approach. *Journal of Educational Statistics*, 1977, *2*, 289-307.

Wilcox, R. R. Prediction analysis and the reliability of a mastery test. *Educational and Psychological Measurement*, 1979, *39*, 825-839.

Wilcox, R. R. A cautionary note on estimating the reliability of a mastery test with the beta-binomial model. *Applied Psychological Measurement*, 1981, *5*, 531-537. (a)

Wilcox, R. R. A review of the beta-binomial model and its extensions. *Journal of Educational Statistics*, 1981, *6*, 3-32. (b)

11 ESTIMATING THE DEPENDABILITY OF THE SCORES

ROBERT L. BRENNAN

INTRODUCTION

The approach to reliability issues discussed in this chapter is based primarily on generalizability theory, which is treated extensively by Cronbach, Gleser, Nanda, and Rajaratnam (1972) and by Brennan (1983). A brief review of generalizability theory is provided by Brennan and Kane (1979), and a recent literature review is provided by Shavelson and Webb (1981).

Applications of generalizability theory to criterion-referenced testing have been discussed by Brennan (1977, 1978, 1981, 1983), Brennan and Kane (1977a, 1977b), and Kane and Brennan (1980). Indeed, this chapter may be viewed, in part, as an integrated summary of much of the work reported in these publications. As such, this chapter provides an introduction to, and review of, a specific psychometric theory for criterion-referenced testing. From another perspective, in terms of the Hambleton, Swaminathan, Algina, and Coulson (1978) trichotomy of types of criterion-referenced reliability, this chapter treats one approach to issues involving the "reliability of criterion-referenced test scores" and, to some extent, the "reliability of domain score estimates."

Since Popham and Husek (1969) challenged the appropriateness of correlation coefficients as indices of reliability for criterion-referenced, domain-referenced, and mastery tests, considerable effort has been devoted to developing more appropriate indices. Most of the these indices have been proposed as measures of *reliability*; in this chapter, however, the more generic term *dependability* will be used to avoid unwarranted associations with classical reliability coefficients.

Appreciation is extended to Dr. Michael T. Kane, who participated in most of the research reviewed here and who offered many insightful comments about drafts of this chapter. This research was partially supported by contracts between the American College Testing Program and the Navy Personnel Research and Development Center, Contract Nos. N00123-77-C-0739 and N00123-78-C-1206.

Probably the most important results of the approach discussed here center around the definition of error variance for domain-referenced interpretations. It is this error variance that principally distinguishes this approach from others that have been proposed, and it is this error variance that is incorporated in the indices of dependability developed and discussed here.

REVIEW OF GENERALIZABILITY THEORY APPROACH

Classical test theory provides a very simple structural model of the relationship between observed, true, and error scores. However, the simplicity of the model necessitates some rather restrictive assumptions if the model is to be applied to real data. Generalizability theory liberalizes and extends classical test theory in several important respects. For example, the theory of generalizability does not necessitate the classical test theory assumption of "parallel" tests; rather, generalizability theory employs the weaker assumption of "randomly parallel" tests. Also, classical test theory assumes that errors of measurement are sampled from an undifferentiated univariate distribution. By contrast, generalizability theory allows for the existence of multiple types and sources of error through the application of analysis of variance procedures or, more specifically, through the application of the general linear model to the dependability of measurement. Consequently, generalizability theory is applicable to a broad range of testing and evaluation studies that arise in education and psychology. The subject of this chapter—namely, the dependability of domain-referenced tests—is only one such application.

Since generalizability theory is unfamiliar to many practitioners, the review provided here is intentionally didactic to some extent. In general, the text provides an outline, without proofs, of the development of theoretical results, with emphasis placed upon the interpretation of such results. For the most part, formulas for estimating results are provided in tables and illustrative examples are reported in sufficient detail to enable the reader to verify calculations. Also, relationships between results for norm-referenced and domain-referenced interpretations are treated to a limited extent. Finally, major emphasis is placed upon results for the simple persons-crossed-with-items design, but a limited treatment of some other designs is provided, too.

Model, Assumptions, and Variance Components for the $p \times i$ Design

Let us assume that the data for a particular test are derived from a random sample of n_p persons from an infinite population of persons and a random sample of n_i items from an infinite universe (or domain) of items. The observed score for any person p on any item i can be represented by the linear model

$$X_{pi} = \mu + \mu_{p}^{\sim} + \mu_{i}^{\sim} + \mu_{pi}^{\sim} + e,$$

where:

μ = grand mean in the population of persons and the universe of items,
$\mu_{p}\tilde{}$ = score effect for person p,
$\mu_{i}\tilde{}$ = score effect for item i,
$\mu_{pi}\tilde{}$ = score effect for the interaction of person p and item i, and
e = experimental error.

Usually there is only one observation for each person-item combination, which implies that the $\mu_{pi}\tilde{}$ and e effects are completely confounded. Cronbach et al. (1972) represent this confounding with the notation (pi, e). Here, in accordance with the notational conventions in Brennan (1983), this confounding will not be indicated explicitly, and this equation may be written as

$$X_{pi} = \mu + \mu_{p}\tilde{} + \mu_{i}\tilde{} + \mu_{pi}\tilde{}. \tag{1}$$

The basic assumptions underlying the model in equation 1 are the typical analysis of variance (or general linear model) assumptions that are well documented by Cronbach et al. (1972) and by most experimental design texts. Briefly, these assumptions are that all effects in the model are assumed to be sampled independently, and the expected value of each effect over the population of persons and the universe of items is set equal to zero. Given these assumptions, equation 1 is the random effects model for the persons-crossed-with-items design, $p \times i$. It is particularly important to note that this model does *not* require any assumptions about the distributional form for the observed scores or any score effects.

Score effects and mean scores. Equation 1 provides a decomposition of the observed score for person p on item i in terms of score effects, or components. In a similar manner, the *average* observed score for person p on a *sample* of items (i.e., test) can be represented as

$$X_{pI} = \mu + \mu_{p}\tilde{} + \mu_{I}\tilde{} + \mu_{pI}\tilde{}, \tag{2}$$

where I denotes the average score for a particular sample of n_i items and, as in equation 1, $\mu_{pI}\tilde{}$ is completely confounded with experimental error.

Following the terminology of generalizability theory, the *universe score* for person p is denoted μ_p and defined as the expected value of the observed score over the *universe* of items. Therefore, using equation 1

$$\mu_p = \mathcal{E}_i X_{pi} = \mu + \mu_{p}\tilde{}, \tag{3}$$

or, equivalently, using equation 2

$$\mu_p = \mathcal{E}_I X_{pI} = \mu + \mu_{p}\tilde{},$$

where the expectation is taken over all possible samples of size n_i from the universe of items.

Similarly, the population mean for item i is

$$\mu_i = \mathcal{E}_p X_{pi} = \mu + \mu_{i}\tilde{}, \tag{4}$$

and the population mean for a test, or set of items, I, is

$$\mu_I = \mathcal{E}_p X_{pI} = \mu + \mu_{I^{\sim}}. \tag{5}$$

Equations 4 and 5, respectively, imply that μ_i is the item difficulty level for the population of persons and that μ_I is the test mean in terms of the proportion of items correct.

In classical test theory, the assumption of parallel tests requires that $\mu_I = \mu_J$, where I and J are two different sets of items, or tests. Here, however, it is *not* assumed that tests are *classically* parallel. Rather, in generalizability theory the assumption of *classically* parallel tests is replaced by the weaker assumption of *randomly* parallel tests. Two tests are randomly parallel if they both consist of random samples of the same number of items from the same universe, or domain, of items.

Defining and interpreting variance components. For each of the score effects, or components, in equation 1, there is an associated *variance component*. For example, the variance component for persons is denoted $\sigma^2(p)$ and defined as

$$\sigma^2(p) = \mathcal{E}_p(\mu_p - \mu)^2 = \mathcal{E}_p(\mu_{p^{\sim}})^2. \tag{6}$$

Similarly,

$$\sigma^2(i) = \mathcal{E}_i(\mu_i - \mu)^2 = \mathcal{E}_i(\mu_{i^{\sim}})^2. \tag{7}$$

and

$$\sigma^2(pi) = \mathcal{E}_p\, \mathcal{E}_i(X_{pi} - \mu_p - \mu_i + \mu)^2 = \mathcal{E}_p\, \mathcal{E}_i(\mu_{pi^{\sim}})^2. \tag{8}$$

These variance components are called *random effects* variance components, because they are derived from the random effects model in equation 1. The sum of these variance components equals the total observed score variance, denoted $\sigma^2(X_{pi})$, which should *not be* confused with the *expected* observed score variance discussed later. Note especially that these variance components are associated with score effects for *single* observations. If, for example, items are scored dichotomously, then the maximum value of any of the variance components in equations 6–8 is .25.

The variance component, $\sigma^2(p)$, assumes a particularly important role here, in that it is the universe score variance, that is, the variance over persons of the universe scores defined in equation 3. In generalizability theory, the universe score variance plays a role like that of the true score variance in classical test theory. Similarly, $\sigma^2(pi)$ is analogous to the usual error variance, for a *single*-item test, in classical test theory. Classical test theory, however, has no quantity analogous to $\sigma^2(i)$, which is by definition the variance of the mean scores for all items in the universe, where each mean is based upon the population of persons. As shown later, $\sigma^2(i)$ plays an especially important role in distinctions between norm-referenced and domain-referenced interpretations of test scores.

By substituting I for i everywhere in equations 6–8, one can obtain the definitions of the variance components associated with equation 2. It is evident that $\sigma^2(p)$, the universe score variance, remains unchanged, and it is easily shown that

$$\sigma^2(I) = \sigma^2(i)/n_i \tag{9}$$

and

$$\sigma^2(pI) = \sigma^2(pi)/n_i. \tag{10}$$

Recall that I denotes an *average* score for a particular sample of n_i items. This is the usual convention in generalizability theory, but if one prefers *total* score variance components, they are obtained by multiplying all variance components by n_i^2.

In equation 10, $\sigma^2(pI)$ is the usual error variance in classical test theory for a test of length n_i. However, $\sigma^2(I)$ in equation 9 is not analogous to any quantity in classical test theory. Indeed, the assumption of parallel tests in classical test theory necessitates that $\sigma^2(I)$ be zero. To appreciate this fact, recall that the assumption of parallel tests requires that, for two different sets of items, I and J, the population means be equal, that is, $\mu_I = \mu_J$ (see equation 5). When this assumption is extended to multiple sets of items (tests of length n_i), it is evident that the assumption is met only if $\sigma^2(I) = 0$. Again, generalizability theory assumes randomly parallel, not classically parallel, tests.

Estimating variance components. In generalizability theory, variance components assume central importance. They are the building blocks that provide a crucial foundation for all subsequent results. From a practical point of view, therefore, the estimation and interpretation of variance components is a matter of considerable importance. In understanding variance components, the defining equations 6–8 are useful, but they cannot be used directly to estimate variance components because these equations are expressed in terms of model parameters, not estimates.

Rather, one usually estimates variance components through an analysis of variance, such as that provided in Table 11.1 for the $p \times i$ design. It is evident from Table 11.1 that $\sigma^2(p)$, $\sigma^2(i)$, and $\sigma^2(pi)$ are estimated using mean squares and sample sizes only; once these variance components have been estimated, equations 9 and 10 can be used to estimate $\sigma^2(I)$ and $\sigma^2(pI)$. (For present purposes, the reader should disregard all references in Table 11.1 to G study and D study, as well as the primes attached to some sample sizes.) Since variance components are unfamiliar statistics for many readers, the lower third of Table 11.1 provides equations for some relatively common statistics in terms of variance components.

Variance components can also be estimated using Venn diagrams. More importantly, however, Venn diagrams provide a useful visual aid to understanding variance components as well as other aspects of generalizability analyses. Figure 11.1 provides the general form of a Venn diagram for the $p \times i$ design, as well as the relationships among areas of a Venn diagram and

Table 11.1. ANOVA for Estimating Variance Components for the Random Effects $p \times i$ Design

Effect, Component, or Source	*df*	*SS*	*MS*	Estimated G Study Variance Component	D Study Sampling Frequency	Estimated D Study Variance Component
Persons (p)	$n_p - 1$	$SS(p)$	$MS(p)$	$\hat{\sigma}^2(p)$	1	$\hat{\sigma}^2(p)$
Items (i)	$n_i - 1$	$SS(i)$	$MS(i)$	$\hat{\sigma}^2(i)$	n_i'	$\hat{\sigma}^2(I)$
Interaction (pi)	$(n_p - 1)(n_i - 1)$	$SS(pi)$	$MS(pi)$	$\hat{\sigma}^2(pi)$	n_i'	$\hat{\sigma}^2(pI)$

$$\hat{\sigma}^2(p) = [MS(p) - MS(pi)]/n_i$$
$$\hat{\sigma}^2(i) = [MS(i) - MS(pi)]/n_p$$
$$\hat{\sigma}^2(pi) = MS(pi)$$

$$\hat{\sigma}^2(I) = \hat{\sigma}^2(i)/n_i'$$
$$\hat{\sigma}(pI) = \hat{\sigma}^2(pi)/n_i'$$

Variance of Observed Person Mean Scores: $\hat{S}_p^2(X_{pI}) = \hat{\sigma}^2(p) + \hat{\sigma}^2(pi)/n_i$

Variance of Observed Item Difficulty Levels: $\hat{S}_i^2(X_{Pi}) = \hat{\sigma}^2(i) + \hat{\sigma}^2(pi)/n_p$

Sum of Observed Item Variances: $\sum_i S_p^2(X_{pi}) = (n_p - 1)n_i[\hat{\sigma}^2(p) + \hat{\sigma}^2(pi)]/n_p = \sum_i X_{Pi}(1 - X_{Pi})$ for dichotomous items

Note: Uppercase P and I represent mean scores, *not* total scores.

Figure 11.1. Venn diagram representation of mean squares and variance components for $p \times i$ design

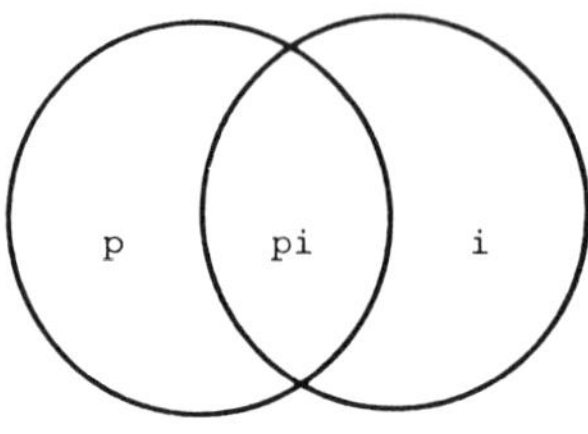

A. General Form of Venn Diagram for p × i Design

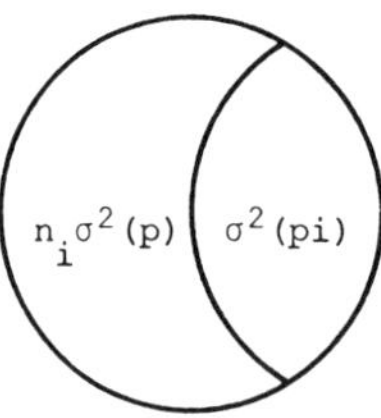

B. Expected Value of the Mean Square for the Effect $\mu_p \sim$: $EMS(p) = \sigma^2(pi) + n_i\sigma^2(p)$

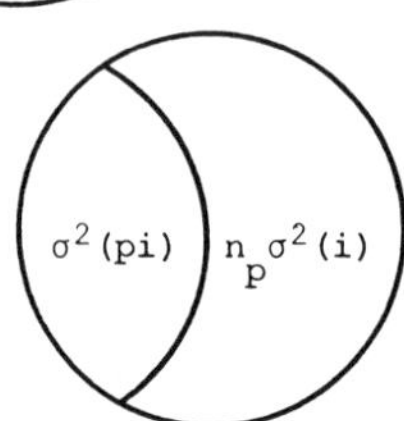

C. Expected Value of the Mean Square for the Effect $\mu_i \sim$: $EMS(i) = \sigma^2(pi) + n_p\sigma^2(i)$

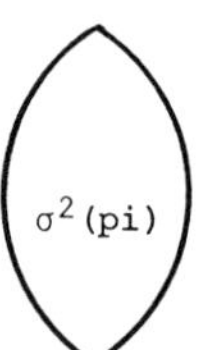

D. Expected Value of the Mean Square for the Effect $\mu_{pi} \sim$: $EMS(pi) = \sigma^2(pi)$

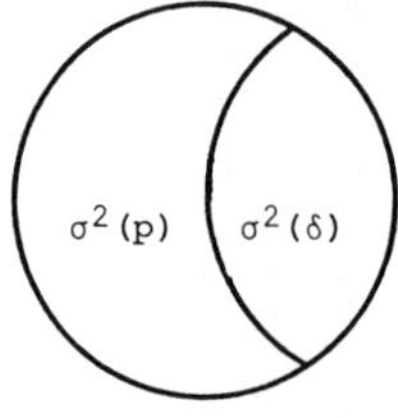

E. Expected Observed Score Variance:

$$\mathcal{E}\sigma^2(X) = \sigma^2(p) + \sigma^2(\delta)$$
$$= \sigma^2(p) + \sigma^2(pI)$$

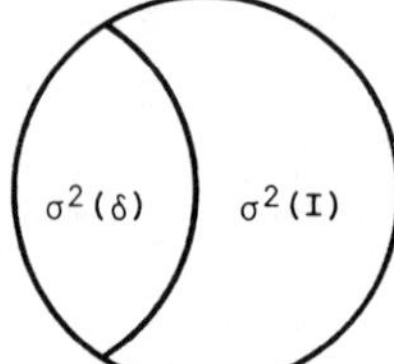

F. $\sigma^2(\Delta) = \sigma^2(\delta) + \sigma^2(I)$
$$= \sigma^2(pI) + \sigma^2(I)$$

certain equations frequently encountered in analysis of variance and/or generalizability theory. As indicated in Figures 11.1A, 11.1B, and 11.1C, circles and their intersections can be interpreted as mean squares, while parts of circles can be interpreted as variance components or simple functions of them. These relationships provide a visual procedure for estimating variance components. From Figures 11.1B and 11.1D, it is evident that subtracting $MS(pi)$ from $MS(p)$, and dividing by n_i, provides an estimate of $\sigma^2(p)$, the universe score variance.

To clarify further the estimation and interpretation of variance components, as well as the notational conventions used here, consider the synthetic data in Table 11.2, which have been studied extensively by Guilford (1954) from the perspective of classical test theory. These data are introduced, not because they are illustrative of any ideal characteristics of a test, but rather because they can be studied in their entirety by the reader, without encountering either trivial results or extensive computational complexity. In particular, using the equations in Table 11.1 and the data in Table 11.2, it is easy to verify the numerical values of the estimated variance components in Table 11.3. It is evident that, for these data, the estimated universe score variance, $\sigma^2(p)$, is slightly less than estimated variance among item mean scores, $\sigma^2(i)$, but neither of these variance components is nearly as large as $\sigma^2(pi)$.

The Error Variance $\sigma^2(\Delta)$ and Domain-referenced Interpretations

One of the distinct advantages of generalizability theory over classical test theory is that generalizability theory allows one to distinguish clearly between two different types of error, denoted σ and Δ. As argued in what follows, δ and its associated variance, $\sigma^2(\delta)$, are appropriate for norm-referenced interpretations, while Δ and its variance, $\sigma^2(\Delta)$, are generally appropriate for domain-referenced interpretations. For the approach developed here to domain-referenced issues of dependability of measurement, this distinction is of crucial importance. Indeed, this approach suggests that classical test theory is generally incapable of distinguishing between norm-referenced and domain-referenced interpretations. I begin with a discussion of $\sigma^2(\delta)$ to enable subsequent comparisons of $\sigma^2(\Delta)$ with $\sigma^2(\delta)$.

The error variance $\sigma^2(\delta)$. In norm-referenced testing, interest is focused on "the relative ordering of individuals with respect to their test performance, for example, whether student A can solve his problems more quickly than student B" (Glaser, 1963, p. 519) or "the adequacy of the measuring procedure for making *comparative* decisions" (Cronbach et al., 1972, p. 95). In this situation, the error for a given person, as defined by Cronbach et al. (1972), is

$$\delta_p = (X_{pI} - \mu_I) - (\mu_p - \mu). \tag{11}$$

In equation 11, μ represents the reference point for making statements about μ_p, and μ_I represents the reference point for making statements about X_{pI}. That is, the raw score, X_{pI}, carries no inherent meaning for a norm-

Table 11.2. Synthetic Data Reported by Guilford (1954, p. 381)

	Item													
Person	1	2	3	4	5	6	7	8	9	10	11	12	Total	X_{pI}
1	1	0	1	0	0	0	0	0	0	0	0	0	2	0.1667
2	1	1	1	0	0	1	0	0	0	0	0	0	4	0.3333
3	1	1	1	1	0	0	0	0	0	0	0	0	4	0.3333
4	1	1	0	1	1	0	0	1	0	0	0	0	5	0.4167
5	1	1	1	1	1	0	0	0	0	0	0	0	5	0.4167
6	1	1	1	0	1	1	1	0	0	0	0	0	6	0.5000
7	1	1	1	1	1	1	1	0	0	0	0	0	7	0.5833
8	1	1	1	1	0	1	1	1	1	1	0	0	9	0.7500
9	1	1	1	1	1	1	1	1	1	1	1	0	11	0.9167
10	1	1	1	1	1	1	1	1	1	1	1	1	12	1.0000
Total	10	9	9	7	6	6	5	4	3	3	2	1		
X_{Pi}	1.0	0.9	0.9	0.7	0.6	0.6	0.5	0.4	0.3	0.3	0.2	0.1	$X_{PI} = .5417$	

$X_{PI}(1 - X_{PI}) = .2483$ $\quad$ $\sum_i X_{Pi}(1 - X_{Pi}) = 2.03$ $\quad$ $\hat{S}_i^2(X_{Pi}) = .0863$ $\quad$ $\hat{S}_p^2(X_{pI}) = .0729$

Coefficient α = KR-20 = .856 $\quad$ KR-21 = .747 $\quad$ $S_p^2(X_{pI}) = .0656$

Note: Uppercase *P* and *I* represent mean scores, *not* total scores.

Table 11.3. G Study and D Study for Random Effects $p \times i$ Design Using Guilford Data and Assuming $n_i = n_i' = 12$

Effect, Component, or Source	*df*	*SS*	*MS*	Estimated G Study Variance Component	D Study Sampling Frequency	Estimated D Study Variance Component
Persons (p)	9	7.875	.8750	$\hat{\sigma}^2(p) = .0625$	1	$\hat{\sigma}^2(p) = .0625$
Items (i)	11	9.492	.8629	$\hat{\sigma}^2(i) = .0737$	12	$\hat{\sigma}^2(I) = .0061$
Interaction (pi)	99	12.425	.1255	$\hat{\sigma}^2(pi) = .1255$	12	$\hat{\sigma}^2(pI) = .0105$
$\hat{\sigma}^2(\delta) = .0105$		$\widehat{E\rho}^2 = .856(5.95)$	$\hat{\Phi}(\lambda = .4) = .807(4.17)$		$\hat{\Phi}(\lambda = .7) = .817(4.47)$	
$\hat{\sigma}^2(\Delta) = .0166$		$\hat{\Phi} = .790(3.77)$	$\hat{\Phi}(\lambda = .5) = .754(3.06)$		$\hat{\Phi}(\lambda = .8) = .875(6.98)$	
$X_{PI} = .5417$			$\hat{\Phi}(\lambda = .6) = .760(3.16)$		$\hat{\Phi}(\lambda = .9) = .915(10.69)$	
$\hat{\sigma}^2(X_{PI}) = .0134$				$\hat{\Phi}(\lambda = X_{PI}) = .747(2.96)$		

Note: Numbers in parentheses following values for $\hat{\Phi}(\lambda)$ are the estimated signal/noise ratios. All estimates of $\sigma^2(X_{PI})$ and $\Phi(\lambda)$ assume $n_p = n_p' = 10$.

referenced test. It is the deviation score, $X_{pI} - \mu_I$, that carries the meaning, and this deviation score is to be interpreted as an estimate of $\mu_p - \mu$.

When X_{pI}, μ_p, and μ_I are expressed in terms of score effects (see equations 2, 3, and 5), one obtains

$$\delta_p = \mu_{pI}\tilde{} \tag{12}$$

with variance

$$\sigma^2(\delta) = \sigma^2(pI). \tag{13}$$

This is the error variance for norm-referenced interpretations of test data, and it is identical to the error variance incorporated in coefficients such as KR-20 and Cronbach's (1951) α, although the derivation of $\sigma^2(\delta)$ is based upon generalizability theory, not classical test theory.

For the illustrative data in Table 11.3, one can see that the estimate of $\sigma^2(\delta)$ is $\hat{\sigma}^2(pI) = 0.0105$. It is well known that the error variance in classical test theory is obtained by multiplying the observed variance by $1 - r$, where r is the reliability of the test. From Table 11.2, for these data, the observed variance is .0729, KR-20 is .856, and, therefore, the error variance is .0729 $(1 - .856) = .0105$, which is identical to $\hat{\sigma}^2(\delta)$.

The error variance $\sigma^2(\Delta)$. In norm-referenced testing, then, our interest is in observed *deviation* scores, $X_{pI} - \mu_I$, which are to be interpreted relative to universe *deviation* scores, $\mu_p - \mu$. In domain-referenced testing, however, our interest is in "the degree to which the student has attained criterion performance" (Glaser, 1963, p. 519), independent of the performance of other students. That is, we are *not* primarily interested in the relative ordering of examinees' universe scores; rather, we are interested in the difference between each examinee's universe score and some absolute standard. In this case, the error for a given examinee is

$$\Delta_{pI} = (X_{pI} - \lambda) - (\mu_p - \lambda) = X_{pI} - \mu_p, \tag{14}$$

where λ is some reference point. Here, no restrictions are placed upon the value of λ except that it be expressed as a proportion of items correct, to be consistent with the previously adopted convention of using mean scores rather than total scores. Usually λ is defined by the user, a priori, and in such cases it is common to speak about *mastery* interpretations, where λ is the mastery cut-off score. However, it will be shown that λ might also be expressed as a population parameter or sample statistic for certain more general domain-referenced interpretations.

When X_{pI} and μ_p in equation 14 are expressed in terms of score effects (see equations 2 and 3), one obtains

$$\Delta_{pI} = \mu_I\tilde{} + \mu_{pI}\tilde{} \tag{15}$$

with variance

$$\sigma^2(\Delta) = \sigma^2(I) + \sigma^2(pI). \tag{16}$$

This is the error variance for domain-referenced interpretations.

It is evident from equations 13 and 16 that $\sigma^2(\Delta)$ is always at least as large as $\sigma^2(\delta)$. For example, for the illustrative data $\hat{\sigma}^2(\Delta) = .0061 + .0105 = .0166$, which is greater than $\hat{\sigma}^2(\delta) = .0105$. Indeed, the difference between $\sigma^2(\Delta)$ and $\sigma^2(\delta)$ is simply $\sigma^2(I)$. Therefore, the two-error variances are equal only when μ_I is a constant for all instances of the testing procedure. The variance component for the main effect for items, $\sigma^2(I)$, reflects differences in the mean score (in the population) for different samples of items. If one is interested only in differences among examinee universe scores, as in norm-referenced testing, then any effect that is a constant for all examinees does not contribute to the error variance. However, for domain-referenced testing, we are interested in the absolute magnitude of examinee universe scores, or the magnitude compared to some externally defined cut-off score. In this case, fluctuations in mean scores for samples of items *do* contribute to error variance.

From another point of view, since all persons take all items for the $p \times i$ design, the effect μ_I- in equation 2 contributes to all examinees' observed scores in the same way. For domain-referenced testing, however, this does not eliminate the item effect as a source of error. For example, if one happens to select an especially easy set of items from the universe of items, the estimates of μ_p and $\mu_p - \lambda$ will tend to be too high. This component of error is taken into account in $\sigma^2(\Delta)$, but not in $\sigma^2(\delta)$.

Although $\sigma^2(\Delta)$ cannot be obtained directly from classical test theory, Brennan and Kane (1977 b) have shown that, for dichotomous data, $\hat{\sigma}^2(\Delta)$ is related to Lord's (1957) formula for the standard error of measurement for a person's score, which in my notation is

$$\hat{\sigma}(\Delta | X_{pI}) = \sqrt{\frac{X_{pI}(1 - X_{pI})}{n_i - 1}}. \tag{17}$$

In effect, $\hat{\sigma}^2(\Delta)$ is the average over persons of the square of Lord's standard error of measurement. The reader can verify this result for the data in Table 11.2. It is also possible to show that $\hat{\sigma}^2(\Delta)$ is an estimate of the generic error variance discussed in Lord and Novick (1968).

Confidence intervals. $\sigma^2(\Delta)$ and $\sigma^2(\delta)$ are discussed extensively by Cronbach et al. (1972), but they do not directly consider $\sigma^2(\Delta)$ in the context of domain-referenced *mastery* testing. Rather, they state:

Classical theory, assuming uniform condition means ($\mu_I = \mu$), ignores the distinction between Δ and δ. Lord (1962) pointed out that condition means are unlikely to be equal when tests are not carefully equated. Lord showed that the variance of the within-person error Δ, over nonequivalent tests, differs from the error variance calculated by classical formulas. . . . A confidence interval of the conventional sort has to be defined in terms of $\sigma(\Delta)$, not $\sigma(\delta)$; only if all tests (or other procedures) yield strictly equal means is it appropriate to use $\sigma(\delta)$. (p. 82)

When Cronbach et al. (1972) speak of a "confidence interval of the conventional sort," they are speaking in the context of using the observed score, X_{pI}, as an estimate of the universe score, μ_p. In this context it is clear from equation 14 that the error variance for a confidence interval is indeed $\sigma^2(\Delta)$. More generally, $\sigma^2(\Delta)$ is the appropriate error variance for a confidence interval when $X_{pI} - \lambda$ is used as an estimate of $\mu_p - \lambda$, independent of the value of λ. However, if the observed score under consideration is the *deviation* score, $X_{pI} - \mu_I$, which is used as an estimate of $\mu_p - \mu$, then $\sigma^2(\delta)$ is the appropriate error variance for a confidence interval. One might say, therefore, that for the score of a *single* examinee on a test, $\sigma^2(\Delta)$ is the appropriate error variance for confidence intervals involving domain-referenced interpretations, whereas $\sigma^2(\delta)$ is the appropriate error variance for confidence intervals involving norm-referenced interpretations.

For the illustrative data in Tables 11.2 and 11.3, a 68 percent confidence interval for the eighth examinee with a score of .75 would extend from $[.75 - \hat{\sigma}(\Delta)]$ to $[.75 + \hat{\sigma}(\Delta)]$. Since $\hat{\sigma}^2(\Delta)$ is .0166, $\sigma(\Delta)$ equals .1288, and this confidence interval is approximately .62 to .88. Alternatively, one could use Lord's standard error of measurement in equation 17 to establish a confidence interval for any examinee with a score of .75. Using equation 17, $\hat{\sigma}(\Delta | X_{PI}) = \sqrt{.75\,(.25)/11} = .1306$, and a 68 percent confidence interval again extends from .62 to .88, approximately. In this case, the confidence interval based upon Lord's standard error of measurement is virtually identical to the interval based upon $\hat{\sigma}(\Delta)$. In general, however, the length of such intervals will differ somewhat, because Lord's standard error of measurement varies for examinees with different scores.

It should be noted that in order to attach a probability statement to a confidence interval, it is necessary to make some distributional assumption. For such purposes, it is traditional to assume a normal distribution, although binomial and compound binomial assumptions are sometimes made, especially in domain-referenced testing. As pointed out previously, these distributional assumptions are not an integral part of generalizability theory, although they are required for the use of error variances in establishing confidence intervals.

The line of reasoning discussed here for identifying the appropriate error variance for a confidence interval for a single examinee's score can be extended to a consideration of confidence intervals for the difference between the scores for two different examinees on two different tests, the difference between the scores for the same examinee on two different tests, and the difference between the scores for two different examinees, on the same test. Table 11.4 summarizes results reported by Brennan (1978) for each of these three cases and for the two different types of error, Δ and δ.

The reader is cautioned *not* to infer from Table 11.4 that all such comparisons are always meaningful or useful. Also, if a measure of change is re-

Table 11.4. Error Variances for Simple Difference Scores

Examinees	Tests[a]	Error is Δ for an Individual Examinee's Score	Error is δ for an Individual Examinee's Score
Different	Different	$2\sigma^2(\Delta)$	$2\sigma^2(\delta)$
Same	Different	$2\sigma^2(\Delta)$	$2\sigma^2(\delta)$
Different	Same	$2\sigma^2(\delta)$	$2\sigma^2(\delta)$

[a] Different tests are, more specifically, different random samples of the same number of items from the same universe of items.

quired, simple difference scores are seldom appropriate (see Cronbach et al., 1972). However, Table 11.4 does highlight one important fact, namely, that $2\ \sigma^2(\delta)$ [*not* $2\ \sigma^2(\Delta)$] is the appropriate estimate of error variance for two different examinees on the *same* test, even when an *individual* examinee's score is to be interpreted in a domain-referenced manner. This result may seem anomalous, but it is consistent with a similar result reported by Lord and Novick (1968, pp. 180–184), who refer to $\sigma^2(\Delta)$ as "generic" error variance. Furthermore, this result is quite reasonable when one realizes that the magnitude of this difference score reflects the *relative* standing of two examinees on the same test. Indeed, such a comparison is *not* properly a domain-referenced consideration.

Indices of Dependability for Domain-referenced Tests

Using generalizability theory it is possible to define two indices of dependability for domain-referenced tests. These indices can be given interpretations that have some similarities with interpretations of classical reliability coefficients and generalizability coefficients. However, since indices of dependability for domain-referenced tests are indeed different from analogous indices for norm-referenced tests, I always refer to domain-referenced indices as "indices of dependability" and to norm-referenced indices as "reliability coefficients" (based on classical test theory) or "generalizability coefficients" (based on generalizability theory). A principal difference is that the domain-referenced indices discussed here incorporate $\sigma^2(\Delta)$, while the norm-referenced coefficients incorporate $\sigma^2(\delta)$. I begin with a brief discussion of norm-referenced coefficients to enable subsequent comparisons of indices of dependability with such coefficients.

Norm-referenced coefficients. Cronbach et al. (1972) define a generalizability coefficient for the $p \times i$ design as

$$\mathcal{E}\rho^2 = \frac{\mathcal{E}_p(\mu_p - \mu)^2}{\mathcal{E}_I\ \mathcal{E}_p(X_{pI} - \mu_I)^2}\ . \tag{18}$$

The numerator is simply the universe score variance, $\sigma^2(p)$, and the denominator is called the *expected* observed score variance (see Figure 11.1E):

$$\mathcal{E}\sigma^2(X_{pI}) = \sigma^2(p) + \sigma^2(\delta).$$

In terms of variance components, therefore,

$$\mathcal{E}\rho^2 = \frac{\sigma^2(p)}{\sigma^2(p) + \sigma^2(\delta)} \,. \tag{19}$$

Technically, $\mathcal{E}\rho^2$ is an intraclass correlation coefficient.

The generalizability coefficient in equation 19 is approximately equal to the expected value of the correlation between randomly selected instances of the testing procedure, where the scores correlated are *deviation* scores of the form $X_{pI} - \mu_I$. (Recall that such deviation scores are inherent in the definition of δ in equation 11.) Also, it is well known that, when the variance components in equation 19 are replaced by their estimates, $\mathcal{E}\rho^2$ is identical to Cronbach's (1951) coefficient α, and to KR-20 when items are scored dichotomously. Therefore, this simple generalizability coefficient is interpretable in much the same way as these classical estimates of reliability, even though the derivation of $\mathcal{E}\rho^2$ is based on the model equation 2, *not* on the classical test theory model.

The generalizability coefficient $\mathcal{E}\rho^2$, can also be expressed as a simple function of the signal/noise ratio:

$$\psi(g) = S(g)/N(g) = \sigma^2(p)/\sigma^2(\delta), \tag{20}$$

where g is used to distinguish this ratio from corresponding ratios for domain-referenced interpretations discussed later. Given equation 20, it is easy to show that

$$\begin{aligned} \mathcal{E}\rho^2 &= \psi(g)/[1 + \psi(g)]. \\ &= S(g)/[S(g) + N(g)]. \end{aligned}$$

The signal/noise ratio $\psi(g)$ is itself a useful alternative coefficient for norm-referenced interpretations. The concept arises naturally in discussing communications systems where the "signal to noise ratio compares the strength of the transmission to the strength of the interference" (Cronbach & Gleser, 1964, p. 468). The signal is intended to characterize the magnitude of the desired discriminations. Noise characterizes the effect of extraneous variables in blurring these discriminations. If the signal is large compared to the noise, the intended discriminations are easily made. If the signal is weak compared to the noise, the intended discriminations may be completely lost. In norm-referenced testing, the signal, $\sigma^2(p)$, is a function of the magnitude of the intended discriminations $\mu_p - \mu$. These intended discriminations reflect the tolerance or sensitivity requirements that must be met if the measurement procedure is to achieve its intended purpose. The noise, $\sigma^2(\delta)$, reflects the *degree of precision*, or the magnitude of the errors that arise in the testing procedure. The signal/noise ratio is, therefore, a measure of the *relative precision* of the testing procedure.

An index of dependability for domain-referenced mastery interpretations. In my treatment of error variance for domain-referenced interpretations, I noted that the differences we want to detect are of the form $\mu_p - \lambda$, and the observed differences are of the form $X_{pI} - \lambda$, where λ is a reference point, or mastery cut-off score. As shown in the preceding discussion, for a norm-reference test the corresponding differences $\mu_p - \mu$ and $X_{pI} - \mu_I$ provide a basis for defining the generalizability coefficient, $\mathcal{E}\rho^2$, equation 19. In a similar manner, an index of dependability for domain-referenced mastery testing can be defined by substituting λ for μ and μ_I in equation 19. The resulting index is

$$\Phi(\lambda) = \frac{\mathcal{E}_p(\mu_p - \lambda)^2}{\mathcal{E}_I\,\mathcal{E}_p(X_{pI} - \lambda)^2}\,, \tag{21}$$

and, in terms of variance components,

$$\Phi(\lambda) = \frac{\sigma^2(p) + (\mu - \lambda)^2}{\sigma^2(p) + (\mu - \lambda)^2 + \sigma^2(\Delta)}\,. \tag{22}$$

Equation 22 was first derived by Brennan and Kane (1977a), who denoted this index "M(C)." Since the derivation is rather involved, it is not repeated here. I simply note that the derivation relies heavily on the fact that the numerator and denominator of equation 21 are expected squared deviations, rather than variances. In this sense, the derivation of $\Phi(\lambda)$ in terms of variance components is similar to the derivation of Livingston's (1972) coefficient. Indeed, it can be shown that equation 21 is identical to Livingston's coefficient when $\sigma^2(\Delta)$ equals $\sigma^2(\delta)$—i.e., when $\sigma^2(I)$ is zero. This is consistent with the fact that Livingston's coefficient is based on the assumption of classically parallel tests, which precludes distinguishing between $\sigma^2(\Delta)$ and $\sigma^2(\delta)$. By contrast, the development of $\Phi(\lambda)$ is based on the assumption of *randomly* parallel tests.

Several characteristics of $\Phi(\lambda)$ are evident from equation 22. First and most importantly, $\Phi(\lambda)$ incorporates the error variance $\sigma^2(\Delta)$, rather than the error variance $\sigma^2(\delta)$ in $\mathcal{E}\rho^2$ (equation 19). Second $\Phi(\lambda)$ will be different for different values of λ. Third, $\Phi(\lambda)$ has an upper limit of one. Fourth, the numerator of $\Phi(\lambda)$ is dependent upon both the universe score variance, $\sigma^2(p)$, *and* the squared distance of the population mean, μ, from the reference point or cut-off score, λ. Clearly $\Phi(\lambda)$ can be positive even when there is *no* variance among examinee universe scores. Suppose, for example, that $\sigma^2(\Delta)$ is positive and all examinees have identical "high" universe scores relative to λ. In this case, $\Phi(\lambda)$ will be positive, reflecting the fact that it is relatively easy to determine correctly whether or not examinees are above the cut-off score. By contrast, in this case, $\mathcal{E}\rho^2$ would be zero.

$\Phi(\lambda)$ can be interpreted in terms of signal and noise concepts in a manner analogous to one interpretation of $\mathcal{E}\rho^2$ discussed previously. In particular, Brennan and Kane (1977b) show that the signal/noise ratio for domain-referenced interpretations, d, is

$$\psi(d) = S(d)/N(d) = [\sigma^2(p) + (\mu - \lambda)^2]/\sigma^2(\Delta), \tag{23}$$

and, in terms of this ratio,

$$\begin{aligned}\Phi(\lambda) &= \psi(d)/[1 + \psi(d)].\\ &= S(d)/[S(d) + N(d)].\end{aligned}$$

Note, in particular, that for domain-referenced interpretations the noise is $\sigma^2(\Delta)$, *not* $\sigma^2(\delta)$, and, when such interpretations are made with respect to a mastery cut-off score, λ, the signal is $\sigma^2(p) + (\mu - \lambda)^2$.

It is clear from equation 23 that the signal/noise ratio for a domain-referenced mastery test, $\psi(d)$, can be large, even if $\sigma^2(p)$ is zero, provided $(\mu - \lambda)^2$ is large relative to $\sigma^2(\Delta)$. In other words, this signal/noise ratio will be relatively large whenever the detection of the signal, $\mu_p - \lambda$, is relatively easy, or equivalently, whenever it is easy to make correct classifications of randomly selected persons. In short, the signal/noise ratio, $\psi(d)$, is a measure of the *relative precision* of a domain-referenced mastery testing procedure, and the index $\Phi(\lambda)$ is a simple monotonic function of $\psi(d)$.

Since $\Phi(\lambda)$ and $\psi(d)$ are monotonically related, the choice between them (if such a choice is required) should be made on the basis of convenience or interpretability. In this regard, the reader should note that, unlike $\Phi(\lambda)$, the signal/noise ratio $\psi(d)$ does not have an upper limit of one. For example, when $\Phi(\lambda)$ is .85. $\psi(d)$ is .85/.15, or 5.67. Whether or not this characteristic of $\psi(d)$, and other signal/noise ratios, is desirable depends upon one's perspective.

A general-purpose index of dependability for domain-referenced interpretations. It is evident from equation 21 that $\Phi(\lambda)$ achieves its lower limit when λ equals μ, the grand mean in the *population* of persons and the *universe* of items. That is, the lower limit of $\Phi(\lambda)$ is simply

$$\Phi = \frac{\sigma^2(p)}{\sigma^2(p) + \sigma^2(\Delta)}\,. \tag{24}$$

In comparing Φ with $\mathcal{E}\rho^2$ one can see that, since $\sigma^2(\Delta)$ is always at least as large as $\sigma^2(\delta)$, the index of dependability Φ must also be less than or equal to the generalizability coefficient $\mathcal{E}\rho^2$. Intuitively, this is a reasonable characteristic of Φ, since domain-referenced interpretations of "absolute" scores are more "stringent" than norm-referenced interpretations of "relative" scores.

The index Φ can also be interpreted in terms of signal/noise concepts in a manner analogous to the interpretation of $\Phi(\lambda)$. For Φ, the noise is still $\sigma^2(\Delta)$, but the signal is $\sigma^2(p)$, resulting in the signal/noise ratio $\sigma^2(p)/\sigma^2(\Delta)$. In this case, the signal reflects universe score differences among persons, independent of any cut-off score. The reasonableness of such a definition of signal for a domain-referenced test may be clarified by the following argument:

> In some cases, a person's score on a domain-referenced test may be used as a descriptive statistic. In other cases, the test may be designed to serve several types of decisions. Under either of these cases, it would be useful to have a general index of the precision of the test, in addition to any indices associated with specific decision procedures. If a particular decision procedure is not specified, the value to be assigned to the signal, or tolerance, must be somewhat vague. However, a natural and useful definition is provided by the magnitudes of the differences that do exist in the population with which the instrument is used. There is strong procedent for this choice in the traditions of physical measurement. General-purpose instruments for measuring length, for example, are typically evaluted by their ability to detect differences of the order of magnitude of those encountered in some area of practice. Thus, rulers are used in carpentry and verniers are used in machine shops. (Brennan & Kane, 1977b, pp. 616–617)

The indices $\Phi(\lambda)$ and Φ as agreement statistics. Previous sections have discussed various distinctions between the domain-referenced indices of dependability, $\Phi(\lambda)$ and Φ, as well as distinctions between these indices and more traditional norm-referenced coefficients. A framework for interpreting $\Phi(\lambda)$ and Φ, and for identifying similarities and differences among these indices and others, has been provided by Kane and Brennan (1980). They discuss two general agreement coefficients, one of which involves a correction for chance agreement. These two general coefficients are

$$\theta = \frac{A}{A_m} \tag{25}$$

and

$$\theta_c = \frac{A - A_c}{A_m - A_c}, \tag{26}$$

where A is observed agreement, A_m is maximum agreement, and A_c is chance agreement. Under very weak assumptions about A, A_m, and A_c, it is possible to show that both coefficients have an upper limit of one.

In general, θ indicates how closely the scores for any examinee can be expected to agree on randomly sampled instances of a testing procedure. By contrast, θ_c indicates how closely such scores can be expected to agree when the contribution of chance agreement is removed. To specify either of these coefficients completely, however, one must define an appropriate agreement function.

For domain-referenced interpretations, one such agreement function is

$$d = (X_{pI} - \lambda)(X_{qJ} - \lambda),$$

where p and q are persons and I and J are sets of items or tests. Briefly, expected agreement (A) is defined by Kane and Brennan (1980) as the expected value of d when p equals q; maximum agreement (A_m) is defined as the expected value of d when p equals q *and* I equals J; and chance agreement (A_c) is defined as the expected value of d for different persons (p and q) *and* for different samples of items (I and J). Given these definitions, Kane and Brennan (1980) derive the results presented in Table 11.5. Note in particular that the agreement coefficient $\theta(d)$ is *identical* to $\Phi(\lambda)$ and the agreement coefficient corrected for chance, $\theta_c(d)$, is *identical* to Φ.

These results imply that the two indices, $\Phi(\lambda)$ and Φ, address different questions about dependability. In general, $\Phi(\lambda)$ indicates how closely, in terms of the agreement function (d), the scores for any examinee can be expected to agree. Φ indicates how closely (again, in terms of the agreement function, d) the two scores for an examinee can be expected to agree, with the contribution of chance agreement *removed*. The index $\Phi(\lambda)$, therefore, characterizes the dependability of decisions, or estimates, based on the testing procedure. The magnitude of $\Phi(\lambda)$ depends, in part, on chance agreement; it may be greater than zero even when decisions based on the testing procedure are no more dependable than the decisions based on marginal probabilities in the population. The index Φ characterizes the contribution of the testing procedure to the dependability of the decisions over what would be expected on the basis of chance agreement. $\Phi(\lambda)$ provides an estimate of the dependability of the decisions based on the testing procedure; Φ provides an estimate of the *contribution* of the testing procedure to the dependability of such decisions. The two indices provide answers to different questions. The issue is not which of these indices is better, but rather which is appropriate in a given context.

Table 11.5 also indicates that the loss, defined in general as

$$L = A_m - A,$$

is $\sigma^2(\Delta)$ for the domain-referenced agreement function d. In effect, therefore, depending upon the perspective one chooses, for domain-referenced interpretations $\sigma^2(\Delta)$ can be interpreted in terms of error, noise, or loss in the measurement procedure.

The approach outlined can also be applied to other agreement functions. For example, Table 11.5 shows that, for the agreement function

$$g = (X_{pI} - \mu_I)(X_{qJ} - \mu_J),$$

both θ and θ_c are identical to the generalizability coefficient, $\mathcal{E}\rho^2$, with the loss, L, being $\sigma^2(\delta)$. In effect, $\mathcal{E}\rho^2$ incorporates its own correction for chance agreement, and $\sigma^2(\delta)$ can be interpreted in terms of error, noise, or loss in a norm-referenced measurement procedure.

Both the d and g agreement functions are consistent with squared-error loss approaches to measurement error. Others have suggested using a threshold loss or agreement function for domain-referenced interpretations (see Subkoviak, chapter 10). As indicated in Table 11.5, for the threshold agreement function, t, the coefficient θ is simply

$$\theta(t) = \Sigma \pi_{ii},$$

Table 11.5. Coefficients for Different Agreement Functions

Agreement Function	Parameters	Agreement Coefficients
Domain-referenced:		
$d = (X_{pI} - \lambda)(X_{qJ} - \lambda)$	$A(d) = (\mu - \lambda)^2 + \sigma^2(p)$ $A_m(d) = (\mu - \lambda)^2 + \sigma^2(p) + \sigma^2(\Delta)$ $A_c(d) = (\mu - \lambda)^2$ $L(d) = \sigma^2(\Delta)$	$\theta(d) = \frac{(\mu - \lambda)^2 + \sigma^2(p)}{(\mu - \lambda)^2 + \sigma^2(p) + \sigma^2(\Delta)}$ $\theta_c(d) = \frac{\sigma^2(p)}{\sigma^2(p) + \sigma^2(\Delta)}$
Norm-referenced:		
$g = (X_{pI} - \mu_I)(X_{qJ} - \mu_J)$	$A(g) = \sigma^2(p)$ $A_m(g) = \sigma^2(p) + \sigma^2(\delta)$ $A_c(g) = 0$ $L(g) = \sigma^2(\delta)$	$\theta(g) = \theta_c(g) = \frac{\sigma^2(p)}{\sigma^2(p) + \sigma^2(\delta)}$
Threshold:		
$t = 1$ if X_{pI} and X_{qJ} result in same classification; 0 otherwise	$A(t) = \Sigma\pi_{ii}$ $A_m(t) = 1$ $A_c(t) = \Sigma\pi_i^2$ $L(t) = \Sigma\pi_{ij}(i \neq j)$	$\theta(t) = \Sigma\pi_{ii}$ $\theta_c(t) = \frac{\Sigma\pi_{ii} - \Sigma\pi_i^2}{1 - \Sigma\pi_i^2}$

Note: Here p and q are different persons; I and J are different random samples of items.

the proportion of persons consistently classified as masters or nonmasters on two randomly selected instances of the testing procedure. When a correction-for-chance agreement is incorporated, the resulting coefficient is

$$\theta_c(t) = \frac{\Sigma \pi_{ii} - \Sigma \pi_i^2}{1 - \Sigma \pi_i^2}$$

where $\Sigma \pi_i^2$ is the sum of the squared marginal proportions of masters and nonmasters in the population. Under the assumption of randomly parallel tests, $\theta_c(t)$ is identical to Cohen's (1960) coefficient kappa. From this perspective, therefore, the choice between Φ and Cohen's kappa as indices of dependability is primarily a choice between two different agreement functions. This issue is discussed more fully later.

Perspectives on indices of dependability. Table 11.6 summarizes three perspectives that have been discussed as a basis for defining and/or interpreting indices of dependability for domain-referenced tests. One perspective involves defining these indices in a manner analogous to the definition of a generalizability coefficient; another is based upon a consideration of agreement coefficients; the third uses signal/noise concepts. Each of these perspectives has two principal features in common. First, the error variance, noise power, or squared-error loss is always $\sigma^2(\Delta)$.

Second, there are *two* distinct indices that can be derived and interpreted, and these two indices address different issues of measurement dependability for domain-referenced tests. In the terminology used by Hambleton et al. (1978) to describe their trichotomy of types of reliability, the index $\Phi(\lambda)$ addresses the "reliability of criterion-referenced test scores," and index Φ is associated with the "reliability of domain score estimates."

Estimating Indices of Dependability for Domain-referenced Tests

The previous section discussed definitions and interpretations of the two indices of dependability for domain-referenced tests, $\Phi(\lambda)$ in equation 22 and Φ in equation 24. In this section I consider *estimates* of these indices.

The $p \times i$ design. Brennan (1979) provides a computer program for performing generalizability analyses with the $p \times i$ design. This program is quite general in that it provides, among other things, estimates of variance components and indices of dependability for models involving sampling of items from either an infinite or a finite universe of items. Here, however, interest is restricted to a consideration of the random effects model, which assumes sampling from an essentially infinite universe of items. For this model, the formulas in Table 11.1 can be used to estimate variance components, and using these estimates, the formulas in Table 11.7 can be used to estimate indices of dependability.

For the most part, the *estimation* of the two indices of dependability for domain-referenced tests, $\Phi(\lambda)$ and Φ, involves a straightforward replacement of variance components with their estimates, as indicated in the first two columns of Table 11.7. There is, however, one exception to this rule. An unbi-

Table 11.6. Indices of Dependability for Domain-referenced Interpretations Given Random Effects $p \times i$ Design

Approach	Indices	Parameters
Generalizability theory	$\Phi(\lambda) = \dfrac{\mathcal{E}_p(\mu_p - \lambda)^2}{\mathcal{E}_I\mathcal{E}_p(X_{pI} - \lambda)^2}$ $\Phi = \dfrac{\mathcal{E}_p(\mu_p - \mu)^2}{\mathcal{E}_I\mathcal{E}_p(X_{pI} - \mu)^2}$	$\mathcal{E}_p(\mu_p - \lambda)^2 = \sigma^2(p) + (\mu - \lambda)^2$ $\mathcal{E}_I\mathcal{E}_p(X_{pI} - \lambda)^2 = \sigma^2(p) + (\mu - \lambda)^2 + \sigma^2(\Delta)$ $\mathcal{E}_p(\mu_p - \mu)^2 = \sigma^2(p)$ $\mathcal{E}_I\mathcal{E}_p(X_{pI} - \mu)^2 = \sigma^2(p) + \sigma^2(\Delta)$
Agreement function: $(X_{pI} - \lambda)(X_{qJ} - \lambda)$	$\theta(d) = \dfrac{A(d)}{A_m(d)}$ $\theta_c(d) = \dfrac{A(d) - A_c(d)}{A_m(d) - A_c(d)}$	$A(d) = \sigma^2(p) + (\mu - \lambda)^2$ $A_m(d) = \sigma^2(p) + (\mu - \lambda)^2 + \sigma^2(\Delta)$ $A_c(d) = (\mu - \lambda)^2$ $L(d) = A_m(d) - A(d) = \sigma^2(\Delta)$
Signal/noise ratios	$\psi(d) = \dfrac{S(d)}{N(d)}$ $\psi_c(d) = \dfrac{S_c(d)}{N(d)}$	$S(d) = \sigma^2(p) + (\mu - \lambda)^2$ $S_c(d) = \sigma^2(p)$ $N(d) = \sigma^2(\Delta)$

Note: $\Phi(\lambda) = \theta(d) = \psi(d)/[1 + \psi(d)]$; $\Phi = \theta_c(d) = \psi_c(d)/[1 + \psi_c(d)]$; and $\sigma^2(\Delta) = L(d) = N(d)$.

Table 11.7. Estimates of Indices of Dependability

Estimate	In Terms of Estimated Variance Components	In Terms of Sample Statistics for a Full-Length Test of Dichotomously Scored Items
$\hat{\Phi}(\lambda) =$	$\dfrac{\hat{\sigma}^2(p) + (X_{PI} - \lambda)^2 - \hat{\sigma}^2(X_{PI})}{\hat{\sigma}^2(p) + (X_{PI} - \lambda)^2 - \hat{\sigma}^2(X_{PI}) + \hat{\sigma}^2(\Delta)}$	$= 1 - \dfrac{1}{n_i - 1}\left[\dfrac{X_{PI}(1 - X_{PI}) - S^2(X_{pI})}{(X_{PI} - \lambda)^2 + S^2(X_{pI})}\right]$
$\hat{\Phi}(\lambda = X_{PI}) =$	$\dfrac{\hat{\sigma}^2(p) - \hat{\sigma}^2(X_{PI})}{\hat{\sigma}^2(p) - \hat{\sigma}^2(X_{PI}) + \hat{\sigma}^2(\Delta)}$	$= \text{KR-21} = 1 - \dfrac{1}{n_i - 1}\left[\dfrac{X_{PI}(1 - X_{PI}) - S^2(X_{pI})}{S^2(X_{pI})}\right]$
$\hat{\Phi} =$	$\dfrac{\hat{\sigma}^2(p)}{\hat{\sigma}^2(p) + \hat{\sigma}^2(\Delta)}$	
$\widehat{\mathcal{E}\rho}^2 =$	$\dfrac{\hat{\sigma}^2(p)}{\hat{\sigma}^2(p) + \hat{\sigma}^2(\delta)}$	$= \text{KR-20} = 1 - \dfrac{1}{n_i - 1}\left[\dfrac{\sum_i (X_{Pi})(1 - X_{Pi})/n_i - S^2(X_{pI})}{S^2(X_{pI})}\right]$

Note: $\hat{\sigma}^2(X_{PI}) = \hat{\sigma}^2(p)/n_p' + \hat{\sigma}^2(i)/n_i' + \hat{\sigma}^2(pi)/n_p'n_i'$.

ased estimate of $(\mu - \lambda)^2$ is *not* obtained by replacing μ, the grand mean, with X_{PI}, the mean over the *sample* of n_p persons and n_i items. Rather, Brennan and Kane (1977a) show that an unbiased estimate of $(\mu - \lambda)^2$ is $(X_{PI} - \lambda)^2 - \hat{\sigma}^2(X_{PI})$, where $\hat{\sigma}^2(X_{PI})$ is the estimated variability of the sample mean. In terms of variance components,

$$\hat{\sigma}^2(X_{PI}) = \hat{\sigma}^2(p)/n_p' + \hat{\sigma}^2(i)/n_i' + \hat{\sigma}^2(pi)/n_p'n_i'.$$

Table 11.7 also reports the estimate for $\mathcal{E}\rho^2$ in terms of variance components, as well as formulas in terms of sample statistics, when items are scored dichotomously. I have already pointed out that KR-20 estimates $\mathcal{E}\rho^2$ when items are scored dichotomously. By contrast, Table 11.7 indicates that KR-21 estimates $\Phi(\lambda)$ when λ equals X_{PI}, the mean for the same of n_p persons and n_i items. This relationship is proved by Brennan (1977). The proof is quite long, but the reader can verify the equality of the two formulas for $\hat{\Phi}(\lambda = X_{PI})$ for the data reported in Tables 11.2 and 11.3. In effect, when items are scored dichotomously, $\hat{\Phi}(\lambda)$ can be no less than KR-21. This fact provides a useful basis for considering the domain-referenced dependability of scores on tests that have been documented with classical reliability estimates only. Similarly, when only sample statistics are available, one can use the second formula in the first row to estimate $\Phi(\lambda)$, for any cut-off score λ. For reasons discussed later, however, it is strongly suggested that whenever possible one report variance components, and estimate indices of dependability, in terms of variance components.

Using the formulas in Table 11.7, the reader can verify the numerical results for the indices of dependability in Table 11.3, based on the illustrative data in Table 11.2. For example, using the estimated variance components in Table 11.3 with the first formula for $\hat{\Phi}(\lambda)$ in Table 11.7, and assuming that λ is .7, one obtains

$$\hat{\Phi}(\lambda = .7) = \frac{.0625 + (.5417 - .7)^2 - .0134}{.0625 + (.5417 - .7)^2 - .0134 + .0166} = .817.$$

Alternatively, since the data in Table 11.2 are dichotomous, one can use the second formula in Table 11.7 with the sample statistics reported in Table 11.2 to obtain

$$\hat{\Phi}(\lambda = .7) = 1 - \frac{1}{11}\left[\frac{.5417(1 - .5417) - .0656}{(.5417 - .7)^2 + .0656}\right] = .817.$$

In a similar manner, the reader can use either of the formulas in the second row of Table 11.7 to verify that $\hat{\Phi}(\lambda = X_{PI})$ is .747, the value of KR-21 reported by Guilford (1954) for the data in Table 11.2. Also, using the formula for $\hat{\Phi}$ in Table 11.6, one obtains

$$\hat{\Phi} = \frac{.0625}{.0625 + .0166} = .790,$$

and using the formula for $\widehat{\mathcal{E}\rho^2}$ one obtains

$$\widehat{\mathcal{E}\rho^2} = \frac{.0625}{.0625 + .0105} = .856.$$

These results illustrate that

$$\hat{\Phi}(\lambda = X_{PI}) \leq \hat{\Phi} \leq \widehat{\mathcal{E}\rho^2},$$

or, when items are scored dichotomously, as they are in this case,

$$\text{KR-21} \leq \hat{\Phi} \leq \text{KR-20}.$$

Table 11.3 also indicates that $\hat{\Phi}(\lambda)$ decreases as λ moves from zero to the sample mean and increases as λ moves from the sample mean to one. This fact is displayed graphically by the dashed line in Figure 11.2. Figure 11.2 also reports estimated values of $\Phi(\lambda)$ for $n_i' = 5$, 10, 15, and 20 items. In effect, Figure 11.2 graphically suggests one of the distinctions in generalizability theory between a G study and a D study. For these illustrative data one can view the G study (or " generalizability" study) in terms of the actual $n_i =$ 12 items in Table 11.2. Some decision maker, however, may be interested in a D study (or "decision" study) involving a different sample of n_i' items where n_i' need not equal n_i. It is for this reason that Table 11.1 distinguishes between n_i and n_i'.

Figure 11.2 was developed using the G study and D study variance components and other results reported in Table 11.8. From Table 11.8 and Figure 11.2 it is evident that increasing the number of items sampled, n_i', has no effect on the universe score variance, $\hat{\sigma}^2(p)$, but increasing n_i' results in decreasing $\hat{\sigma}^2(I)$, $\hat{\sigma}^2(pI)$, $\hat{\sigma}^2(\delta)$, and $\hat{\sigma}^2(\Delta)$. Furthermore, these decreases in $\hat{\sigma}^2(\Delta)$ cause the indices of dependability $\hat{\Phi}(\lambda)$ and $\hat{\Phi}$ to increase.

The i:p design. Another way in which G studies and D studies can differ is in terms of the data collection design. Until now, we have implicitly assumed that both the G study and the D study use the crossed design, $p \times i$. We will continue to assume that variance components have been *estimated* from the crossed design, but now we will assume that the D study employs a design in which each person is administered a different random sample of n_i' items. This design is denoted $i{:}p$, where the colon is read "nested within."

Suppose, for example, that as a result of some G study, estimated variance components are available for the $p \times i$ design, but decisions are to be made based upon administering different random samples of n_i' items to each examinee. This frequently occurs in computer-assisted test construction (Lippey, 1974) or computer-generated repeatable testing (Lord, 1977). Under these circumstances, the linear model for item scores in the D study is

$$X_{i:p} = \mu + \mu_{p^\sim} + \mu_{i:p^\sim}, \tag{27}$$

where experimental error is confounded with the item effect $\mu_{i:p^\sim}$. The model for mean scores over n_i' items is obtained by substituting I for i everywhere in

Figure 11.2. Estimates of $\Phi(\lambda)$ for various numbers of items based on Guilford (1954) data

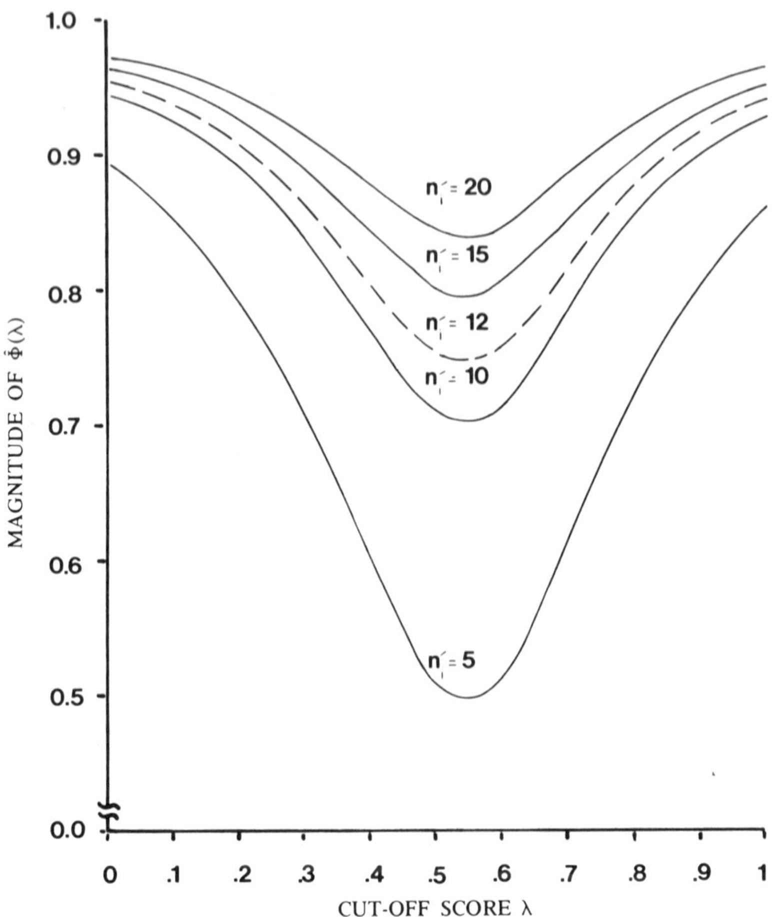

equation 27. Cronbach et al. (1972) discuss the *i:p* D study design extensively, and Kane and Brennan (1980) extend their discussion to considerations in domain-referenced testing. Here, I simply summarize some of the more important results.

In comparing the *i:p* design in equation 27 with the $p \times i$ design in equation 1, one can see that the effect for items nested within persons, $\mu_{i:p}$~, in the *i:p* design represents the confounding of μ_i~ and μ_{pi}~ in the $p \times i$ design. Also, the expected value, over persons, of the observed score for the *i:p* design equals μ, the grand mean in the *universe* of items, but for the $p \times i$ design, this expected value equals μ_I, the mean for the *sample* of n_i items.

Table 11.8. D Studies for Random Effects $p \times i$ Design Using Guilford Data for $n_i' = 5, 10, 15, 20$

Effect, Component, or Source	Estimated G Study Variance Component	D Study Variance Component			
		$n_i' = 5$	$n_i' = 10$	$n_i' = 15$	$n_i' = 20$
Persons (p)	.0625	.0625	.0625	.0625	.0625
Items (i)	.0737	.0147	.0074	.0049	.0037
Interaction (pi)	.1255	.0251	.0126	.0084	.0063
$X_{PI} = .5417$	$\hat{\sigma}^2(\delta) =$	.0251	.0126	.0084	.0063
	$\hat{\sigma}^2(\Delta) =$	.0398	.0200	.0133	.0100
	$\hat{\sigma}^2(X_{PI}) =$	.0235	.0149	.0120	.0106
	$\widehat{\mathcal{E}\rho}^2 =$	.714	.832	.882	.908
	$\hat{\Phi} =$	.611	.758	.825	.862
	$\hat{\Phi}(\lambda = X_{PI}) =$	.495	.704	.792	.838
	$\hat{\Phi}(\lambda = .7) =$	.617	.784	.850	.885
	$\hat{\Phi}(\lambda = .8) =$	.727	.851	.898	.922
	$\hat{\Phi}(\lambda = .9) =$	.808	.898	.931	.948

Note: All estimates of $\sigma^2(X_{PI})$ and $\Phi(\lambda)$ assume $n_p = n_p' = 10$.

Figure 11.3 provides a Venn diagram representation of the variance components and mean squares for the $i{:}p$ design. From Figure 11.3, one can see that for the $i{:}p$ design, *both* $\sigma^2(\delta)$ and $\sigma^2(\Delta)$ equal $\sigma^2(I{:}p)$. Furthermore, it is easy to show that

$$\sigma^2(I{:}p) = \sigma^2(I) + \sigma^2(pI),$$

where variance components to the right of the equality are for the $p \times i$ design (see equations 9 and 10). Clearly, then, given estimates of $\sigma^2(I)$ and $\sigma^2(pI)$ for a G study employing the $p \times i$ design, one can easily estimate $\sigma^2(\delta) = \sigma^2(\Delta)$ for a D study employing the $i{:}p$ design. Furthermore, so long as items are sampled from the same universe, the universe score variance, $\sigma^2(p)$, is identical for both designs. It follows that the domain-referenced indices of dependability for the nested design are identical to those for the crossed design, and the generalizability coefficient, $\mathcal{E}\rho^2$, for the nested design is identical to Φ for the crossed design.

These results imply that the dependability of a domain-referenced testing procedure is not affected by whether the D study uses the crossed design, $p \times i$, or the nested design, $i{:}p$. The aim of domain-referenced testing is to provide point estimates of examinee universe scores rather than to make comparisons among examinees. The dependability of each examinee's score is determined by the number of items administered to that examinee, not by how many items or which items are administered to other examinees. Administering the same items to all examinees, in any instance of the testing procedure,

Figure 11.3. Venn diagram representation of mean squares and variance components for $i:p$ design

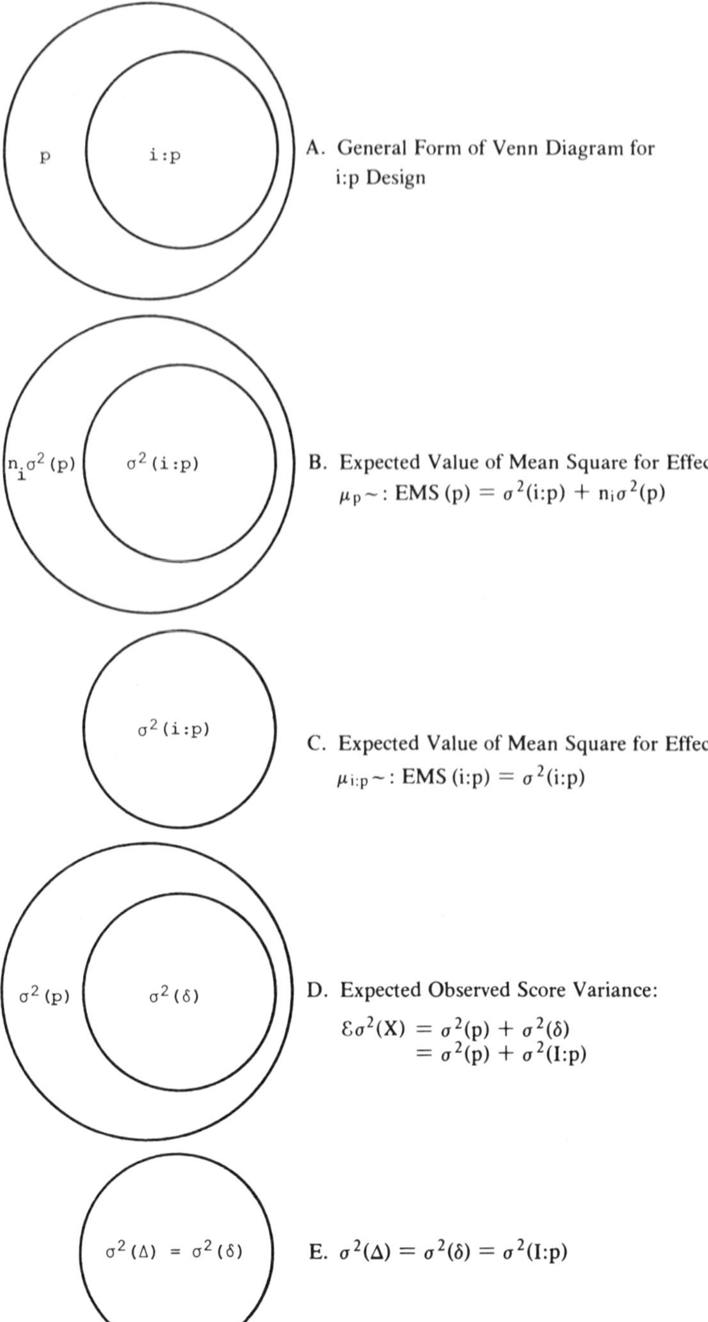

improves the dependability of norm-referenced interpretations but does not improve the dependability of domain-referenced interpretations. Furthermore, the use of different samples of items for different examinees will tend to improve estimates of group means. If, therefore, domain-referenced tests are to be used for program evaluation, the selection of independent samples of items for different examinees provides *more* dependable estimates of group means without any loss in the dependability of estimates of examinees' universe scores.

An Example with Considerations of Extensions to Other Designs

In previous sections a simple set of synthetic data have been used primarily to illustrate computational procedures and results for the $p \times i$ design, with some considerations given to the $i{:}p$ design. Here, the theoretical framework discussed before is applied to a large real data base for one of the instruments in the Adult Performance Level (APL) Program. The APL Program is an objectives-based assessment program developed by the American College Testing Program (ACT) and designed to measure the life skills proficiency of adults. Rather than emphasizing purely academic knowledge, the APL Program focuses on functional competency as manifested in basic tasks that are relevant to everyday living.

The APL Program consists of six instruments: the APL Survey (ACT, 1976) and five Content Area Measures, or CAMs, (ACT 1977). All items in all instruments are scored dichotomously (correct = 1, incorrect = 0). The data base analyzed here is for the adult version of the APL Survey only, and this data base consists of the responses of 2,432 adults to each of the $n_i = 8$ items in each of the five content area subtests of the APL Survey. These subtests are in the areas of Community Resources, Occupational Knowledge, Consumer Economics, Health, and Government and Law. Actually, the 2,432 examinees are only a subset of the entire data base, and the analyses reported here are only illustrative of a number of analyses of these data (see Brennan, 1978). For these reasons, these analyses should not be interpreted as a validation of the APL Program.

Table 11.9 reports mean squares and estimated variance components for the $p \times i$ design for each of the five content area subtests of the APL Survey. From Table 11.9 it is evident, for example, that there is considerably less variability among items in the Health Content area than in the other areas. Table 11.10 reports variance components, error variances, summary statistics, and indices of dependability for each of these subtests when the number of items in any subtest is $n_i' = 8$ or $n_i' = 20$.

Consider, for example, the last row of Table 11.10, which provides estimates of $\Phi(\lambda)$ when the criterion level is .75, in terms of the proportion of items correct. For the APL Survey with $n_i' = 8$ items, the values of $\hat{\Phi}(\lambda = .75)$ are somewhat low by conventional standards, suggesting that domain-referenced decisions based on the eight items and a criterion level of .75 may not be very dependable for these subtests. For this reason, ACT has developed

Table 11.9. G Studies for the Five Subtests of the APL Survey Using the $p \times i$ Design

		Mean Squares					Estimated G Study Variance Components				
Effect	*df*	s_1 = CR	s_2 = OK	s_3 = CE	s_4 = H	s_5 = GL	s_1 = CR	s_2 = OK	s_3 = CE	s_4 = H	s_5 = GL
p	2431	.38121	.52279	.50769	.65299	.54843	.0322	.0459	.0440	.0631	.0477
i	7	50.74109	62.34850	79.60269	18.03560	84.19510	.0208	.0256	.0327	.0074	.0346
pi	17017	.12371	.15540	.15548	.14858	.16689	.1237	.1554	.1555	.1486	.1669

Note: The five subtests are as follows: s_1 = Community Resources (CR); s_2 = Occupational Knowledge (OK); s_3 = Consumer Economics (CE); s_4 = Health (H); and s_5 = Government and Law (GL).

Table 11.10. D Studies for the Five APL Content Areas Using the $p \times i$ Design with $n_i' = 8, 20$

	D Study Variance Component									
	Community Resources (CR)		Occupational Knowledge (OK)		Consumer Economics (CE)		Health (H)		Government and Law (GL)	
Effect	$n_i' = 8$	$n_i' = 20$	$n_i' = 8$	$n_i' = 20$	$n_i' = 8$	$n_i' = 20$	$n_i' = 8$	$n_i' = 20$	$n_i' = 8$	$n_i' = 20$
p	.0322	.0322	.0459	.0459	.0440	.0440	.0631	.0621	.0477	.0477
i	.0026	.0010	.0032	.0013	.0041	.0016	.0009	.0004	.0043	.0017
pi	.0155	.0062	.0194	.0078	.0194	.0078	.0186	.0074	.0209	.0084
$\hat{\sigma}^2(\delta) =$	.0155	.0062	.0194	.0078	.0194	.0078	.0186	.0074	.0209	.0084
$\hat{\sigma}^2(\Delta) =$	.0181	.0072	.0226	.0091	.0235	.0094	.0195	.0078	.0252	.0101
$\widehat{\mathcal{E}\rho}^2 =$	.675	.839	.703	.855	.694	.849	.772	.895	.695	.850
$\hat{\Phi} =$	.640	.817	.670	.835	.652	.824	.764	.890	.654	.825
$X_{PI} =$	.7753	.7753	.6615	.6615	.6472	.6472	.6780	.6780	.5694	.5694
$\hat{\sigma}^2(X_{PI}) =$	.0026	.0010	.0032	.0013	.0041	.0016	.0009	.0004	.0043	.0017
$\hat{\Phi}(\lambda = X_{PI}) =$	.620	.812	.654	.831	.629	.819	.761	.889	.633	.820
$\hat{\Phi}(\lambda = .50) =$	.853	.937	.753	.886	.724	.872	.824	.924	.657	.834
$\hat{\Phi}(\lambda = .75) =$	.625	.816	.691	.852	.682	.849	.776	.897	.751	.886

Note: All estimates of $\sigma^2(X_{PI})$ and $\Phi(\lambda)$ assume $n_p = n_p' = 2432$.

the five Content Area Measures (CAMs) mentioned previously, which are considerably longer versions of each of the five subtests in the APL Survey. ACT (1977) reports, for each CAM, estimates of $\Phi(\lambda = .75)$ that exceed .90.

Now, suppose one wanted to consider constructing a 100-item version of the APL Survey. It would be of interest to estimate error variances and indices of dependability for the five subtests in this new version of the survey. These estimates are also provided in Table 11.10 under the columns headed $n_i' = 20$. The last row of Table 11.10 indicates that $\Phi(\lambda = .75)$ is estimated to be in the .80s for each content area subtest.

This discussion has been couched in terms of indices of dependability. In my opinion, it is especially important to consider also the error variances, $\hat{\sigma}^2(\Delta)$, for each of these subtests, which are reported in the fifth row of Table 11.10. The square root of these error variances, or the standard errors, are the estimates used in establishing confidence intervals about the examinees' proportion-correct scores. For $n_i' = 8$ items, these standard errors range from .13 to .16, approximately; and for $n_i' = 20$ items, the range is about .08 to .10.

It is important to note that the preceding discussion does *not* address domain-referenced issues of dependability for the *entire* 40-item APL Survey. Thus far, I have considered such issues for each subtest or content area only. By analogy with classical approaches, one might conduct a $p \times i$ analysis in which all 40 items in the survey were *not* differentiated by content area. To do so, however, would confound certain estimates and induce some ambiguities, because such an approach fails to reflect the fact that items are *nested* within subtests in the universe. Classical test theory cannot directly take into account such nesting, but generalizability theory can. Furthermore, the approach to domain-referenced interpretations discussed here has been extended by Brennan (1983) to *any* balanced design, and Crick and Brennan (1983) provide a computer program for estimating variance components and indices of dependability for any balanced design.

For the entire 40-item APL Survey and the data base discussed here, each person responded to every one of the $n_i = 8$ items in each of the $n_s = 5$ subtests. This design is denoted $p \times (i{:}s)$, where, as before, the colon is to be interpreted as "nested within." Figure 11.4 provides the Venn diagram and structural model for this design, along with formulas for the estimated random effects G study variance components. Note that for this design there are five independently estimable sources of variance, whereas for the $p \times i$ design there are only three. A principal advantage of the $p \times (i{:}s)$ design is that it enables one to distinguish effects due to items *within* subtests from effects due to subtest means.

Table 11.11 reports results for four different D studies of the entire APL Survey using the $p \times (i{:}s)$ design. The reader interested in a detailed consideration of procedures for obtaining these results can refer to Brennan (1978, 1983). Here, I simply consider some of the more important aspects of these results. Basically, Table 11.11 reports four different D studies: two in which

Figure 11.4. Venn diagram, model, and estimated random effects G study variance components for $p \times (i:s)$ design

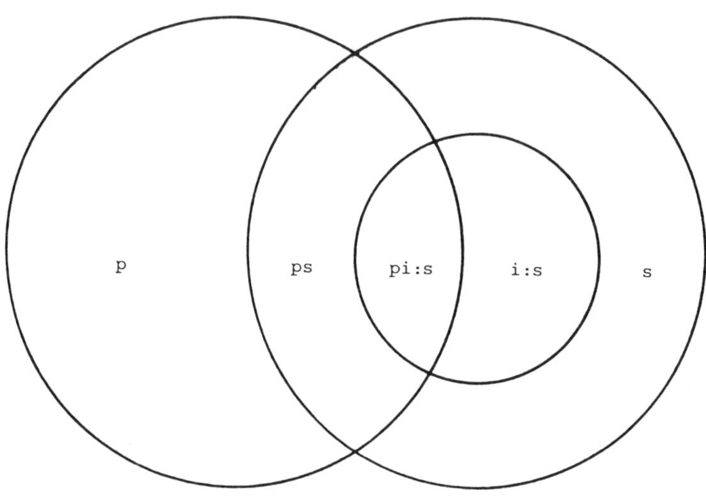

Model:

$$X_{pi:s} = \mu + \mu_{p\sim} + \mu_{s\sim} + \mu_{i:s\sim} + \mu_{ps\sim} + \mu_{pi:s\sim}$$

where experimental error is confounded with $\mu_{pi:s\sim}$.

Estimated Random Effects G Study Variance Components:

$$\hat{\sigma}^2(p) = [MS(p) - MS(ps)]/n_i n_s$$
$$\hat{\sigma}^2(i{:}s) = [MS(i{:}s) - MS(pi{:}s)]/n_p$$
$$\hat{\sigma}^2(s) = [MS(s) - MS(i{:}s) - MS(ps) + MS(pi{:}s)/n_p n_i$$
$$\hat{\sigma}^2(ps) = [MS(ps) - MS(pi{:}s)]/n_i$$
$$\hat{\sigma}^2(pi{:}s) = MS(pi{:}s)$$

the five subtests are considered random with $n_i' = 8$ and 20 and two in which the subtests are considered fixed with $n_i' = 8$ and 20. To say that these five subtests are random is to imply that we are interested in generalizing to some essentially infinite universe of potential subtests. (See Brennan 1983 for considerations in sampling from a *finite* universe.) By contrast, if subtests are considered fixed, then our interest is only in the actual subtests in the APL Survey. Table 11.11 illustrates that when subtests are considered fixed, indices of dependability are larger and error variances are smaller than when subtests are considered random. This is not to say that subtests here *should* be considered fixed. Such a decision is generally not a psychometric issue; it is a judgment that must be made by a decision maker with a particular universe of generalization in mind.

Recall that the estimates of $\Phi(\lambda)$ for each subtest with a criterion level of .75 and eight items were somewhat low by conventional standards (see Table 11.10). From the last row of Table 11.11, however, one can see that for the

Table 11.11. D Studies for APL Survey Using Design $p \times (i:s)$

			D Study Variance Components			
			Subtests Random ($n_s' = 5$)		Subtests Fixed ($n_s' = 5$)	
Effect[a]	MS	G Study Variance Component	$n_i' = 8$	$n_i' = 20$	$n_i' = 8$	$n_i' = 20$
p (2432)	1.84829	.0414	.0414	.0414	.0414	.0414
s (5)	106.02210	.0024	.0005	.0005		
$i:s$ (8)	58.98439	.0242	.0006	.0002	.0006	.0002
ps	.19105	.0053	.0011	.0011	.0011	.0011
$pi:s$	.14857	.1486	.0037	.0015	.0037	.0015
		$\hat{\sigma}^2(\delta) =$	.0048	.0026	.0037	.0015
		$\hat{\sigma}^2(\Delta) =$	.0059	.0033	.0043	.0017
		$\hat{\sigma}^2(\tau)$[b] $=$	.0414	.0414	.0425	.0425
		$\widehat{\mathcal{E}\rho^2} =$	.896	.941	.920	.966
		$\hat{\Phi} =$	.875	.926	.908	.962
		$X_{PI:S} =$	.6663	.6663	.6663	.6663
		$\sigma^2(X_{PI:S}) =$	.0011	.0007	.0006	.0002
		$\hat{\Phi}(\lambda = X_{PI:S}) =$	.872	.925	.907	.961
		$\hat{\Phi}(\lambda = .50) =$	.920	.954	.942	.976
		$\hat{\Phi}(\lambda = .75) =$	.889	.935	.919	.967

[a] Numbers in parentheses are G study sample sizes; i.e., $n_p = 2432$, $n_s = 5$, $n_i = 8$.
[b] $\hat{\sigma}^2(\tau)$ is the universe score variance, which is identical to $\hat{\sigma}^2(p)$ when subtests are random, and equals $\hat{\sigma}^2(p) + \hat{\sigma}^2(pS)$ when subtests are fixed.

entire 40-item APL Survey, $\hat{\Phi}(\lambda = .75)$ is .89 or .92, depending upon whether subtests are considered random or fixed, respectively, and for a 100-item version of the survey these estimates are on the order of .95. Again, I suggest that such results be used in conjunction with the estimates of the error variance $\sigma^2(\Delta)$. From Table 11.11, it is evident that these estimates are relatively small.

SUGGESTIONS FOR FUTURE RESEARCH

In considering suggestions for future research, it is desirable first to summarize some of the more salient features of the approach reviewed in previous sections. Basically, this approach may be viewed as an extension of generalizability theory to domain-referenced interpretations. As such, it is applicable to numerous data collection designs including the simple $p \times i$ design, and it enables one to make concrete and meaningful distinctions between norm-referenced and domain-referenced interpretations—distinctions that resolve a number of ambiguities in other approaches. To a large extent, such distinctions are made possible by, and indeed the approach is based upon, differentiating between two different types of error variance. There are, nevertheless, a number of issues that remain to be researched. Some of these are summarized in the following.

Distributional Assumptions

It has been argued that one of the advantages of generalizability theory is that it is distribution free. That is, the error variances and indices of dependability discussed here can be defined and estimated without any assumptions about the form of the distribution of universe, observed, or error scores. Nevertheless, for some purposes, such as establishing confidence intervals, distributional assumptions are required. For classical norm-referenced interpretations, it is traditional to assume that errors of measurement are normally distributed. It has been pointed out by many, however, that for domain-referenced interpretations such an assumption may not be optimal. In particular, the binomial or compound binomial distribution may be a better choice for domain-referenced interpretations (see Jarjoura, 1983). However, as yet, this distributional assumption has not been extensively studied in the context of the approach to domain-referenced interpretations discussed here.

Loss Functions

The approach to domain-referenced interpretations suggested here explicitly incorporates a squared-error loss function. It has been noted previously that other researchers have suggested using a threshold loss function (see Subkoviak, chapter 11). Some issues involved in choosing a loss function for domain-referenced interpretations have been discussed by Kane and Brennan (1980). Briefly, they argue that the threshold loss function is appropriate whenever the only distinction that can be made usefully is a *qualitative* distinction between masters and nonmasters. If, however, different degrees of mastery and nonmastery exist to an appreciable extent, the threshold loss function is not appropriate because it ignores such differences (see also Brennan, 1981).

In many (but *not* all) educational contexts, differences between masters and nonmasters are not purely qualitative. Rather, the attribute that is measured is conceptualized as an ordinal or interval scale, and the examinees may possess the attribute to varying degrees even though a single cut-off score is used to define mastery. In this context it is important that examinees who are far above or below the cut-off score be classified correctly. The misclassification of such examinees is likely to cause serious losses. The misclassification of examinees whose level of ability is close to the cut-off score will involve much less serious losses. Current techniques for setting the cut-off score are not very precise, and the choice of a cut-off score is, to some extent, arbitrary. It is, therefore, relatively less important that the testing procedure correctly classify examinees whose level of skill is close to the specified cut-off score. The domain-referenced indices suggested in this chapter reflect these considerations.

This is *not* to say that squared-error loss is always preferable to threshold loss, or vice versa. Indeed, in some contexts both seem somewhat inappropriate; therefore, one potential line of research involves examining the applicability of other loss (or utility) functions. To do so, however, is by no means trivial in theory or in practice.

Cut-off Scores

Shepard (chapter 7) treats some procedures that have been proposed for establishing a cut-off score, λ. A number of issues encountered in the application of such procedures have yet to be studied extensively. One such issue involves the effect of disagreement among cut-off score "setters" on the dependability of domain-referenced interpretations. More specifically, most procedures for establishing a cut-off score necessitate some type of subjective judgment(s) by experts. The validity and practical utility of such procedures may rest heavily upon the extent to which the experts agree in their judgments. Moreover, when λ is defined as the average of the experts' judgments, Brennan and Lockwood (1980) have suggested that some types of measurement dependability are affected by the extent to which experts disagree.

The Brennan and Lockwood (1980) study is based upon an application of generalizability theory to the Angoff (1971) and Nedelsky (1954) cut-off score procedures. To examine the effect of rater disagreement on measurement dependability they developed a modification of the index $\Phi(\lambda)$, which incorporates a term reflecting disagreement among raters. They found that $\Phi(\lambda)$ generally decreases as rater disagreement increases. The Brennan and Lockwood study is a preliminary attempt to combine, in a systematic manner, some issues associated with cut-off score procedures and measurement dependability for domain-referenced tests. Such issues need to be examined more thoroughly.

Other Issues

There are a number of issues in generalizability theory that are currently receiving considerable attention, including alternative procedures for estimating variance components, especially for nonorthogonal designs, and issues of validity viewed from the perspective of generalizability theory (see Kane, 1982). Since the approach to domain-referenced interpretations discussed here is based, in part, on generalizability theory, it follows that studying these issues may shed additional light on domain-referenced interpretations.

Also, the approach to dependability discussed here has not yet been extended to a consideration of multiple cut-off scores used simultaneously in a single instance of a testing procedure. To address this issue may necessitate some multivariate considerations of considerable complexity.

GUIDELINES FOR PRACTITIONERS

If the previous section provides suggestions for those who might extend the approach described in this chapter, then this section is addressed to those who would apply the approach as it currently exists. Of course, these two audiences overlap to some extent—perhaps to a considerable extent. Indeed, practitioners frequently generate the questions that lead to research topics, and sometimes the same people answer these questions. In any case, any set of guidelines for practitioners is likely to raise questions while it proposes suggestions. Also, the viability of such suggestions depends upon the role of the practitioners, to some extent, and certainly on the context within which the practitioner exists.

Finally, in considering the applicability of a set of guidelines, it is useful to consider the perspective of the person making the suggestions. The first two subsections that follow expand upon two issues that seem important to me, when one views issues of measurement dependability for domain-referenced tests, in the context of generalizability theory.

Nature of a Domain of Items and Parallel Tests Assumptions

In previous sections, no assumptions have been made about the nature of the domain, or universe, of items except that it is sufficiently well defined that one can reasonably consider the items in a test to be a sample from the domain. In particular, for the approach suggested and reviewed in this chapter, there is no requirement that the item mean scores, or difficulty levels in the population, have any particular distributional form, and there is not requirement that $\mu_I = \mu_J$ for two different tests, or sets of items, I and J. In short, I have assumed randomly parallel, as opposed to classically parallel, tests.

Clearly, if all items in the universe are homogeneous in difficulty levels, then certain simplifications of results will occur. However, it is not necessary to require such conditions. Indeed, for domain-referenced testing (and many would argue for norm-referenced testing, too) the domain of items should be specified by content matter specialists, and these specialists should *not* be constrained to include items in the domain only if they have a constant difficulty level in some population. Now, when the items in a domain vary in difficulty, it is impossible for all tests (i.e., random samples of the same number of items) to be classically parallel. Therefore, it can be argued that the assumption of classically parallel tests is not only unnecessary but also frequently unreasonable, at least for domain-referenced testing.

Some object to the assumption of randomly parallel tests in that tests are not usually built by a strict process of random sampling from a domain of items. Even so, the assumption of randomly parallel tests is a useful idealization. Although the items of a particular test may not have been drawn at random, one can usually conceive of a universe of items from which the test items might have been drawn (see Cronbach et al., 1972, pp. 359–360, 366–370, for further details).

This discussion has been couched in terms of random sampling from an undifferentiated domain of items. This is the simplest case to consider, but it is by no means the only possibility. For example, items may be randomly sampled from a stratified universe, as illustrated in the previous discussion of the

$p \times (i{:}s)$ design. In such cases, analyses are more involved, but the argument is essentially unchanged.

Score Interpretations and Domain Specification

From the point of view of generalizability theory, a test is simply a random sample of items from some domain. Therefore, the existence of a domain (or universe of generalization) does not provide a clear basis for distinguishing between norm-referenced and domain-referenced testing. Rather, in my opinion, the fundamental distinction between norm-referenced and domain-referenced testing is a distinction in score use and interpretation. To avoid verbal complexity, it is common to speak of "tests" rather than "interpretations, or uses, or scores"; however, the distinction should be kept in mind.

Some writers differentiate between norm-referenced and domain-referenced tests in terms of the procedures used for constructing items. Such procedures affect domain specification. Suppose a group of test developers uses one procedure to construct items for what they call a "domain-referenced test" and a different procedure to construct items for what they call a "norm-referenced test." Even if both tests are for the same *general* content area, the domain of items will almost certainly be different for the two tests. In such a case, differences in test content are attributable to differences in the *two domains*, or universes of generalization, not to any inherent differences in norm-referenced and domain-referenced interpretations per se. Indeed, in such a case, one could provide norm-referenced and domain-referenced interpretations for scores on tests sampling either domain.

Also, a number of researchers and practitioners have suggested differential criteria for identifying "acceptable" items for norm-referenced and domain-referenced tests (see Berk, chapter 5). It is not my purpose here to evaluate such criteria, but it is clear that different criteria will usually produce different tests, or sets of "acceptable" items. To be more specific, once one changes the criteria for item acceptability, the domain, or universe of generalization, is likely to change. Consequently, when the criteria for item acceptability differ, the differences in the tests themselves are most directly attributable to differences in the specification of the universe of generalization. To summarize, in my opinion, differences between norm-referenced and domain-referenced testing are best thought of as differences in score interpretation, while different procedures for item construction and different criteria for item acceptability usually imply different domains, or universes of generalization. Once a universe of generalization is specified and items are sampled from it to form a test, then the scores on the test can be given either a norm-referenced or a domain-referenced interpretation. It may well be that practitioners find certain universes of generalization interesting or useful primarily for domain-referenced interpretations, while they find other universes interesting or useful primarily for norm-referenced interpretations. Even so, it seems best to differentiate between norm-referenced and domain-referenced testing *principally* in terms of score interpretation. Otherwise, one is likely to confound differences in score interpretations with differences in universes of generalization, which result from different item construction and/or identification procedures. This is *not* to mitigate, in any way, the importance of such procedures. The point here is that such procedures affect the universe of generalization and do not necessarily imply a distinction between norm-referenced and domain-referenced interpretations *per se*.

Indices of Dependability

I have considered two indices of dependability, $\Phi(\lambda)$ and Φ, for domain-referenced interpretations, as well as two corresponding signal/noise ratios. As discussed previously, indices of dependability and signal/noise ratios are monotonically related by simple equations. From a technical perspective, therefore, it is of little importance whether one emphasizes indices of dependability or signal/noise ratios. However, $\Phi(\lambda)$ and Φ have characteristics that are more familiar to most practitioners; therefore, the following discussion will be couched in terms of indices of dependability.

Basically, three different approaches have been discussed for defining and interpreting $\Phi(\lambda)$ and Φ. These approaches are based upon developing these indices in three ways: (*a*) in manner somewhat analogous to the development of a generalizability coefficient, (*b*) through signal/noise concepts, and (*c*) as special cases of two general agreement coefficients. In terms of interpretability, I suggest that the "agreement" approach may be the easiest for most practitioners. However, interpretations in terms of signal/noise concepts may be more informative for people familiar with measurement procedures in the physical sciences. Finally, people familiar with generalizability theory may find the first approach to be the most straightforward.

Regardless of the approach practitioners prefer in interpreting $\Phi(\lambda)$ and Φ, it is crucial that practitioners differentiate between $\Phi(\lambda)$ and Φ. These two indices address *different* questions about the dependability of decisions based on the testing procedure. $\Phi(\lambda)$ indicates the dependability of decisions based on the testing procedure, while Φ characterizes the *contribution* of the testing procedure to the dependability of such decisions. Therefore, both indices should be reported, and practitioners should be careful not to confuse them.

Actually, of course, there are an infinite number of possible values for $\Phi(\lambda)$, depending upon the cut-off score, λ. For many domain-referenced tests, therefore, it is best to report as many values of $\Phi(\lambda)$ as there are cut-off scores that might be used in particular contexts. Better still, one might report a $\Phi(\lambda)$ "curve" (see, for example, Figure 11.2). Indeed, several curves might be reported if the number of items, in any given instance of the testing procedure, can be altered.

In interpreting the magnitudes of any specific values of $\Phi(\lambda)$ and Φ, practitioners should keep in mind that $\Phi(\lambda)$ is dependent upon the universe score variance, $\sigma^2(p)$, the error variance, $\sigma^2(\Delta)$, and the quantity, $(\mu - \lambda)^2$; and Φ is dependent upon $\sigma^2(p)$ and $\sigma^2(\Delta)$. Interpretations based solely upon the magnitude of $\Phi(\lambda)$ or Φ seldom provide a sufficient basis for good decision making.

Variance Components

In previous sections, considerably more space has been devoted to indices of dependability than to variance components. Such indices have practical as well as theoretical value. However, variance components and associated error variances are likely to be the most important results, because they frequently provide the most important basis for making decisions. Therefore, the central role that variance components play in domain-referenced interpretations should not be overlooked. Indeed, according to the *Standards for Educational and Psychological Tests* (APA/AERA/NCME Joint Committee, 1974), "The estimation of clearly labeled components of score variance is the most informative outcome of a reliability study, both for the test developer wishing to improve the reliability of his instrument and for the user desiring to interpret test scores with maximum understanding" (p. 49).

For these reasons, it is recommended that variance components, and especially the error variance, $\sigma^2(\Delta)$, be reported in documenting the technical characteristics of a domain-referenced test. Furthermore, it is recommended that users give at least as much consideration to variance components as they give to indices of dependability in making judgments about the applicability of domain-referenced tests in specific contexts, for specific purposes. Finally, it is recommended that test developers carefully consider variance components, and especially error variance, in their deliberations about the optimal length of a domain-referenced test. Minimizing error variance is by no means the only relevant consideration in defining test length, but it is one important consideration.

Other Issues

Decisions about the appropriateness of particular loss functions cannot be made on the basis of a test *per se*. Such decisions are intimately involved with a consideration of the purpose and context of the testing procedure. For this reason, it is impossible to make a statement about the universal applicability of either squared-error loss functions or threshold loss functions, for domain-referenced interpretations. Prudence would suggest, therefore, that when ambiguity exists with respect to choice of a loss function, practitioners should interpret results cautiously. Indeed, it is sometimes advisable to report and interpret results based upon more than one loss function when ambiguity in choice of loss function exists.

In previous sections, an effort has been made to demonstrate relationships between sample statistics and other well-known quantities on the one hand and $\Phi(\lambda)$, Φ, and $\sigma^2(\Delta)$ on the other. For example, Table 11.7 illustrates that $\hat{\Phi}(\lambda = X_{PI})$ equals KR-21. Such relationships are not of fundamental theoretical importance, but they can be used advantageously as a "rough and ready" way to estimate dependability for some domain-referenced interpretations. Indeed, this is the principal reason such results have been reported here. Again, however, it is strongly recommended that whenever possible one report variance components, and estimate indices of dependability, in terms of variance components.

APPENDIX: GLOSSARY OF SYMBOLS

Symbol	*Definition*
$\times$	"Crossed with"
:	"Nested within"
p, i, s	A person, item, or subtest
P, I, S	A *set* of persons, items, or subtests
n	G study sample size
n'	D study sample size
MS	Mean square
SS	Sum of squares
X_{PI}	Observed mean score over persons *and* items, expressed as a proportion of items correct
$\mathcal{E}$	Expected value
Σ	Summation
λ	Cut-off score
μ	Grand mean in population and universe
μ_p	Universe score for person p; expected value of observed score for person p, over universe of items
μ_i	Population mean for item i; expected value of observed score for item i, over the population of persons
$\sigma^2(p)$	Universe score variance, or random effects variance component for persons
$\sigma^2(i)$	Random effects variance components for items
$\sigma^2(pi)$	Random effects variance components for the interaction of persons and items
$\sigma^2(\Delta)$	Variance of differences between observed scores and universe scores
$\sigma^2(\delta)$	Variance of differences between observed deviation scores and universe scores expressed in deviation form
$\mathcal{E}\rho^2$	Generalizability coefficient
$\Phi(\lambda)$	Index of dependability for domain-referenced mastery interpretations
Φ	General-purpose index of dependability for domain-referenced interpretations
θ	Agreement coefficient *not* corrected for chance agreement
θ_c	Agreement coefficient corrected for chance agreement
ψ	Signal/noise ratio *not* corrected for chance
ψ_c	Signal/noise ratio corrected for chance
A	Expected agreement

A_c	Chance agreement
A_m	Maximum expected agreement
L	Loss or expected disagreement
d	Domain-referenced agreement function
g	Norm-referenced agreement function

REFERENCES

American College Testing Program. *User's guide: Adult APL survey*. Iowa City, IA: Author, 1976.

American College Testing Program. *Technical supplement: APL content area measures*. Iowa City, IA: Author, 1977.

Angoff, W. H. Scales, norms, and equivalent scores. In R. L. Thorndike (Ed.), *Educational measurement* (2nd ed.). Washington, DC: American Council on Education, 1971. Pp. 508–600.

APA/AERA/NCME Joint Committee. *Standards for educational and psychological tests* (rev. ed.). Washington, DC: American Psychological Association, 1974.

Brennan, R. L. *KR-21 and lower limits of an index of dependability for mastery tests* (ACT Technical Bulletin No. 27). Iowa City, IA: American College Testing Program, 1977.

Brennan, R. L. *Extensions of generalizability theory to domain-referenced testing* (ACT Technical Bulletin No. 30). Iowa City, IA: American College Testing Program, 1978. (Also, NPRDC Technical Report. San Diego, CA: Navy Personnel Research and Development Center, 1978.)

Brennan, R. L. *Handbook for GAPID: A FORTRAN IV computer program for generalizability analyses with single-facet designs* (ACT Technical Bulletin No. 34). Iowa City, IA: American College Testing Program, October 1979.

Brennan, R. L. *Some statistical procedures for domain-referenced testing: A handbook for practitioners* (ACT Technical Bulletin No. 38). Iowa City, IA: American College Testing Program, 1981.

Brennan, R. L. *Elements of generalizability theory*. Iowa City, IA: American College Testing Program, 1983.

Brennan, R. L., & Kane, M. T. An index of dependability for mastery tests. *Journal of Educational Measurement*, 1977, *14*, 277–289. (a)

Brennan, R. L., & Kane, M. T. Signal/noise ratios for domain-referenced tests. *Psychometrika*, 1977, *42*, 609–625; Errata, 1978, *43*, 289. (b)

Brennan, R. L., & Kane, M. T. Generalizability theory: A review. In R. E. Traub (Ed.), *New directions for testing and measurement* (No. 4): *Methodological developments*. San Francisco: Jossey-Bass, 1979. Pp. 33–51.

Brennan, R. L., & Lockwood, R. E. A comparison of the Nedelsky and Angoff cutting score procedures using generalizability theory. *Applied Psychological Measurement*, 1980, *4*, 105–126.

Cohen, J. A coefficient of agreement for nominal scales. *Educational and Psychological Measurement*, 1960, *20*, 37–46.

Crick, J. E., & Brennan, R. L. *Manual for GENOVA: A generalized analysis of variance system* (ACT Technical Bulletin No. 43). Iowa City, IA: American College Testing Program, 1983.

Cronbach, L. J. Coefficient alpha and the internal structure of tests. *Psychometrika*, 1951, *16*, 292-334.

Cronbach, L. J., & Gleser, G. C. The signal/noise ratio in the comparison of reliability coefficients. *Educational and Psychological Measurement*, 1964, *24*, 467-480.

Cronbach, L. J., Gleser, G. C., Nanda, H., & Rajaratnam, N. *The dependability of behavioral measurements: Theory of generalizability for scores and profiles*. New York: Wiley, 1972.

Glaser, R. Instructional technology and the measurement of learning outcomes: Some questions. *American Psychologist*, 1963, *18*, 519-521.

Guilford, J. P. *Psychometric methods* (2nd ed.). New York: McGraw-Hill, 1954.

Hambleton, R. K., Swaminathan, H., Algina, J., & Coulson, D. B. Criterion-referenced testing and measurement: A review of technical issues and developments. *Review of Educational Research*, 1978, *48*, 1-47.

Jarjoura, D. *Confidence and tolerance intervals for true scores* (ACT Technical Bulletin No. 42). Iowa City, IA: American College Testing Program, 1983.

Kane, M. T. A sampling model for validity. *Applied Psychological Measurement*, 1982, *6*, 125-160.

Kane, M. T., & Brennan, R. L. Agreement coefficients as indices of dependability for domain-referenced tests. *Applied Psychological Measurement*, 1980, *4*, 219-240.

Lippey, G. (Ed.). *Computer-assisted test construction*. Englewood Cliffs, NJ: Educational Technology Publications, 1974.

Livingston, S. A. Criterion-referenced applications of classical test theory. *Journal of Educational Measurement*, 1972, *9*, 13-26.

Lord, F. M. Do tests of the same length have the same standard error of measurement? *Educational and Psychological Measurement*, 1957, *17*, 510-521.

Lord, F. M. Test reliability: A correction. *Educational and Psychological Measurement*, 1962, *22*, 511-512.

Lord, F. M. Some item analysis and test theory for a system of computer-assisted test construction for individualized instruction. *Applied Psychological Measurement*, 1977, *1*, 511-512.

Lord, F. M., & Novick, M. R. *Statistical theories of mental test scores*. Reading, MA: Addison-Wesley, 1968.

Nedelsky, L. Absolute grading standards for objective tests. *Educational and Psychological Measurement*, 1954, *14*, 3-19.

Popham, W. J., & Husek, T. R. Implications of criterion-referenced measurement. *Journal of Educational Measurement*, 1969, *6*, 1-9.

Shavelson, R. J., & Webb, N. M. Generalizability theory: 1973-1980. *British Journal of Mathematical and Statistical Psychology*, 1981, *34*, 133-166.

BIOGRAPHICAL NOTES

RONALD A. BERK is Professor of Education and Director of the Johns Hopkins University National Symposium on Educational Research (NSER). He received his Ph.D. degree from the University of Maryland in 1973. Prior to joining the faculty at Johns Hopkins, he taught elementary school in the District of Columbia (1968–1972) and served as an evaluator in the Montgomery County (MD) School System (1973–1976). Professor Berk has authored or co-authored more than 50 journal articles, the DeGangi-Berk Test of Sensory Integration (Western Psychological Services), and, most recently, *Screening and Diagnosis of Children with Learning Disabilities* (Charles C Thomas). He has also edited three books and has been a reviewer for several journals and publishing companies.

ROBERT L. BRENNAN is Director of Measurement Research for the American College Testing Program in Iowa City. He received his Ed.D. degree from Harvard University in 1970. He was Research Associate at Harvard from 1968 to 1971 and Assistant Professor of Education at SUNY at Stony Brook from 1971 to 1976. Dr. Brennan's research on generalizability theory and criterion-referenced measurement has been published in numerous journals and in his book, *Elements of Generalizability Theory* (ACT). He has served as a reviewer for various measurement journals and as advisory editor to the *Journal of Educational Measurement* and *Applied Psychological Measurement*. Dr. Brennan has also directed American Educational Research Association training sessions on generalizability theory and applications.

RONALD K. HAMBLETON is Professor of Education and Psychology and Chairman of the Laboratory of Psychometric and Evaluative Research at the University of Massachusetts, Amherst. He earned his Ph.D. degree from the University of Toronto in 1969 and has been a member of the University of Massachusetts faculty since completing his studies in Toronto. Professor Hambleton served as advisory editor to the *Journal of Educational Measurement* from 1974 to 1980. Presently he serves as advisory editor to the *Journal of Educational Statistics* and *Applied Psychological Measurement*, editor of the review section of the *Journal of Educational Measurement* (1984–1986), chairman of the American Psychological Association Public Affairs Committee, and APA's representative to the International Test Commission. His present research interests are in the areas of item response theory and criterion-referenced testing. With more than 100 publications to his credit, Professor Hambleton recently co-authored (with

H. Swaminathan) the book *Item Response Theory: Principles and Applications* (Kluwer-Nijhoff).

JASON MILLMAN is Professor of Educational Research Methodology at Cornell University and is principal investigator of Automating Achievement Testing in Computer Assisted Testing, a project funded by Control Data Corporation. He received his Ph.D. degree from the University of Michigan in 1960. In addition to publishing extensively in the areas of educational measurement, research, and evaluation, Professor Millman has held several elected offices in professional associations, including president of the National Council on Measurement in Education, and has served as editor of *Educational Researcher* (1964–1968) and the *Journal of Educational Measurement* (1968–1971) and as consulting editor on several other publications. He has also conducted numerous workshops, including two on criterion-referenced measurement for the American Educational Research Association, and consulted with roughly 50 national, state, local, and professional organizations on educational measurement and evaluation projects.

ANTHONY J. NITKO is Professor of Educational Research Methodology at the University of Pittsburgh and is coprincipal investigator of the Domain-Referencing and Microcomputers in Classroom Testing Project, which is funded by the National Institute of Education. In 1982 he conducted a month-long measurement seminar for the chief examiners and the professional staff of the Malawi Certificate Examinations and Testing Board at Zomba, Malawi, Central Africa. He was a Research Associate at the Learning Research and Development Center from the time he completed his doctorate at the University of Iowa in 1968 through 1974. During that period he directed test development and evaluation projects for individualized and adaptive learning environments. Professor Nitko has been a testing and measurement consultant for a number of organizations and agencies, most recently the American Council on Education and the U.S. Army. He has also authored or co-authored several books, chapters, and journal articles, including the textbook *Educational Tests and Measurement: An Introduction* (Harcourt Brace Jovanovich).

W. JAMES POPHAM is Professor of Education at the University of California, Los Angeles, and Director of IOX Assessment Associates. He received his Ed.D. degree from Indiana University in 1958. He taught at Kansas State College of Pittsburg from 1958 to 1960 and San Francisco State College from 1960 to 1962. Professor Popham is a past president of the American Educational Research Association. He has authored over 200 research papers, articles, and monographs, 20 books, including *Criterion-Referenced Measurement* and *Modern Educational Measurement* (Prentice-Hall), and 20 filmstrip-tape programs for preservice and inservice teacher education. He has also received numerous awards for excellence in teaching and research. From 1978 to 1981 Professor Popham served as founding editor of the AERA journal *Educational Evaluation and Policy Analysis*.

GALE H. ROID is Director of Research for Western Psychological Services in Los Angeles. He received his Ph.D. degree from the University of Oregon in 1969. He was an Assistant Professor at McGill University from 1969 to 1972 and was Research Professor in the Teaching Research Division, Oregon State System of Higher Education, from 1972 to 1979. Dr. Roid has authored or co-authored more than 30 journal articles, book chapters, and research papers in educational and psychological measurement. One of his most recent publications (with T. Haladyna) is the book *A Technology for Test-Item Writing* (Academic Press). Dr. Roid has also been the recipient of several federal research contracts, has consulted with the military on test construction procedures, and has made editorial contributions to numerous published tests and computerized scoring programs.

LORRIE A. SHEPARD is Associate Professor of Education and Chairperson of the Research and Evaluation Methodology Division at the University of Colorado, Boulder. She is also the immediate past president of the National Council on Measurement in Education. She received her Ph.D. degree from the University of Colorado in 1972. Prior to joining the faculty at the university, Professor Shepard was Research and Evaluation Specialist in the California Department of Education (1972–1974). She has authored numerous articles and book chapters on criterion-referenced testing, test item bias, and, most recently, learning disabilities identification. She has also served as editor of the *Journal of Educational Measurement* (1977–1980) and as a frequent reviewer for several other journals. Professor Shepard is currently co-editor of the *American Educational Research Journal*.

MICHAEL J. SUBKOVIAK is Professor of Educational Psychology at the University of Wisconsin, Madison. He received his Ph.D. degree from SUNY at Buffalo in 1972. He was Director of Psychological Testing and Chief Statistician for the U.S. Army in Vietnam from 1970 to 1972 and Director of Testing and Evaluation Services at the University of Wisconsin from 1977 to 1979. Professor Subkoviak has published extensively in the areas of educational evaluation and psychometric theory, particularly multidimensional scaling. He has also served as a reviewer for numerous measurement and research journals, and is an advisory editor to the *Journal of Educational Measurement*.

INDEX